HEART AND BLOOD

HEART AND BLOOD

*Living with
Deer in
America*

Richard Nelson

*Alfred A. Knopf
New York
1997*

THIS IS A BORZOI BOOK
PUBLISHED BY ALFRED A. KNOPF, INC.

http://www.randomhouse.com/

Owing to limitations of space, all acknowledgments
for permission to reprint previously published material
may be found following the index.

Library of Congress Cataloging-in-Publication Data
Nelson, Richard K.
Heart and blood : living with deer in America / by
Richard Nelson. — 1st ed.
p.   cm.
Includes bibliographical references.
ISBN 0-679-40522-4
1. Deer—United States.   2. Deer—United States—Psychological
aspects.   3. Deer hunting—United States.   I. Title.
QL737.U55N45   1997
799.2'765'0973—dc21   97-2814   CIP

Manufactured in the United States of America
First Edition

This book is dedicated
to Nita, in enduring love and partnership,
to Mom and Dad, Ethan, Keta, and our family of friends,
and to the deer, who so richly embellish our lives.

There, wandering—over the fallen oak leaves
          Black-tailed deer.
One, two, three, four.

As the fifth deer
I follow them.

Somewhere
Right now
—I'm sure—
The world sleeps very well.

—NANAO SAKAKI

CONTENTS

Beginnings   xi

Prologue   3

ONE   *Tracking the Deer*   10

TWO   *Crossing the Wild Edge*   53

THREE   *Excess and Restraint*   91

FOUR   *Embattled Sanctuaries*   122

FIVE   *The Backyard Wilderness*   157

SIX   *The Deer Capital of Texas*   183

SEVEN   *Opening Weekend*   218

EIGHT   *In Search of Eden*   249

NINE   *The Hidden Harvest*   289

TEN   *Heart of the Hunter*   312

Epilogue   342

Bibliographic Essay, Information Sources,
    and Acknowledgments   353
Literature Cited   365
Index   377

The buck stands atop a rise, darkly silhouetted against broad-trunked oaks and maples strung with garlands of freshly opened leaves. He watches nervously but holds his ground, as if my stillness has assuaged his fears. Since I let myself become visible at the edge of a pine glade 15 minutes ago, I've kept still as a rock, positioned exactly as he first saw me. A mule deer or blacktail would probably have forgotten about me by now, or forgiven the intrusion and gone about his business, but this whitetail keeps me fastened here, gathering dew, as the sky over central New York State brightens to amber and vermillion.

The deer's molting coat looks thin and scruffy, winter gray mixed with the fox red of emerging summer fur. His forehead is so sparsely furred it looks almost bare; his ears have pinkish, translucent centers and narrow black borders; and his antlers are thick and stumpy, with short, round tines densely cloaked in velvet.

At last he turns casually away, leaning down to nibble tender shoots of grass, and when he looks up again a tuft of silvery dandelion fuzz clings to his chin like a beard. Every few seconds—as if he's twinged by a dissipating memory—he abruptly raises his head and stares at me, focusing his outsized ears for the slightest betraying sound.

After one of these inspections, he turns away and opens his mouth for a long moment, stretching his jaw muscles or perhaps yawning. At intervals he bends around to lick his shoulder, parting the hairs and exposing their whitish shafts; then he shivers like a horse shooing flies. Apparently distracted by itchiness related to the molt, he scruffs his flank with a hind leg, pulling out clumps of fur that drift away like feathers. Each time he raises a leg to scratch I can see his male parts, sheathed in soft white fur. And once, he bends around to scratch with a rear hoof just below his shining obsidian eye, moving so delicately and precisely that he never closes the eye.

At last, the buck seems wholly relaxed, browsing through the luxuriant grass without fear or distraction. But then, without apparent cause, he startles to full, trembling alertness and half crouches as if he'd been jolted by electricity. And he stares intently—not at me but off toward the still-unrisen sun, where he's apparently caught an incongruous sound or a flash of movement. Following the line of his gaze, I see nothing and hear nothing, yet I trust his judgment and assume we're no longer alone. A full minute passes before the source of his trepidation becomes clear.

Jogger. A woman dressed in crimson shorts and matching sweatshirt trots along the nearby road with a smallish terrier leashed beside her. The two come quietly toward us, passing beneath arched tree limbs, passing splendid green yards bordered in tulips and daffodils, passing houses with morning newspapers on their porches.

The buck holds his ground for a moment, then stamps one forehoof, whirls, and bounds off between two houses, vaulting effortlessly over a backyard fence and slipping through a curtain of white lilacs like an eagle disappearing into a cloud.

A short while later, I hike to a rise overlooking broad sweeps of hills and farmlands, all shimmering beneath the freshly risen sun. Looking westward into the continent, I dream of deer in the valleys, deer amid mossy alpine heights, deer on burned droughty plains, deer in riverbank glades, deer on bouldery scree slopes, deer among cactus forests, deer neck-deep in waving green grass, deer rattling through cattails, deer lingering silently among ferns and salal, deer raking burnished antlers on sumacs, sapling pines, palmettos.

I dream of solitary deer, does with fawns, yearlings in pairs and threes, clusters and herds of deer; resting, running, leaping, playing, jousting, grazing, browsing, sleeping, hiding, and dying deer.

I dream of deer wandering the pathless wild, deer slipping quietly through suburban yards, deer crossing farmland highways, deer leaping at the sound of a hunter's step.

I dream of an entire continent, sprawling off to the earth's curved edge, alive and thronging with deer, all woven together with humankind in bonds of heart and blood.

I'm not sure exactly when I became obsessed with deer.

I remember standing between Mom and Dad on the front seat of our '49 Ford peering over the dash as a whitetail bolted across a Wisconsin hay field like snow whirling in a gale. And I remember poking handfuls of grass through a chain-link fence at the Madison, Wisconsin, zoo, feeling the grass plucked away by a deer who stood taller than I did and seemed docile as a barnyard calf. Those two images are burned into my mind: one of a powerful, elegant, and utterly wild creature; the other of a beautiful, tame, and profoundly innocent being. Many years later, as a student at the University of Wisconsin, I also became intrigued with deer as a wildlife species much studied by biologists and game managers. And yet, the animal itself had always remained elusive, cryptic, remote.

It wasn't until I settled in a small village on the North Pacific coast that deer took full possession of my heart. If one experience stands out above all others, it was an encounter with three blacktail does feeding placidly in a broad muskeg during a torrential rainstorm. Perhaps it was the gale and downpour, or perhaps my gradual, circumspect approach—but instead of dashing away, the deer allowed me to come within 10 yards and trail them around for perhaps an hour. This was the first time I realized I could get close to wild deer, and it opened a deep craving that has never waned.

It may seem paradoxical that I also began hunting deer around this same time, but the two experiences are intricately connected. I had learned, while living among Eskimo and Indian people in northern Alaska, that a hunter's keenest edge is knowledge of the animal he stalks, knowledge based on years of close and careful observation. I had also been apprenticed to Koyukon Indian elders, who believe that animals are imbued with spirit, power, and awareness beyond anything known in my own culture. These years as a student of Indian and Eskimo hunters profoundly influenced my own relationship to deer—my intense desire to learn more about them, my commitment to depending on them as food, and my appreciation for the vast dimensions of their beauty.

As my intellectual and emotional connections with deer strengthened, so did my curiosity about them—and I began devoting myself completely to this interest. For several years I traveled to various parts of the country, learning how people live with deer in modern America, taking guidance from farmers, ranchers, suburb dwellers, Native American elders, hunters, writers, biologists, land managers, social scientists, animal rights activists, wildlife watchers, and many others. This book came from the experiences I had, the teachings I was offered, and the books and articles that accumulated on my shelves.

It's important to say that I am not a biologist, although I've listened eagerly to what biologists have to teach us about deer. My interest in these chapters is to explore the relationships between people and deer in our shared homeland. Often, nowadays, these relationships are snarled in conflict, brought on especially by the tremendous increases of both human and deer populations. Serious problems have arisen over deer in the suburbs, in nature preserves, in farmlands and ranch country; there are endless debates about plans to control, reduce, or limit deer numbers; and controversy simmers over the emotional issue of hunting.

I have approached these subjects as someone passionately involved with the natural world, as a wildlife watcher and conservationist, as a subsistence hunter, as an anthropologist fascinated with humankind and our relationships to wild animals, and as a citizen of my nation and place. I have also given myself a visible role in these chapters, sometimes as a participant, sometimes as an observer, sometimes as a commentator. And I have carried into each of these stories my own background, perspectives, and biases. For this I beg the indulgence of people who hold differing views, and I hope that I've treated each of my guides, teachers, companions, and subjects respectfully.

During three years of travel and research for this book and three years of writing that followed, I incurred more debts than I could ever imagine repaying. Most of the information, experiences, and interpretations contained in these pages came to me through the kindness of others. For this I can only return my sincerest gratitude and pass along to the best of my ability what was so generously given.

In the book's final section—which includes a bibliographic essay and listing of information sources—I specifically acknowledge many people who contributed material for each chapter. At the outset, however, I want to mention a few who played especially important parts in shaping this book and helping me sustain the energy it required.

My sincere, heartfelt, and enduring thanks:

To Nita Couchman, who traveled along or tended the hearth at home; who watched, listened, discussed, advised, read, and edited; who made this whole endeavor possible, and did it with gentleness, insight, judgment, and encompassing love. To our son, Ethan, who grew into the strength and independence of manhood during these years. To Shungnak, who taught me so much about tracking and seeing deer; and to Keta, who knows the deer in ways I can't even imagine and must also love them, if excitement in their presence is any clue.

To my parents, Robert and Florence Nelson, who gave the project a Midwest headquarters, whose encouragement made all things seem attainable, whose love was as certain as sunrise, and whose home was always bedrock for our lives; and to Dave Nelson, Jean Breedlove, and Mark, Jodi, and Kelsey Kubale, who all strengthened that bedrock.

To the book's editors, Bobbie Bristol and Karen Deaver; to my agent and adviser, Susan Bergholz; and to Bert Snyder; they have guided this book from beginning to end with insight, understanding, sensitivity, and friendship.

To the donors, board members, and staff of foundations who provided support for this work: the Lannan Foundation, the National Endowment for the Arts, and the Institute for the Study of Natural and Cultural Resources. Whatever the practical importance of funding, it is equally significant as a gesture of affirmation for the writer who labors in solitude and struggles to maintain confidence.

To the Native Alaskan elders and hunters who vitally influenced my life and taught me a different way of seeing the natural world—especially Catherine Attla and Steven Attla, Joe Beetus, Fred Bifelt, Eliza Jones, Tony Sam, Cue Bifelt, Lavine Williams, Edwin Simon and Lydia Simon, Waldo Bodfish and Mattie Bodfish, Wesley Ekak, Wayne Bodfish, Dempsey Bodfish, Weir Negovanna, Sam Herbert Jr., Moses Peter, Harry Carroll—and the people of Huslia, Hughes, Wainwright, and Chalkyitsik, Alaska.

To Gary Nabhan, Barry Lopez, Pattiann Rogers, and many other writers whose work and counsel have meant so much to me throughout these years; to Marion Gilliam and everyone associated with the Orion Society; and to the community of people who celebrate the natural world, work for its protection, and urge us toward a more responsible engagement with the earth.

To Mark Gorman and Nancy Knapp, Steve Reifenstuhl and Andrea Thomas, Robert Rose and Barbara Teepe, John Straley and Jan Straley—who strengthen the life in which this work is embedded and whose friendship expands the embrace of home.

To those who hosted, guided, instructed, or assisted me in so many crucial ways: Dewitt Daggett, Larry Evers, Bart Gillan and Debbie Gillan, George Gmelch and Sharon Gmelch, Donald Harvey and Elaine Harvey, Mike Hughes, Buzz Kemper, Jodi Kemper, James Mlsna, Mark Mlsna, Felipe Molina, Lee Swenson and Vijaya Nagarajan, Robert Reifenstuhl and Chris Reifenstuhl, and Mark Weller; and a particular note of gratitude to Isabel Stirling for her bibliographic virtuosity.

To the biologists and agency professionals who willingly shared information and perspectives gained through years of research experience:

William Armstrong, Terry Bowyer, Beverly Bryant, Mark Ellingwood, Eugene Fowler, Michael Gillingham, Thomas Hanley, David Hardy, Fielding Harwell, Dan Hirchert, William Ishmael, Matthew Kirchoff, David Klein, Floyd Lemley, Harry Libby, Thomas Lindberg, Mark Lowery, Rodney Marburger, Dale McCullough, John Olson, Wade Owens, Katherine Parker, Brian Peck, David Reihlman, John Schoen, Laine Stowell, Kevin Wallenfang, and Raymond Winchcombe.

To Robert Rose, whose drawings in chapter one illustrate the differences between North American deer, and, more importantly, bring to life their wild elegance and beauty.

I claim nothing in this book as my own, except the pleasures that so abounded as I learned about deer and people in America. On the other hand, I take sole responsibility for every error of fact and inference, and for whatever misguided conclusions I may have drawn. According to ethnographer Hans Himmelheber, the Yup'ik Eskimo people of Nunivak Island used to finish stories by asking their listeners' forgiveness:

May all my small mistakes go into their places and make little noise.

And finally, to each reader of the following chapters, I am grateful for your attention, for your companionship, and for your interest in deer and the natural world.

HEART AND BLOOD

PROLOGUE

Summer dawn comes gently, wreathed in birdsongs and soft rhythms of surf. I force open my eyes, check my watch, and stare at the tent's dim, gray wall. Four a.m. I feel like I've been run over by a herd of buffalo. One of those restless nights in camp, hearing every stitch and scuttle in the nearby woods, thinking of the brown bear tracks and fresh heaps of scat on the beach 50 feet away. But Keta never barked as she would for bear. I reach out to rub her warm fur, grateful for the company. The noises must have been something small—a mink or marten, possibly an otter.

Fifteen minutes later, I step out into the pallid light. Instinctively, I glance through the surrounding woods, then look both ways along the beach, checking first for the dark hulk of a bear and then for deer. Nothing moves, except a batch of scoter ducks diving and bobbing near the kelp beds. The North Pacific sprawls away beyond rocks and islets, brooding-gray, rippled by an offshore breeze. Ragged overcast hides the mountaintops, crawls into clefts and valleys, fingers the high emerald meadows.

Keta wags her tail and looks into my eyes, begging to get started. She's been excited since we anchored in the cove and made camp last evening. A man and a border collie may be vastly different creatures, but Keta and I have some important things in common: we get along easily, we love being outdoors together, and we're both truly fixated upon deer. Around these enthusiasms we've shaped a rich working partnership.

Not far from the tent a narrow game trail leads into the forest. Keta flounces ahead, nose to the moss, checking last night's olfactory news. She looks like an oversized fox and moves with similar grace and energy. Her fur is silky and flowing, glossy black, with a flash of white around the neck. She also has a fox's erect, attentive ears, acute as radar, reliable cues to sounds far beyond my hearing. But her eyes . . . unmistakably those of a border collie: bright and intense, given to the predatory stare herders call "hard eye," used by these quick-minded dogs to control sheep and other stock. Since we adopted Keta from a Wisconsin dog pound a couple years back, we've trained her to suppress her chase-and-herd instincts, while encouraging her extraordinary aptitude and enthusiasm for finding animals.

When I point at my heel, Keta moves close to me. Together we examine a patch of moist ground embossed with the single hoofprint of a deer, so crisp edged it must be from last night. For all I know, it could have been made five minutes ago; but Keta nuzzles the track casually, showing there's little scent. And more important, her calm demeanor indicates that no deer smells linger in the air.

The path winds through a labyrinth of massive trees—spruce, hemlock, and cedar—with a dense canopy that holds back the dawn. I feel vulnerable in the near darkness, knowing I share the top of the island's food chain with a cannier and far more powerful creature than I am. It's another reason to appreciate Keta's acute senses and warning bark. The deeply shaded forest is robed in moss, with a sparse undergrowth of head-high blueberry, huckleberry, and menziesia shrubs. Sapling conifers grow atop the moldering trunks of trees pitched down by winter storms.

Slats of light open between the trees ahead. And as we approach the woods' edge, the quiet is broken by a Swainson's thrush, unfurling the north country's most exquisite song. It has a dazzling, flutelike beauty, as if there were rainbows pinwheeling through the thickets, as if the breeze were laden with dense ambrosial smells, as if auroral light pulsed through every bough and needle of the thrush's tree. Easing away, I feel a twinge of regret: it's late July and soon the thrushes will fall silent.

The forest ends abruptly at the flank of a broad muskeg—a boggy meadow with scattered ponds and solitary, stunted shore pines. Beyond the muskeg's far edge, the volcanic mass of Kluksa Mountain heaves up from the lowland, like Kilimanjaro looming over the African savanna. I stand for a long while, scanning the muskeg and probing its tangled fringe until my arms ache from holding the binoculars. No sign of deer . . . so I turn north, moving slowly and meticulously upwind, entering a stretch of pine glades and grassy openings. It's an ideal place to spot deer because the view is spacious and unimpeded, but there's also plenty of cover to make shy animals feel secure.

As I cross swales and pockets of low ground, the saturated moss squashes under my feet—a subtle noise for me, but loud as shattering crystal for a deer. I angle toward a low ridge hoping for drier ground. We've had a stretch of rainy weather, not unusual in a place where the average year brings 100 inches of precipitation. Without omnipresent clouds and wetness we couldn't have this temperate rain forest and its lavish community of life.

Now . . . rather than staying close, Keta sidles off and lifts her nose as if there's a faint musk drifting in the breeze. She comes reluctantly when I gesture toward my heel. Taking her cue, I pause and watch ahead, then move when a sigh of wind in the trees covers the sound of our footsteps. Luckily, the ridge is well drained and densely carpeted in sphagnum moss, so it's fairly quiet going.

Keta's behavior telegraphs the scent's increasing strength: she moves forward, catches herself and looks back, falls in beside me, then shunts away to my left or right like someone pacing at a line she's been warned not to cross. She probes her nose into the breeze, occasionally reaching to the side for a stronger ribbon of scent. She hesitates and stares intently, aware that something is nearby but unable to pick it out. And most telling of all: she leans back and anxiously lifts a forepaw, possessed by her desire to charge off but yielding to the discipline she's learned, as if an inner voice were ordering her to wait.

By this time I'm convinced it must be a deer. If it were a bear, Keta would refuse to keep still and she'd woof suspiciously, deep in her throat. I edge along, furtive and stalking, as if I'd already seen the animal. At one point I even try sniffing the air, but for me there's not a hint of smell. It's strange, being completely numb to a signal that's as obvious to Keta as walking into a cloud of smoke. I stop for several minutes to study the ravel of shrubs and trees and openings ahead. But despite Keta's certainty, the place looks vacant to me.

A familiar sound breaks my concentration: the high-pitched, staccato cries of a bald eagle. The bird's great size creates an illusion of slowness as it soars across the muskeg and lifts to the peak of a tall snag. There it perches, black body silhouetted against the clouds, white head blazing, saber eyes peering down at us like an owl watching voles scurry through the grass.

Then, as I'm about to take a step, something catches my attention: a cinnamon-colored patch in a gap between sapling pines, sharper edged and with a brighter rusty tinge than the billows of moss I often mistake for deer. Yet this time I feel sure . . . and a look through binoculars confirms it.

I ease behind a slender tree trunk that breaks my profile, then hold an opened palm toward Keta, like a policeman stopping traffic. In our silent language it means "lie down and stay." The deer is about 30 yards off, hidden from Keta by a patch of shrubby pines. Without Keta I surely would have approached too quickly, made too much noise, and frightened the animal away.

A few minutes later the deer steps into plain sight. She's a heavy-bodied doe, facing upwind and away from us, head down, feeding avidly as a cow in summer pasture.

Slowly . . . slowly, I lift my binoculars, and she fills up the field of view. Her coat is light reddish tan. I can pick out every long, coarse summer hair on her flank and the remnants of winter fur that haven't shaken free. I can see the rise and fall of her ribs, the thin white fur and ripe bulge of her belly, the graceful arch of her neck, the angular shape of her hindquarters, the sculpted muscle and sinew of her legs. I can see the shaggy, white fringe of her tail, and the sooty fur on its tip for which the black-tailed deer is named. I can see the pale white markings beneath her chin, the gray fur and translucent skin of her enormous funnel-ears. And when she turns I can see her slender, elongated face, the conspicuous dark patch on her forehead, the twitching of her muzzle, the brightness of her great, shining eyes.

She leans down to graze, nuzzling back and forth amid the starbursts of yellow daisies, the violet blush of laurel, the snowy clusters of bog orchids, the leathery green of Labrador tea, the delicate dancing blades of grass. So exquisite is she—like a rose petal on a sheet of jade—that it takes a supreme act of self-control to keep myself from jumping up and shouting aloud.

But like Keta, I hold a tenuous grip on myself, standing still in the warm, swaddling breeze, holding the binoculars to my eyes, clinging to the tender and brilliant beauty of these moments. The doe is totally unaware of us, contentedly plucking what appear to be deer cabbage leaves and stems of sedges. Her eyes move this way and that as she feeds, revealing the dusky white crescents at their edges. At one point she bends her body in an arc, lifts a hind leg, and scratches her shoulder, leaving a disheveled spot in her fur. She seems wholly uninterested in looking around. It's as if nothing could disturb her seclusion; nothing could lift the curtain of security and contentment that surrounds the deer in the embracing freedom of her world.

I turn to look into Keta's eyes. Firmly now, I point to a low spot behind the little hillock where we stand. She folds back her ears, tucks her tail, and walks away, stopping several times to face me, sad eyed and pleading, but obedient. When I give the hand signal, she lies down.

I start again toward the deer, working my feet through brittle blades of grass to the silent moss below, taking care not to brush against the little pines, hesitating between each step, always closely watching the doe to be sure she's busy feeding . . . so the sound of her picking and chewing will mask the unavoidable squish and crumple of my bootsteps. I have rarely seen a deer so focused on eating; she's looked up only twice since I saw her.

I've now come within 30 feet of the doe after crossing open terrain where I could sidestep patches of crunchy lichen, spongy potholes, and raspy clumps of crowberry, but here the easy going ends. Between us is a cluster of sapling pines spaced tightly enough so that I'll have to worm through without scratching against their branches. I stand at the barrier's edge, alternately regarding the prospects and watching the deer. By an amazing stroke of luck she still has her hindmost parts toward me. If she faced my way I'd have to keep still as a rock, and even then it's likely the game would be up.

I know myself as a predator, know the hunter inside me, know the communion of meat and blood that shapes my body from those of deer. And considering how I've stalked this animal—slipped through the boundaries of her solitude, hidden my inimical shape, and used the wind to conceal my encroaching footsteps—I wonder that I can feel so innocent.

Perhaps it's because I haven't brought a rifle, not even for protection against blundering into a bear. I've come here to hunt only with my eyes, a luxury of the twentieth-century world, where freezers and grocery stores foster the illusion that life sustains itself without taking other life. Today I nourish only my soul, and the beauty of this encounter is what feeds me. I wonder if hawks and herons, wolves and killer whales are ever astounded by the loveliness, the grace, the perfection of their prey.

The doe lifts her head and gazes absentmindedly toward me, without blinking, as I stare back through the binoculars. She has enormous, elegantly curved lashes. Her globed eyes stand out from her face so she can look forward along her snout. And the morning sky reflects on their polished ebony surface the way clouds shimmer on still water.

I look from her eyes to the landscape they encompass: the green tangle at her feet; the surrounding meadows; the sodden muskegs that bed and nourish her; the forest that shelters her from rain and wind and snow; the dense thickets that shade and conceal her; the nearby shore, where kelp left by winter storms helps to carry her through the lean months; and the veering tundra heights of Kluksa Mountain, where she finds lush browse and seclusion in the long summer days.

During these moments, I sense—in a way that lies beyond words—how the deer is made from the world in which she lives, how this world is shaped by her existence within it, and how each is deeply infused with the other's wildness.

But now, looking back at the doe, I find that something has gone awry. She's standing in a rigid pose: head raised, ears wide in a listening V, body hardened and tense, tail flared to show its white underside, eyes fastened on me. What could have frightened her, since I haven't moved, haven't given a hint of my presence, haven't left the concealment of a bushy pine? Then I realize she isn't looking at me at all, but *past* me, and I hear a shuffle in the grass.

I know immediately that Keta must have forgotten her instructions or chosen to ignore them. Sure enough, she's on the move. And to make matters worse, she isn't just slipping up behind me; she's zigzagging excitedly, weaving herself through streamers of scent, still trying to spot the deer beyond the hedgy pines.

Before Keta settles at my side, the doe breaks into a stylized mechanical strut, heading up the slope toward a scatter of trees and underbrush. There's nothing to lose, so I imitate the soft, sheeplike bleat of a fawn.

She stops . . . then turns and steps deliberately back toward us, as if I were pulling a line attached to her neck. Ears honed, nervously flicking her tail, she then angles off, moving parallel to us along the rise, stopping occasionally to stare from the half concealment of shrubs and tree trunks. She's caught by an insuppressible curiosity, yet I can almost feel the quavering intensity of her fear, the tension that simmers eternally inside her, and the whetted blade of her alertness. She moves toward us like a droplet of oil trembling on a hot skillet.

The call keeps her from dashing off but can't ease her alarm. She moves slowly and silently like a cloud drifting along the hillside. At intervals the doe stretches forward, as if she's pushing her nose through a spiderweb. She looks at us repeatedly, but seems less trusting of her eyes than of the telling evidence a different sense will give her. I know exactly what she's trying to do and vainly wish for a way to change it.

She reaches into the eddying air as if to nip a handful of leaves, lifting her snout in little jerks. Before this she's found nothing of consequence. But finally . . . inevitably, she collides with the dark omen of our scent. For a deer, this obliterates all question. She cringes back, thrusts her nose forward again, pinches down her ears, and stares accusingly toward us. With utmost dignity she raises one foreleg and slowly turns aside. Then she bounds to the crest of the slope, springs effortlessly over a fallen log, and hushes away amid green veils, as if she's vanished into the cloud of her own breath.

I stand for a while, watching the empty spot where she disappeared and giving Keta a chance to settle down. Moments ago the deer filled up this meadowy enclave with her presence. She seemed as wild as Kluksa Mountain's smoldering volcanic core. We stood here together, snared in each other's gaze: two quick-minded creatures, our bodies and souls wedded to the same island. I felt that we were more alike than different, and for the duration of a single gust that whispered in the trees, I thought I knew her.

But in the vast quiet she leaves behind, I am fairly overwhelmed by a deeper sense, recognizing the distances between our worlds and acknowledging the impenetrable depths of the deer's mind.

Reflecting on this encounter afterward, I realize that deer have always lingered somewhere beyond my understanding, elusive as moonlight on water. Enchanting, fascinating, beloved, bewildering strangers. Yet I am driven to know about them, to comprehend their lives more fully, to fathom more clearly my own relationship to them, and to consider their existence as wild animals on a continent they have shared intimately— for thousands of years—with humankind.

No scientist, no shaman, no stalker, no sentimentalist will ever understand the deer . . . and for this I am truly grateful. I am possessed by a powerful curiosity about this animal, but what I desire most is to experience and acclaim its mysteries. In our explorations of scientific and practical information about deer, we should always keep in mind what the elders and philosophers teach: that while knowledge dispels some mysteries, it deepens others.

ONE

TRACKING THE DEER

No other creature seems more a shape
of the moonlight than does the deer.
—ARCHIBALD RUTLEDGE, 1918

W hat sort of animal is a deer and how does it live? There is an
almost limitless array of answers, reflecting the infinitely complex dimensions of a living creature. We know deer by their outward appearance—the elegantly shaped body, long supple legs, innocent face,
great dark eyes, graceful movements, controlled power and agility. We
know them by their habits: creatures of the forests and meadows, farmlands and mountains, often half visible at the edge of sight, elusive as a
fading breeze at dusk. We know them by expressions of their nature: shy,
gentle, alert, quick, tense, wild. Most people are intrigued and delighted
by deer, drawn toward them in mind and heart.

A consideration of deer natural history adds many traits to the ones
listed above: physical characteristics revealing the origins of deer and

establishing their position in the animal kingdom, physiological processes that sustain them as living organisms, behavior patterns and yearly biological cycles that define their way of life, ecological relationships and seasonal rounds of activity integrating them with the surrounding environment.

As a starting point for understanding the relationship between people and deer, it's first essential to learn about deer as organisms, to explore what is known about their life history. On this subject there is a staggering amount of information. Terry Bowyer, a University of Alaska biologist who had studied California mule deer, once told me: "Deer are the *Drosophila* of wildlife management." *Drosophila* is the scientific name for fruit flies, widely used in genetic research, and the subject of scientific books and articles numbering in the thousands. Bowyer pointed to a bulky file cabinet on the far side of his office: "That's full of papers about deer—you're welcome to look through them." He dug more articles from his desk and pulled book after book from the shelves, including a couple as hefty as encyclopedia volumes. "Yes," he concluded, "there's no shortage of biological literature about deer."

Beginnings

People in every culture have drawn from observation, insight, and imagination to explain the origins and evolution of animals. For example, Native American traditions richly describe the beginnings of deer in elaborate stories called myths or legends, considered to be the source of profound truth and wisdom. In Western societies we've largely abandoned similar stories carried down by our own ancestors, replacing them with the scientific, evolutionary account—which is a mystery and celebration in its own right.

Deer belong to a tremendously varied assemblage of herbivorous, or plant-eating, mammals called ungulates. Over the course of evolution, these creatures developed long and powerful legs, while the number of toes gradually decreased. The remaining toes became greatly elongated and lifted up so only their tips, which we know as hooves, make contact with the ground. In all likelihood, the most important advantage of these highly evolved legs is speed to escape from predators.

Taxonomists use the number of toes to distinguish two quite different orders of ungulates. Most diverse by far is the order Artiodactyla—meaning "even toed"—which includes pigs, hippopotamus, camels, chevrotains (mouse deer), antelopes, giraffes, pronghorn, sheep, cattle, goats, and buffaloes, as well as the true deer. The artiodactyls live throughout Africa, Europe, Asia, South America, and North America. They are all ruminants, or cud chewers, meaning they have a complex, multichambered stomach and a digestive process that involves regurgitating food to break it down by repeated chewing. Artiodactyls have an even number of hooves, usually two. By contrast, members of the Perissodactyla—including horses, rhinoceroses, and piglike tapirs—have an odd number of toes. For example, a horse runs on the tip of one long, powerful, intricately specialized toe, while a deer sprints and leaps on paired, slender middle toes.

From studies of fossils, paleontologists have reconstructed an evolutionary history of the deer family, or Cervidae. The first true deer were small, herbivorous animals who appeared some 20 million years ago in temperate woodlands of Europe and Asia. Over the next few million years, cervids diversified and spread into North America, crossing the Bering Strait during one of several periods when lowered sea levels opened a corridor of dry land. Like their closest relatives—the giraffes—early deer had low-crowned teeth, indicating a preference for the woody browse diet found in forest and brush country. By contrast, the bovids (cattle, buffaloes, sheep, goats, and antelopes) developed the high-crowned teeth of grazers and adapted to life in open, grassy terrain.

Ancestral deer were relatively short legged and stocky, with a face we would recognize, except for short tusks that were in fact enlarged upper canine teeth. A few living Asian species—the musk deer, muntjacs, and water deer—still have these peculiar tusks, which move in their sockets and are apparently used in feeding. During their early evolution, ancestral deer lacked the attribute for which they are now best known: they had no antlers. How these beautiful embellishments evolved, or why, remains a free field for speculation. Some biologists suggest they originated for defense, and that antlers gradually became larger as the canine tusks disappeared. Other scientists, perhaps the majority, believe that although antlers function for combat and defense, their primary purpose is to display a male's physical prowess and increase his chances to mate with females.

Regardless of their purpose, what began as small bumps on a primitive deer's skull gradually became elongated into carrotlike stalks, then developed a glorious variety of tines, forks, and palpations. These appendages culminated in the largest deer that ever lived—*Megaloceros giganteus,* the Irish elk. A stag in his prime hulked more than seven feet tall at the shoulder and the span of his antlers measured up to 14 feet, greater than the length of a compact station wagon. Some have theorized that dysfunctionally huge antlers contributed to the Irish elk's extinction, about 11,000 years ago. There is no evidence to support this idea, but in science a house vacant of facts is usually haunted by theories.

Antlers are found exclusively on members of the deer family and only on males, except for the relatively small, slender antlers carried by female caribou and reindeer. Aside from their beauty, the most remarkable characteristic of antlers is that they are shed and regrown every year. Horns, by contrast, are permanent fixtures that keep growing throughout an animal's life. Characteristic of the bovids, horns are found on both sexes, have an elegant but unbranched design, and consist of a bone core sheathed in keratin, the same material as fingernails. Antlers are solid bone, arising from small knobs called pedicles, which develop on a buck deer's skull several months after birth. It takes a tremendous amount of energy to grow a new set of antlers every year, be it the modest rack of a whitetail buck or the monumental adornments that added a hundred pounds to the weight of an Irish elk. Whether for protection or sexual advertisement, antlers must have conferred a strong evolutionary advantage to offset their nutritional cost.

Over a prodigious span of geological time, the cervids radiated into five separate lines, or subfamilies, containing about 40 modern species (taxonomists disagree on the exact number). Of these, some 24 are found in Eurasia, reflecting the great age of the deer family in that part of the world. Several Eurasian species—notably red deer, fallow deer, and sika deer—have been locally established in North America for commercial sport hunting and venison production. Another 10 members of the Cervidae are indigenous species restricted to South and Central America.

North America has only five native species. Three of these—moose, elk, and caribou, or reindeer—are also found in Europe and Asia. This book deals with the two remaining species, familiar animals known to most North Americans simply as "deer." Except for a few relocated populations established during the past century, our deer live exclusively in the Western Hemisphere. We have two species of deer, but they are divided somewhat confusingly into three types: white-tailed deer *(Odocoileus virginianus)*, mule deer *(Odocoileus hemionus)*, and two distinctive mule deer subspecies collectively known as black-tailed deer *(Odocoileus hemionus columbianus* and *Odocoileus hemionus sitkensis)*.

The scientific name *Odocoileus* is an apparent misspelling of the Greek, *odontocoileus,* meaning hollow or concave tooth. A French-American naturalist, Constantine Samuel Rafinesque, devised this name in 1832 after he picked up a single deer tooth in the Virginia woods. Since deer teeth are not hollow, we might charitably guess that Rafinesque's specimen was from an old deer, giving it a deeply worn, concave surface. The whitetail's rather provincial specific name, *virginianus,* commemorates the source of Rafinesque's scavenged tooth. Our other species is more appropriately named: *hemionus,* from the Greek for "mulelike," a reference to the animal's generously proportioned ears.

According to eminent Canadian biologist Valerius Geist, our first deer—the whitetail—evolved in North America about four million years ago. Elk, moose, and caribou arrived considerably later, as did the venerable mammoths and mastodons. Interestingly, fossilized remains suggest that ancient whitetails looked nearly identical to those we see today. And whereas scores of large mammals became extinct during the Ice Age, white-tailed deer persisted, then thrived in an array of newly vacated ecological niches. Here, says Geist, is the true measure of an animal's success—its ability to survive for a very long time and through periods of dramatic environmental change.

We might remember, for the sake of comparison, that humans first walked across the Bering land bridge into North America sometime between 12,000 and 30,000 years ago. On the geological scale, this makes us relative newcomers. However, it also means that people and deer have lived together on this continent for a very long time, and not as distant strangers but in the constant, intense relationship of predator and prey.

Valerius Geist believes that black-tailed deer separated from their whitetail ancestors somewhere along the West Coast about a million years ago. Much later—perhaps as little as 7,000 to 14,000 years ago—a further divergence from the original blacktail type gave rise to the mule deer. Geist is convinced that this happened through hybridization between blacktails and whitetails. Details of this evolutionary story are hard to assemble, however, because fossil bones from all of our deer look so much alike. Perhaps, then, mule deer should be classified as a subspecies of black-tailed deer, instead of the other way around. In any case, all three types are closely related. Where mule deer and whitetails inhabit the same territory, as they do in parts of the West, they regularly interbreed, but most, if not all, of their hybrid offspring are sterile.

When we look at a deer, whether in the backcountry or the backyard, we see the living embodiment of wild nature on our North American continent—an animal whose evolution was shaped over several million years by the unique ecological circumstances of this landscape. And in the elegant and complex reciprocity of things, deer have also influenced the evolution of their own surrounding natural community. For example, they have probably affected characteristics of growth, reproduction, and dispersal in some of the plants they eat. On the other side of the equation, they have affected the behavior and lifeways of animals who prey on them, such as mountain lions, wolves, and bears.

Because humans have likely been the most important predators on deer for many thousands of years, we ourselves—and the hunger in our bellies—may have influenced the evolutionary sculpting of this creature. Selective pressures from human hunting would have favored traits such as acute senses, secretiveness, wariness and escape behaviors, camouflaging coloration, cryptic patterns of body movement, and fleetness of foot.

Rumps and Racks

Most people who live in North America have seen deer for themselves, either in the wild or in captivity, but relatively few can distinguish among whitetails, mule deer, and blacktails. At first glance all three types look nearly the same, but knowing a few basic differences in appearance, behavior, and geographic range makes them fairly easy to tell apart.

Whitetails are by far the most widespread North American deer species. They've been seen in all 48 contiguous states, eight Canadian provinces, throughout Mexico and Central America, and into northern South America. Draw a line from the western borders of Manitoba and Minnesota, down through the central states to Louisiana, and any native deer east of that line is a whitetail. West from there things get more complicated, a puzzlework of fingers and offshoots. For example, whitetails live in a few small pockets along the Columbia and Umpqua rivers in western Washington and Oregon, far removed from their compatriots east of the Cascade Mountains.

Both whitetails and mule deer are found in a broad swath from western Canada and the Rocky Mountain states, south to New Mexico, Arizona, and adjacent Mexico. Mule deer have to themselves most of the Great Basin, eastern and southern California, and Baja California. Finally, black-tailed deer inhabit the Pacific coastal strip from southeastern Alaska to central California.

In recent times white-tailed deer have begun expanding westward in the United States and Canada. For example, whitetails have become common in the Canadian prairie provinces, while mule deer have declined or vanished. The same process is under way in places like Montana, Wyoming, Colorado, and Texas—especially in habitats changed by human activity, such as agricultural lowlands. Valerius Geist believes this process might eventually cause the extinction of the mule deer. The large but easily hunted mule deer bucks are often killed each fall, he says, and this allows smaller but more elusive whitetail bucks to breed with female mule deer. Because the hybrid offspring are infertile, mule deer decline and whitetails take over. Whether or not this theory is correct, there's no question that the adaptable white-tailed deer is moving into areas of the West where it's never been seen before.

The simplest way to characterize North American deer distribution is this: whitetails in the East, mule deer in the West, a mix of both in the Rockies, and blacktails along the Pacific coast.

Where different types of deer live together, they tend to segregate by habitat. In much of the West, whitetails occupy wooded river bottoms, low-elevation valleys, agricultural lands, and other areas affected by humans. Mule deer prefer more open, brushy country and high mountain terrain, migrating down to the valleys during winter. So a glance at the surroundings can be the first clue about a deer's identity.

The best way to tell our deer apart is by checking their heads and tails, not necessarily in that order. Whitetails end in a flourish—a long, wide, graceful tail, mostly brown on the upper side, with a white border that bristles when the animal is nervous or agitated. This conspicuous fringe is one of the easiest and surest ways to identify a white-tailed deer. When truly frightened, a whitetail "flags," raising its tail to show the brilliant white underside, waving it to and fro as the deer bounds away.

By contrast, a mule deer's tail is small, narrow, and understated; its color is creamy white on both sides except for the black tip; and surrounding the tail is a large, whitish rump patch. Of all the traits that separate whitetails from mule deer, this rump patch might be the easiest to see from a distance. Ironically, the hindquarters of an undisturbed mule deer look much whiter than those of a whitetail, but anyone who has seen the conspicuous flag of an alarmed white-tailed deer understands how it got the name.

The tail of most black-tailed deer is about halfway between the other two in size and shape, white on the underside and along the edges, usually with a black stripe down the middle of the upper side, and always black on the tip. When frightened, a blacktail may flag like a whitetail, although often not so vertically and wagging less from side to side as the animal dashes off.

At the head end, mule deer are distinguished from other species by the trait for which they're named—outsized, mulelike ears. The antlers are also diagnostic. Mule deer and blacktails have forked tines, or points, branching from the main beam of each antler, and the entire rack seems to reach upward like a tree. Whitetails have single tines, like vertical fingers arranged along a nearly horizontal beam. Mule deer bucks also develop much larger and taller racks than whitetails. With a little practice one can easily see the differences in typical deer, but antlers can be tricky because they're highly variable. This lavish individuality has much to do with the mystique of antlers among some hunters.

A cautionary note. These traits aren't always as distinctive as they sound, nor does a given species look the same everywhere. There are about 30 subspecies of white-tailed deer in North and Central America (plus another 8 in South America), and between 7 and 11 subspecies of mule deer. These are regional varieties, marked by subtle differences in size, color, and other characteristics. In the West, there are also hybrids between whitetails and mule deer, or between mule deer and blacktails. This variability and mixing can make for confusion, especially in places like California, western Texas, and parts of the Rockies.

Size is not a reliable way to distinguish types of deer. In our largest subspecies, the Rocky Mountain mule deer, mature bucks measure about 42 inches high at the shoulder and average around 200 pounds. Record mule deer scale close to 500 pounds. Adult whitetail bucks from the Northeast measure a couple of inches shorter and average about 160 pounds. Our largest whitetails come from the midwestern United States and adjacent Canada. A prodigious buck taken in Minnesota weighed 511 pounds; by comparison, one of the largest from New York scaled 388 pounds. Black-tailed deer are smaller, especially in the north; for example, adult bucks in southeast Alaska average about 150 pounds. A record Sitka blacktail from coastal Alaska weighed 253 pounds, and the largest Columbian blacktails scale around 300 pounds. (These figures are close approximations, calculated from hunter-killed deer that were field-dressed before weighing.)

Among white-tailed deer, average size is considerably larger in the north than in the south. For example, in a New Hampshire study the average weight of prime adult (four-and-a-half-year-old) whitetails was 245 pounds for bucks and 145 pounds for does. Compare this with the Key deer of extreme southern Florida—a diminutive whitetail subspecies—in which adult bucks average about 80 pounds and does, 60 pounds, both sexes standing just over two feet at the shoulder. Generally speaking, does are about 30 percent smaller than bucks in all of our deer species.

The tendency for deer to be largest in northern regions and progressively smaller toward the south is explained by a biological principle called Bergman's Rule, which states that body size in a given species increases with distance from the equator. Larger animals have less surface area relative to their total body mass, which conserves heat, saving energy and improving their chances of survival in cold climates. Smaller animals have relatively more surface area, promoting dissipation of heat, an adaptive advantage in perennially hot climates.

While this may be true, the size of deer within a given population is also influenced by other factors, especially nutrition. Well-fed animals—meaning those in good habitat with relatively low deer population—grow faster and become much larger than animals competing for survival in poor or overpopulated habitat.

Leaving their physical attributes aside, whitetails and mule deer (including blacktails) are very different creatures whose overall looks and behavior often give them away at a glance. The first time I saw both species together was in the Rocky Mountain Arsenal, a huge tract of grassland and brushy woods on the outskirts of Denver. Even at a hundred yards, there was no mistaking the lean, sinewy whitetails, especially when they sprinted away, bright flags erect and waving. As we watched, I suddenly realized how we got the American expression "hightailing it" to describe a quick retreat. The animals vanished without pausing to look back.

Not far off was a group of mule deer. By comparison, their bodies were thick and muscular; they moved more slowly and deliberately; and they had an almost placid demeanor, regarding us with benign interest as we approached. Instead of running when we got too close, they bounded off, springing with all four legs at once like jumping mechanical toys. And they didn't go far before stopping to gaze at us, altogether unlike the disappearing whitetails. Only mule deer and blacktails have this unusual, bouncy gait, which is called "stotting." Biologists believe stotting evolved as a way to escape predators—it allows sudden upward leaps, unpredictable changes of direction, effective use of obstacles like bushes or rocks, and quick ascent of steep slopes in the hilly western country.

Whitetail differs from mule deer as piccolo differs from flute, oboe from saxophone, violin from viola. Each animal has a clear and resplendent beauty of its own. But I must admit, on that day in Colorado I was struck above all else by the exquisiteness of the white-tailed deer: their narrow faces, slender necks, lithesome bodies, and incredibly gracile legs. I saw in them the quintessence of all that is elegant about deer.

And I saw how deeply the wildness runs through them, even against a backdrop of fences and steel buildings. These whitetails were so flinchy and high-strung, it seemed a wonder they could live at all, could contain within themselves such incandescent energy and alertness. It was as if their nerves and veins were wound so tightly they might all snap at once, as if they might spontaneously explode in moments of illimitable fear. But instead, their power was released in great, suspended, arcing leaps, as the deer flung themselves like dark moons over the earth's far edge.

Natural Virtuosity

It seems that a beauty like the deer's should be rare and hidden. Yet of all the animals who inhabit North America, deer are among the most widespread and abundant. Interestingly, we seldom appreciate the loveliness of common things—like seagulls, crows, and dandelions—but we care fervently about deer, which attests to their extraordinary qualities. Research on attitudes toward nature affirms that Americans and Canadians value deer more highly than any other wild creature.

I met a biologist who for two years had studied deer at the Rocky Mountain Arsenal, and he'd closely observed the area's many human visitors as well. When a tour bus squeezed by us on a narrow road, he wryly commented: "People who want this area protected emphasize that it's a place where you can see eagles, and they say eagles are the most important reason to keep it wild. Maybe so. But I'll tell you what most visitors want to see when they come through here. They take a look at an eagle or two sitting in a tree. Then, what's the biggest thrill for them is the deer. Everybody's heard about the deer, and that's what they really want to watch."

Such a gift, then, that wild deer live within a short drive of almost every household on this continent. The only areas *not* inhabited by deer are in the far north of Canada and Alaska—places sparsely populated by humans as well. There is no more convincing testimony to the remarkable adaptability of deer than the vast extent of their homeland. Deer of one type or another occupy a bewildering array of natural habitats, "so diverse as to defy generalization," writes the biologist Olof Wallmo.

Perhaps best known are whitetails of the eastern temperate forests, thriving in the same moderate conditions that appeal to millions of our own kind. But subspecies of white-tailed deer also range from near tree line at 60 degrees north latitude in Canada, down across the equator, to 10 degrees south latitude in Brazil. Both whitetails and mule deer inhabit

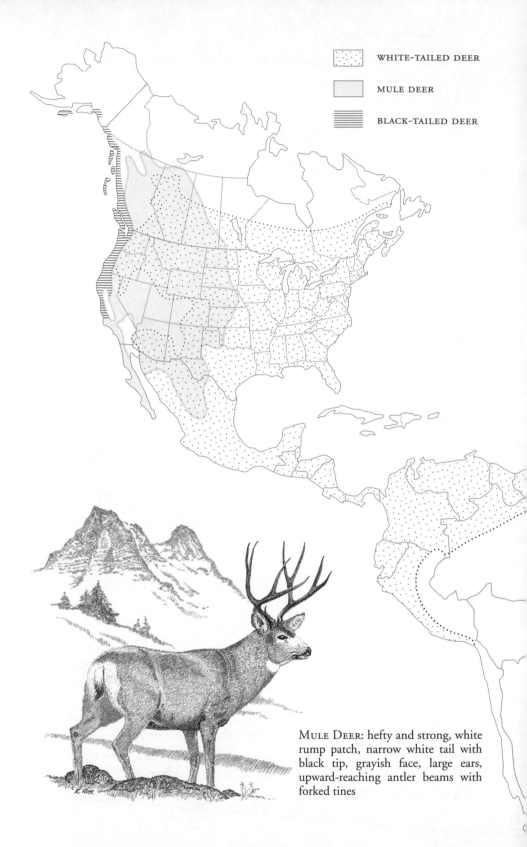

WHITE-TAILED DEER

MULE DEER

BLACK-TAILED DEER

MULE DEER: hefty and strong, white rump patch, narrow white tail with black tip, grayish face, large ears, upward-reaching antler beams with forked tines

A PORTRAIT OF ELEGANCE
AND ADAPTABILITY

A marvel of adaptation, North America's three types of deer range from the subarctic to the equatorial tropics, and from the wilderness to the suburbs.

BLACKTAIL: resembles mule deer, especially in southern range, but generally smaller and stockier build, browner rump, medium-width tail with black midline and tip, dark face, shorter antlers with forked tines

WHITETAIL: lean and graceful, brown rump, long and wide brown tail with white fringe, white underside of tail shows when flagging, dark face with white eye rings, forward-reaching antler beams with unforked tines the low deserts of Arizona and California, where shade temperatures reach 115 degrees Fahrenheit in summer and yearly rainfall may total less than 5 inches. At the other extreme, mule deer near the border of Alaska and British Columbia sometimes experience temperatures of 70 below zero or colder. And North Pacific coastal black-tailed deer flourish in temperate rain forests saturated by almost 200 inches of precipitation annually.

Deer live in the sagebrush steppes of Wyoming, the longleaf pine forests of Georgia, the mountain meadows of Alberta, the coastal chaparral of California, the deciduous forests of Pennsylvania, the northern deserts of Oregon, the tallgrass prairies of Nebraska, the boreal forests of Quebec, the oak savannas of Texas, the plateau scrublands of Mexico, the coastal plains of Nicaragua, the tropical forests of Brazil, and a myriad of other environments.

One key to this flexibility is the deer's amazing range of diet, which collectively includes thousands of plant species. Deer can eat and digest nearly anything that grows, from delicate ferns to thorny devil's club, from juicy squash to bristling evergreen boughs, from succulent corn to papery lichen. Though it seldom happens, deer are reliably known to eat animal flesh, especially fish. For example, whitetails on Michigan's North Manitou Island eat small fish called alewives that sometimes wash in large numbers onto the beaches. During these periods, researchers estimated, alewives made up 30 to 50 percent of the deer's diet. Naturalist Sigurd Olson watched a doe eating black suckers up to 14 inches long after killing them with her front feet. An Idaho biologist discovered where white-tailed deer had pawed through the snow to eat wintering colonies of ladybug beetles.

Another key to deer's adaptability is their versatile brain and body. Deer have adapted their life cycles and their entire behavioral repertoire to surroundings as radically different as sheltering forests and open plains, deserts with almost no water and swamps with almost no land, scalding shadeless heat and unrelenting subarctic cold. For many thousands of years, deer have also accommodated—with extraordinary success—the habitat changes wrought by humankind. They thrive not only in remote, pristine wildlands but also in farm and ranch country, in every sort of park and commons, in rural parishes, in suburbs, and even in city neighborhoods.

The biologists Charles Nixon and Lonnie Hansen found central Illinois whitetails doing well in "one of the world's most intensively farmed regions," where corn and soybean fields take up 86 percent of the land,

and less than 10 percent is patchy woods. Not only do the crops provide rich feed for deer, but just as important, the vast "corn forest" gives them virtually limitless cover. But consider this: After harvest time only the scattered woodlots are left, while the cultivated land is reduced to bare, raw earth, and so it remains until crops grow again the following year. Every fall, hunting reduces deer numbers to a level that can be supported by wild plants and leavings in agricultural fields, and the next summer, extremely high fawning success replenishes the population. These twentieth-century Illinois whitetails have adapted to a world almost totally different from the one that sustained their ancestors here 150 years ago.

In recent decades, deer have become more and more tolerant of people, and large numbers of them have abandoned the ancestral life of forest and field. Pressured by growing populations of their own kind, deer began moving into attractive habitat around the edges of towns, where they found a wide selection of edible plants and a warm welcome from human residents. Later, as deer continued to increase, they began infiltrating the urban world itself. In fact, these animals have become entirely too adaptable for some people's taste—dodging traffic at dusk, feasting in yards and gardens, oblivious to householders' complaints of freshly browsed roses, nipped delphiniums, and shorn lettuce. Millions of North Americans are discovering for themselves that deer can live almost anywhere.

Long before deer started moving in on people, we were moving them around, putting their adaptability to yet another test. North American whitetails have been transplanted to Finland, Czechoslovakia, Cuba, the Virgin Islands, and other islands of the Caribbean. Between 1901 and 1905, New Zealanders interested in hunting imported about 50 whitetails, and the animals reproduced so enthusiastically in this predator-free environment that by 1926 all protection was removed in hopes of controlling their population. Incidentally, these deer quickly adapted their biological cycles to the Southern Hemisphere's reversed seasons; they now rut in April and May rather than November or December, and they give birth in December and January instead of June or July.

During the 1960s, 40 black-tailed deer from Oregon were introduced to the Hawaiian island of Kaua'i. The island's mountainous interior is covered with a nearly impenetrable forest, where reclusive blacktails eat savory plants like guava, passion fruit, uki uki, and shoots of koa trees. Unlike the New Zealand whitetails, these deer have increased slowly, and by 1990 their population appeared stable at about 400 animals.

Few wild creatures are as versatile and successful as North America's

deer. Whether shaped by the ineluctable processes of evolution, the clev-
erness of Grandfather Raven, or the wisdom of God, deer are a paragon
of genius in wild design.

Population, Pestilence, and Predators

The adaptive virtuosity of deer is reflected not only in their widespread
occurrence but also in their abundance, past and present. It's extremely
hard to estimate North America's total deer population in pre-Colonial
times, but accounts by early European travelers and settlers leave no
question that deer were plentiful. "Of . . . Deare, in some places there are
a great store," wrote Thomas Harriot, an Englishman who visited Virginia during the 1580s. He also noted, comparing New World deer to
those in Britain, "They differ from ours onely in this, their tailes are
longer, and the snags of their hornes looke backward." Writing about
Carolina whitetails in 1682, Thomas Ashe commented: "There is such
infinite Herds that the whole country seems but one continued park."
Daniel Boone told John James Audubon that during the 1780s in the
Green River country of Kentucky, "You would not have walked out in
any direction for more than a mile without shooting a buck."

Estimates of North America's total deer population in 1500 A.D. have
ranged from 50 million down to 25 million. Some biologists think these
figures are all too high, and they believe deer are more numerous today
than ever before, thanks to regulated hunting and creation of open habitats by land clearing. The present United States deer population is vari-
ously calculated at 15 million to 25 million.

Looking more closely, we discover striking differences in the number
and density of deer from one area to another. Population mosaics are incredibly complex, reflecting the diversity of habitats, hunting effects,
land uses, and deer management policies. Biologists often refer to an environment's "biological carrying capacity," meaning its ability to sustain
a given density of deer over the long term; and nowadays they also speak
of "social carrying capacity" to indicate the maximum abundance of deer
that people in a given area will tolerate (due to problems like agricultural
crop damage).

In southern Wisconsin, for example, farmlands dominated by open
fields with little protective cover may have relatively few deer—perhaps
15 per square mile. But in neighboring townships where hilly terrain creates a mix of woods and fields, densities may reach 70 to 80 deer per
square mile. On a continental scale, regional densities vary from near

zero at the northern limits of the deer range in Canada and Alaska up to 300 deer per square mile in parts of central Texas.

Whitetails are by far the most abundant of our deer, in total numbers as well as population density. They do best in mixed habitats, especially forest or brushland mingled with open meadows and agricultural fields, where they find a wide diversity of food plants and plenty of shelter. Highest populations are in places like the upper Midwest, New York, and Pennsylvania, locally down the East Coast to the deer-rich farmlands of Georgia and Alabama, and westward into parts of Texas. Areas of lower abundance for all deer include sprawling, shelterless agricultural lands and arid regions like the Great Plains, western deserts, sagebrush prairies, and coastal chaparral.

Deer populations also fluctuate over time, adding another dimension to this complexity. They're affected by long-term changes such as loss of habitat diversity resulting from forest regrowth in the East, competition with livestock in the West, and urban expansion everywhere on the continent. In the shorter term, populations may drop suddenly because of severe winters, drought, disease, and human or animal predation, and they usually increase when these conditions are reversed. It's safe to say that deer numbers are never constant in a given locale.

Of course, the population of deer is enormously important from a human standpoint: their value to wildlife watchers and hunters is beyond calculating, they have great impact on agricultural crops, they can be harmful or beneficial to natural habitats, and they have even become a factor in American suburban life. What amounts to a biological research industry has developed from our efforts to understand relationships between deer and people, and to find ways of managing deer numbers.

A key factor is the deer's remarkable capacity to reproduce and multiply. Consider Dale R. McCullough's studies at the George Reserve in southern Michigan, a tract of woods, swamp, and meadow covering 1½ square miles, enclosed by a deer-proof fence 11½ feet high. Because deer cannot enter or leave the enclosure, and because they have no animal predators, this is a perfect laboratory for population and ecology research. Beginning in the 1960s, biologists used controlled hunting to gradually reduce whitetail numbers within the reserve, and by 1975 only about 10 remained, most of them fawns. At this point researchers stopped all hunting and let the population grow on its own. In 1980, just five years later, they counted 212 whitetails inside the George Reserve.

On good range, a wild deer population can double every two years, despite deaths from car collisions, animal predators, and buck hunting seasons. Biologists in many parts of the United States have found it impossible to stabilize growing deer populations unless hunters are allowed (if not encouraged) to take does.

Of course, deer populations are not always vigorous and healthy. Deer are susceptible to a long list of diseases and parasites, some capable of reaching epidemic proportions. In 1976, an outbreak of epizootic hemorrhagic disease reportedly killed thousands of deer in the Dakotas, Nebraska, Kansas, and Wyoming, and over a thousand more died from the disease that year in New Jersey. Foot-and-mouth disease is another deadly illness, originally transmitted to deer from cattle and pigs. In 1924, more than 22,000 deer were killed in a California effort to stop the spread of the disease; of these, about 2,200 animals had lesions showing they were infected.

Other diseases that can seriously impact deer numbers include bluetongue, encephalitis, anthrax, anaplasmosis, and salmonellosis, and deer may be afflicted by a whole menagerie of parasitic worms, nematodes, larvae, mites, and ticks. Recently, deer have become notorious as intermediate hosts for *Ixodes scapularis,* the deer tick, the main carrier of Lyme disease—an illness that is extremely dangerous to humans, as well as to dogs and cattle, but apparently has no effect on deer.

It's important to note that in any wildlife population, a certain number of individuals are bound to die from infectious diseases, but rarely do illnesses become epidemic. Many diseases and parasites only reach lethal proportions when the deer population is extremely high and animals are weakened by poor nutrition. As long as their numbers are well balanced with the environment, most deer are strong enough to heal themselves or to resist infection altogether.

We often hear that sick, stressed, old, or very young deer are the ones most likely to be killed by animal predators, and biological evidence reveals this to be true. But there's no question that healthy adult deer are also taken, despite being wonderfully equipped to elude pursuers. Predators, of course, have evolved for millions of years to overcome the defenses of their prey, giving rise to a tense, uneasy, constantly shifting balance. This is the stone on which the blade of life is whetted to its keenest edge. Ecology and evolution—those fundamental processes of nature—center around the splendid reciprocity of one life being passed along to another.

A deer's first defense against predation is its alertness: its acute senses of smell, hearing, and sight; its remarkable ability to hide in dense vegetation, to blend with the surroundings, and to slip silently away. Once I followed two small blacktails through a stretch of woods and shoreline on a calm winter day. I stayed within 20 feet of the deer as they crossed patches of crunchy gravel, crusted snow, and dried grass. My footsteps rattled like spilled marbles, while the two animals were so magically quiet I could scarcely hear them. It was as if something inside them absorbed the sounds of their own existence. They were like mist: tangible and lovely, but able to drift noiselessly through the world.

This should be no surprise, I thought. Just as animals evolve sensitive hearing to detect approaching predators, they also evolve the capacity to keep silent so predators have difficulty finding them. Surely quietness was a major factor in the deer's evolutionary design: legs and hooves developed partly as organs of noiseless locomotion; muscles, nerves, and mind were shaped by the imperative for silence.

If these subtle tactics fail, deer have other means of escape. "To a deer, whether he runs up a steep hill or runs downhill, the terrain is flat and even," explained Navajo elder Claus Chee Sonny. "This is so because deer travel on lightning." A whitetail can sprint 35 to 40 miles per hour for short distances and sustain speeds of 20 to 25 miles per hour; mule deer and blacktails are about 5 miles per hour slower. On level ground, horizontal leaps of more than 20 feet have been measured for mule deer, and it's not uncommon for whitetails to jump over fences 8 feet tall. In New York, biologist C. W. Severinghaus found tracks of a white-tailed deer that stayed airborne for 29 feet horizontally (on a slight downgrade), while leaping over a log 7½ feet high. Deer also willingly take to the water, and they can swim both far and fast. On the North Pacific coast, it's common to see blacktails crossing channels several miles wide, and some does swim to small islands where they raise their fawns away from brown bears or wolves.

Before hunters and trappers exterminated them from much of North America, wolves were probably the most important animal predator on deer, especially in the East. It's difficult to know how wolves might have influenced deer populations in earlier times, but modern studies indicate that each year's fawn production successfully balances against losses to wolves.

To study relationships between wolf and deer populations, biologists Harry Merriam and David Klein released two captive wolf pairs in 1960 on Coronation Island, off the southeast Alaska coast. This 32-square-mile island had no other predators and was rarely visited by hunters, which allowed the blacktail population to reach moderately high levels and to severely overbrowse the forest's brushy understory. Coronation's poorly fed deer measured about 20 percent smaller than their counterparts on larger islands nearby, and the absence of predators had made them fairly tame.

One of the wolf pairs had 11 pups the first summer—a litter of extraordinary size, doubtless reflecting the wolves' equally extraordinary food supply. Before long, Klein told me, this burgeoning wolf population "proceeded to really hammer the deer," something that can happen when prey populations are extremely dense. At one point, biologists found that deer bones and fur made up 95 percent of the wolves' droppings. A year after wolves were introduced, Coronation's deer had become "very spooky," recalled Klein. "Their whole behavior had changed."

Four years after the wolf pairs were released, biologists counted between 9 and 13 wolves on the island, but the deer had practically vanished and the vegetation showed dramatic regrowth. "If you walked all day you might see one or two fresh deer tracks," Klein said. Not surprisingly, wolf droppings had fewer deer remains and showed evidence of beach scavenging, such as clamshells, seal bones, and fish bones. Most telling of all, biologists found wolf remains in some droppings, indicating cannibalism. By the mid-1970s, wolves had vanished from Coronation, but enough deer survived to repopulate the island. Recent studies by Steven Lewis, Klein's student, show renewed overbrowsing and a decline in the average size of Coronation blacktails.

Northern deer are most susceptible to wolf predation during winter, especially when they're weakened by deep snow and cold. Even on snow, a healthy adult deer can usually outrun a wolf, but fawns and older animals are much more vulnerable. Should a wolf manage to overtake a prime deer, the outcome is still undecided. The wolf biologist David Mech saw a whitetail successfully fend off a wolf by charging and kicking with its front feet; once it literally bowled the wolf over. In northeastern Minnesota, Mech and Patrick Karns found that wolves seldom have a significant impact on whitetail populations, except during extreme winters, and studies in Glacier National Monument showed that mule deer made up only a small part of the wolves' diet.

Deer are better matched against coyotes, a smaller but far more numerous relative of the wolf. Coyotes regularly prey on fawns, and they can also kill larger deer weakened by severe winter conditions or poor habitat. In some areas—especially western grasslands where livestock overgrazing has damaged natural cover—coyotes may take enough fawns to significantly reduce deer numbers. But research in many other places has shown that coyote predation has little effect on overall deer population levels. Consider the work of William F. Porter in the Adirondacks of New York, where coyotes first appeared in about 1920 and have now become fairly common. During a 20-year period after 1970, deer made up about 90 percent of the coyotes' diet in this area. At the same time, deer populations went from about 25 per square mile down to 5 per square mile following heavy winters, then back up to about 20 per square mile in the mid-1980s.

Mountain lions, formerly widespread but now mostly limited to the West, are a master predator on deer, which are by far their most important prey. Yet here again, research shows that lion predation is seldom the main influence on deer numbers. In one area of central Utah, biologists concluded that after mountain lions were reduced by at least 50 percent, hunters altogether may have taken 6 to 18 more deer per year, an increase of 1 to 4 percent from the average harvest of 447 deer. In short, control of mountain lion numbers had little effect on either the deer population or hunting success.

Other animals occasionally known to take deer include bobcats, bears, and eagles; once again, fawns are the most likely prey. I haven't yet mentioned the single most important nonhuman predator on deer in North America today. This, of course, is the domesticated dog. We might think stray or feral animals are the main culprits, but in fact, docile, well-mannered house pets allowed to run loose probably do a larger share of the killing. Well-known deer researcher John Ozoga writes: "Dogs are most perilous to young fawns, but they frequently kill adult deer, apparently for 'sport,' and their chasing of undernourished deer during late winter likely contributes to additional stress and death of some deer that might otherwise have survived." Dog predation has little effect on deer populations, but for many people it is a potent emotional and ethical issue.

As we've seen, animal predators are not a prime determinant of deer numbers, except in local areas and where deer populations are out of balance with their habitat. This is true even when deer make up a high percentage of the diet for wolves, coyotes, or mountain lions. As long as the environment is in good condition, each year's reproduction makes up for animals taken by predators, and in this way a diverse wildlife community is sustained. Most biologists conclude that reducing predation is not a very effective way to maintain or increase deer populations. In fact, deer are often *more* numerous (and healthier) in the presence of animal or human predation than they are in its absence. The real key is to use the environment in ways that keep all animal populations healthy—including deer, livestock, predators, other wildlife, and people.

Which brings me to the final point, a reminder that human beings are the dominant predator on North American deer, and the only one capable of dramatically influencing deer populations. This is as true today as it probably has been for thousands of years.

Seasons of the Deer

Almost everywhere on our continent, deer experience dramatic changes in their surrounding environment and in their own biology during the course of a year. It's hard to generalize about these changes, because each species is distinct and every area has its own ecological rhythms. For any broad statement about seasonal patterns, we could pour out a boxful of exceptions. I've chosen to illustrate the yearly round with perhaps the most "typical" example, or at least the most familiar one: white-tailed deer in the midwestern United States. And I've pointed out some variations in comparative notes about other regions.

SPRING

In the Midwest, after the protracted cold and snow of winter, spring comes as a holy time, filled with glory and resurrection. Clouds of geese whirl up from black and stubbled fields. Cricket frogs and spring peepers flood the air with choruses of sound. In the floodplain forests, new leaves unfold like butterfly wings, veined and tender and luminous. Each day brings an earlier sunrise, showered with the songs of robins and redwing blackbirds, the ventriloquial thumping of ruffed grouse. Wreathed in cool mists at dawn, footloose deer wander through a fresh-born world.

Whitetails of the Great Lakes country usually enter spring in a somewhat bedraggled condition. They've survived months of cold temperatures and sparse food supplies, draining their reserves of fat, maintaining themselves in a state of suppressed metabolism and lowered activity. During March or April, northern deer trek from wintering areas to their summer range, usually a distance of 5 or 10 miles, but sometimes as much as 50 miles. In balmier southern climates there's no need for seasonal movements, and deer may spend their entire lives on a few square miles of land. At the other extreme, mule deer in the mountainous West often migrate 50 to 100 miles from low elevation wintering areas to the high slopes where they feed on lush summer vegetation.

It's pleasant to imagine the freedom deer must experience at this season, released from the stress of cold temperatures, unbroken snow, and a constant diet of woody browse. After the snow melts, midwestern whitetails haunt meadows and woodlots, grazing on tender shoots of grass and sedges, an assortment of broad-leaved plants, tightly coiled fiddlehead ferns, and many other emerging plants that provide a nutritious deer's salad of succulent leaves and early greens.

Although most does became pregnant the previous fall, slow winter metabolism limits development of their unborn young. As late as March, the 100-day whitetail embryo typically measures just 8 inches and weighs under 10 ounces, but surging metabolism and abundant spring food bring on sudden growth. By May, the 180-day fetus is near full term, almost 20 inches long and weighing about 6 pounds. Deer normally have full, round bellies, so even at this stage there's little outward evidence of a female's condition. The biologists Michael Gillingham and Katherine Parker, who lived intimately with hand-raised blacktails in southeastern Alaska, found it almost impossible to tell if a doe was pregnant right up to the day she gave birth. For all of our deer, the normal gestation period is between 200 and 210 days, with an extreme range of 187 to 222 days. Poorly nourished does may carry their young for an extra week or more, compared with does who are well fed.

The nutritional drain of carrying young keeps females looking angular and bony despite spring's luxuriance. At the same time, males quickly replenish fat they lost while rutting the previous fall and couldn't regain in the pinch of winter. Whitetail bucks go through another change at this time. By April, nubs of new antlers begin growing from each pedicle. Developing antlers are full of blood vessels and nerves, and they're covered with frizzy skin called velvet. Under ideal conditions—uncrowded range with plenty of food—antlers may grow at the incredible rate of a half inch per day. According to John Ozoga, this makes them "one of the fastest-growing structures in the animal kingdom."

Diet and inheritance, much more than age, determine the eventual size of a deer's antlers. For example, a first-year buck can develop anything from slender spikes to an impressive 10-point rack. In a New York study, three-year-old bucks occupying good habitats averaged 8-point racks, but in poor habitats antler development generally lagged a year behind, and many bucks never grew large racks at all. Texas biologists studying antlers in captive whitetails found that some bucks grew exceptionally large antlers while others fed the same diet had small racks.

These traits were passed from generation to generation, showing that antler size and shape are influenced by genetic inheritance as well as nutrition.

Although antlers are made of bone, in the velvet stage they're tender and easily damaged, so bucks avoid brushing them against anything hard. Single deformed antlers—a fairly common sight—are often caused by such accidents. Interestingly, if a buck has an injured or missing leg, one of his antlers is likely to be stunted, crooked, or oddly shaped, and it's often on the side *opposite* his abnormal leg. Biologists suggest this is caused by "complex neurological relationships," meaning they have yet to figure it out. Female deer occasionally grow antlers, usually permanent, velvet-covered spikes. Known causes include abnormal production of sex hormones, especially testosterone, as well as genetic anomalies that affect the animal's entire reproductive system. Some antlered does give birth to fawns, nurse them, and behave normally as mothers.

Early spring is a social time for whitetails, when animals of both sexes and all ages are often seen together. John Ozoga's Michigan studies indicated that deer living in the same area have distinct social groups and know each other by sight and scent. The does form matriarchal "clans," including an elder female, several generations of her daughters, and their fawns. Ozoga explains that a number of these family groups share a single homeland, or "ancestral range," and sometimes all of the groups join up for a while. Whitetail does apparently spend their lives keeping close company with female relatives. Their one solitary period comes near the beginning of summer, as fawning time approaches. Mature bucks hang out together in fraternal groups of two to six for most of the year, and only during the fall rut do they become loners.

During late May or early June, as preparation for giving birth, the northern whitetail doe isolates herself on a small territory, driving off other deer, including any of last year's young who are still tagging along. For the next month to six weeks, she'll defend a territory of 10 to 20 acres against all intruding deer. This hideaway is often the same area where she gave birth in previous years.

Fawns are usually born in the seclusion of deep woods or thickets, so people rarely witness the event. A doe either stands or lies down while giving birth, and the process generally takes 15 to 30 minutes. On entering the world, an infant deer is slick and wet and very dark, but its fur quickly dries and lightens to the familiar russet color, arrayed with 250 to 350 camouflaging spots. The newborn whitetail weighs six to nine pounds in northern areas and a bit less in the south.

On the best midwestern farmlands, about 50 percent of one-year-old does give birth to fawns, while in poor or overused habitats most does are two years old before they have offspring. Regardless of their age, malnourished does have lower conception rates and less chance of carrying their fetus to full term. Among wild deer in Upper Michigan, infant mortality was as high as 70 percent after a hard winter. A study of captive animals revealed that mothers kept on a starvation winter diet gave birth to fawns averaging about four pounds, and 90 percent of the newborns died. By contrast, fawns of well-nourished mothers averaged nearly eight pounds at birth, and 95 percent survived.

Healthy females pregnant for the first time usually have a single fawn, but twins are the norm afterward, triplets are not uncommon, and quadruplets as well as quintuplets have been recorded. Whitetail does may continue raising young until they're very old—12 years or even more.

Shortly after giving birth, the mother deer thoroughly licks her infant, eats the afterbirth, and cleans the surrounding area, consuming any plants soiled with blood or fluid to eliminate scents that could attract predators. Fawns give off no detectable smell and lie absolutely still to escape notice if danger comes near. Many people have reported seeing dogs or wild predators pass right by a fawn without noticing it—so the strategy does work.

Gangly newborns start walking and nursing in a very short time— usually 30 minutes to an hour after entering the world. For a day or so the mother produces thick, high-protein colostrum milk, containing antibodies that help the fawn resist disease until its own immune system develops. Following birth, a mother whitetail leads her young into concealment, usually keeping twins in separate places, presumably to avoid the chance of a predator stumbling across both of them at once. The doe and her infant become imprinted upon each other, creating a nearly inseverable bond, much as a baby duck or goose becomes fixed on its mother and trails her everywhere. Similar to young ducks or geese, a fearless little fawn is susceptible to imprinting on other animals for the first few days, including humans, so it's important to leave young deer strictly alone. And it's true, as almost everyone has heard, that does occasionally abandon offspring that have been touched or handled by people.

Fawns are usually left by themselves in secure bedding places, although the mother seldom wanders far. To keep up with the nutritional drain of nursing, a doe spends as much as 70 percent of her time eating, and she visits her fawns to nurse only two or three times a day at the beginning, a bit more often later on. While suckling, the little ones wag their tails excitedly and thump their noses against the udder. Compared to cow's milk, a doe's milk is richer in protein, dry solids, and energy, and it contains about twice as much butterfat. Nursing fawns grow very fast, doubling their birth weight in about two weeks and tripling it within a month. During each visit the doe also cleans her youngster, and she stimulates urination and defecation by licking under its tail. Afterward she leads the fawn to a clean, scent-free place a short distance away.

Dangers abound for the stripling deer. About 10 percent of fawns are stillborn or die quickly from genetic defects or accidents, and they face many other threats, including disease, abandonment, and predatory animals. A threatened fawn bawls for its mother, who comes quickly and may try to lead the predator away, or, as we've seen, she might even charge the intruder, striking at it with her sharp hooves. One observer saw a whitetail doe closely following a black bear that was carrying her dead fawn in its jaws.

When they're about 2 weeks old, fawns start eating plants, and by 5 weeks their ruminant digestive system is in full operation. At 10 weeks or so, the young deer are functionally weaned and can live on their own; nonetheless, some mothers tolerate occasional nursing well into the fall. As their offspring become more independent and nurse less frequently, does finally start to gain weight, putting on fat reserves they'll need for the winter ahead.

Fawns are quick to develop the brilliant speed and jumping ability of their kind. Within a few days they can outrun a human, and at about two weeks they're faster than a dog. They often show their stuff, playfully darting, bucking, dodging, and sprinting back and forth in games that look like tag.

I once saw a young California blacktail dashing around at incredible speed, weaving through a maze of trees and bushes, as if an imaginary playmate were hot on her heels. Suddenly, she'd stop and strike an odd, frozen pose—legs askew, head high, eyes open wide, ears pinched back—then she'd burst off as though someone had whacked her with a stick. She whirled around the older deer, apparently begging them to join the chase, but they just watched and kept out of the way. Everything about this young deer reminded me of the spontaneous frolics of a half-grown puppy.

SUMMER

The tentative warmth of midwestern spring gives way to the throbbing heat of summer days, the muggy nights adrift with fireflies and chanting whippoorwills. Painted turtles crawl up on sun-warmed banks to crane their necks and dig holes for their ivory-colored eggs. A flush of growth surges through the land; forests and fields swell up in green billows, like the crests of thunderheads. Whitetails retreat to forests and shady thickets in the heat of day and emerge with the cool compassion of dusk.

As summer comes on, deer shed their dense, grayish winter coat, replacing it with thinner, reddish-colored fur. Since shedding and regrowth happen at the same time, the animals often look ragged and patchy, almost as if they're diseased. All deer undergo these seasonal molts, but in northern areas summer fur comes later and lasts for a shorter time, compared to deer in warmer climates. Each hair in the winter coat is hollow—a tiny column of trapped, highly insulative air—and beneath the long outer hairs is a dense, woolly undercoat. The summer pelt is composed of solid hairs and has no undercoat, giving the deer a sleek, athletic appearance, showing the bulge and cleavage of muscles, the hard crooks of bones.

These warm months offer a nearly limitless assortment of foods, which are at their nutritional peak early in the season. Deer seem to enjoy a varied diet and sample widely as they roam from one patch of vegetation to another. They also have an unexplained but well-documented ability to choose the most nutritious plants; unlike us, they seem to prefer what's best for them. Ready access to food does not mean deer have a laissez-faire existence during summer—most of the time they're busy feeding. At intervals through the day and night, deer stop eating in order to ruminate, or chew their cud, and to rest in secure bedding places, many of which are favorite spots they visit time and again.

During this bounteous season, each whitetail keeps to a fairly small area, averaging 200 acres or less. Among all of our deer species, adult males usually spend summer apart from the females, although some yearling whitetail bucks break the pattern, joining the does after fawns are born. Deer are steadfastly devoted to familiar home territories, and in areas where they migrate, individual animals usually come back to the same place each summer. It seems that females, with the added physiological drain of nursing fawns, occupy areas where nutritious food is most abundant, while bucks relegate themselves to lower-quality habitat.

Out West, mule deer bucks take to the open high country, but many does stay at lower elevations, where bushy thickets and forest give protective cover to their fawns. Similarly, along the North Pacific coast, most blacktail bucks retreat for summer to meadowy alpine heights, while does can be seen anywhere from mountaintops to lowland forests and estuary meadows.

Each individual deer has a home range, either one area it inhabits year-round or separate areas occupied seasonally. This range is not an exclusive, defended territory, but more like a neighborhood occupied or visited by other deer. In general, the home range of white-tailed deer is smaller than that of mule deer or blacktails. A whitetail usually stays within a radius of one mile on its seasonal home range, although actual size and shape vary according to local geography, food abundance, and other environmental factors. Within a given population, does usually have smaller ranges than adult bucks. Also, whitetails living in open environments often occupy larger areas than those inhabiting forested country, and individual deer tend to have smaller, more stable home ranges in mild southern climates, as compared to deer in the northern states or Canada.

A study of Texas whitetails found that does had an average home range of less than a hundred acres, compared to over a thousand acres for bucks. During their lifetimes, most individuals moved no more than a mile and a half from their birthplace. Deer are often powerfully devoted to their home grounds. Relocated animals—such as those trapped in urban areas and released to the countryside—often find their way back, covering distances of 20 to 100 miles. The most impressive example I've found was a Texas whitetail taken from the Aransas Wildlife Refuge in 1942 and set free 350 miles away, near the town of Sheffield. About two years later the same deer was trapped back at Aransas.

Shortly after fawns are born, they start exploring the area around their secluded nursery, and they roam farther afield as the weeks pass, learning more and more of the landscape. At two months, they follow their mother about half the time, and by autumn they stick with her wherever she goes. We can't get inside a deer's mind, but it's reasonable to assume that by watching the elders, fledgling animals gain important knowledge for survival—how to get around on the home terrain, follow migratory routes, avoid dangers, find the best foods at each season, and behave toward others in their social group.

Among all of our deer, fawns gradually lose their spots in late summer, and by September are about the same color as adults. In the richest midwestern farmlands, six-month-old bucks often weigh 90 to 100 pounds, and some reach 170 pounds or more. This is exceptional growth, of course. Buck fawns in many areas average 70 to 80 pounds, and does somewhat less. On the Northwest Pacific coast, I've often seen blacktail fawns in winter who looked no bigger than a medium-sized dog and probably weighed about 40 pounds.

By mid-July, adult bucks have grown almost full-sized antlers, but they're still sheathed in velvet. Each animal's rack is like a fingerprint—with its own peculiarities of shape, size, and tine arrangement—and these inherited characteristics are much the same year after year. Antlers may also have subtle or striking anomalies, such as asymmetrical shape and extra tines, sometimes many of them, including "drop tines," which jut downward instead of up. In any case, a buck's antler growth is strongly affected by the spring and summer food supply, especially his intake of calcium, phosphorus, and protein (notably collagen). For example, whitetail bucks on New York's Fire Island develop large racks despite having limited space, overbrowsed habitat, and limited food sources. Biologists suggest their exceptional antler development might result from the island's soils, which are very high in calcium and magnesium.

Above all, normal antler growth, hardening, and loss of velvet are determined by the male hormone, testosterone, which the animal's body produces in increasing amounts between August and October. If a buck fawn is castrated he will never develop antlers; an adult buck castrated after shedding will grow a set the next year, but they'll be permanent and will retain their velvet; and an antlered buck castrated after losing the velvet will shed his adornments within a week and never have antlers again.

Deer reach peak body and antler size between 4½ and 8 years of age; afterward their strength and prowess gradually decline. In heavily hunted areas such as the Midwest, whitetails (especially bucks) seldom live more than two years, but in the absence of hunting, deer usually die from winter stress between the ages of 8 and 15, and a few have reached 20 years of age. A tame blacktail doe on Gambier Island, British Columbia, was about 22 when she died in the winter of 1938–39. Often the condition of a deer's teeth are crucial to its longevity. In the hill country of Texas, for example, I saw hunter-killed whitetails 8 or 9 years old whose teeth had been worn almost to the gums. Deer in this condition have difficulty eating and are not likely to survive the next winter.

Patterns of wear on deer's teeth are so predictable that by a quick examination biologists can estimate an animal's age. Fawns are aged by the irruption and replacement of milk teeth, which happens on a regular schedule from birth to about 17 months. Adult deer have a curved row of incisor and canine teeth in the lower front jaw (the upper jaw has no front teeth), then a long toothless gap in the upper and lower jaws, and behind the gap matched rows of premolars and molars. Because molars are grinding teeth they're especially good indicators of a deer's age: the sharp cusps gradually become dull and eventually flatten, after which the whole tooth wears down, becoming shorter each year.

Aging by tooth wear takes practice, and on older animals it isn't very precise. To age a deer more accurately, a thin section cut from one tooth is examined under a microscope, revealing cementum layers added each year like tree rings. At field stations where hunters are required to check in deer, it's only possible to make age estimates on the basis of dental replacement and wear. Biologists use this information to develop population profiles vital for assessing deer numbers, managing harvests, and studying deer ecology.

Among midwestern whitetails, adult bucks and does usually stay in separate groups through summer, but during August, some of the prime, fat, powerful males start showing up in territories occupied by matriarchal clans. This is an early sign of the mating season, which builds gradually toward a peak in late fall, bringing dramatic changes in deer behavior. Deer have far more complicated social lives than most people realize. Within each group there is a hierarchy, older animals usually holding dominant positions over their juniors. Biologists have learned to recognize many ways that deer show deference, aggression, or "courtesy" toward one another. When two deer meet, for example, they often approach slowly, touch noses, and lick or groom one another. Other courtesies include avoiding direct eye contact, holding the ears partway back, and half crouching to show submissiveness. On the other hand, there's no shortage of threat and aggression among deer, displayed in gestures like direct stares, laying the ears far back, holding the head especially high or low, and putting one hoof up on another deer's back.

Deer are also surprisingly loquacious, but their voices are so soft that people rarely hear them. Whitetails use at least a dozen distinctive sounds to communicate with each other. I've already mentioned, for example, the way a fawn bleats to call for its mother. A doe's soft grunts can also bring wayward youngsters quickly to her side. Members of adult groups make barely audible, low-pitched bleats or mooing sounds to keep in touch or to find one another.

During aggressive confrontations, whitetails make low, guttural grunts. One of the few sounds people commonly hear is a series of explosive, wheezy snorts, which all of our deer species make when they feel threatened by a human or predator. Alarmed deer also stomp one forefoot, which makes a deep, thumping sound easily heard at short range. During the rut, whitetail bucks have a repertoire of deep grunts and baritone snorts audible from a short distance away. Skilled deer hunters attract bucks by imitating these sounds with their voices or with mechanical calls.

By summer's end, northern whitetails on uncrowded range have reached peak condition. Their bodies are full and fat, their muscles are tense and hard, and they're ready to begin the rituals of mating.

FALL

Midwestern autumn is an incendiary time, as if summer's growth had reached the point of bursting. The sun is a cool fire adrift in pale-clear skies. Freshening winds scrawl darkly over the faces of ponds. Mallards veer away through curtains of cattail, and blackbirds swarm up from the fields like blown leaves. In the flare of sunset, whitetails slip from the edges of cornfields, from thickets of purple-leaved sumac, from fields of silky milkweed, from golden-mantled forests—to feed beneath the unveiling stars.

By early September along the northern borderland of states and provinces, both whitetails and mule deer begin to shed their summer fur and grow a thick winter coat. The prime bucks molt first, followed by young animals of either sex, then does with fawns. Sometime between middle and late September, whitetail bucks start thrashing their antlers against bushes and boughs, first tearing away the velvet and then polishing the newly exposed bone to a stained-ocher gloss. The velvet is gone within about 24 hours, so it's unusual to see a buck partway through the process, with bloody strips dangling from his rack. In more southerly regions, all of these changes generally come a few weeks later.

Whitetails often congregate in large numbers during September and October, to share abundant forage in the woods and fields. Wild nuts and fruits are wholesome deer foods, as are cultivated crops like apples, corn, soybeans, and many others. Wherever oak trees grow, highly nutritious acorns make up a large percentage of the fall diet in good years, not only for whitetails but also for mule deer and blacktails. Fallen leaves can be an important autumn food, except those from tannin-rich species like oak, hickory, and elm. If all goes well, male deer have broad, round backs by early October, showing they're heavy with fat. Does, adolescents, and fawns reach peak condition after the adult bucks, usually in late fall or early winter.

In most of North America, deer show early signs of the rut—breeding season—during September. By this time, males have begun establishing an order of dominance, based on strength, antler size, and aggressiveness. Yearling bucks, intimidated by other males and abandoned by their mothers, often leave their old home territory and settle as far as 20 miles away. Interestingly, these youngsters may become sparring partners with much larger bucks, who engage them in low-key shoving matches, as if they're practicing for the serious competition ahead.

As autumn deepens, bucks surging with testosterone become more and more aggressive. In early fall they don't actually fight but display their prowess with ritual postures: walking stiff-legged, staring directly at an adversary, laying their ears back, and approaching each other with lowered antlers. Usually the smaller buck averts his eyes, crouches, and turns away to show submission. Also at this season, male whitetails, blacktails, and mule deer make signposts to advertise themselves. With their antlers, they rub the bark off trees and bushes, leaving conspicuous white patches, and sometimes they twist or break branches as well. In the process they deposit chemical scents, or pheromones, from glands on the forehead. No one understands exactly what these scents and signposts mean, but John Ozoga describes them as personal calling cards identifying each deer to others who happen by.

Among whitetails, the prime high-status bucks make far more rubs than their subordinates do, and it's widely believed, especially by hunters, that big bucks habitually choose larger trees for rubs. Compared to whitetails, mule deer "horn" bushes more often—snapping and rattling branches, then listening for replies from challengers. Incidentally, rubbing and horning can damage or kill small trees, so it's a nuisance in people's yards and a costly problem in orchards.

Only white-tailed deer make another kind of signpost—the scrape. Rutting bucks paw the ground, leaving bare circular depressions two or three feet in diameter, easily seen in the fall woods if you know what to look for. Sometimes you find a series of them, almost in a straight line. Biologists believe that while scraping, a buck leaves identifying scent on the ground from glands between his hooves. Scrapes are usually made beneath an overhanging branch or twig four to six feet off the ground, and as part of his ritual the buck rubs this branch against the sides of his face. Researchers have long suggested this deposits another marking scent, and they've recently discovered glands inside the nostrils that may be the source.

Bucks of every species also urinate on their tarsal glands, marked by patches of dark fur inside the hock on each rear leg. This produces a strong-smelling musk that signals a male's presence in the area. Whitetails often urinate near scrapes, which probably adds to the identification provided by other glands. Biologists suspect that the mingled odors of urine and tarsal glands help attract females to a buck.

Obviously, scent plays an important role in mating and other aspects of social life among deer, but because our own sense of smell is so rudimentary, we can never fully comprehend this dimension of their world. During every minute of their lives, deer are immersed in a rich and complex array of smells: clouds and curtains of it, rivers and ribbons of it, mingled and interwoven threads of it. We might imagine that scent for deer is like taste for us—sweet, sour, astringent, delicate, piquant, syrupy, bitter, strong, faint—each smell filled with significance, much as words and gestures carry meaning for us.

Among northern whitetails, rutting activity increases during October and peaks in November. Dominant bucks grow belligerent toward one another and are now likely to fight in earnest. These encounters usually begin with a stiff, sidling approach, each animal holding his ears back, grunting and threatening. If neither one submits, the two bucks might suddenly clash, bodies crouched, legs braced, heads down, antlers meshed, powerful necks twisting. The antagonists push, pull, and circle, sometimes so violently that they flatten vegetation and tear up the ground. After a few minutes one buck usually jerks free and bounds away, while the panting victor either stands proudly or gives chase, still trying to gore his opponent.

Fights can be intense and spectacular, but they're also rare in comparison to the measured sparring that settles most questions of status. Nevertheless, by the end of rutting season a prime buck is likely to bear an assortment of wounds, which can be serious or even life-threatening. Rarely, the antlers of two bucks lock together during a fight, and if they can't separate they'll eventually starve, die of exhaustion, or fall to predators.

Of course, the point of all this is sex, because dominant bucks have more opportunities to mate than do their underlings. Female deer breed only when they come into estrus, which lasts a very short time, about 24 hours. A doe approaching her peak roams almost constantly, covering as much as 20 miles in a night, increasing the likelihood she'll meet a desirable buck. Her urine contains scent broadcasting her condition, a fact seldom lost on the local cadre of males. As a doe's crucial time approaches there's likely to be an impatient buck treading right behind her, awaiting his moment, monopolizing her attention while keeping other bucks at bay. Until she's ready she won't let him get too close . . . and sometimes she'll try hard to get rid of him.

One fall, I camped in a Texas park where regular handouts had partially tamed the local whitetails. It happened to be the height of rutting season, and any doe giving off an alluring scent was escorted by a suitor, whom she usually ignored as long as he kept a distance. If he got close enough to sniff under her tail she'd turn aside or scamper off a short ways, but sometimes the buck drove his intended to the point of desperation. Occasionally I'd see a harried doe burst at top speed from the underbrush and sprint from one end of the campground to the other with a libidinous buck in pursuit, both of them openmouthed and panting.

Every time one of these pairs careened through the labyrinth of tents and mobile homes, an audience of startled campers, mostly retired folks, put aside their morning coffee and watched with ardent fascination. You could almost feel the rising heat of empathy in the Texas air, as each onlooker silently cheered for the pursuer or the pursued.

After smelling the urine of a female in estrus, a buck may stretch out his neck, curl his upper lip, and inhale deeply, as if to analyze the scent, apparently to judge the doe's readiness. When she reaches full estrus, a doe and her male consort usually move someplace away from other deer for a day or two, where they mount and mate repeatedly.

Valerius Geist describes young mule deer bucks trying a clever strategy to separate these pairs. First they'd bound toward the two deer, snorting as if something had alarmed them, and when the doe bolted off they followed her, apparently hoping for a chance to mate. But every time, the master buck came right along, chased the crafty suitors away, and regained his protectorate over the doe. Among whitetails, blacktails, and mule deer, the bond between mating pairs is a temporary thing; afterward they go their separate ways. Unlike the American elk, dominant bucks do not accumulate harems during the mating season, although whitetails living in open country such as the Texas grasslands show a tendency toward harem formation.

If a doe fails to breed successfully, she'll come into estrus again 28 days later, and then a third time after another month if she still hasn't mated. Because of these late pregnancies, some fawns are born in July, even August, which means they'll be small, underdeveloped, and vulnerable during the winter ahead. In any case, these repeated estrus cycles stretch the northern rutting season into December, although after November it dwindles considerably.

Among deer, mating takes precedence over almost everything, and males in the rut are so distracted they seldom even bother to eat. Midwestern whitetail bucks lose up to 20 percent of their fat, and in southeastern Alaska, most adult blacktail bucks have no body fat left when mating ends. Exhausted and depleted as winter sets in, male deer are sus-

ceptible to predators as well as starvation. Rutting season, with its atten-
dant distractions and wandering, also puts thousands of deer in the paths
of cars, as many commuters can attest. And of course, hunting seasons in
most states coincide, at least in part, with the rut.

In warmer places like the southeastern states and California, rutting
often comes later and may be spread over a longer period. Where temperatures change little throughout the year, as in tropical South America,
cycles of individual deer are much less synchronized, so antler growth,
mating, and fawning can happen during any month. Deer often become
reclusive after the rut, resting and feeding, keeping out of sight in dense
thickets. With diminishing testosterone levels, northern whitetails drop
their antlers in December and January. Antlers are cast one at a time, and
usually the larger animals shed first. From now until April, when fresh
velvety nubs start growing, it's hard to tell a buck from a doe. In southern and western states, deer may drop their antlers as late as March or
April.

WINTER

With rumbling gales and stinging snow, cold weather comes down like a
maul against the north country. Skeletal forests hiss and clatter in the
wind. On calm days, a stunned silence lays heavy across the land, broken
occasionally by the whispers of chickadees and the dry, distant cawing
of crows. Each day new messages are written on the deepening snow,
in tracks of gray squirrel, cottontail rabbit, meadow vole, and red fox.
Deer lie deep in the cedar swamps, shadowless under the gaunt winter
moon, shrouded by the haze of their own breath, abiding the long night's
passage.

In most northern regions the first heavy snows push deer toward their
wintering grounds. Fall migrations of mule deer in the western mountains are usually fast paced and deliberate, following well-known routes
from high country to lowlands. Farther east, whitetail movements are
more subtle, covering relatively short distances over a longer period of
time. Filtering in from all directions, white-tailed deer move over the
pitch and swale of land to congregate in the same sheltered areas they've
used for many years, perhaps for generations. John Ozoga's studies of
Michigan deer show that related does and their fawns group together
after the rut. Following the others toward winter grounds, youngsters
learn migratory routes they'll use throughout their lives.

Traditional wintering areas, called "deer yards," are well known in the
rural Midwest and colder regions of the Northeast: often these are in

dense stands of conifers, such as hemlock, spruce, pine, balsam fir, or, best of all, northern white cedar. Studies show that white cedar not only provides excellent shelter but is also the one food that can carry Great Lakes deer through an entire yarding season without need for anything else. Whitetails congregate in yards for three to four months, depending on the winter's severity, and seldom wander more than a mile. If snow accumulates deeper than two feet, it's very hard for deer to move around, and they're likely to stay within areas of a hundred acres or less. Because deer rely on the same wintering yards every year, it's very important that these areas be identified and protected.

To fully understand what winter habitat means to deer, biologists C. W. Severinghaus and E. L. Cheatum suggest we look at it in human terms. First, imagine that 90 percent of our houses became unusable during the coldest and most stressful months, forcing us to crowd into the remaining 10 percent. And to make matters worse, 90 percent of the grocery stores were closed because of snow and other factors, so all of us had to survive on 10 percent of the normal food supply. This is the predicament northern deer face each year.

A theory that winter yarding habits originated mainly for protection from wolves is supported by studies of deer in the north country of Minnesota. Concentrated in a yard, deer share a network of trails through the snow, which helps them escape predators and reach feeding areas. In winter congregations, there are also more eyes, ears, and noses alert for danger. But even where trails are available, snow hampers mobility of deer, so they're quite vulnerable. Besides pursuing deer in deep snow, some predators intentionally drive them onto smooth ice, where their hooves give very poor traction. Also, a deer is liable to fall spread-legged on the ice and dislocate both hips, an injury that means certain death.

During the cold months, deer conserve heat by curling up for the night in sheltered beds, preferably under coniferous trees that inhibit skyward radiation of warmth, and they're most active in the daytime, taking advantage of sunshine and milder temperatures. Of course, their winter diet is heavily constrained. If the snow isn't too deep, deer paw down to find whatever remains from last summer's vegetation, but in the absence of leafy greens they depend on buds, stems, twigs, needles, and other woody browse. This dry diet explains why their winter droppings are small, oblong pellets, altogether different from the moist, soft, and much larger scats produced by a diet of fresh summer greenery.

When it's tough going, deer become competitive, and larger, more aggressive animals often drive others away from food. In general, this puts dominant bucks atop the pecking order, lesser bucks and does in the middle, and fawns at the bottom. By standing on their hind legs, adult bucks can feed on branches and boughs up to seven feet above the ground, which gives them yet another advantage over the smaller animals.

In the depths of a hard winter, all deer in the group eat less palatable and less nutritious foods such as aspen, birch, alder, hemlock, maple, balsam, pine, and other trees or bushes. They sometimes prune shrubs to a scrawny, conical shape, leaving the lower branches untouched beneath the snow. Deer also nip everything to the highest level they can reach, making conspicuous "browse lines" in forests, woodlots, plantations, and orchards. Come spring, anyone who looks closely can pick out this evidence of hard times in deer country.

Unquestionably, winter can be a lethal season, especially in years with prolonged cold spells and deep snow. Regardless of conditions, all northern deer undergo a natural metabolic slowdown in midwinter, akin to a walking hibernation, considerably improving their chances to survive. The deer eat, sleep, move around, and carry on their social lives, but there is an overall slackening of pace and intensity so they need about 30 percent less food. Under the best circumstances, with unlimited access to food, deer still lose up to 15 percent of their body weight in the course of winter, and declines of 20 to 25 percent are not unusual when their diet is constricted. If weight losses reach 30 percent or more, some deer begin dying from exposure and starvation. In general, the better a deer's condition at the start of winter, the better its chances of surviving a drastic weight decline.

Deadliest times are at the beginning of winter or near the end—especially in February and March, when the animals' metabolism is returning to normal and their food needs increase. This is when severe weather or prolonged deep snow can be disastrous for deer. Even mild winters bring death in the deer community, taking especially the tender young, the infirm elders, the injured and diseased, and the careless. Also, loss of fetuses by malnourished does takes an invisible toll on the population. And a tough winter's aftermath continues into the following summer, when underdeveloped and poorly fed newborns succumb to malnutrition, abandonment, disease, or predators.

The biologist A. Starker Leopold estimated that a severe winter may kill as many as two million deer in the United States. Even during milder years, regional outbreaks of cold weather and heavy snowfall can cause hundreds or thousands of deaths, especially in overcrowded and heavily browsed habitat. This happened a few years ago in eastern Oregon, when a hard winter pushed large numbers of mule deer out of the high country, crowding them into the Malheur River and Burnt River valleys. In mid-February, the writer Barry Lopez and I drove to the area from his home on the Mackenzie River, hoping to gain a better sense for the harsher side of deer life. What we saw was something not comprehensible by reading mortality statistics or newspaper stories.

Conditions had eased a bit from previous weeks, but hard-packed snow still covered the scrubby slopes and the dappled sagebrush flats. Along Highway 20 east of Juntura, we began spotting deer in pairs and trios, then in bunches of 10 or 15, and later in herds numbering as high as 60 animals that drifted over the swales like migrating caribou. From a distance, we caught no signs of hardship or privation, but a few deer allowed us close enough to see their sharply ridged backs and bony hips—the sculpted angularity of hunger.

These sightings did not prepare us for the discoveries we'd make when we stopped to explore on foot. First, along a bend of the Malheur River we saw three gaunt deer standing beside a fourth—that one a dark, disheveled carcass sprawled on the gravelly bar as if it had toppled in midstride.

Nearby, we came across a fawn of the previous year with tiny button antlers, lying flat on his belly in the middle of a frozen pond, forelegs crooked sharply back, neck stretched forward, chin on the ice, and hind legs splayed out on either side. Almost certainly, the starveling had slipped, dislocated his hips, and lain helpless until he died. Perhaps it was the afternoon sun, or perhaps his own body heat, that melted the ice around him so he sank down an inch and then froze solidly in place.

On a snowy embankment a few feet above the pond lay another fawn with caved-in skull and shattered foreleg—killed as she tried to cross the highway. Marrow in the center of her broken leg was not solid and creamy white, as in a healthy deer, but gelatinous and bright scarlet: the telling sign of starvation. Perhaps there was mercy in her sudden, violent death.

Farther east, on the narrow benchland between river and highway, Barry came across a fully grown deer, frozen in his snowy bed at the edge of a sage thicket. A few yards off was a buck fawn, tightly curled like a puppy, as if he were only resting among the bushes, his eyes open and glazed, his body not yet hardened from the cold, and a cluster of fresh, marble-sized droppings under his tail, where they had spilled as he relaxed in death just hours before.

Suddenly, a fawn burst from a clump of brush 20 yards from us, dashed a short distance, and collided with an old, sagging fence. By a quirk of fate, one foreleg snared itself between two strands of barbed wire, so she spun around and hit the snow with a thump. There she lay, twisted onto her back, so weak she couldn't try to pull herself free. Yet she held up her head, kept her ears erect, and looked straight at us. Was this the unassailable dignity of the doomed? Was she simply too dazed or too exhausted to sustain fear? Or was she asking for a deliverance that only we—or the night's oncoming cold—could give her?

We stood watching, as if we, too, had suddenly grown numb, while the fawn's head slowly tilted backward and down until it rested on the snow, and her glistening black eyes closed, as if to shut out the world or yield herself to it. The temperature would drop close to zero tonight; another month, at least, remained of winter; and no miracle on earth could keep this little deer alive. We knew that, even as Barry gently held her while I released her leg from the fence. Shaky as a newborn, she struggled to her feet, took a few steps, toppled onto the hard-packed snow, and barely lifted her head. Her gaze seemed empty, as if she saw nothing at all, as if life still flickered inside her body, but not her mind.

From Eskimo and Indian people, I had learned how to make an animal's death instant and painless, in a way the cold and snow and starvation could not do. When this was finished, her eyes seemed peaceful at last, and in sadness but not regret, I whispered an apology for what we had done.

Backtracking the fawn's short run, Barry found where she had been resting when we came along—a small round depression melted into the snow under a gnarled sage. Beside it lay the frozen carcass of an adult buck, which the fawn had pressed herself against, perhaps for warmth before he died and for some lingering comfort afterward. I picked up her body—soft and cooling, loosely filled with frail bone and webs of emaciated muscle—and laid her back where she had been, in company with the buck.

Leaning close, Barry remarked on the difference between our fates. For us, the night's descent would bring the certainty of warm, secure shelter and ample food, while deer faced the vagaries of hunger and cold, competing for browse with their own abounding kin.

On down the road, Barry and I would see hundreds of lean but still living deer, and we'd find others for whom the winter's misery had ended. Some had expired from hunger and withering cold; some had been killed by a lethal dietary change after eating hay intended for livestock; some had blundered into the paths of cars and trucks, including a doe whose broken belly revealed two perfectly shaped, hairless, pink fetuses; some, languishing and addle minded, had tumbled to their deaths from high cliffs or ledges; and some had been taken by coyotes—the tale of their demise written in tracks converging on the snow, in drifts freshly stained with blood, in half-eaten carcasses and gnawed bones scattered amid the sage thickets.

One other deer, the most pathetic of all, had tried to jump over a barbed-wire fence, but her hind leg became twisted between the upper-most strands—and there she hung, bent double at the hips, until she died. Her head lay on the ground, her neck was sharply bent, her eyes were dried and sunken, as if to mask the unthinkable agony of this death. Straining against the taut, pinioned wires, Barry and I managed to pry her raw-boned body free. Then we turned away, following her own hoof-prints back to the road, which she had crossed just before encountering the fence.

Much as it rends the human soul to witness starving deer, long experience proves that artificial feeding usually does more harm than good. First of all, as Barry and I saw in Oregon, the sudden change of diet may be fatal to deer because their digestive system can't adjust that quickly. A truly humane feeding program would have to start long before starvation set in, then continue until wild foods again became available. Because there are usually thousands of hungry animals spread over huge areas of snowbound terrain, feeding simply isn't practical or affordable. And even if it worked, supplemental feeding would just allow more deer to repro-duce the following year, adding to the overpopulation that caused star-vation in the first place. The key to winter deer survival is a healthy environment, and the key to a healthy environment is balance between deer numbers and their habitat.

Inevitably, the hard knot of winter unravels. Snow melts in the bright March sun, windrows of needle ice glisten along lakeshores, and the air fills with an anthem of dripping, trickling, flowing water. Deer congre-gate on south-facing slopes to luxuriate in the warmth and graze on bare patches opened by the thaw, taking advantage of newly available food just as quickening metabolism stimulates their appetite. A benign tran-quillity permeates the world at winter's end. But in distant fields and woodlots, foxes gnaw remnant flesh from deer bones exposed by the dwindling snow.

We should remember that every region, indeed every local area, has its own version of this cycle. For example, southern Florida whitetails experience little more than a trace of winter, and so the dominant influences on their population are nonseasonal, including car collisions, urban development, habitat availability, and access to fresh water for drinking. In most of California, winter is a time of rain, mild temperatures, and abundant feed, but *summer* brings months of drought and decreasing food supplies. An important factor limiting California deer populations is the fact that fawns are born in the lean, stressful summer months, diminishing their chances of survival.

Despite these variations, and others of a less dramatic sort in every part of North America, deer in most areas have a seasonal round much like that of whitetails in the Great Lakes region. For example, black-tailed deer in the mountainous rain forests of our North Pacific coast inhabit a world that seems totally different from midwestern cornfields and woodlots. Yet these animals go through the same biological cycles, at almost the same time, and in almost the same way as their distant farmland counterparts. This includes the trial of winter survival, as I have often seen on the island where I weave my own seasonal cycle together with that of black-tailed deer.

The Fawn's Eyes

Twenty-five degrees, calm, and clear. January sun lays a tender apricot blush on the snowfields of Kluksa Mountain. My boots hiss softly in the deep powder. A week of snow has concentrated deer along the shore, where there's less accumulation under the big coastal trees, and close by, piles of kelp washed onto the beach provide a ready source of food.

After leaving the boat in a tiny cove this morning, Keta and I came across a good-sized buck, lean and bony from the rut, feeding on snarls of seaweed. There were two raw, pale spots on his forehead—roots of the antlers he'd recently shed in the nearby woods or muskegs. Those bare spots brought back childhood memories of an old Norwegian man our family sometimes visited on weekends. One of his fingers was a stump, neatly healed around the exposed end of the bone, so it looked like a button surrounded by pink flesh.

We left the buck, hiked down the shore, and soon encountered a lone doe standing just above the driftwood, then a doe and fawn who ran when we stepped noisily on a patch of gravel exposed by the ebbing tide. When I imitated a fawn's call, the doe reappeared at the trees' edge, fixed her eyes and ears on us, stretched out her neck, and called back in a low, soft voice, like the gentlest mooing of a cow, barely audible above the

surging waves. Then she stared intently toward us, as if she expected a
fawn to appear and follow her. Seeing only these two strangers, she finally turned, angled up the steep bank, and vanished without looking
back.

Now we've hiked a quarter mile along the beach without seeing more
deer, but I expect some in a broad, crescent-shaped cove around the next
point. Sure enough: two fawns and a doe. Moving very slowly, using
boulders and driftwood logs for concealment, we sneak closer. Then,
while all three deer are busy feeding, heads down amid kelp mounds, I
step with Keta into the open.

During cold weather and snow, our blacktails become less vigilant and
seem to abandon their normal wariness. If you keep absolutely still until
they relax, move while they're not watching, and gradually let yourself
become a visible part of the surroundings, they'll sometimes accept your
intrusion and act as if you no longer matter. This peculiarity would make
them vulnerable to predators or to hunters with exceptional patience,
but the risk must be outweighed by the survival value of keeping calm
and conserving energy. In any case, all three deer hold us in a protracted
stare, then gradually settle back to feeding.

After a while, one of the fawns ambles up into the woods and disappears, but the other fawn stays behind, close to the doe, indicating this
pair is a mother and her offspring. Some young ones rejoin their mothers after the rut, and some are more independent. Watching the deer
move around makes Keta so excited I worry she'll bolt after them, so I
ease into a crouch and gently stroke her fur. From the way her body trem-
bles, I wonder that it doesn't hum like an electric wire. Holding out one
hand, I give her the signal to lie down on lava bedrock washed bare by
the tide. She obeys reluctantly, her attention still fastened on the deer.

After I've gone a ways toward the animals, I slowly turn to check on
her, and for a moment she seems to have vanished. Then I realize my
mistake. Her black fur perfectly matches the lava, the white ring around
her neck resembles a patch of snow, and her bright, blazing eyes gleam
like ice crystals clinging to the rocks. Over the next 20 minutes, I work
closer to the doe and fawn, taking one step at a time, letting my presence
soak in. Keta holds absolutely still, but at intervals I reach a hand behind
my back and reaffirm the signal to lie down.

Both deer are standing at the abrupt edge between snow and sand, the
highest reach of last night's tide, rooting around in a snarl of kelp, pulling
out flaccid strands and chewing them up into their mouths like cold
spaghetti. Early on, they were occasionally struck by moments of fear,

but while I've come closer they've grown more relaxed, as if I'm just another deer or an irrelevant, innocuous, movable object. The distance between us narrows to 50 feet, 30, 20, 15. Then I stop, keep very still, and watch.

The doe is medium sized for an island blacktail, three feet tall at the shoulder, probably about a hundred pounds, sleek furred, smooth, and round—unusually fat for midwinter. The fawn looks about half her size, with long, dainty legs and a body not much larger than Keta's. I watch the rise and fall of their chests, the blinking of their eyes, the muscles working in their jaws.

After some minutes, they bend toward each other until their noses touch, and the fawn licks his mother's face. She leans down, closing her eyes while the tiny pink tongue caresses her fur, ranging from cheek to forehead. But shortly, another impulse takes over: the doe shunts away, lifts a foreleg, and rests it on her fawn's back, asserting her claim to the kelp. In response, the fawn steps a few yards away and begins to feed again.

Then, without apparent reason or forewarning, the little one lifts his head, funnels his ears, and reaches his muzzle toward me—all in curiosity, without a trace of fear. He angles toward my right side, turns sharply, and comes straight my way. I have no time to think, except to wonder if I might try to touch him should he come within reach. His hoofsteps on a patch of frozen gravel sound crisp and brittle as wrinkling paper.

The approaching fawn keeps his forelegs angled slightly outward, as if he might abruptly swerve away, but he comes on without wavering, and pauses only when he reaches the edge of a shallow tidewater pool a few feet wide. For a moment his image is splendidly reflected, as if there were a fawn on the shore and another in the sky.

Then his hoof touches the pond, breaking the mirror, and he steps across, halting about three feet away. The pale tips of his ears are no higher than my waist. He looks up into my face and seems all eyes: black and wet and shining eyes; eyes filled with sunlight and snow, dark rocks and shimmering water; eyes like the clear, limitless dome of a midnight sky; eyes that take my image into the fawn and spin me through the networks of his mind, as my own eyes have brought the fawn inside me.

At the island's edge, in the glare of winter sun, amid the sounds of surging waters, with the breeze eddying between us, the fawn and I share a moment of pure bewilderment.

After a few minutes, the little deer straightens and turns, crosses deliberately in front of me, and circles to my side, keeping the same distance. I could now reach out to touch him, but have no inclination to do so and feel sure he'd startle if I tried. When the fawn stops, I glance back at Keta, still crouched against the rocks, tense as a wishbone bent to the shattering point.

Slowly now, the fawn moves around behind me . . . and there he collides with the bitter, drifting pall of my scent. Almost involuntarily, he winces back. He shoves his muzzle into the scent once more, like someone who tastes a sizzling pepper twice to affirm a sensation that barely seems possible. He recoils, turns end for end, follows his earlier tracks around to my front side, and pauses to stare at me like a deceived child. Then he struts away, flagging the bright underside of his tail, a perfect miniature of an adult deer making a frightened but honorable retreat.

Oddly, when the fawn reaches his mother's side, he relaxes and bends down to pick at the kelp. But the watchful doe has taken on the fear he seems to have forgotten, although she acts as if it had nothing to do with me. Her body stiffens; her ears shift one way and the other; then she turns and leads him up the beach, across the snow-covered driftwood, into the tangled shroud of forest.

I wait a moment to be sure they've gone, then signal for Keta. She dashes up, snuffles the fresh-tracked snow, wags her tail, nuzzles my hand, fidgets, and rubs against my side, looks bright eyed into my face, then stares toward the place where the deer vanished, begging me to follow. I kneel down and give her a hug, whispering thanks in her ear.

My body is filled with energy and elation. I feel joy and gratitude for this winter day, this wild country, this blessed companionship of animals.

CROSSING THE WILD EDGE

Ask now the beasts, and
they shall teach thee.
—JOB 12:7

Down the Back Channel

Circumstances can change fast for an Alaskan traveler. One minute, the research biologist Thomas Hanley and I sat comfortably aboard a warm, plushy jet, and the next, we shivered outside a tiny airport terminal in a gale that made 15 degrees above zero feel more like 30 below. About 150 miles south of Juneau, we had first glimpsed the town of Wrangell as our plane made its final descent over the broad, whitecapped waters of Zimovia Strait. The community, stretched along several miles of island shore, looked much bigger than its listed population of about 2,500. From the air, we also saw evidence of Wrangell's economic mainstays: commercial fishing boats clustered in a small harbor near midtown and a large sawmill complex exhaling a pall of steam and smoke, surrounded by thousands of fresh-cut logs.

The biting cold encouraged quick introductions, but immediately I felt at ease with Hanley's fellow researchers, two young biologists, Michael Gillingham and Katherine Parker, as well as their assistant, Lisa Shively. We all crammed inside Mike and Kathy's truck for a quick ride to the harbor, then worked up a sweat hauling gear down a long, steep ramp onto the dock. Mike supervised loading the Forest Service skiff, a broad-beamed aluminum 19-footer with a boxy cabin, powered by a 150-horsepower outboard.

Boat travel is perilous in any season here, but especially so in mid-February with a northeaster gusting off the Stikine River Flats. Knowing that to capsize meant almost certain death in the frigid waters, we carefully balanced our load while Mike gave the engine a final check. After we found places to hunker amid bags and boxes inside the cabin, Mike guided the boat through a narrow gap in the jetty. Everyone's grip tightened as our little craft confronted a mass of steep, racing seas. The engine growled, the hull lurched and pounded, and saltwater spray quickly froze to an opaque rime on the cabin windows.

After what seemed an interminable beating, we passed the northern tip of Wrangell Island and found blessedly calm water in Eastern Passage, locally known as the Back Channel. Our boat cabin was no warmer than the frozen surroundings, but it sheltered us as we whisked across the water at high speed, slicing through mirrored images of mountain and forest. Our route took us along the inland edge of southeastern Alaska's panhandle, identified on maps as the Alexander Archipelago, a complex lacework of fjords and bays and inlets; 10,000 miles of coastline nesting 1,000 islands, some scarcely bigger than a house and some larger than the state of Delaware. Everywhere, the land is mountainous, with great rivers twisting through the valleys and icefields splayed among the peaks. Fringing the lower slopes and shorelines is a great forest of coniferous trees, the mother of life on this northern terrain.

Tom and I stood outside the cabin for a while, enjoying the scenery and talking above the outboard's whine. He's in his forties, of medium build, with a dense crop of salt-and-pepper hair. The principal wildlife biologist for the U.S. Forest Service's Pacific Northwest Research Station in Juneau, Tom is internationally recognized as an expert on the ecology and nutrition of deer. Months before, he had told me of the study he was directing on Channel Island, about 15 miles south of Wrangell, involving black-tailed deer raised by hand, so people could walk around with them recording the food they ate, the habitats they preferred, and the changes in their behavior at each season.

Most of southeastern Alaska is designated the Tongass National Forest, and the dominant land use is clear-cut logging. Old-growth forests are crucially important to deer in the Tongass, especially during winter, because the canopy of huge trees protects animals against harsh weather, prevents deep accumulations of snow, and furnishes a variety of essential foods. Not surprisingly, almost all research on southeast Alaska deer has considered the effects of habitat loss due to depletion and fragmentation of ancient forest—and Tom Hanley's project, formally called "The Nutritional Basis for Habitat Selection by Black-Tailed Deer," was no exception. He hoped to learn about the relationships between food, forests, and deer survival, and his method was to examine what he calls the physiological ecology of deer.

Basic to the study was measuring how much energy a deer takes in as food, and balancing that against the energy it expends to locate food, move around in deep snow, maintain body warmth, and meet other needs. This balance of energy gain and loss, which ultimately determines a deer's survival, is profoundly influenced by the quality of its environment.

For some years, Tom and his colleagues had studied deer ecology by observing wild animals from a distance and by piecing together such bits of evidence as the material in their droppings. They also worked with tame deer in pens, focusing on particulars like the digestibility of different food species or the ways plant fibrousness affects the rate of a deer's foraging. "With those approaches you tend to see deer as averages rather than individuals," he acknowledged, "like machines or programmed robots, constantly at work to balance energy intake against energy loss."

But on Channel Island, the researchers could study "real deer" living on their own in a wild environment, so the resulting ecological portrait came entirely from nature. This had already affected Tom's thinking about deer, notably his realization that each animal is an individual with its own peculiarities of behavior and physiology. For example, the researchers were finding that just like us, some deer are far more efficient than others at accumulating fat—a lament among ice cream lovers but an important survival advantage for wild animals.

Also, the Channel Island blacktails sometimes made unexpected choices. "From the standpoint of biological efficiency, it appears that they only do what they 'should' when there's deep snow, which makes food hard to find—really tough conditions. That's when their decisions start costing a premium and when they get very serious about behaving in optimal ways. But when conditions are relaxed they seem to have more flexibility than I'd given them credit for. Instead of doing what seems most efficient, they do lots of different things. Sometimes they just mess around, like when they hang out on the beaches for no apparent reason. Or they'll eat kelp that has little nutritional value for deer, like our own snacking."

Having made countless trips between Wrangell and Channel Island, Kathy and Mike knew every shoal, point, and bay along our route. I realized how lucky Tom had been to find people who were not only skilled biologists but also capable of handling enormous practical and logistical challenges, as well as long periods of solitude. One thing Tom had asked of Kathy and Mike was a guarantee that they wouldn't quit until the two-year project was finished, but he needn't have worried. If they had any regrets, it was that only six months remained.

We had now traveled deep into the fjordlike chasm of the Back Channel. Nearby on our right were the timbered slopes of Wrangell Island, and across a mile or two of water that plunged more than 700 feet deep stood the ragged, icy peaks of Alaska's mainland. Finally, we entered a wide, mountain-rimmed bowl that looked like a dead end except for a narrow outlet leading farther into the mazy waterways of the Inside Passage. Rising amid the dark, rippled waters, like a pebble in the toe of a sock, was Channel Island—about three quarters of a mile long and several hundred feet high, its steep sides cloaked in forest. I stared into the dark crowds of trees, knowing the deer were there, hidden from sight, listening as we passed.

When we slowed not far offshore, Tom recalled his difficulties finding an island that met all of his criteria for the study. Channel Island was the ideal size, 157 acres, or one quarter square mile—large enough to support the required number of deer. It also satisfied his other needs: good forest cover, a variety of plant communities, plenty of snow in the winter, and reasonable access from a town. No bears or wolves lived on Channel Island, nor were they likely to pay it a visit, so researchers didn't have to worry that study animals would contribute more to a predator's diet than they would to science. As Tom listed the characteristics of his research site, I was reminded that every island—indeed every natural place—is unique.

It was late afternoon, so rather than dally for a closer look, we turned toward the bay's far corner. Shortly we entered a pocket of smooth water about 200 yards wide, with Sweets Island on one side and an enormous mountain wall on the other. High above were broad-faced peaks capped by fields of snow, awash in crimson from the low winter sun. I wondered if anyone could conjure up a more idyllic setting, just when Mike announced, "There's home."

Tucked against Sweets Island was a long, narrow house, neatly fitted atop a floating metal barge, as if it were perched on a rock at the tide's edge. After fastening the skiff to an attached dock, we scuffled inside. The first thing to catch my eye was a colorful ersatz movie poster taped on the kitchen wall. "Oh yeah, I cut that from a magazine," chuckled Tom. It had two spotted deer with fiercely predatory eyes, gaping jaws, and sharp fangs lunging toward a terrified, slightly clothed, abundantly cleavaged woman. The title, slashed underneath in flaming orange letters, read: BLOODBATH OF THE KILLER FAWNS.

Aside from its miniature kitchen, the house contained two bunk-office-utility rooms and a storage shed packed with equipment. Electricity was supplied by a portable generator, a large oil stove provided heat, and drinking water came from town in hefty plastic jugs. Mike and Kathy shared these tight quarters with their assistants, so their work demanded tolerance for isolation, a knack for working harmoniously with assistants, and willingness to accept little privacy for months at a time.

Mike is Canadian born and educated, built more for basketball than hockey, with curly red hair and beard, an easy laugh, and a lightning sense of humor. You could pick up Mike's brightness in his words, but with Kathy you felt it as much as you heard it. She's a tallish woman in her thirties, with long brown hair, dark eyes, and a gentle feminine grace. From conversations with Tom, I knew she is not only a talented biologist but has a rare gift for dealing with the sensitivities of wild animals.

While the rest of us settled in, Mike pulled six scuttling Dungeness crabs from a trap in the middle of the bay, assuring unanimous agreement about the dinner menu. The biologists went over details of their project as we feasted that night, and I noticed they talked about the deer not so much as a class of animal but as a group of individuals, each with its own peculiarities, reminding me of nothing so much as gossip. Again and again, amid the crunch and pop of crab legs, I heard names—Tornado, Osage, Kake, BlueMoon, Paladin, Heidi, Cherry, Hawkins, Pia, and Falstaff—the 10 Channel Island deer. Aside from assistants who stayed for varying periods of time, the deer were Kathy and Mike's closest companions, and after following them around for almost two years, the biologists had become intimately acquainted with each animal. Perhaps this explained why they'd given the deer names, departing from the usual practice of identifying study animals with code numbers.

Later, I went out into the stinging cold. Enormous, snowy peaks ghosted against the sky, and from the Big Dipper's rim, I traced a line almost directly overhead to the North Star. Knowing wolves lived on the mainland as well as on nearby Wrangell Island, I listened in vain for a yip or howl, but the prodigious, enveloping silence was a gift nearly as rare. Then I thought of the deer so close at hand, surrounded by the same night, the same waters, the same breathless winter chill. I couldn't help smiling as I headed back inside.

In the Company of Deer

The next morning was hoary and clear, 10 degrees Fahrenheit with a northeast wind spilling through canyons that led back into the Canadian interior just 20 miles across the mountains. You could feel the boreal cold needling against your face, rushing down your throat, seeping through your clothes. It defied logic that our gust-darkened bay was not frozen over. Only the snowless shore, periodically washed by high tides, revealed that we were on a saltwater tendril of the North Pacific.

After bundling up, we made the choppy mile-and-a-half crossing to Channel Island and anchored in the protection of a small point. Nailed on several trees were boldly printed signs reading: CHANNEL ISLAND—CLOSED TO DEER HUNTING, with a short explanation of the research. Mike commented that deer were currently scarce around Wrangell, a town where almost everyone eats wild meat and fish. It was hard to put worries aside, he confessed, although remarks about "those fat bucks on Channel Island" seemed only good-natured teasing, and so far the deer had been left strictly alone.

Out on the point was a simple plywood hut, painted government brown. Uninsulated and bare floored, it brimmed with a deadening, bony cold, but we crowded inside to escape the wind. Mike lit the propane heater, though it seemed a futile gesture. At times the hut had been a vital refuge when sudden gales and rough seas prevented the research crew from getting home. It contained an assortment of computer and radio equipment—the complex technology considered necessary for modern biological research. In earlier times, naturalists relied almost exclusively on their eyes and ears, huge doses of patience and determination, and minimal tools: field glasses, notebooks, pencils. As I perused the electronic gear, I felt a romantic pull toward that older way, which seemed most elegantly suited to the study of wild creatures.

Shortly after we arrived I heard Lisa's voice outside the hut, like someone greeting a friend: "Pia! Hello, Pia." A medium-sized doe walked casually into the beachside clearing. The animal paused a moment, then waded through the drifts straight toward Lisa the way I'd often seen one deer join another. It was as if my senses had gone awry. This deer looked identical to the wildest of her kind, but she approached Lisa without a trace of fear. When they met, Lisa rubbed the doe affectionately and nuzzled her face against the deer's.

Lisa was a soft-spoken, lightly built woman in her mid-twenties, who had recently finished her master's degree and would soon begin doctoral studies in biology. Like many young scientists, she allowed her feelings to live openly alongside her objective, professional self. When we talked about the work, it was clear she felt lucky to be on Channel Island, enjoyed the research, and had a strong personal devotion to the deer.

I eased closer, half expecting the doe would dash away, but she paid me slight attention. She looked alert and healthy but very lean—her spine made a subtle ridge and angular bumps revealed the bones of her pelvis. At the same time, I saw a conspicuous leather strap around her neck with a small metal box attached: her radio collar. Bands of colored tape wrapped around the collar's loose end identified the doe as Pia. I confess it seemed all wrong, like a blaring neon sign atop a wilderness mountain. Yet the deer, who had worn it most of her life, seemed as oblivious to the collar as I am to the shoes on my feet.

Lisa explained that a transmitter inside the box sent a constant signal. Using a receiver and handheld directional antenna, researchers could track this signal to find her. It also indicated whether a deer was moving or keeping still—in other words, feeding or bedding—information received by a continuous recorder on Sweets Island. Because each radio collar transmitted on a different frequency, individual animals were identified by their signals.

Pia stepped up on the hut's front porch, then wandered back to us, sniffed our clothes, and licked our hands. Her tongue was firm, strong, rough like a cat's. I found this unabashed friendliness from a deer confusing, but reminded myself that deer are sociable animals and Pia was raised in a group that included humans along with her own kind.

Just then two more deer emerged from the woods—a yearling doe named Kake and a two-and-a-half-year-old buck named Falstaff—both wearing collars. "The deer know our boat," Mike commented, "and they'll often come when they hear it, particularly now, when no one's been around for a week and they're stressed by snow and cold." Kathy suggested one other reason: "Possibly because Mike and I raised them, they come to us for the sense of security, especially in hard times. It's the same as a fawn going to its mother or a child to its parent."

We all marched into the woods, single file, up a steep snow trail. The path twisted between lofty spruce and hemlock trees with a dense understory of blueberry and huckleberry bushes. The three deer mixed right in among us, as if we were members of their troop or they were members of ours. I couldn't decide if this was a heightened realization of the natural or a descent into something profoundly unnatural; it was like the dream world of Henri Rousseau—lambs and lions keeping company.

Tom explained that his original captive blacktails in Juneau had been "orphans," fawns picked up by people who thought they were abandoned, not realizing the mother was probably nearby. The first deer brought to Channel Island were born to those penned animals and flown down just a month later. Several died the first winter and one was eaten by a bear after it swam off the island, leaving five who were now two and a half years old. The next spring Mike and Kathy had arrived and raised nine more fawns, five for the island and four sent back to Juneau as a "control group." The Juneau animals were kept in a fenced enclosure and given unlimited food, to compare the condition and growth of deer under optimum nutritional circumstances with that of deer living naturally on Channel Island.

The Juneau deer had a secure, comfortable existence, safe from predators, eating all they wanted—but permanently confined. And the Channel Island group lived amid the wildness most deer are born to, but they faced the perils of a natural environment and the prospect of a shorter, harder life.

Mike and Kathy led us to a large platform scale in a clearing atop the rise. Offering little handouts of raisins, or simply crinkling the plastic raisin bag, Kathy enticed each animal onto the scale. She gave only a few tidbits so the deer's normal food intake wouldn't be affected. The scale provided a tangible measure of winter's toll. Pia had lost several pounds in just a week. Falstaff was stable, but since his peak before the September rut he'd dropped more than 30 pounds.

Although it was only February, most of the deer had declined about 20 percent in weight. This equaled the weight lost by does during the whole previous winter, but it was still short of a 30 percent loss by the largest bucks in that year. Kathy said one buck who scaled 130 pounds in the fall was now down to 90 pounds. Here was a scientist reciting data from her research, but you couldn't miss the concern in her voice.

Hunger-stressed deer erect the fur on their forehead, so their faces look dark and round like a fawn's. Eventually they begin stumbling on flat ground and have difficulty jumping over downed logs. Last winter this happened to Kake, Mike recalled. The symptoms hadn't appeared this year, but Mike worried that some of the deer were getting close. If severe conditions persisted, death from starvation was a possibility.

This was a tough issue, and although no decisions had been made, there were practical and ethical reasons to consider keeping the deer alive with supplemental food. Researchers had brought these animals to Channel Island, so perhaps they had incurred a responsibility to prevent them from dying. Also, the number of animals in a study can affect the validity of its results, so starvation losses could adversely affect a project that had cost considerable money, to say nothing of the researchers' time and efforts.

On the other hand, perhaps animals should be allowed to die in the interest of research. After all, one of the project's main goals was to study effects of snow, a crucial element of deer ecology. During severe winters in southeast Alaska, hundreds of deer—even thousands—starve to death because snow buries their food and limits their mobility. Wasn't the research designed to let natural conditions prevail?

Nobody mentioned the matter of personal attachment to the animals, but it drifted invisibly through the conversation. This was an agonizing dilemma: on the one hand, a biologist's obligations to the animals without whom research would be impossible. And on the other, a scientist's commitment to the unfaltering pursuit of objective knowledge.

After weighing the deer, we followed a network of trails deeper into the island. Again the animals joined our little parade, sometimes mixing in, sometimes wandering aside to nibble at blueberry or huckleberry twigs. Kathy led the way and stopped at intervals to switch on the telemetry receiver. Standing close, I could hear metallic pings in her earphones, surging and fading as she turned the antenna, growing louder as we approached the still-invisible deer.

Only nine of the animals had radio collars, because one, a buck named Hawkins, was too wild. Unlike the others, he often wouldn't allow people close enough to record what he was eating, so there was no reason to give him a collar. It was also an ethical issue, because Kathy and Mike worried they'd never get his collar off when the study ended. So Hawkins was a phantom deer, a noncollaborator, sometimes tolerant of human company and sometimes not. Interestingly, he was unsociable with deer as well as people, often staying alone in the least accessible parts of the island, joining others mostly during the rut.

At the far end of Channel Island we located two more does and lured them to a large plywood box. For the reward of a few raisins, the deer tolerated being shut inside and hoisted by a rope-and-pulley system with a scale attached. In these ticklish situations, it was Kathy who tenderly coaxed and calmed the deer, drawing on that sixth sense that told her when to push and when to ease back.

Around me the deer seemed least comfortable, doubtless because they knew a stranger when they saw one. They were tolerant as long as I moved slowly, and they liked being rubbed on the chin, neck, or chest. If I touched a deer's back or rump, she'd sag gracefully so my fingers barely made contact. Perhaps they'd learned to do this when slipping under low branches or logs, or it might be a submissive response, the way a deer crouches when an aggressive member of the social group puts one foreleg on its back to assert dominance.

As far as I could tell, the mannerisms of these creatures were identical to those of the wild deer I had followed almost obsessively at home. If I moved gently, I could put my nose beside theirs, watch them browsing shrubs, hear the soft rush of their breath, see how they'd close an eye when it touched a branch. Deer have incisors—sharp front teeth—only on the bottom jaw, and a thick, fleshy pad on top. Yet they easily grasped and plucked twigs, then moved the food back to chew it with their crenelated molars and premolars. From this range, I could hear every sound of snapping twigs and grinding teeth, even the liquid gulps when they swallowed.

Kathy said deer feel most secure around people who aren't standing fully erect, and they did seem to relax when I crouched or knelt in the snow. From this low vantage, I noticed how they spread the two toes of each front hoof an instant before it touched the powdery surface, creating a snowshoe effect and making their tracks appear quite large for medium-sized deer.

When we left the second scale, Kathy and Mike discouraged the deer from following so they wouldn't waste precious energy when they could be feeding and resting. In this cold weather, with a couple feet of snow even under the canopy of trees, the deer's lives were that close to the margin. But Kake and Pia insisted on staying with us.

On normal study days, people followed deer around, not vice versa. Tom explained that each researcher was randomly assigned a deer for that particular day and would stay with it, recording every bite the animal ate, the duration of feeding and resting periods, vegetation communities it favored, even the number of times it chewed. Everything was logged on notebook-sized portable computers and transferred to a main computer at the day's end. "In winter," Kathy added, "the deer often feed continuously for five to six hours at a stretch. Then they bed down for a while to rest and rechew their cud. You hope they stop around midday, because otherwise you're so busy with the computer that you can't eat lunch."

Preferred foods—tender, low-growing, evergreen plants—are mostly buried under snow during the cold months. So deer rely on twigs and boughs, which are harder to eat and less nutritious, just when they need the most energy to keep warm and move around in the snow. This is why winter deer survival hinges on drawing energy from fat and protein accumulated during the previous growing season, and on the metabolic slowdown that happens regardless of weather or food availability.

Also, the more stressed deer are by winter conditions, the less skittish they are, perhaps because their minds are torpid or because evolution has favored deer who are less apt to spook and run when their survival depends on conserving energy. In summer, Mike suggested, even the relatively tame Channel Island animals might not be so calm around an outsider like me.

Outsider. This brought an unsettling thought. Since I first heard about the Channel Island study, I had wondered what would eventually become of the deer. Last night Mike and Kathy said they should be released into the wild, in a place seldom or never visited by hunters. But would that be possible? Because he hadn't worked so intimately with the deer, Tom took a more practical view, stressing the difficulty of moving them to a "safe" area. If interested biologists could be found, the animals might be used for other studies. But Mike and Kathy wondered if it was reasonable and practical to bring these free-ranging animals into captivity, or if any other researchers would want to continue studies with the deer on Channel Island.

Their sentiments brought to mind the story of a biologist doing physiological research on a group of hand-raised deer. This biologist worried about how the animals would be treated after his work was finished, since decisions on their use were made by the research facility. It's safe to say that deer in most projects are treated humanely, but in some cases they've been starved, chilled, relentlessly exhausted, or euthanized for postmortem investigations; they've had their brains manipulated, glands removed, legs intentionally broken, coats shaved, bodies implanted with transmitters, and stomachs fitted with portholelike fistulas, to name a few of the procedures used in animal research. He quietly arranged a solution to ensure that none of this happened.

These deer were too tame for release in the wild, so he found a game farm that would take them in. Security at the research facility was strict because of threats from animal rights activists. As his study neared completion, the biologist and a colleague spent some late nights training the deer to calmly leave their pens and enter a truck. Then, at four a.m., he and his collaborator drove into the research facility, loaded their cargo, and made a clean getaway. After some adjustments the animals fared well in their new home.

I wondered if most wildlife researchers would go to such lengths on behalf of their animals. I'd been told by another biologist, "Many scientists lose their humane feelings after a while, so there aren't a lot of captive deer who end up in retirement. The solution might just be a twenty-two rifle, or the animals may get used in some type of experiment where they're fed a certain diet, then killed and ground up to analyze their muscles and bones."

There was no question about Mike Gillingham and Kathy Parker's commitment to the Channel Island deer, but releasing them would not be a simple matter. How would they live up to their convictions when the time came? Looking at Kake and Pia, who had trailed us all day, I wondered what their fate would be.

Travels with Cherry

Winter put on a different face the next day—woolly overcast, temperature rising to the twenties, and opaque snow squalls bearing down over the mountains. Only the wind was unchanged, blustering out of the east, wheezing and winnowing around the research hut, shaking clumps of snow from high boughs. A solitary deer abandoned the sheltering forest to greet us: Falstaff, the buck we'd met yesterday. Mike assigned Lisa to work with him, which meant she'd stay close for about six hours, recording his activities on her computer. It must be a familiar drill for the deer, I thought, noting that he paid his new partner scant attention as they wandered down the shore and disappeared through the alders.

Next, Mike put on earphones, aimed the telemetry antenna this way and that, and gestured toward the island's south end. "It's set for Osage's radio collar frequency . . . he's down that way." We trudged into the forest, Tom and I on Mike's heels, following a trail packed troughlike into the knee-deep snow. Gusts murmured in the treetops, but among the crowded trunks we felt only a gentle breeze. After a couple hundred yards, the telemetry beeps were very strong. We peered into a labyrinth of branches, boughs, and wind-thrown trunks, all gloriously embroidered with snow. As far as I could tell, we were alone in the forest, but the clairvoyant electronic gear said otherwise.

"Ah, there you are," said Mike warmly, looking toward our left. "Come on, Osage." Now I saw the deer, half hidden in a patch of shrubs, surrounded by mounds and pillows of snow, not more than 30 feet away. Osage waded over to join us and Mike gently rubbed his face. For several minutes we stood there—an unlikely cluster of three men and a deer—then Osage moved off into the brush with Tom close behind, his shadow for the day. Once they'd gone far enough so the deer wouldn't tag after us, Mike and I shuffled on.

"I'm betting Cherry's up here somewhere," Mike predicted. "She usually stays high on the island, like our wild buck Hawkins. But her signal's so strong it's hard to get a clear direction." We paused every few yards to study the snow-clouded forest, but saw nothing. Mike and I left the trail, wallowed up a hillside, and tightroped along a fallen trunk suspended eight feet above the ground, giving us a clear view of the surroundings.

Mike peered up the slope and smiled. "I see you, Cherry . . . those two wiggling ears." Deer have an almost magical ability to vanish amid their surroundings, and I'd never seen anyone with Mike's skill at picking them out. At last I saw her, mostly concealed by a snow-covered bush, staring down at us. "Cherry doesn't come like some of the others do, so you'll have to go to her. She's also a bit wild or shy, which means it's best not to push things. Let her slowly get used to you."

Last summer Cherry had had her first fawn, Mike recalled, but it was born late, and since nobody had seen the little one for a while, they wondered if it was still alive. Although I couldn't record data like the others, Mike wanted me to follow Cherry in case she joined up with her offspring. Perhaps he was just letting me feel useful or inventing a harmless task to keep me occupied, but if so, I appreciated the kindness.

Cherry appraised me skeptically and slipped into a thicket when I came within 30 feet. Her nervousness was surprising, said Mike, but he also admitted being pleased. "We've always hoped the deer would be afraid of strangers and this is our first test. The wilder they are, the better their chances to survive once this is over." After a final reminder to go easy, Mike left Cherry and me to sort things out for ourselves.

The doe quickly settled back to browsing, but she kept a watchful eye and moved off whenever I got closer than 20 feet. Her shoulder was about the height of my waist, she weighed perhaps 75 pounds, and she had a thick, dense coat, uniform gray-brown except for the white belly fur and creamy patches on her neck. I was struck by the perfect elegance of her form, the rich texture of her fur, the gentle and sensitive movements of her legs.

Of course, she had a radio collar, marked with strips of cherry-red tape. I still found the collars jarring, although they weren't much different from those we so easily accept on dogs. It wasn't how they looked, but what they *meant*. I felt inwardly pained to see a collar—symbol of human control—on an animal whose wildness meant so much to me. Iñupiaq Eskimo and Athabaskan Indian people, with whom I had lived, believed radio collars violate a wild creature's dignity. Some told me that animals so afflicted were better off taken by hunters and used as food, putting an end to the insult. We might see the ethical problems more clearly if someone suggested using radio collars to study the daily movements of people. Yet I understood why radio collars were essential for the Channel Island project and I knew ethical treatment of the deer was among its highest priorities.

Cherry had vanished behind a knot of jackstrawed windfalls, but her tracks were easy to follow. I poked my fingers inside them to feel the snow, still sugar-soft, unlike hardened, crusty prints that were a day or two old. Within a few minutes I reached the trail's end, where the doe stood in her latest tracks like a pencil at the end of a sentence. Following Mike's instructions, I talked soothingly and knelt down to make myself small.

Cherry fed enthusiastically on a cluster of sapling hemlocks, but from a slender tree about 20 feet tall she took a single nip and moved on. In all likelihood, her brief sampling of the larger tree was a matter of whimsy, but I remembered Tom explaining that after repeated browsing, some shrubs and trees may produce chemicals whose taste discourages animals like deer. Evidence is too scant to generalize, yet when certain plants grow large enough so that protection is unnecessary, the chemicals are no longer produced.

Cherry gazed off through the woods, ears funneled toward sounds I couldn't detect. Perhaps it was another deer, but how could she hear an animal as quiet as herself? Moving as close as possible and listening carefully, I picked up the cottony hiss of her hoofsteps, the rhythmic *crunch-crunch-crunch* of her jaws. Her cheek muscles bulged and her ears shivered each time she chewed. A dusting of snow fell onto her back from an overhanging branch, and a couple minutes later she shook it off, in a spasm that started with her body and moved forward to her head and floppy ears. Even her intense shaking was practically noiseless.

Next she moved into a huckleberry patch, threading herself through a lattice of twigs, reaching out to tug and browse, pausing again to listen. I could only assume she heard clicks, snaps, scratches, whisks, peeps, or rustles that informed her about the surroundings. But for me, the snow-laden forest was completely hushed, as if this natural community carried on its daily business without a trace of sound.

As I watched the deer, I wondered if nature is not so much a secret or hidden place as it is a quiet place. To know about the natural world, we should become still enough to hear a doe's footsteps in powdery snow, or a fawn's bleat from its bed in the thicket, or the rasping of a vole's teeth on tender shoots, or the breeze shivering through an owl's feathers. Listening somewhere beyond the clangor of machines, we might rediscover what the deer has not forgotten.

Just before noon, Cherry stopped beside a huge spruce on a ledge with a fine view of the forest below. A perfect bedding place, I hoped, attentive to my growling stomach. Almost immediately she turned around several times, scratched the snow as if she were preparing the spot, then lay down, bending her forelegs under and coming to rest on her belly, in the fashion of a cow rather than a dog.

I sat about 10 feet away on a cushion of hemlock boughs and we both got busy with our lunches. For the deer, this involved reworking food she'd gathered and stored over the past few hours. I saw a little bulge zoom up her throat and into her mouth—this was a wad of plant material, called a bolus. After chewing for a minute or two she swallowed, the bulge slipped back down her throat, and seconds later another one came up. It looked as if mice were running up and down inside her esophagus.

Like other ruminants—including cattle, sheep, goats, and antelopes—deer process their food in a complex four-chambered stomach. While feeding intensively, a deer chews each mouthful only enough so it can be swallowed. This minimizes foraging times, when wild animals are especially vulnerable to predators. According to Tom Hanley, it also allows the deer to spend more time lying down, which burns about 20 percent less energy than the animal uses while standing up.

As a deer feeds, rough particles of plant material accumulate in two large stomach chambers called the rumen and reticulum, which contain billions of microscopic protozoans and bacteria. Eventually the deer moves to a secure place, often a thicket or overlook, to regurgitate the

plant material and microbes for rechewing. This process, called ruminating, further mixes the organisms with the food, while also breaking
the material into smaller particles so microbes can more easily digest its
cellulose.

Deer can't survive without their souplike community of many different microbial species. Each species is adapted to certain foods, so as a
deer's diet shifts seasonally there are corresponding changes inside her digestive system. During winter, for example, microorganisms that thrive
on succulent greens and leaves are replaced by others adapted to the various species of browse. Starving deer given hay or other emergency foods
often die with their stomachs full, partly because of inadequate microbial
adaptation, and because of intestinal or stomach impactions, digestive-
tract infections, or low nutritional values.

The rumen and reticulum function as a single large fermentation
chamber, where microbes digest the vegetable mash. When food particles
are small enough to move on, the mixture of digested cellulose and other
plant materials—along with a flush of the microorganisms themselves—
passes to the omasum and abomasum. In these two chambers, and in the
small intestine, everything is further digested and absorbed as it is among
nonruminant animals like dogs, cats, or humans.

Now, think about this process. The deer maintains a churning swarm
of tiny organisms inside her stomach. She feeds vegetable material to
these organisms, they make the plant nutrients available to her, *and then
she digests some of the organisms along with everything else.* So the deer is
like a yogurt culture on the hoof, propagating billions of microscopic organisms that then become her own food.

Cherry ruminated for about an hour, and by that time, though I was
bundled like a nomad from the Siberian steppes, cold had crept down to
my skin. Perhaps the deer was also chilled, because she abruptly stood,
arched her back the way a dog stretches, and went to work on the nearby
shrubs. A few yards from her bed she left a pile of droppings. The little
pellets felt cool within five minutes, even when I pushed my fingers
down inside them. From this I learned that warm scats on the snow mean
a deer is very close, as long as you haven't frightened it away.

For the next hour, Cherry meandered from one patch of brush to another. She was totally aloof and, reminiscent of my failures in adolescent
courtship, moved away if I got closer than 10 feet. I was getting frustrated, wishing a friendlier deer like Kake or Pia would come along. Then
I found a clump of pale-gray strands, draped like miniature Spanish moss
over a low branch. Earlier, Tom had identified these hairlike wads as

lichens called old man's beard—though he used their scientific names, *Usnea* and *Alectoria*. They're a nutritious favorite of southeast Alaskan blacktails, but since they usually grow on branches well above a deer's reach they're only available when storms blow them down.

I noticed Cherry watching as I pulled the lichen free; then her eyes fixed on the dry, puffy snarl. Holding out my hand, I talked gently and eased closer. She hesitated, lifted her nose, stepped my way. The temptations and awkwardness of teen love came to mind again. Keeping her body as far away as possible, Cherry leaned out to pull the offering from my fingers. Then she turned, pinched back her ears, and trotted about 30 feet. While chewing the lichen she squatted to urinate, a deer's expression of anxiety.

Cherry worked her way toward the island's shore, where I found many branches festooned with beard lichen, gathered more, and stuffed it in my pockets. Then I eased toward her, trying to look harmless and sincere, and sure enough she came to tug it away. When I drew back my hand she moved closer, nuzzling greedily as if she found my tactics irritating. Excited now, I knelt down and held the frizzy stuff next to my face. The deer came boldly until her hooves punched into the snow beside my leg. Her furry cheek brushed against my skin; her nose touched my chin and lips; her eyes looked directly into mine. I saw no iris, no pupil, just a shining black pool filled with reflections of the forest when she looked one way and with my silhouette when she looked another. The elation of a first kiss surged through me.

But my bliss was to be short-lived. Suddenly the doe tensed, dashed off a few yards, and looked back as if I had betrayed her. At the same instant, another deer stepped from behind a huge fallen tree trunk a few yards away, and then a second appeared. I was amazed that two deer had come within 10 feet before I noticed a thing. The stripes on their collars—red and black, yellow and black—identified them as Kake and BlueMoon, both does. According to Kathy they'd been keeping company for several months.

From the moment they arrived the two were almost fearless, and while they crowded close to mooch lichen, Cherry kept her distance. I knew from last night's discussion that Cherry had once dominated all the deer. "Merciless," said Kathy. "She'd just beat up everybody. Kake took it for a while but then fought back. And before you knew it, Cherry dropped to the bottom of the social order, even though she's heaviest of the does."

Cherry was also the smartest, Kathy and Mike agreed. And in keeping with her antisocial ways, she would cleverly frustrate the researchers.

Sometimes she'd refuse to get on the scale until everyone walked away; then she'd stand on it and look at them as if she were playing a game. Also, the study occasionally required urine samples, collected with a small vial fastened to the end of a stick. One day, Cherry decided not to cooperate. "When she saw you coming with the stick she'd just pee forever, until her bladder was empty," Mike complained. "After that, every time you got a step away, she'd squirt a little bit and walk off, so you couldn't get any. She was annoyed and letting you know it."

Cherry grew solitary after losing her dominant position. It was the only way she could escape constant harassment, stay clear of flailing hooves, and have uncontested access to food. The fact that Cherry shunned both people and deer added to my impression that the researchers belonged in some way to the deer's social group. And considering how much time they spent together, it seemed as if the animals belonged to the biologists' social group as well.

Cherry wandered out of sight, so I stayed with Kake and BlueMoon for a while. Mike had described BlueMoon as an unaggressive deer, close to Cherry at the bottom of the hierarchy, but unlike Cherry, she loved company. BlueMoon was also the most gymnastic Channel Island deer—"a dainty monkey," Mike called her—who would fearlessly clamber along cliffs and scamper around on fallen trunks, so it was hard for the researchers to stay with her. Mike suggested this allowed her to feed without competition from higher-status deer.

Kake was dominant in the deer hierarchy, along with a large buck named Paladin. Kathy suggested Kake and BlueMoon made ideal friends because they stood at opposite ends of the social scale, so neither had anything to prove to the other. "Kake never beats up on BlueMoon," she explained, "and BlueMoon knows if she's with Kake nobody gets after her."

It was clear from last night's conversation that Kake was the researchers' favorite deer. "She's very sensitive, affectionate, and she's really committed to humans, which can make things hard," Kathy said. "On the one hand, it's nice to have an animal return your affection; but on the other hand, you're relieved when she'll just go and be a deer, partly because that's what she's supposed to be, but partly because you know she'll be able to take care of herself when this is over."

Not long after joining Kake and BlueMoon I started feeling loyal toward Cherry, perhaps because we'd spent much of the day together, or because she was more challenging, or because I assumed an outcast deer must be lonesome. She hadn't gone far, and when I came within sight she walked straight toward me. Rather than flatter myself, I suspected lichens could be the main attraction. Nonetheless, she'd abandoned her fear, so I could roam around with her, savoring the pleasure of being close to this lovely creature.

I was struck by the wonderful oddness of this—a deer accepting human company, even going out of her way to be with me. After all, I am a hunter. On most days, I eat the flesh of her kind. Because of this I was somewhat embarrassed, as if I'd taken advantage of her naïveté. I wondered if gaining such closeness with deer would make hunting difficult for me, but this didn't seem likely. I had always loved deer, not only as wild, beautiful creatures but also as a source of my own existence; as animals who elevate my senses, enrich my spirit, and nourish my body. My feelings toward deer were wholly unlike the attitude that cows are simply beef on the hoof or that wheat is nothing more than unprocessed flour.

As I watched the Channel Island deer, I sought fuller comprehension of an animal I am made from—the life outside me that becomes the life within me. Beyond this, I reached toward intimacy with a wild creature who engages my soul more deeply than any other. If this seems contradictory, then the whole living process is a contradiction. We love apart from ourselves that which we also kill to sustain us: great trees become our houses and furniture, flowering plants become our vegetables and fruit, fellow creatures become our food and clothing. The situation is not fundamentally different for a deer. Plants who die to feed her also make her bed, conceal her from predators, shelter her from storms, and surely pleasure her senses.

By three o'clock the winter light was fading beneath towering trees and thick layers of cloud. Everyone would be waiting at the anchorage, but it was hard to leave Cherry after a time so lavish and fascinating. At times I'd felt a shared familiarity of mind with this deer, empathizing with her shyness during those early hours or with the appetite that brought her boldly when I offered lichens. But now, as she vanished into a thicket without looking back, there seemed a vast, indecipherable distance between us.

Science and the Heart

We were all tired after being out in the cold and waddling through snow in our heavy clothes. Squeezed around the tiny kitchen table that night, we treated ourselves to another backwoods feast. The meal helped restore body and mind, which in turn heightened my understanding of the

Channel Island research: just like deer, we tried to balance energy intake against each day's energy loss.

No one seemed surprised when I reported that Cherry's fawn hadn't shown up; they agreed it had probably died. I mentioned that Cherry spent almost the entire day eating, and I wondered if this was typical. Mike estimated that on ordinary winter days, the deer spent about half their time feeding and the other half lying down to ruminate, then added, "They're like constant chewing machines; seldom will they just lie around and do nothing." Even after dark they wouldn't rest for long, as revealed by radio collar signals charted on the Sweets Island recording device. This was less true in the summer, when abundant forage made life easier, so the animals had more time to loaf, relax, or sleep.

"What happens during winter storms and cold snaps?" I asked. "Do the deer simply hunker down?" Not for the whole day, Kathy replied. "During heavy snowfalls they're likely to trudge around and look for food, even though energy costs are really high doing that. But when it's very cold and blowing—wind chills of twenty-five to thirty-five below zero—they just tend to lie in their curled position and shiver. The food's out there to be found and you wish they'd go after it, but there must be something about comfort."

I thought of the penned blacktails in Juneau, with their abundance of nutritious food. Later, when Tom took me to see them, I was impressed by how big and portly the deer looked. Their main role, as far as I could tell, was to be on permanent vacation: eat, drink, and be measured. Tom pointed out that despite unlimited access to food, they chose to eat only half as much during winter as they did in summer, reflecting the automatic slowdown in their metabolism.

From discussions with biologists and explorations of scientific literature, I knew captive deer weren't always so lucky. For example, penned animals have been used to study winter starvation—a major cause of death and a critical factor in deer population dynamics. I'd seen articles about these investigations, most of them published during the 1960s and 1970s in professional wildlife journals.

Here's an example from the northeastern United States. To study how natural shelter affects winter deer survival, whitetail fawns were confined in three fenced enclosures, one having patchy thickets, the second providing moderate cover, and the third densely wooded. Food was kept "below an estimated maintenance level and . . . reduced as the season passed." In other words, the fawns were intentionally starved. Out of 21 deer, 3 became so weak they died, and in spring the survivors were killed to measure fat content in their marrow. Afterward, researchers found they couldn't draw meaningful conclusions, because access to shelter was not sufficiently different in the three impoundments.

A more ambitious project was undertaken at a midwestern wildlife research facility. To study how food deprivation affected survival of fetuses and fawns, 168 captive does were divided into groups receiving high-, moderate-, and low-level diets. As winter progressed, 43 pregnant females either starved to death, died of accidents, or were "sacrificed" so researchers could study their reproductive tracts. ("Sacrifice" is the term of choice among animal researchers; ironically, its Latin roots mean "to perform a religious or holy act.") Except for deer killed intentionally, researchers tried to prevent emaciated does from dying in order to observe full gestation and fawning. Illuminating the project's challenges, they wrote: "Keeping deer alive after they had reached the critical nadir of physical wretchedness was a difficult, demanding task, not readily appreciated."

Thirty-seven fawns born to these animals died of "nutritive failure," mainly because dissipated mothers could not or would not care for them. "If the fawn was unable to obtain milk, it bleated plaintively while following the mother. After a few hours the fawn then lay quietly in a semi-torpid state until it died." Reading these words, I marveled at the phenomenon of dispassionate scientific observation—the supremacy of empirical knowledge over humane or ethical impulse—especially among people who you might assume were drawn to their discipline by love for the natural world.

But the project I remembered most vividly was a study of rumen microorganisms in starving deer, conducted at a university in the West. Nine adult mule deer were first kept on a wholesome diet, then divided into three groups, put in small enclosures, and never fed again. Members of one group were kept together and allowed to eat each other's feces. The second group was penned together and allowed to eat dirt from the floor as well as feces. This meant that members of both groups could ingest each other's rumen microbes. Animals in the third group were individually isolated in concrete-floored cages, and they ate nothing but their own feces. The first deer expired after 16 days, seven more died between day 20 and 37, and the last died 47 days after feeding stopped. So they could immediately draw rumen fluid, researchers watched closely as each animal approached death.

An article about the project concluded: "These results agree with the literature indicating that [the] number of viable [rumen] bacteria declines during starvation." Simply put, the study supported what was already known. Furthermore, because wild animals are never entirely without food, the experiment "did not completely simulate naturally occurring starvation." In other words, information gained by starving these deer to death was of limited value.

As I read this article I imagined people coming each day to observe as the deer weakened and collapsed. What struck me was not just the animals' protracted suffering—after all, agonized death is ubiquitous in the natural world—but the thought that it was done so methodically, that science could morally encompass this behavior, and that such a course was followed as a means to more intimately understand nature.

It seems, from articles in recent wildlife journals, that scientists either have stopped intentionally starving animals or now avoid mentioning it's been done. One hopes that a more humane ethic has emerged to guide wildlife research. According to one biologist, "If they're going to publish your articles, some journals now require that you treat animals in accordance with certain rules." But he added, "The rules aren't very stringent. They basically say you have to keep animals alive and maintain sanitary conditions, and I assume they prohibit you from starving them."

When I asked another biologist about starvation research, he told me: "It's not a kind of study I like, but if treating a few deer that way allows you to understand why twenty-five or thirty thousand animals are starving on winter range, and how you can help to prevent that, then it's justifiable by my lights. But if you're simply repeating previous studies, I would find that abhorrent." There are also biologists for whom no amount of information justifies this kind of suffering. Of course, each researcher strikes a different balance between humane considerations and the demands of scientific inquiry.

In the floathouse that night, I felt lucky to be with people who were committed to rigorous, meticulous science but who treated animals with respect and care, recognizing them as collaborators in a quest for knowledge. To fully understand our world, I thought, we must exercise not only the intellect but also the heart.

Our conversation went on for hours, until an epidemic of yawns brought on talk of tomorrow's plans, so Mike switched on the marine weather forecast. The prediction was unexpected and ominous: intensifying cold with northeasterly gales that could persist for days. My spirits sank. To avoid becoming stranded, we'd have to leave for Wrangell the next morning.

Awaiting sleep, I stared into the prodigious blackness, listened to the music of water lapping against the barge, and imagined the great peaks heaved up around us—the shelter of rock and forest, the freedom of animals living beyond human eyes, the mystery of a wildness known only to itself.

Return

I went back to Channel Island in September, seven months after my first visit. Fresh off the jet, I picked out Mike's bramble of red hair moving through the airport crowd. Tom Hanley couldn't come this time, but Mike had with him a colleague and friend, Norman Barichello, a biologist with the Yukon Department of Natural Resources. Intense and sometimes rowdy conversation started as soon as we climbed into the pickup's front seat. Norman and Mike were old pals from their college days in Canada. They made ideal sidekicks—witty and frivolous one minute, serious and thoughtful the next. I was outnumbered, a Yank anthropologist in the clutches of two Canuck biologists, and they didn't let me forget it.

This time, rather than boating to Channel Island, we drove logging roads that followed the shore of Zimovia Strait and then twisted across Wrangell Island toward a skiff landing on Eastern Passage, within sight of the floathouse. In one place we pulled off for a ridgetop view of forested mountains and glittering fjords, country so pristine it jarred our senses, as if we'd driven back through time.

But a few miles farther on, the twentieth century overtook us: our road opened into a sprawling, newly shorn clear-cut. Where primordial forest had stood for thousands of years, the land was ripped and raw and suppurating, without a single standing tree. Wanting a closer look, we forced our way through snarls of slash, climbed across helter-skelter tree trunks left to rot, and stood atop amputated stumps. Surrounding hills gaped with a maze of clear-cuts, as if scavengers had gnawed the flesh from the earth itself. I struggled to imagine anything that might redeem such a wasteland, and thought this was a place where blindness would be a gift.

Kathy met us at the landing with a small skiff, and as we approached the floathouse Lisa came out to help unload our gear. What a contrast to winter: the forests were lush and alive, the weather benign and unthreatening. Calm waters behind Sweets Island reflected emerald alpine meadows. When a silvery fish leapt several times in midbay, Lisa explained that salmon were on their way to spawn in a nearby river. That evening we regaled ourselves with conversation and watched the long northern sunset smoldering on mountaintops still patched with snow.

Some days before this, Kathy and Mike had made an important decision: with Norman and me around to help, it was time to begin releasing deer. Because of cost and logistics they'd given up hope of transporting the animals to a secure, faraway locale. Their new homes would be within 20 miles of Channel Island, places we could reach with the big skiff. Like their wild compatriots, the deer would have to become savvy about bears, wolves, and hunters. You couldn't miss the gravity in Mike's and Kathy's voices as they outlined plans for capture and relocation. There were practical worries, to be sure, but mostly I sensed their anxiety over the deer's future and their anticipation of separating from animals they knew so intimately after two years of almost daily contact.

Next morning, a layer of dense fog hovered 20 feet above the floathouse cove. We peered through a crevice between slick water and sagging mist, closed at its far edge by the dark forest wall. When at last the fog withered, all of us piled in the boat and crossed to Channel Island. As I walked across a field of knee-high grass near the research hut, I remembered deer wading through drifted snow to greet us last winter. This time no hungry animals came from the forest, so it was our job to find them.

It didn't take long. Up near the scale we found Kake, the affectionate doe, and nearby was her fawn—an entrancing duplicate of his mother, about one third her size, dainty legged, short faced, with the same dense sorrel coat. He nibbled tender leaves and peered at us from billowing thickets, keeping a shy distance, but eventually let us come within 10 feet, close enough, Mike figured, to catch him with a large net. Fawns and mothers must be released together, but how would we capture both at once? Raised by their own kind rather than humans, the striplings fairly trembled with wildness, unlike their calm and trusting elders.

As if to demonstrate the point, Kake followed Kathy's crinkling raisin bag to the platform scale and let herself be weighed. At the same time, a prime buck ambled down the trail and came right in among us. He carried thick, sharply curved antlers with three polished, bony-gray points on each side and main beams colored a rich burnt ocher, as if they'd been stained with blood. "That's Paladin," Kathy told Norman and me. "He's three years old, the number one buck and overall dominant deer on Channel Island." He certainly looked the part, brawny and muscular next to the doe, bristling with patrician confidence. Kathy lured him onto the scale. "At the end of winter he weighed eighty-nine pounds," she reported, "and now he's at a hundred forty-seven, a fifty-eight-pound gain."

It had been a tough winter, Mike recalled, with persistent cold and deep snow. My companion Cherry had dropped from 104 pounds to 85 pounds, surviving an 18 percent weight loss. Her missing fawn was never seen again, but this summer she'd raised two healthy offspring. Later compilation of research data would reveal that the Channel Island black-tails experienced winter weight losses of 14 to 31 percent. "We've learned that deer are incredibly resilient animals," concluded Mike. "They can thrive despite going through tremendous stresses every year."

Summer had been kind: the deer looked fat and well muscled, appropriately alluring for the mating season just ahead. Even now, two months before the rut, Paladin flexed and surged with maleness. It didn't matter who you were—doe, fawn, or human—he'd approach with his head down, presenting his antlers, stiffened tail twitching up and down, offering a silent challenge. When Mike rubbed his forehead, the buck shoved hard and hooked with his antlers. "Don't ever get your face near those points," Kathy warned. "Also, never keep your back toward him, and be especially careful when you stoop down, because that elicits aggression."

Crouching probably triggered the same response as a rival buck lowering his head to invite a joust. I couldn't resist giving it a try and Paladin did exactly what his nature dictated. When he got within two feet—antlers poised to skewer my delicate hide—I scuttled out of reach. He stopped and raised his head as if nothing had happened. It was hard to put this straightforward aggression together with his gentle, innocent, tenderly handsome face. His behavior didn't mesh with the popular stereotype of deer as peaceful and harmless creatures. Kake was under no such illusion. Whenever he approached, she'd tuck her tail like a submissive dog and slip to a safe distance. During all this, Kathy told of a woman biologist who was punctured by a mule deer seriously enough to need stitches.

When Kake and her fawn wandered off, Mike suggested I follow. Unlike Cherry the past winter, Kake accepted me without hesitation, even when I leaned close enough to feel her breath against my cheek. She meandered up a steep hillside, munching continuously, as if she were in the gardens of paradise, where all was edible and delicious. Swaddled in deep thickets, the doe feasted on menziesia leaves, twisted stalk, wild lily of the valley, and mushrooms. She nipped outsized skunk cabbage and devil's club leaves, sculpting their edges like someone taking bites out of a tortilla. Her droppings, processed from succulent summer foods, were large and soft, unlike the dry, marble-sized pellets left by deer feeding on dry winter browse. Because of higher moisture intake she urinated more often than she would during winter; the water was clear as a mountain stream and puddled noisily.

Kake's fawn seemed very independent until he lost track of his mother. Then he cried in a soft, plaintive, extremely high-pitched voice, but Kake paid no attention. Nor did she allow him to nurse, though he tried repeatedly, always sneaking up from behind. Once she lifted a hind leg over the fawn and attempted to move away, but her leg came down unceremoniously atop his head and almost knocked him over. Weaning had started back in July, but obviously the youngsters weren't ready to accept it.

On a hillside sheltered by enormous spruce, Kake and her fawn bedded down in a peaceful, hidden spot, oceanic in its green stillness. Sitting on the moss beside Kake, I could hear her stomach rumble, a sound uncannily like distant thunder on a muggy summer night. After she ruminated for a while, soft white foam gathered around her lips, droplets of clear saliva slipped down her chin whiskers, and viscous strands of drool shimmered to the ground. I remembered Kathy saying that deer froth and salivate like this after they've eaten skunk cabbage.

Later that afternoon I found Mike tracking BlueMoon through a maze of shrubs and fallen trees, tapping keys on his portable computer, using a complicated letter-and-number code to record the habitat she was in, the species she ate, how many "plant units" she took, and how long she chewed. "Okay, that's species thirteen, devil's club," he muttered, "about two plant units. Now she's walking . . . standing . . . taking multiple bites of species twenty-one . . . then back to thirteen, about four plant units." Other codes were logged for each time she drank, defecated, or urinated, and for how long she spent grooming, nursing, running, playing, standing, lying down, and ruminating. And, the ultimate in deer minutiae, Mike even counted the number of chews for each bolus—generally about 60.

"On this job, you feel like someone who can't walk and chew gum at the same time," Mike said with a laugh. "Some days it's pouring rain, you've had no chance to eat lunch, you're crawling around the underbrush, you're totally fried—you're still trying to punch in data without missing one thing the animal does."

Mike, Kathy, and Lisa went through this routine each working day, accumulating huge amounts of information for later analysis. They also kept track of weather conditions, vegetation patterns, snow depth, deer weights and body condition, and radio collar data on the animals' movements. Sorted and analyzed by computer, this mass of data would eventually yield calculations of energy gain and expenditure among the Channel Island deer. It was a bewilderingly complex process, and to carry it off, these biologists had developed an impressive array of talents, from fluency with advanced technology to the delicate art of working cooperatively with animals.

Deliverance

"I guess this is it," Mike declared when we arrived on Channel Island the next morning. He and Kathy looked at each other for a long moment. I was reminded of parents about to send their children into the world—that odd mix of excitement and dread. Of course, this project was based on hard-minded, objective research, but the scientific process is never purely intellectual, and no scientist is—or should attempt to be—wholly disconnected from human emotions. Mike pursed his lips, sad eyed and serious, then mustered a smile. We left him with Kathy in the research hut.

When they emerged, Kathy sketched a plan: "Since we've got Norm and Dick to help, we'll try the most difficult releases first. That means does with two fawns—Cherry or Heidi." She switched on the telemetry receiver and listened intently. The loudest pings confirmed what Kathy had expected: Heidi was fairly close, probably near her favorite stretch of shore. While the other deer could turn up anywhere, this doe favored one place so much that the crew had named it "Heidi's Beach."

Sure enough, we found her in heavy woods behind the beach and the two fawns grazing in tall grass that rimmed the stony shore. Knowing what it means to love a place, I felt a sharp twinge of sadness: if our plan succeeded, Heidi would be permanently uprooted from her home. But the options were clear: live somewhere else or face hunters sure to visit Channel Island after the study ended. Like a Pied Piper, Lisa crinkled a raisin bag to lure Heidi toward the fawns. Once their mother was nearby, the fidgety twins felt secure enough to let people come closer. Lisa, Norman, and I hunkered in the grass while Mike eased toward one fawn and Kathy toward the other. Each of them carried a wide-hooped net Mike had fashioned for the job.

The two fawns strayed apart and kept a wary distance from their stalkers. Mike and Kathy wanted to make their moves simultaneously so one tyke wouldn't be frightened by the other's capture. Kathy's deer relaxed first so she stayed close to it, looking over her shoulder, waiting for the other to calm down. Knowing it was his move, Mike pitched the net as

soon as he got within range . . . and his aim was perfect. The fawn leapt
frantically against tangling mesh, but Mike hugged her against the soft
grass so she couldn't injure herself.

The capture happened so fast that before Kathy knew what happened
the netted fawn let out a piercing, panicked wail. Almost instantly, Heidi
bounded up the beach, snorting loudly. Kathy didn't have a chance, as
her loose fawn dashed for the woods. Meanwhile, Norman and I ran to
the boat, fetched a large plywood crate, and carried it up to Mike.

All three of us labored to unsnarl the tiny deer, who squirmed and
bleated and flailed her hooves. I was surprised by the strength and intensity of her struggles. But far beyond this, I was amazed by the pounding of her heart. It was incredibly fast, perhaps 300 beats per minute, and
loud enough to be heard easily from 3 feet away. In fact, I probably could
have heard it from 10 feet. The terror in the panicked hammering of that
fawn's heart is something I will never forget. I imagined the sound elevated and multiplied, drumming out across the waters, drumming up
against the mountainsides, drumming far into the valleys—as if the heart
of earth itself were trembling in fear of us.

Norman lifted the crate's sliding door while Mike eased the deer inside. She clattered around briefly and then became quiet. I peeked in
through a crack at the top of the door—her ears were erect, her eyes wide
and blinking. She was either calm or exhausted, or she had resigned herself to whatever might come next. Lisa and I stayed behind while the others trailed Heidi into the forest, assuming she'd reunite with her missing
fawn. Half an hour later, Mike came breathless from the woods to tell us
Kathy had caught the fawn on a nearby beach. We drove the boat around
a rocky point, found Kathy and Norman with the fawn inside a gunny
sack, and carried another crate up to them. This youngster rattled and
clacked inside the box for about 15 minutes before quieting down.

The water was silky calm, glazed with deep coniferous green, as if the
forest had dissolved into it. Our next job would be easy. Heidi had relaxed since her initial fright and a few raisin treats kept her close. Now
Kathy prepared a hypodermic syringe with a small dose of light tran-
quilizer called Rompun. "We only use ten percent of the recommended
dosage," she explained. "You couldn't do this with wild deer because it
takes about twenty minutes to work and has no effect on a truly frightened animal." Speaking gently, she eased next to the doe. Heidi twitched
at the needle's jab but then stood peacefully. After giving the drug time
to work, Kathy maneuvered Heidi into the crate, removed her radio collar, and shortly the deer flopped down in a groggy daze.

Mike seemed lost in his own thoughts. Earlier, as he held the netted fawn and watched the other escape, his face had been scrawled with anguish and distress. Norman and Kathy talked about the emotional strain of capture-and-drug operations. They described wild animals being pursued by helicopter, darted with potent drugs, their blood drawn and their bodies probed, then tags or collars attached before they were released.

"I just hate that cowboy biology," a researcher once told me, "but some people enjoy it. After a while, the animal isn't even an animal for them; it's a target."

Animal deaths from drug overdoses, exhaustion, or other accidents are common in field studies using capture-and-release methods. While I couldn't know how "most" biologists judge such things, once again I was pleased to be among people committed to treating animals with care and respect. This was not only good ethics, Norman asserted, but also good science. How valuable is knowledge gained by manipulating and manhandling animals, versus that gathered through close, careful, sustained observation under natural circumstances? Norman suggested that the older and less intrusive approaches could yield insights as valid as those possible with today's technology-based, quantitative approaches.

When I talked with Dr. David Klein, a respected wildlife biologist at the University of Alaska, he described caribou migration studies using satellite-tracked radio collars and observers monitoring herds from airplanes. These methods can yield valuable information, he judged, "but I also think it's important to maintain a close association with the animal and get a *feeling* for its relationship to the environment." Assessing the Channel Island research, Klein said, "Mike and Kathy are doing a good job with high tech, but they're also following the deer around, coming closer to the animal's perspective."

Some biologists voiced concern that the hand-raised Channel Island deer had never learned from their natural mothers, so their behavior or feeding patterns might differ from those of fully wild animals. But Tom Hanley cited studies of other ungulates showing that although hand-reared animals learn more slowly, after a year or so they behave virtually the same as those raised by mothers. Also, the Channel Island project was designed to study the internal physiology of deer, and according to Tom, this makes behavioral questions irrelevant, because physiological processes are not affected by the animal's "wildness" or "tameness."

"Time to get on with it," Mike announced. During previous weeks, he and Kathy had scouted widely, looking for good deer habitat away from major boat routes, keeping in mind each animal's special character and needs. For Heidi's family, they'd chosen a protected bay with good southern exposure, lush vegetation, and little sign of bears or wolves. Later on, they'd take one or two of Heidi's favorite companions to the same place. After loading and securing the crates, we headed off through the mountain-walled channels. Along the way, Kathy predicted Heidi would adjust well to her new situation. "Remember how she snorted and ran after we caught the fawn? Heidi's grown to like people and tolerate them, but she's a deer first."

After landing in a deep, quiet cove, we hefted our odd cargo back beneath the trees. There, in the cool shadows of hemlock and spruce, we waited for Heidi to recover full alertness. Kathy rubbed the doe's neck and talked soothingly, but Heidi stayed inside the crate, as if she were confused or reluctant to leave Kathy's reassuring company. When at last she walked out, she headed straight for a devil's club bush and bit chunks from the broad parasol leaves. Still we waited, until she looked bright eyed and fully coordinated. Then Mike and Kathy asked us to stand back while they released the two fawns.

The little ones dashed from their cages, stopped about 10 yards away, peered back as if nothing had happened, then scampered to their mother and began munching beside her. The vegetation was lavish and dense, without so much as a nibbled leaf, indicating no deer had been around this summer. If their new home was unfamiliar, it was also like being turned loose in a supermarket.

Kathy said she felt relieved—no animals hurt, the whole family together, and the habitat nearly ideal. Our day had been so intense and all-consuming that there wasn't time to think about sadness. "It's probably better that way," she mused, watching the deer slip off amid curtains of shrubbery. The moment they disappeared we hurried for the boat to make sure they wouldn't abandon the woods in an effort to stay with us.

"From now on a crinkling bag spells disaster," warned Mike as we left the bay. We hoped the blacktails' inherent wildness would resurface in the absence of human contact, nurtured by this forested mountain terrain. We hoped they'd flee the sounds and scents of unknown predators, of unfamiliar outboard engines or strange human voices. Of course, none of us would ever know. And that, I suppose, was a mercy.

Paladin's World

Morning leaned down from a heavy sky, raindrops dimpling slick water in the Back Channel. Thin shards of cloud drifted along mountainsides, as if you could see the land's breath. Mike and I climbed a steep slope on Channel Island's south end and found two bucks keeping company. Paladin watched disinterestedly as we approached, then returned to his browsing. Bedded 10 feet away was Osage, dreamily chewing his cud. Mike had work of his own today, so he wished me well and threaded off into the woods.

I knelt down a few yards from the two animals, letting them grow accustomed to my presence. Osage was a lovely buck, but a year younger and far less imposing than the regal Paladin, so I was surprised when he abruptly stood, lowered his sapling rack, and strode confidently toward Channel Island's reigning potentate. Their mismatched antlers met with a dull clack. Legs bent so their bellies nearly touched the ground, the bucks jammed powerfully against each other, tearing divots of moss and breaking bushes as they circled. Osage quickly yielded and scrambled off, half crouched, ears back, tail between his legs. After a few pursuing steps Paladin relaxed, as if the aggression were drained out of him.

Lightly built Osage looked more like the champion's mascot than his sparring partner, but practice sessions are common between unequal bucks. "Play fights," Kathy and Mike called them, in contrast to the prolonged, intense frays between evenly matched bucks during peak rut. After losing a particularly savage battle with Paladin last year, Falstaff swam off to the mainland. The crew tracked him with telemetry and brought him back, where he assumed a lower position in the island's hierarchy. Losing an animal like Falstaff—raised by hand, wearing a radio collar, and part of a growing data inventory—would have been a great loss to the project. He simply couldn't be abandoned.

Paladin ambled away from Osage, feeding contentedly along a little rise, where a drooping spruce bough caught his attention. Pushing his head against the stiff, twiggy branches, he raked his antlers back and forth with strong, deliberate movements that gave the impression of a much larger animal. Above all, it looked as if thrashing this way felt good to him—really good, like scratching a profound itch. At intervals he'd stop to sniff the bark and load up on his personal fragrance. Surging with virility, he erected his body hair, then quickly opened and shut his preorbital glands. The winking glands looked strange, like cracking a little door at the corner of each eye, exposing a sheath of pinkish flesh inside.

I wanted to see more sparring but Osage lay down and Paladin roamed off, nibbling leaves and fronds, occasionally nuzzling the moss for mushrooms or crunchy fern rhizomes. Every noise seemed magnified in the enveloping silence: his rack ticking against branches, twigs snapping under his hooves, and papery noises when he tore chunks from skunk cabbage leaves. A little spruce branch hung for a while in his antlers like a crumb in someone's beard, and occasionally a twig or leaf dropped onto his back but didn't stay for long. I remembered Kathy saying that a deer's coat never becomes dirty or grimy, as dirt or debris rarely clings to the dry hairs, and deer regularly lick themselves—so your hand feels perfectly clean after rubbing their fur.

I followed Paladin over a ridge to the island's east side, where I suddenly heard the yammer of chain saws and the roar of logging trucks among broad hills across the channel. It was a jarring contrast to the silence of a deer moving beneath ancient, sheltering timber, following a pattern of life that had gone on here for millennia. At intervals I heard the thunder of falling trees and from an opening I saw a dark smear of emptied mountainside. As Jeremiah 25:37 reads: "The peaceable habitations are cut down . . ." Many centuries would pass before those places would again be clothed in giant forest with small, brushy openings created by storm-toppled trees, the montage of habitats vital for healthy deer populations along this coast.

Another tree fell and pandemonium echoed along the mountainsides, fading to a numb silence. The buck raised his head, listened for a moment, then reached out and plucked an elderberry leaf.

Later on, as I followed Paladin along a game trail, he gave an intriguing glimpse into his mind. When we came upon a smaller path that joined our trail from the right, the buck went a few steps beyond it, paused and stared off into the woods, then turned around and took the other track. That trail angled up to a ledge with a perfect deer bed, worn to bare earth, overlooking the nearby forest. After feeding briefly, Paladin lay down in the bed. It was no stretch to believe he chose this trail because he felt like ruminating and knew exactly where to go. Mike later commented that Channel Island's deer almost always bedded in places they had used before, and among these were "ancestral beds" that deer had used for many generations.

Of course, most deer populations have a long history on their home terrain, and as evidence of their habitation we find established beds or trails, as well as vegetation affected by decades or centuries of browsing. In New York, the biologist C. W. Severinghaus reported deer trails mapped as early as the 1890s still being used during the 1950s. And from early plantation records, Archibald Rutledge concluded that deer paths around his South Carolina home had been in use for more than 300 years. Deer become expressions of the land that nurtures them, as surely as the land itself reflects their presence. In this sense, each place and each community of animals is like no other on earth.

Curled in his bed, Paladin seemed relaxed and drowsy. Twice he yawned widely, bleating at the same time the way people sigh during a good yawn, then put his head down like a tired dog, although his ears never stopped moving. Only when I rubbed under his neck did he close his eyes, reveling in pleasure. By contrast, he hooked his antlers at my arm if I touched a front hoof, as if I'd triggered his male aggression. When he calmed down I knelt close and listened to his chewing and licking, his strong huffy breaths.

Paladin raised his head and looked out through the forest, where afternoon light blinked between enormous tree trunks. Whatever it was— this companionship we shared—he remained always and ever a prime buck deer, master of his domain. I couldn't help dwelling on a painful thought: that the unhinging of his world loomed ahead. These were Paladin's final days on Channel Island and I was the last human to share his close company. He rested quietly in the shadows and watched as I left by the trail he'd shown me.

Crossing the Wild Edge

It was a glorious morning, blue chasms between pearly clouds, juncos and chickadees teetering through high boughs. The previous day, we had captured Pia, her fawn, and a buck named Tornado, then released them many miles away. When we returned to Channel Island we found Hawkins, the elusive, uncollared buck, standing in the open as if he'd been waiting for us. "Ah, a gift from God!" exclaimed Mike. "We were afraid we'd never get him off Channel Island." We took Hawkins where we had released the others, and Tornado showed up just after we opened the crate. This meant Hawkins would have a companion while the drugs wore off—another stroke of luck.

Today was my last with the crew, so Mike and Kathy wanted to move a couple of strong, heavy bucks. Using telemetry, Mike found Osage and lured him into the sunny meadow with BlueMoon tagging along behind. Rather than face the inevitable, we hung around with the two deer, took their pictures, and savored some bucolic moments together. Finally, Kathy maneuvered Osage to a flat place and injected the Rompun. Soon as the buck went down, Lisa removed his radio collar and Kathy gave him a dose of worm medicine. One important step remained before putting him into a crate.

Legal hunting in this area was restricted to antlered bucks, so any deer flashing a conspicuous rack was a prime candidate for the dinner table . . . especially if he didn't have a buck's normal wariness. It was much safer to look like a doe, so Mike and Kathy chose to saw the antlers off each buck. The operation was painless and fairly quick, and the antlers would grow back next year, but no one liked doing it. After Osage was uncrowned it would take quite an eye to notice his discreetly hidden manhood.

Kathy looked discontented when we finished. It bothered her, she said, to immobilize the deer, to handle and manipulate them, to remove the buck's antlers, and to turn their lives topsy-turvy. Mike agreed: "Doing this stuff makes me sick to my stomach."

We didn't have the luxury of relaxing once Osage was inside a crate, because telemetry showed Paladin was just back in the woods. Shortly he traipsed out behind Mike, and again Kathy handled the delicate work of injecting Rompun. After about 10 minutes Paladin slouched down heavily in the tall grass. It was hard to watch a proud, independent animal reduced to such helplessness. We gently restrained the deer when he seemed only half conscious: Kathy nested his head, Lisa wrapped a piece of cloth over his eyes, Mike wielded the hacksaw, and I straddled his body. He struggled for a few minutes, bleating pathetically, then relinquished his fate to us.

I sprawled across the deer's back, wrapped my arms around his neck, and held his forelegs so he wouldn't try to stand. Pinning him this way, I realized our bodies were about the same size. He felt familiar, like hugging a person in a fur coat. I pressed my cheek against his dense, odorless hair and felt the warmth emanating from his skin, the thick muscles of his shoulders, the hard angles of his pelvis, the heavy rise and fall of his ribs, the taut bulge of his belly. I put my ear on his chest and heard air gusting through his windpipe like wind in a canyon.

Mike sawed through the base of each antler, then filed off the sharp edges of their pale-gray stumps. Kathy tied the antlers together and tagged them with Paladin's name, while the rest of us eased him into a crate. After a few tussles, Mike said, the bucks would realize they'd been disarmed and would keep a safe distance from wild, antlered deer. Perhaps next year Paladin would vie for dominance in his new territory, but for now his only challenge was to stay alive.

An hour later we skimmed at full throttle down the glassy waters of Blake Channel. Massive, timbered slopes impinged on either side, as if we were in a canyon several thousand feet deep. A bald eagle flecked the sky, turning pirouettes above velvet tundra meadows. Seals bobbed up to watch us pass, globed eyes opened wide, nostrils flaring and closing, slick fur shining in the sun.

Finally we entered the broad reach of Bradfield Canal, a fjord riven 15 miles into the Alaskan mainland, and Mike turned toward a heavily wooded valley on the north side. A shallow stream riffled across the tidal flat, its banks lined with gulls and crows. There were salmon everywhere: some fresh from the sea, making bright-silver flashes as they leapt from the salt water; others spawned out, mottled and dying among rocks in the stream; and still more dead and rotting where they'd been left by the falling tide. "Looks like a good place for bears," I thought aloud. Mike nodded. Gorged with salmon, the bears probably wouldn't bother to stalk deer, and hopefully by the time spawning ended the deer would be wild enough to stay clear of predators.

Sweating and puffing, we wrestled the two crates across a maze of boulders and into the woods. Osage looked fully alert and calm, lingered near us for a while, then ambled off into his new world. You had to look closely to see the bright spots where his antlers had been, but we knew any big deer would sorely tempt a poacher—there were no guarantees. Paladin, still fuzzy minded, stepped out tentatively when Mike opened his crate. Kathy urged him farther into the woods and up a mossy slope, where he stood for a long time, ears laid back, half-opened eyes peering down at us. "That means he feels bad," she explained.

We held our distance, talking quietly, keeping watch in case a bear showed up before Paladin's mind cleared. "When you bottle-raise a deer and take control of it," Kathy reflected, "you owe it the best possible life, not just during your work but after it's finished." The Channel Island deer might seem independent and skittish, she added, but they weren't much afraid of people, having been treated with care and sensitivity throughout their lives. In some way, we all felt like his betrayers.

Paladin had become more alert. His erect ears turned this way and that, as if he were listening first to our reassuring voices and then to the jumble of unfamiliar sounds. Mike and Kathy agreed the time had come, so they retreated quickly, hoping the bucks wouldn't follow us into the open. I paused momentarily at the trees' edge and glimpsed Paladin, staring toward the thicket where we'd last seen Osage. I understood that his rightful place was here, restored to the wildness that had always simmered inside him. This was exactly how the Channel Island research should end. Having obliged the interests of his human companions, he was now free to be completely, exclusively, a wild deer . . . even if that meant feeding a bear or wolf somewhere in the valley beyond.

I imagined the two bucks listening as our engine's noise faded to a murmur and then turned my attention to a great, leaning mass of mountains reflected on the waters before us. No one spoke a word until long after we'd turned north into Blake Channel. Then Mike heaved a deep breath and shook his head: "Well, four to go." Kathy stood outside the boat's cabin, staring up at the vertiginous peaks, long brown hair blowing delicately against her cheek. How did she feel, I asked. "Sad," she half whispered, and that was all.

My respect for these people, and for their work, had grown enormously during the times we'd spent together. Above all, I admired the standards they set for the conduct of research. They demonstrated that exacting, systematic, objective science can be—indeed, should be—carried out in the presence of fundamental human virtues: ethical commitment, sensitivity, thoughtfulness, and love for that which is studied.

Instead of going straight home, Mike took us into a wide, shallow bay. Idling along in five feet of crystal water, we watched the gray, sandy bottom pass beneath us, the ivory flecks of clamshells, the gnarled hulks of sunken logs. Finally Mike cut the engine and as we drifted on the satiny calm he glassed the slopes with binoculars. "Look there!" he exclaimed, pointing to a broad, Irish-green meadow surrounded by rocky peaks. In the center of the meadow were three pure white mountain goats, gleaming like stars in a distant galaxy, cradled in their own world but clearly visible from ours.

I glanced at the empty crates lashed to our deck. Despite all the stress and sadness of separation, I couldn't help smiling. A thought rollicked through me like a fawn in summer grass: free and alive!

Postscript

When field studies ended on Channel Island, the research project was far from done. It would take several more years to analyze huge volumes of data and then write articles for publication, making results of the study available to other scientists, wildlife managers, and foresters; in this way, Channel Island's blacktails would increase our overall understanding of relationships between deer and habitat.

One day I received from Mike, Kathy, and Tom a packet of articles they'd submitted to professional journals, reporting on various aspects of the Channel Island research. One article, titled "An Accurate Technique for Estimating Forage Intake of Tractable Animals," explained methods used to estimate and record amounts of plant material eaten by the deer.

This information would be valuable for biologists who might want to adopt the same methods for studies of nutritional ecology.

Another article—"Seasonal Patterns in Body Weight, Composition, and Water Transfer Rates for Free-Ranging and Captive Black-Tailed Deer in Alaska"—summarized yearly changes in the deer's physical condition. It revealed, for example, that during winter the deer had lost between 70 and 82 percent of their body fat and 10 to 15 percent of their protein reserves, demonstrating how energy stored from summer's foraging was critical to keep them alive through the cold months.

Some results of the study were bafflingly technical, as in the article "Do Urinary Urea Nitrogen and Cortisol Ratios of Creatinine Reflect Body Fat Reserves in Black-Tailed Deer?" Urine samples collected from the deer were used to test a hypothesis that levels of certain chemicals in the urine are valid indicators of an animal's physical condition, but Channel Island results showed the technique was not reliable. On the other hand, urinary chemicals did indicate how much energy the deer were gaining from their habitat at sampling time, which suggested the tests might be useful in ways that hadn't been expected.

Core results of the project were summarized in an article titled "Foraging Efficiency: Energy Expenditure Versus Energy Gain in Free-Ranging Black-Tailed Deer." The mass of data compiled on Channel Island's deer over two years revealed that foraging efficiency during the summertime depended mainly on how much energy they took in: they ate a lot, gained more energy than they used, and put on weight. But in winter, foraging efficiency was mainly determined by how much energy the deer expended, and the overall balance was negative. In other words, they gained less energy from food than they used to find it, to keep warm, and to move around in deep snow. Fat reserves built up through summer were essential to keep the deer alive during cold months. The path of survival was narrow and precarious.

It was interesting to view the Channel Island blacktails from this scientific perspective—their daily lives encapsulated by graphs, charts, calculations, and technical language. This elevated the animals to a kind of immortality, gave them significance beyond the specific place they'd inhabited, and revealed aspects of their lives that only became visible from the examination of data collected over long periods of time. It added rich and fascinating dimensions to the deer I'd seen during my visits on Channel Island.

As I finished the last article, I had a vivid memory of Cherry beneath a deep-green canopy of forest, stepping cautiously toward me in the powdery snow, leaning out, and pressing her nose against my hand. Her breath puffed into the chill Alaskan air, her nostrils flared to take in my scent, and her eyes mirrored the wildness all around. During those moments, I wondered if the full truth of her—and of the deer itself—would always remain somewhere beyond our grasp. Almost involuntarily, I closed my eyes and let the lightning brilliance of her beauty fade, until I could bear it once again.

THREE

EXCESS AND RESTRAINT

When Daniel Boone goes by at night
The phantom deer arise
And all lost, wild America
Is burning in their eyes

—STEPHEN VINCENT BENÉT

People of the Deer

The interwoven history of people and deer in North America began long before Europeans laid eyes on this continent. For thousands of years, Native American people relied on the deer as a vital part of their cultural, spiritual, and economic lives. According to tradition, their relationship with deer began in an ancient time, when plants, animals, and the earth itself were taking their present forms. Each Indian community has its own account of these beginnings, detailed in epics whose meaning and importance compare with that of Genesis for the Christian world.

The ethnographer Karl Luckert was told one of these stories by Claus Chee Sonny, a Navajo elder, medicine man, and teacher of the Deer Huntingway religious tradition. According to this tradition, the Deer

Gods themselves taught the First People how to hunt and how to act properly toward animals. There was a hunter waiting in ambush, and he had been told by Wind that deer would appear to him in single file. He had four arrows: one made of sheet lightning, one of zigzag lightning, one of sunlight roots, and one of rainbow.

Then the first deer, a large buck, came with many antlers. The hunter got ready to shoot the buck. His arrow was already in place. But, just as he was ready to shoot, the deer had transformed himself into a mountain mahogany bush. . . . After a while, a mature man stood up from this bush. He stood up and said, "Do not shoot! We are your neighbors. These are the things that will be in the future when human beings will have come into existence. . . ." And he told the hunters how to kill and eat the deer. So the hunter let the mature Deer-man go at the price of his information. . . .

Then the large doe, a shiny doe, appeared behind the one who had left. The hunter was ready again, to shoot the doe in the heart. But the doe turned into a cliffrose bush. A while later a young woman stood up from the bush. The woman said, "Do not shoot! We are your neighbors. In the future, when man has been created, men will live because of us. Men will use us to live on." So then, at the price of her information, the hunter let the Doe-woman go. . . .

Then a young buck, a two-pointer, came along. And the hunter got ready to shoot the two-pointer. But the deer transformed himself into a dead tree. . . . After a while, a young man stood up from the dead tree and said, "—in the future, after man has been created, if you talk about us in the wrong way, we will cause trouble for you if you urinate, and we will trouble your eyes. We will trouble your ears if we do not approve of what you say about us." And at the price of his information, the hunter let the young Deer-man go.

Then the little Fawn appeared. The hunter was ready to shoot the Fawn, but the Fawn turned into a lichen-spotted rock. . . . After a while, a young girl stood up from the rock and spoke: " . . . I am in charge of all the other deer people. If you talk bad about us, and if we disapprove of what you say, I am the one who will respond with killing you. I will kill you with what I am. If you hear the cry of my voice, you will know that trouble is in store for you. If you do not make use of us properly, even in times when we are numerous, you will not see us anymore. . . .

"These are the things which will bring you happiness. When you kill a deer, you will lay him with the head toward your house. You will cover the earth with plants or with branches of trees, lengthwise, with the growing tips of the plants pointing the direction of the deer's head— toward your home. So it shall be made into a thick padding, and the deer shall be laid on that. Then you will take us home to your house and eat of us. You will place our bones under any of the things whose form we can assume—mountain mahogany, cliffrose, dead tree, lichen-spotted rock, spruce, pine, or under any of the other good plants. At these places you may put our bones. You will sprinkle the place with yellow pollen. Once. Twice. Then you lay the bones. And then you sprinkle yellow pollen on top of the bones. This is for the protection of the game animals. In this manner they will live on. . . ."

The Deer Huntingway stories also tell how to properly use deer and show respect toward them, and they give these final instructions from the divine deer people:

> Everything of which we are made, such as our skin, meat, bones, is to be used. . . . Anything that we hold on to, such as the earth from the four sacred mountains, the rainbow, the jewels, the corn, all the plants we eat, will be in us. Our bodies contain all these. And because of this we are very useful. . . .
>
> The usefulness of the deer is the foundation which has been laid; it serves as an example for other things. This is what is meant when we say that the deer are first in all things. We are in the gods who are mentioned, in the mountains, in the rainbows, in the roots of sunlight, in the lightnings. . . . For this reason, an unwounded buckskin—of a deer not killed by a weapon—shall be used in the sacred ceremonies. Also, we are in all the plants. In this manner, even the insects are associated with us. . . . All livestock lives because of the deer. That is what keeps the animals moist, breathing, walking about, and altogether alive.
>
> And animals are our food. They are our thoughts.

Showing respect and veneration toward animals is one dimension of the hunter's way; another is the practical imperative to kill, butcher, and use them. Surprisingly, very little has been recorded about Native American methods of deer hunting, or about the extensive knowledge of deer behavior and biology that Indian people have accumulated through generations of close observation. I believe that, for any tribe heavily dependent on deer, a comprehensive record of this knowledge could fill several hefty volumes.

The historical literature portrays Indians, above all, as masters of still hunting: a solitary man in the forest, armed with bow and arrow, slipping like a phantom through light and shadow, stopping every few yards to watch, waiting for the flicker of movement that reveals a deer, then cannily stalking within range. There is also a romantic but accurate image of the hunter disguised as his prey, covered with a whole or partial deer hide, his own head embellished with antlers.

"They manage to put on the skins of the largest [deer] which have before been taken, in such a manner, with the heads on their own heads, so they can see out through the eyes as through a mask." So wrote Jacques Le Moyne de Morgues in 1564 about Florida Indians, and he continued,

"Thus accoutred, they can approach closer to the deer without frightening them. They take advantage of the time when the animals come to drink at the river, and, having their bows ready, easily shoot them."

This tactic was used by many tribes, but published descriptions leave us to imagine the intricate knowledge and cunning that enabled hunters to slip right in among the animals and take whichever they preferred. An expert hunter can seemingly penetrate the mind of his prey, anticipating what the animal will do, reacting to the slightest blink or gesture, as the tangible and metaphysical distance between them fades. When Navajos hunted this way, for example, they drew from the spirit as well as the intellect—disguising themselves in the sacred hide of a deer killed by suffocation rather than with arrows or bullets.

Of course, it took another kind of virtuosity to get such a hide. Deer are great sprinters over short distances, writes Barre Toelken, but at a jogging pace they can't match the endurance of a highly conditioned human. So if a hunter can get a deer into open country, he follows at a steady run until the animal becomes exhausted. "When the deer is finally caught," Toelken explains, "he is thrown to the ground as gently as possible, his mouth and nose are held shut, and covered with a handful of pollen so that he may die breathing the sacred substance. And then—I am not sure how widespread this is with the Navajos—one sings to the deer as it is dying, and apologizes ritually for taking its life, explaining that he needs the skin for his family." Neighboring Hopi Indians, who use horses to encircle and chase down deer, say that ritually smothering the animal allows its spirit to go home "and so to live again on earth."

Most tribal hunters who ran deer to exhaustion probably killed them with a bow and arrow, or in later years a rifle. During the 1880s in Wisconsin, the naturalist John Muir witnessed such a hunt: "In winter, after the first snow, we frequently saw three or four Indians hunting deer in company, running like hounds on the fresh, exciting tracks. The escape of the deer from these noiseless, tireless hunters was said to be well-nigh impossible." During times of heavy snowfall, Indians on snowshoes could easily overtake animals foundering in the deep, powdery drift. Another man reported watching a Wisconsin Indian kill four deer with a tomahawk after chasing them onto clear, slick ice. People also used dogs to trail, chase, and hold deer at bay until hunters caught up.

Solitary bowmen often waited along trails, at watering spots, near mineral licks, and in other places where animals were likely to come within range. They also attracted deer to these stands using calls carved from wood or bark, shaped like miniature horns and usually fitted with a reed. In southeastern Alaska, a Tlingit Indian man showed me how to call black-tailed deer by blowing on a bunchberry leaf held between his tongue and the roof of his mouth. Nowadays, most Tlingit calls are made by splitting a finger-sized stick lengthwise and sandwiching a rubber band in a widened space between the halves. The high-pitched buzz, which sounds like a bleating fawn, attracts does year-round and bucks especially during the fall rut, when they're craving female company. There are also descriptions of Indians clashing antlers to "rattle in" bucks during the rut, a method popular among many hunters today.

Native Americans also caught deer by setting snares in game trails, each snare fastened to a bent tree and triggered so the captured animal was snapped up off the ground. On the subject of "deare" in his 1637 book, *New English Canaan,* Thomas Merton wrote: "The Salvages take these in trappes made of their naturall Hempe, which they place in the earth where they fell a tree for browse; and when hee rounds the tree for the browse, if hee tread on the trapp hee is horsed up by the legg, by meanes of a pole that starts up and catcheth him."

Although we pay most attention to solitary hunting, cooperative hunts might have brought in more deer. Many tribes used drives or surrounds, especially in fall and early winter when deer provided venison for the lean months ahead and when their thick fur was ideal for warm clothing. Sometimes a circle of drivers would work through the woods and brushlands—shouting, beating sticks together, or howling like wolves—eventually crowding the surrounded animals into a small area. Women and children joined these hunts as drivers or to help with the butchering, but it seems that men did most or all of the killing.

In the eastern United States and Canada, Indians also drove deer between converging wooden or stone fences. Some of these in upstate New York were as long as 3 miles, and a couple in northern Wisconsin measured 12 and 15 miles. The barriers funneled into a tight passageway where animals got caught in snares, plunged into pitfalls, or ended up in a corral surrounded by archers. During the fall of 1615, Samuel de Champlain saw a fence in southern Ontario "made of great wooden stakes eight or nine feet in height" and fifteen hundred paces long, narrowing to a cul-de-sac only five feet wide. The fence was built by about 25 Hurons, who then made early-morning drives every other day for approximately a month, bringing in a total of 120 deer. "I can assure you," Champlain declared, "one takes a peculiar pleasure in this mode of hunting."

Champlain also described another kind of drive he saw among the Huron people:

Four or five hundred savages placed themselves in line in the woods until they reached certain points which jut out into the river; then marching in their order with bow and arrow in their hands, shouting and making a great noise to frighten the animals, they keep on until they come to the end of the point. In this way all the animals are compelled to throw themselves into the water, unless they pass through the line at the mercy of the arrows which are shot at them by the hunters. Meanwhile the savages posted in the canoes . . . easily draw near the stags and other animals.

In much of North America, Indians used fire to drive game toward hunters, especially when the vegetation dried out in spring and fall. Near Groveland, New York, in the late 1700s, one chronicler saw about 500 Iroquois people encircle an area of almost 50 square miles, then set fires to push deer and other animals toward hunters in the middle. In the southeastern United States, Indians burned the forest floor to force deer, bears, and other game onto peninsulas or narrow isthmuses where hunters waited. Farther west, Navajos would designate men to run around a wide circle lighting fires, closely followed by others who kept the flames from spreading outward. Hunters waited until deer bunched in the center and then brought them down with arrows.

In the Navajo Stalking Way tradition, if the first deer taken on a hunt is a buck, a turquoise bead is placed between its antlers; if it is a doe, a white shell bead is put on its head. A prayer is spoken, first asking for the deer's return and for luck in future hunts, then reminding the animal that it has been treated respectfully. The prayer goes in part:

> To the home of the dawn you are starting to return
> With jet black hooves you are starting to return
> By means of zigzag lightning you are starting to return
> By the evening twilight your legs are yellow
> That way you are starting to return
> By the white of dawn your haunches are white and that way
>   you are starting to return
> A dark tail be in your tail and that way
>   you are starting to return
> A haze be in your fur and that way you are starting
>   to return
> A growing vegetation be in your ears and that way
>   you are starting to return
> A mixture of beautiful flowers and water be in your
>   intestines and that way you are starting to return
> May turquoise be in your liver and abalone shell the
>   partition between your heart and intestines
>   and that way you are starting to return

May red shell be your lungs and white shell be your windpipe
   and that way you are starting to return
May dark wind and straight lightning be your speech
   and that way you are starting to return
There you have returned within the jet basket
   in the midst of the beautiful flower pollen
Pleasantly may you have arrived home
Pleasantly may you and I both continue to live.

In many Native American tribes, the annual cache of deer hides was as essential as their supply of venison. The skins were used for all sorts of clothing—jackets, shirts, robes, skirts, leggings, breechcloths, shawls, moccasins, hats, and mittens—and for countless other items, like tepees, blankets, bags, thongs, and drums. Exactly how many hides people needed each year is a matter of speculation. One scholar has suggested, for example, that the 18,000 Huron Indians, when first contacted by Europeans, used about 62,000 deerskins each year, but some believe this number is too high. In 1750, when the Cherokee Indians (numbering fewer than 10,000 people) were probably overhunting for trade with Europeans, they sold about 25,000 deer hides per year.

Indians had uses for almost every part of a deer. From antlers they made arrow and spear points, needles, stone tool flakers, clubs, beads, household utensils, and glue. Thread and bowstrings were made from twisted deer sinew. Bones were fashioned into dozens of implements, from hide fleshers to fishhooks to flutes. Deer hair was used for insulation and embroidery; teeth for pendants and corn shellers; hooves for glue and rattles; heads for ceremonial masks. Whatever people didn't make into something, they most likely ate: tongue, heart, liver, kidneys, testicles, marrow, and various organs—even stomach contents, among some peoples. They rendered deer fat into tallow, which was then stored in containers made from the animal's stomach, bladder, and large intestine.

And of course there was venison, a reliable year-round food in thousands of Indian villages and encampments. For many tribes, deer meat was a dietary staple—boiled, roasted, dried, or pounded into pemmican, prepared with all sorts of other foods according to traditional recipes. In some areas, low deer numbers could mean hardship or starvation for Indian communities, and it's not surprising that historians and archaeologists have rated deer the most important of all game animals, especially among tribes east of the Mississippi. A substantial percentage of the animal fragments unearthed in some prehistoric sites are deer bones, teeth, and antlers. At the Buffalo Village site in West Virginia, 44 percent of all animal remains were from deer, and archaeologists calculated that venison accounted for almost 90 percent of the meat eaten by people who lived there. In New York, deer accounted for 33 percent of the faunal remains and about 55 percent of the "biomass" eaten by Indians who inhabited the Kipp Island site. Many other excavations in the eastern United States show that deer were the most important animal, often followed by wild turkey and bear. Deer were less important in areas like the Great Plains, where people relied on buffalo, or in coastal communities dependent on fish and shellfish.

The Pueblo Indian writer Simon Ortiz once told me that Acoma people call the deer by a kindred term meaning "Our Mother." This suggests another way that Native Americans have measured the animal's importance, and it may be the most telling of all.

As Euro-American commerce infiltrated the frontier, Indians were drawn into an expanding market for wild game. Trade usually focused on furbearing animals, but deer could be equally important at times. By the 1700s, Indians in many areas not only had access to hunting rifles, they also used deer hides as currency to buy those guns. In 1716, Cherokees trading around Charleston, South Carolina, paid 35 deerskins for a rifle, 16 for a Duffield blanket, 5 for an ax, 3 for a hoe, and 1 for 30 rounds of ammunition. Competition for deer hides may even have caused wars between neighboring tribes, and it's likely that Indians played a role in the overhunting that depleted deer populations, especially in eastern North America.

The fact that tribes participated in this disastrous era of wildlife exploitation has led some to doubt that Native Americans ever had a conservation ethic. It's hard to get a clear perspective on those times because cultures, economies, and environments were all being radically changed—if not threatened or destroyed—creating unimaginable pressures on tribal communities. But I believe the ethnographic accounts show overwhelmingly that conservation is (or was) deeply embedded in traditional Native American lifeways.

The beliefs and practices followed by many tribes are much like those I learned from Koyukon Indians in Alaska. During several years of traveling and hunting with Koyukon people, I saw them consistently limit their take of animals like moose, caribou, bear, wolf, beaver, lynx, and other furbearers, as well as waterfowl and fish. They used all sorts of modern technology—including rifles, shotguns, snowmobiles, and nylon fishnets—so they could easily have overharvested. But people explained that they restricted themselves because killing to excess or wasting game can deplete wildlife populations and affront the spirits that protect each animal. For the offender, this can mean poor hunting or trapping luck, sickness, or even death. It became clear to me that conservation, precisely as we understand it in Western ecology, is a founding principle of Koyukon subsistence life. "The country knows," a village elder once advised me. "If you do wrong things to it, the whole country knows. It feels what's happening to it."

Native American communities, like any others, have sinners and law breakers as well as puritans and conformists. The same is true for whole societies: sometimes they closely follow their own rules and sometimes not. It's unrealistic to expect that Native Americans were *never* guilty of waste, overharvest, or environmental damage, and it's equally mistaken to suggest that if any transgressions took place, we should conclude Indian tribes had no conservation ethic. In our own society, does the existence of theft show that we have no sense of property rights? Does violent crime reveal that we have no sanctions protecting human life? Like all societies, we do our utmost to eliminate dangerous or misguided behavior, but absolute control is never possible.

Native Americans, living intimately with the natural world and depending on it for a livelihood, understood the dangers of overexploitation and tried to prevent it. This is why they developed principles of sustainable use and consciously sought to maintain balanced relationships to the environment. I don't mean to imply, however, that Indian people had no impact on their surroundings: they harvested enough animals and plants to alter the makeup of wild communities, they cut down trees for firewood and settlements, and they cleared forests for agriculture.

Furthermore, Indians regularly used fire to manipulate their environment, a practice so widespread that it altered the ecological face of pre-Columbian North America. Almost everywhere east of the Mississippi, for example, tribal burning maintained prairies and meadows, thinned out forest understories, and created a more open landscape in areas that would otherwise be covered by unbroken woodland. Indian people recognized that burning stimulated the growth of useful plants, allowed easier travel and hunting, and (most important) benefited game populations. Western biologists have confirmed the ecological value of controlled burning, and fire has been used as a tool for scientific wildlife management in many states, such as Arkansas, South Carolina, Missouri, Ohio, Texas, Arizona, Idaho, California, and others.

Like all people, Indian tribes affected their surrounding environment, and individuals or communities sometimes breached their own mandates against overusing game or damaging habitat. But the fundamental balance between Native Americans and their environment is demonstrated, above all else, by the land itself. When the first Europeans arrived on this continent, they found such abounding wildlife and witnessed such pristine natural beauty that they called this place a "wilderness," as if no one had ever lived here.

Excess and Restraint

In 1623, when Governor William Bradford of Plymouth Colony married his second wife, Alice, neighboring Wampanoag Indians joined the wedding celebration. Among them came the leader Massasoit, plus "four other kings and about six score hunters with their bows and arrows," bearing contributions of deer and turkey. "We had about twelve pasty venisons, besides others," wrote Emmanuel Altham in a letter to Sir Edward Altham, "[and] pieces of roasted venison and other such good cheer in such quantity that I could wish you some of our share." Amid these joyous and innocent occasions, the devouring of America's frontier began.

Whites, like the Indians before them, used venison and deer hides as a medium of exchange. In 1794, the fledgling state of Franklin (later known as Tennessee) paid its officials in deerskins: 1,000 per year for the governor, 500 for the chief justice. Residents of Franklin could also pay their land taxes in deerskins, each hide being equal to six shillings.

Deer harvests soon reached massive proportions, driven mostly by commercial markets, and by the early 1800s (according to historical studies by Richard McCabe and Thomas McCabe), white-tailed deer had declined by 35 to 50 percent from pre-Columbian levels. Between 1776 and 1850, the number of Americans increased from 1.5 million to more than 23 million. European immigrants swarmed across the land, cutting and plowing, building and fencing, hunting and trapping.

At the same time, however, settlers increased deer habitat by opening the forest and clearing fields. This, along with decimation of Indian tribes, must have prevented a more catastrophic decline of deer and perhaps allowed whitetails to rebound temporarily in some areas. In any case, it was fish and wildlife—deer above all—that nourished the flash flood of humanity. Farmers, lumberjacks, trappers, traders, and townspeople throughout the frontier subsisted on wild as well as cultivated foods. A Minnesota newspaper editorialized in 1896: "Great country this for game in and out of season. We have venison . . . any time we take the trouble to have it brought in. Nothing like enjoying the good things on the frontier while they last and before civilization makes the game scarce."

A new profession, market hunting, supplied meat and hides to those who didn't harvest for themselves. Around 1830, in midwestern states like Illinois and Missouri, venison sold for two or three cents per pound and deer carcasses for about a dollar, giving rise to our popular expression "one buck," meaning a dollar. Deerskins were used to make hats, gloves, pants, waistcoats, shoe uppers, leatherstockings, rugs, upholstery fabric, saddles, handbags, and more. Other salable parts of deer included hair for stuffing saddles and furniture, and antlers for buttons, knife handles, racks, stands, cloth sizing, and ammonia manufacture.

Market hunting peaked shortly after the Civil War, fueled by the growing human population, widespread use of repeating rifles, construction of railroad networks, and availability of refrigerated rail cars for shipping meat. It was a slaughter, plain and simple, greatly escalating the damage already done to wildlife over the previous 300 years. From 1850 until about 1900, the American people went on a binge of exploitation described by the McCabes as "the period of greatest hunting pressure on wildlife *ever.*"

In the early days, deerskins went mainly to Britain and other European countries. For example, 2.5 million pounds of hides, taken from about 600,000 deer, were shipped from Savannah to England between 1755 and 1773. A century later the primary markets were American cities like Chicago, Omaha, Boston, Cleveland, Cincinnati, New York, and Philadelphia. In 1880, from the state of Michigan alone more than 100,000 deer carcasses were sent to urban markets. Six tons of venison went by rail from Lichfield, Minnesota, to Boston just during the month of December in 1882. A single Texas trader, operating near present-day Waco, shipped at least 75,000 deerskins between 1844 and 1850. One commercial hunter in St. Cloud, Minnesota, reportedly took 4,800 pounds of venison during the 1858–59 season. Also in Minnesota, a father and son claimed 6,000 deer between them during the year 1860.

Deer were taken with snares, deadfalls, leghold traps, poison, and pitfalls; hunted at night by torch and jacklight; pursued by men on foot, on horseback, in wagons or sleighs or boats; trailed by hounds, decoyed with tame deer, lured to salt or grain. They were taken all year long, without regard to season or limit. People who bemoaned the losses amounted to a faint voice in a land overswept by thoughtlessness and disregard.

Chief Luther Standing Bear of the Oglala Sioux lamented,

> We did not think of the great open plains, the beautiful rolling hills, and winding streams with tangled growth as "wild." Only to the white man was nature a "wilderness." . . . When the very animals of the forest began fleeing from [his] approach, then it was that for us the "Wild West" began.

In 1868, the price of venison undercut that of beef or pork, which explains why deer provided common table fare in cities as well as countryside. Commercial harvests of truly astounding proportions took place especially in the Midwest, where deer remained abundant after they'd become scarce closer to the eastern markets. And as game populations ebbed, venison took on added meaning as America's own cuisine, spiced with a twinge of nostalgia for the vanishing frontier. At the Maxwell House restaurant in Nashville, Tennessee, "Saddle of Minnesota Venison with Red Currant Jelly" was featured on the Christmas dinner menu in 1879; no price was listed.

The decline and extermination of deer began in the populous Northeast, then spread west and south, affecting different regions at different times. As early as 1638, just 18 years after the Pilgrims stepped ashore, Plymouth Colony records show that deer numbers were dropping. The first law protecting deer in post-Columbian America was passed by the town of Portsmouth, Rhode Island, in 1646: "that there shall be no shootings of deere from the first of May till the first of November; and if any shall shoot a deere within that time he shall forfeit five pounds."

Other colonies soon picked up the idea. "The killing of deer at unseasonable times of the year hath been found very much to the prejudice of the Colonie," stated a preamble to Connecticut's 1698 limited-season law. "Great numbers of them have been hunted and destroyed in deep snowes when they are very poor and big with young, the flesh and skins of very little value, and the increase greatly hindered."

Between 1698 and 1738, closed seasons were established in Massachusetts, New York, Pennsylvania, and North Carolina. Elsewhere, laws restricting deer harvests came later—for example, Alabama (1803) and Louisiana (1857) in the South; Wisconsin (1851) and Kentucky (1861) in the Midwest; Texas (1881) and Oregon (1899) farther west. In 1873, Maine became the first state to establish bag limits on deer; and later on, as whitetails became rare, deer hunting was completely prohibited in many states, such as Kansas (1908) and Tennessee (1911). Bounties were enacted in hopes of eradicating wolves, mountain lions, coyotes, and other predators—mainly to protect livestock and people, although almost everyone figured this would also benefit wild animals like deer.

The first publicly funded game wardens, called "deer reeves," were employed by North Carolina in 1738 and Massachusetts the following year, but legislatures in many states didn't fund enforcement until 50 to 100 years after they had set up game laws. The undisputed champion of delay is Virginia, which established a deer hunting season in 1699 but didn't get around to hiring game wardens until 1916, an interval of 217 years. I haven't been able to learn if this reflected a law-abiding citizenry or a frugal hand at the state treasury.

In most areas, the lag between law and enforcement gave a free field to market hunters and did little to nurture healthy deer populations. The U.S. Bureau of Biological Survey estimated in 1890 that 300,000 whitetailed deer remained in this country. By this time, according to the McCabes, people seldom hunted whitetails because they rarely saw any, and conditions were little better for mule deer and blacktails in the West.

Finally, in 1900, a federal regulation called the Lacy Act was passed, prohibiting interstate commerce in game taken in violation of state law. This effectively brought an end to commercial hunting—and none too soon. Almost everywhere in North America, wildlife had been slaughtered for the market without mercy or forethought, including not only deer, but elk, bears, turkey, ducks, geese, grouse, quail, all sorts of furbearers, and every species of bird whose feathers could decorate a lady's hat. The passenger pigeon and buffalo, once among the most abundant creatures on earth, had been hunted to the verge of extinction. In the process, they became icons of a world nearly obliterated by an orgy of human greed.

To Native American people, the continent was like a vandalized home, emptied of family and furnishings. "Our village was healthy and there was no place in the country possessing such advantages, nor hunting grounds better than those we had in possession," recalled Black Hawk, chief of the Sac and Fox Indians. "If a prophet had come to our village in those days and told us that the things were to take place which have since come to pass, none of our people would have believed him."

When Black Hawk spoke these words, in 1833, few people beyond tribal communities were ready to listen. Within a few decades, however,

Euro-Americans would begin to acknowledge the devastation they had wrought—and this set the stage for a rebirth of conservation on the American land.

As early as the 1860s, according to historian John Reiger, some "sportsmen" started to hunt and fish not for income, not purely for sustenance, but also for the pleasure of engaging themselves in this way with the outdoors. As wildlife populations dwindled, these people increasingly lamented the excesses of market hunting, as well as the destruction of forests, wetlands, and other wild habitats. Their cause was promoted especially by outdoor magazines, which first appeared in the 1870s. One such periodical, the *American Sportsman,* described a hunter of the new style: "Quantity is not his ambition; he never slays more than he can use; he never inflicts an unnecessary pang."

Writing for *Field and Stream* in 1873, Charles Hallock called for uniform game laws, more watershed protection, less water pollution, and development of scientific forest management. He also criticized poachers, hunters who killed for "fun" without understanding the animal or its environment, and hunting only for meat without concern for the subtler pleasures and ethics of fair chase. During this era, hunters and fishermen were the citizens most immediately affected by destruction of wildlife and habitat. "Except for sportsmen," Reiger contends, "only a tiny number of Americans had any real interest in conservation before the turn of the century." So it was mainly hunters and fishermen who formulated the new conservation ethic, who became the first and most prominent voices for responsible use of wildlife, and who advocated preservation of natural habitats.

In the 1870s, sportsmen formed hundreds of organizations to protect and propagate wildlife. They poured money and energy into establishment of game preserves, somewhat on the model of artificially stocked "deer parks" that had graced country estates as far back as Colonial times. One of the first preserves was Blooming Grove Park, covering 12,000 acres in rural Pennsylvania. Established in 1871, the park was intended to support populations of game animals, birds, and fish for the specific benefit of a hunting and fishing membership. According to John Reiger, Blooming Grove Park was also the first place where "systematic forestry" was attempted in the United States.

While decimation of wildlife continued in many areas, private groups set up other preserves modeled on Blooming Grove Park, with their own closed seasons and bag limits. Also, as far back as 1857, fishermen and hunters had advanced the idea of a forest preserve in the Adirondacks, where logging and settlement would be prohibited. The ensuing debate provided fertile ground for the idea of publicly owned wildlands set aside for hunting, fishing, and recreation. When victory came at last, it was not in the Adirondacks but in the far-flung mountains and valleys of Yellowstone, designated the world's first national park in 1872. Thirteen years later, in 1885, New York's legislature established a 715,000-acre Adirondack preserve.

Development of the conservation idea and nature awareness in America involved a cadre of prominent men originally drawn to the outdoors by hunting or fishing. Among them were John James Audubon, Gifford Pinchot, George Catlin, Frederick Jackson Turner, John Quincy Adams, Frederick Law Olmsted, Francis Parkman, Washington Irving, William Cullen Bryant, Horace Greeley, Albert Bierstadt, Thomas Moran, Henry Van Dyke, Ernest Thompson Seton, C. Hart Merriam, and John Burroughs. Henry David Thoreau disavowed hunting but loved to fish; and although John Muir shot many an animal as a boy, he later became passionately opposed to hunting.

Women played an important though less public role in the early conservation movement, especially working for protection of birds threatened by the millinery trade. Other women influenced American attitudes toward nature through their success as writers and illustrators—notably Elmira Phelps, Florence Merriam, Olive Thorne Miller, and Mabel Osgood Wright. As far back as 1850, Susan Cooper (daughter of novelist James Fenimore Cooper) wrote in her popular book, *Rural Hours,* that preserving an old forest is as important as saving an ancient monument. It would take another century, however, before women gained prominence as public spokespersons for environmental responsibility, a role triumphantly affirmed in 1962 with the publication of Rachel Carson's *Silent Spring.*

Environmental historians consistently point to one person, George Bird Grinnell, as a dominant figure in the emergence of America's conservation movement. Grinnell was a Yale educated naturalist, also a hunter and fisherman, who became widely known as publisher of *Forest and Stream* magazine from 1880 until 1911. Besides publishing articles on hunting and fishing, Grinnell used the magazine as a forum to promote every sort of environmental cause. He fought against the excesses of market hunting and the destruction of forests, proposed a system of county game wardens supported by fees from hunters, crusaded for both strict wildlife protection and exclusion of commercial interests from Yellowstone Park, supported John Muir's fight against the Hetch Hetchy dam in California, and championed the idea that forests, game, and fish on public lands should be used in carefully regulated, sustainable ways.

Drawing from his sizable magazine readership, Grinnell founded the Audubon Society in 1886 principally to fight against the slaughter of wild birds for the millinery trade. After some early lapses and rekindlings, the organization grew into a major political force, and among its early efforts was helping to assure passage of the Lacy Act, which did so much to protect deer, birds, and other wildlife. Along with his friend Theodore Roosevelt and a group of prominent New Yorkers, Grinnell cofounded the Boone and Crockett Club in 1887. Its objectives were to promote hunting and exploration, to advance knowledge of natural history, and to "work for the preservation of the large game of this country, and, so far as possible, to further legislation for that purpose, and to assist in enforcing the existing laws." Described by Reiger as "the first private organization to deal with conservation issues of national scale," the Boone and Crockett Club fought against arcane and destructive hunting practices and for complete protection of wildlife in Yellowstone National Park.

While George Bird Grinnell played a key role in formulating the American conservation movement, President Theodore Roosevelt made conservation a part of national policy. There is ample reason to gasp over Roosevelt's early exploits as a hunter, but he eventually recognized—with Grinnell's help—that animals like the buffalo, antelope, grizzly bear, and deer desperately needed protection from overhunting. Roosevelt was also influenced by the chief of the Forest Service, Gifford Pinchot, who was himself a sportsman in the Boone and Crockett vein. Environmental milestones of Roosevelt's presidency included the addition of 100 million acres to what became known as national forests, establishment of five national parks and 17 national monuments, and creation of a national wildlife refuge system including more than 50 separate areas. The refuges, modeled somewhat on private reserves, were intended to protect habitat, foster healthy wildlife populations, and assure public access for hunting and fishing.

It's important to remember that figures like John Muir, who were not hunters or fishermen, profoundly influenced American attitudes and policies toward the environment. But it's equally significant that hikers, campers, mountain climbers, canoeists, birdwatchers, naturalists of all sorts—women and men—allied themselves with hunters and fishermen who had adopted the "sportsman" ethic and recognized the urgency of protecting wildlife and habitat. Commercial and subsistence hunting were among the root causes of ecological destruction in North America, but a different generation of hunters now became leading advocates for environmental restoration. It's safe to assume that many of these hunters were motivated, beyond everything else, by a concern for the continent's most important large game animal: the deer.

After several dark centuries, an ethic of restraint, moral engagement with nature, responsible and rationally managed environmental uses, and respect toward the wild community had once again emerged in North America. It's intriguing to imagine how Indian people felt as they watched this unfolding of the European mind, this recovery of a wisdom that had seemed forever lost. Perhaps essential knowledge comes almost inevitably from the land itself, from the waters, and from the plants and animals who nourish us in so many ways. It would seem so, judging by the combined history of our continent's ancient and modern inhabitants. This may help us understand what Chief Joseph of the Nez Perce said more than a century ago:

> The earth and I are of one mind. The measure of the land and the measure of our bodies are the same.

From the Vanishing Point

Perhaps in a few remote places deer populations remained unaffected by the exploits of Euro-Americans. But otherwise, one story is repeated with fascinating regularity across the continent: after invasion and settlement came staggering overharvest and dramatic environmental change, leading to scarcity or complete extermination of deer. Then conservation measures allowed deer to increase, in many cases to the point of serious overabundance. Deer populations remain excessively high in some areas, while in other areas regulated hunting and habitat management have brought a sustainable if tenuous equilibrium.

The history of whitetails in New York is a good example. Although most biologists believe large tracts of virgin forest would have supported relatively few deer, regular burning by Indians had created extensive areas of mixed grassland and woods throughout the eastern United States, including New York. In 1687, Baron LaHouton wrote of Chautauqua County, near Lake Erie: "I cannot express what quantities of deer and turkeys are to be found in these woods and in the vast meads that lie upon the south side of the lake." Clearing by European settlers favored deer at the outset, but by 1880, 75 percent of New York's forest had been cut down, leaving scant cover for whitetails, and unregulated hunting took a further toll.

The litany of decline and disappearance was heard everywhere. "It is fair to suppose that there are not a dozen deer in [the] whole Catskill region," an 1887 report concluded. In 1913, it was a newsworthy event when someone spotted five whitetails in eastern Rensselaer County, and throughout western New York, deer had been totally extirpated before the nineteenth century ended. Similar stories came from neighboring states like Vermont, which lost most of its deer by 1840, though a few survived thanks to the complete ban on hunting between 1865 and 1887. In Pennsylvania and New Jersey, whitetails dwindled close to extinction at the turn of the century.

Some eastern states eventually reestablished deer by importing animals from near and far. For example, private individuals in New Jersey purchased and released hundreds of whitetails from states like Maine, Virginia, Wisconsin, and Michigan. Vermont's deer population stems mostly from 17 animals released near Rutland in 1878. Pennsylvania brought in about 1,200 deer, and Kentucky imported some 2,600, in a flurry of projects that hopscotched deer from one state to another.

New York's whitetails sank to their lowest numbers during the 1880s and 1890s, but some animals survived in places like the Adirondacks and, curiously, Long Island. Then the tide began to turn. Market hunting dissipated, mainly because there weren't enough deer to make it worthwhile, and the state employed game wardens to enforce increasingly restrictive laws. Also, by 1900 thousands of marginal farms had been abandoned, and as fields disappeared beneath trees and shrubs, deer found huge areas of rapidly improving habitat.

From this point on—despite occasional setbacks during harsh winters—whitetails spread naturally from areas where they had survived, and soon populations blossomed throughout New York. In the state's western counties, where deer had once been extinct, farmers complained by the 1940s that they'd become a nuisance. Despite increasingly liberal hunting regulations, the state's deer numbered 450,000 in 1978, then soared to almost a million by 1993, aided by mild winters and forest regrowth. Since the 1980s, conflicts have intensified over damage to crops in rural areas, to shrubs and gardens in suburbs, and to wild vegetation in parks or preserves. There's no question about it: white-tailed deer have made a big comeback in New York State.

Of all the stories about decline and recovery of deer, none is better known or more intriguing than the Kaibab episode. According to turn-of-the-century records, roughly 4,000 mule deer lived on the sprawling Kaibab Plateau, just north of the Grand Canyon in Arizona. By the 1890s, as many as 20,000 cattle and 195,000 sheep were also grazing the area on federal leases, but when Theodore Roosevelt designated the Kaibab a refuge in 1906, livestock grazing ended and an ambitious predator control program was set up for the benefit of game. Almost 5,000 coyotes were shot, trapped, or poisoned, along with 781 mountain lions, 554 bobcats, and 20 wolves. Textbook versions of this story blame removal of predators for the eruption of deer numbers that followed, but ecologist Graeme Caughley points out that elimination of livestock overgrazing might have been just as important. In any case, the deer exercised their remarkable ability to multiply.

How many mule deer lived on the Kaibab during the peak years, around 1925, is a matter of widely differing opinion; estimates range from 30,000 to 100,000. But without question, deer had severely degraded their habitat, and experts of every stripe concluded something had to be done. Since part of the area was now inside a national park, shooting deer was deemed unacceptable. Salvation appeared in the person of Zane Grey, the western novelist, who organized over 100 local cowboys and Navajo Indians, figuring to drive 8,000 deer from the Kaibab, down into the Grand Canyon, across the Colorado River, then up onto the canyon's browse-rich south rim.

Everyone was poised and ready on December 16, 1924: drift fences had been set up, drivers armed with all sorts of noisemakers sat high in the saddle, and Paramount Pictures showed up to film the action. On signal, the ragged line of horsemen spurred their mounts, and in a cacophony of hoots and bells the chase began. In the early going, herds of up to 500 deer were seen milling ahead of the drivers, but unlike cattle, the deer quickly outran their pursuers, wheeled back through the lines, and left a weary mob of wranglers to face the canyon's edge alone. A second try brought the same result: not one deer left its home grounds.

Over the next couple winters, thousands of deer starved on the Kaibab for lack of browse, and about 15,000 were shot or live-trapped during a five-year effort to get the population down. Around 1930, the federal government intensified deer hunting and stopped killing predators, which further reduced the herd and boosted habitat recovery. There is disagreement over how many deer were left when the proverbial dust settled, but the decrease was substantial. Since that time, a healthy balance between deer and their environment has been restored on the Kaibab. And Zane Grey's name rests comfortably on his reputation as a story-

teller, while his exploits as a wildlife manager have remained blessedly
obscure.

The Forest and the Deer

Deer have a wonderfully complex relationship to the forest. Among our
first ecological lessons is that they are creatures of the edge, drawn to the
abundant feed of open places but equally dependent on sheltering woods
or thickets. The forest edge is in constant flux, partly because of natural
processes like wildfires and climatic changes, partly because of human activity. Since Western technology and culture swept over the face of North
America, forest margins have ebbed, surged, and shifted as never before.

When Europeans first arrived, a variegated forest of deciduous and
coniferous trees covered much of our continent, and the pattern was
made even more complex by thousands—perhaps millions—of natural
or Indian-made clearings throughout the woodlands. Open country prevailed in the western prairies and deserts, relegating trees to river valleys
or mountain heights. In 1600, North America had about 850 million
acres of forest, but by 1900 fewer than 580 million wooded acres remained. According to the environmental journal *Forest Watch,* American
farmers cleared, on the average, 13.5 square miles of woodland every day
between 1850 and 1900; much of this was accomplished by the ancient
means of fire.

Of course, trees were also felled by ax and crosscut saw, then ripped
into lumber or split and stacked for their most important use, fuel. In
1850, wood supplied the United States with over 90 percent of its fuel,
but by 1970 the figure had dropped to just 3 percent as people shifted to
coal and then oil. This, along with wildfire control, encouraged widespread regrowth of forests. By the 1950s, fire consumed less than 5 million wooded acres each year, compared with more than 40 million acres
annually at the beginning of this century.

Another cause of change in our forests might come as a surprise. In
1910, more than one third of all U.S. farmlands grew feed (notably hay)
for something like 50 million horses, the power behind most private and
commercial transportation. Needless to say, cars and trucks put an end
to that. In places like upstate New York, land used for hay wasn't much
good for other crops, so it went fallow. In fact, millions of acres in eastern North America gradually reverted to woods, a vital factor in the population growth of white-tailed deer—and all because horses disappeared
from the American road.

Improvements in farm technology also affected the forests. Before 1920, land was relentlessly cleared to feed the increasing human population, but after that, farmers started growing more food on the same acreage. Plowed soil in the United States increased from about 20 million acres in 1800 to some 400 million acres in 1920. The rate of increase has slowed considerably since then, but lands are still being cleared. For example, more than 3,000 square miles of Louisiana bottomland forest—prime deer habitat—were cut between 1962 and 1974, mainly for soybean fields.

More croplands will be needed in the future, given the high rates of soil erosion, changing attitudes toward use of chemical pesticides and fertilizers, depletion of fossil groundwater, and a worldwide human population growth of 95 million people—a number equal to the entire population of Mexico—every year. Although deer often do well on agricultural land, they also need plenty of surrounding cover in woods, marshes, and thickets, so it's important to preserve a balance between wild and cultivated acreage.

In addition, commercial logging profoundly affects forests in many parts of North America today. Like agriculture, timber cutting can improve habitat for deer, but this depends on where and how it's done. For example, in the north country of Minnesota and Wisconsin, large tracts of uniform second-growth forest—marginal habitat for deer—may be improved when clear-cutting opens the canopy and brings on a flush of shrubby forage. But to favor deer over the long run, it's essential to recut these tracts often enough so nutritious browse isn't shaded out by homogeneous stands of young trees. Also, each tract should be partially logged in patchwork patterns over many years, to develop a mix of small, different-aged cuts. This sort of logging, although it's seldom done, can create a diversified environment with abundant food and shelter, which benefits not only deer but other wildlife as well.

Ecologically responsible logging is a complicated process that must be designed for the local environment. In northern Wisconsin, for example, high whitetail numbers that follow typical, large-scale clear-cutting can threaten important plant species like Canada yew, eastern hemlock, northern white cedar, and several kinds of wild orchid. By overbrowsing the forest and changing its composition, deer also jeopardize other wildlife species, including songbirds like the Blackburnian warbler, Canada warbler, and yellow-bellied flycatcher. Ecologists William Alverson, Donald Waller, and Stephen Solheim have proposed concentrating timber cuts in some parts of Wisconsin's national forests, while leaving other tracts unlogged and controlling deer numbers to encourage forest regrowth. If these woodlands are allowed to reach ecological maturity, deer will decline on their own, creating natural sanctuaries for species jeopardized by overbrowsing.

Whatever the public appeal of environmentally sensitive logging, it's safe to say that for most timber companies profits take precedence over deer, biodiversity, and other uses of the land. Many timber businesses dislike the inconvenience of logging small patches to create a mosaic of different-aged cuts, because clearing large areas all at once brings the highest profit. But "even-age" logging usually means boom and bust for deer: plentiful browse for a few years, after which young trees close the canopy and shade out nutritious undergrowth. There are thousands of examples, probably millions, banked up against highways throughout North America. Almost everyone has seen dense stands of evergreen trees, their trunks neatly aligned, beneath them a mat of brown needles and very little else. These tracts are ecological barrenlands, far less nurturing to wildlife than any natural forest community, regardless of age.

In parts of the American and Canadian West logging may favor deer, but in others it can be quite harmful. This is strikingly true in prairie country, where narrow braids of trees along river courses are often the only available shelter. A cottonwood grove or willow patch can be the crux of survival for deer whose world is dominated by open range, pastures, or checkerboard croplands. Nevertheless, these shady copses are destroyed to enlarge fields and improve grazing. Between 1960 and 1980, for instance, agricultural clearing eliminated about 15 percent of the forested land in Kansas and Nebraska, and losses continue at a rate of 1 to 3 percent each year. In Rocky Mountain states like Montana, deer rely on old-growth coniferous forests for shelter and browse during times of heavy snow. Clear-cutting forces them to wallow in deep powder, unable to reach buried food, exposed to winds and bitter cold. The result is fewer deer.

If responsible logging has been slow to come on public lands like our national forests, it's been even slower in the private domain. A few small companies are committed to selective harvesting of trees, which maintains not only their logging business but also a permanent, healthy forest community. These are the exceptions. Many corporations manage their lands as tree farms—vast stands of only one or two species, which are cut long before they reach full maturity, permanently eliminating the old-growth forests that once supported a diverse natural community.

Also, over the past few decades, companies owning huge tracts in states like Montana and Alaska have clear-cut on a scale not witnessed since the dark days of an earlier century. Apparently their motives are rooted in that same era: cut as many trees as possible for immediate profit, then either hold the wasted land or sell it at bargain prices. In such places, there is no tomorrow for the fallers, choker setters, truck drivers, and mill operators who cast their lot with the industry. And the future is bleak for deer on land where it takes many decades, if not several centuries, to replace an old-growth forest.

It's a sad but simple truth that most of America's primeval forests have vanished. Wildlife researchers John Schoen, Olof Wallmo, and Matthew Kirchoff contend that our original woodlands were largely destroyed before anyone with a botanical or ecological perspective came along to describe them. By 1920, something like 90 to 95 percent of the virgin forest was gone from the eastern United States, and by 1950, no significant stands were left. What remained was a patchwork of second-growth woods dominated by large, even-aged trees. Individually these trees might be quite old, but taken as a whole, they constituted an immature ecological community, without the diversity brought on by death and decay of true elders, century after century.

This explains a treasured American myth—that European settlers found here an unbroken forest of oceanic dimensions. It's been claimed that a squirrel could have rambled through treetops from Maine to Michigan (or south to Florida) without once touching the ground. Because the closed canopy would shade out nutritious undergrowth, biologists have assumed deer were relatively scarce in this immense forest, but it's hard to balance this opinion against reports of early travelers who marveled at the abundance of deer.

As we've seen, however, these woodlands were interrupted everywhere by agricultural fields, grassy meadows, and other openings made by Native Americans. This alone might have created enough edge to support impressive deer populations. Although Schoen and his colleagues make no mention of Indian clearing, they believe old-growth eastern forests were riddled with small breaks where trees fell from old age, disease, storms, river meanders, and other natural events. Deer would find lush forage beneath this perforated canopy. Today, natural openings like these are still found everywhere in ancient, unlogged forests of coastal Alaska and the Pacific Northwest, allowing deer to thrive where they would otherwise be rare. These last primeval forests give us a glimpse of the New World as it was before Columbus, and they bring us to the most controversial logging in North America today.

The Tongass National Forest stretches along 500 miles of southeastern Alaska's coast, a country of mountains and waters, where steep-walled ridges hover beside fjords studded with islands and coves. Streams fed by 100 inches of rain per year twist through glacial valleys and across tide flats. It is a land of the ancient and enormous, dominated by a great, silent, living mass of trees—Sitka spruce, western hemlock, Alaska cedar, red cedar.

Bald eagles nest on stick platforms woven into high boughs or fixed atop broken snags overlooking the shore. In season, millions of salmon return to enact rituals of spawning and fall prey to brown bears that hunt along the riffles. Every wild species that lived here when Europeans arrived is still here: river otter, marten, mountain goat, wolf, raven, hawk owl, varied thrush, marbled murrelet. Moving like shadowy wraiths among the trees are Sitka black-tailed deer, one of the animals most intricately dependent on old-growth forest.

The temperate rain forests of southeast Alaska are one of the rarest environments on earth and among the most productive. In some areas, the total weight of living material on a given area of land exceeds that of tropical forests. While North Americans have fought to save rain forests in distant lands, our own have rapidly dwindled. About 96 percent of the primeval rain forest in Oregon has been destroyed by logging, and 75 percent is gone in neighboring Washington.

I caught a glimpse of this one morning on a jet lofting away from Seattle. Mount Rainier, with a smooth disk of lenticular cloud drawn over its summit, stood enormous against the blue bend of sky. Tiers of mountains pitched away toward the eastern and western horizons, range beyond range, like swells at sea. I peered down on peaks and ridges, broad mountain swales, valleys laced with fog. It could have been a taste of pure glory, but arrayed beneath us was clear-cutting on a colossal scale. Whole mountain complexes had been reduced to scab lands, with little scrawls of trees left behind like fleeting moments of conscience. Gaping cuts were littered with stumps and slash, the way buffalo bones had once been left to bleach on the prairie. Off into the hazy distance they reached—strips, triangles, parallelograms, squares, rectangles, as if the land had been disfigured by a cookie cutter. Logging roads looped back and forth along the slopes like the tracks of worms.

There was death and pallor on those mountains, their vacant faces tilted toward the sky.

> And I brought you into a plentiful country, to eat the
> fruit thereof and the goodness thereof; but when ye
> entered, ye defiled my land and made mine heritage an
> abomination. (Jeremiah 2:7)

I tried to imagine a more powerful demonstration of ecological havoc. If wildfire burned an area this size, it would be judged an appalling catastrophe. The great oil spill in Prince William Sound—a modern paradigm of environmental disaster—would pale by comparison, affecting a fraction of the wildlife over a much shorter span of time. I was astonished that the intentional and virtually complete destruction of these forests could be sanctioned by governments and carried out in the name of beneficial industry. When overcast closed like a curtain beneath us, my mind drifted toward places farther north, where the same process is under way.

Southeastern Alaska contains the largest tracts of uncut temperate rain forest left on earth. But here, too, the valleys echo with chain saws. Up to 17,000 acres have been destroyed in a single year by clear-cutting, and in some areas the mazy archipelago of islands, mountains, and fjords looks much like the mutilated lands of Washington and Oregon. Stumps and young regrowth now cover about one million acres of southeastern Alaska, and each year the devastation continues. If nothing is done to stop it, almost 4,000 square miles of ancient forest may be clear-cut. These figures include the Tongass National Forest and former Tongass lands conveyed to Alaskan Native Corporations.

From the standpoint of both logging and wildlife, all rain forest is not created equal. Most of the Tongass is in fact mountainous, unforested terrain consisting of bare rock, glacier, boggy muskeg, alpine tundra, or high-elevation scrub. According to the U.S. Forest Service, which oversees the Tongass, only one third of the land supports commercially useful trees, and a mere 4 percent contains the "high-volume old-growth" coveted by logging companies and essential to many wildlife species. In river valleys and along lower mountain slopes grow the oldest, largest trees, soaring to heights of 100 feet or more, with trunks up to 9 feet in diameter. These venerable giants have lived 300 to 800 years, and some sprouted more than 1,000 years ago.

But more important, the *forest itself* is far older than its individual trees, looking much the same today as it did 10,000 years ago. Although small patches constantly change—as trees naturally die and regrow—the character of the ancient forest remains fairly constant. Standing snags and fallen trunks play a vital ecological role, nourishing a tremendous variety of plant and animal life, from invisible microbes to nesting birds, from tiny ferns to half-grown trees rooted in the rich, moldering wood. In fact, there is more living material inside one of these "dead" trunks than in the trunk of a live tree standing next to it.

For black-tailed deer, the death and toppling of trees is significant in another way. Powerful storms set the forests waving like fields of grass, rocking trees until their roots snap and trunks come flailing down. These windfall openings are soon richly clothed in new undergrowth providing abundant forage—one of two key habitat elements for deer in this region. The other critical element is sheltering trees.

During winter, deepening snow pushes blacktails down off the slopes and they concentrate in heavily forested areas. Even here, six feet of snow can accumulate on the open ground beneath canopy gaps, in muskegs or meadows, and in clear-cuts. But the umbrella of boughs in an old-growth forest intercepts so much snow that only a fraction accumulates on the ground, which means deer can move around easily and find enough browse to carry them through lean months. According to John Schoen and Matthew Kirchoff, this is why blacktails live almost exclusively in ancient forests throughout winter and spring.

Many other animals also depend on the forest and are harmed by clear-cutting. For example, southeast Alaska has the world's highest densities of brown bears and bald eagles. The eagles nest in trees averaging 400 years old, almost always near salt water and often in prime logging areas. During summer months, brown bears and black bears haunt old-growth forest in valleys near salmon spawning streams, but in some areas, bear deaths have increased dramatically due to intense hunting along logging roads. Also, clear-cutting causes siltation and streambed changes that harm salmon populations and the animals that depend on them, as well as commercial fishing and tourism businesses.

To learn more about how clear-cutting affects deer in the Tongass National Forest, I hiked with Matthew Kirchoff into the Lemon Creek valley a few miles outside Juneau. Matt is lean and angular, soft-spoken, with a lingering trace of upstate New York in his speech, and a gentle manner that's as engaging as his agile scientific mind. After many years of research, he is considered a leading expert on relationships between deer and logging in southeastern Alaska. Crusty snow rattled underfoot as Matt led the way up an old logging road with sheer mountain walls towering on either side, their upper slopes brilliant in afternoon sun.

Matt picked a trail that curved into a stand of slender-trunked spruce about 30 feet tall, their needles bundled in frost. "This area was clear-cut twenty-five years ago and it's well on the way to becoming an even-aged forest," he explained. "You've still got a few openings where seedlings were slow to sprout, but as the trees grow they'll close the canopy. Then essentially no wildlife will be able to live here except red squirrels and a few birds. It's barren and unproductive, and will stay like this for a very long time."

Although he was summarizing decades of meticulous scientific research, I caught a palpable sense of loss in Matt's voice. And during pauses in our conversation I didn't hear so much as a single bird's twittering, as if the silence were meant to underscore his conclusions.

Farther on, we crossed a stream in a narrow ravine where no trees had been cut, and here we stood beneath towering spruce with trunks four to five feet across. Peering into the heights, I saw that each bough was laden with snow, as if we had entered an enormous tunnel beneath layers of drift. There was snow underfoot, to be sure, but not more than an inch or two.

"These are probably two- to three-hundred-year-old trees," Matt estimated. "Big spruce grow well along streams, where their roots can go deep in the gravel soil. That's why you notice there aren't many blowdowns here. Trees also help to stabilize the stream. If they're cut down, the stream meanders, buries seedlings, and prevents new trees from getting started."

Climbing up the other side of the ravine, we entered a different sort of forest, dominated by lanky hemlock and spruce with trunks 10 to 14 inches in diameter. Scattered around us were broad, flat-topped stumps capped with sphagnum moss. "This stand was cut about sixty years ago," said Matt. "Essentially nothing grows under these trees—just moss and a few ferns. Deer can't live in a place like this. They've got a good canopy to reduce snow depth, but there's nothing for them to eat." I kept a careful watch for deer tracks, yet saw not a trace of them, nor of those of any other animal.

I looked off through the pillared maze of trunks, the labyrinth of branches and boughs. For most of us, this forest would epitomize the loveliness and abundance of nature, the certainty of rebirth after logging that happened almost a human lifetime ago. There was beauty even in the stumps and in the decomposed slash that showed as faint ridges under a blanket of moss. Yet the biological truth was starkly different: here was a forest nearly emptied of plant and animal life, a desert in a land of perpetual rain. It defied intuition and testified to the way science reveals subtle, invisible, but essential truths.

Near the end of a short midwinter day, we emerged from the forest and trekked into a snowy meadow embroidered with bare-branched wil-

lows. Matt gestured toward the hillside we had just descended. "You see
the big trees way up along the ridgetop? That timber has never been
logged. Then, just below it, there's a dividing line where the smaller trees
begin—that's the old clear-cut we hiked through. But you have to look
closely to pick out the difference." Then he asked, "Do you think the
tourists, or even most people who live around here, would notice? It all
seems like the same forest to them, and it looks like nothing's wrong.

"The whole process is hard for people to understand," Matt conceded.
"After you clear-cut a forest in southeast Alaska, you get a short period
when it's wide open, when plant growth really takes off." I remembered
Tom Hanley, the Forest Service ecologist, saying that although deer feed
in recent clear-cuts, shrub species that dominate these openings are high
in tannin, so they're hard for blacktails to digest. To make matters worse,
deep winter snows virtually exclude deer from scrubby regrowth areas.

"Following these early stages," Matt continued, "you get the type of
forest we saw back on the hillside. When the canopy closes twenty to
thirty years after logging, there are almost no understory plants for deer
to eat. You've got an even-aged, second-growth forest that's going to last
two hundred years or more. During that time, the habitat that's essential
for winter survival of deer is *gone.*"

In the Tongass National Forest, clear-cut tracts are scheduled to be
logged again in 100 to 125 years. Paul Alaback, a respected plant ecologist,
believes it takes 300 to 500 years for a southeast Alaskan forest to reach
ecological maturity—the stage called old-growth. An old-growth forest is
dominated by very large trees, as you would expect, but the forest is hon-
eycombed with small openings created when trees topple in storms or die
of other causes. In a given area there are openings of every age, each rep-
resenting a particular stage of regrowth—weeds and shrubs in new clearings, trees of varying sizes in older ones—so the whole forest is a highly
diverse community offering both food and shelter for deer. Clear-cutting
every 100 years—or even half as often—means keeping those tracts in a
second-growth stage, so they're permanently lost for deer. Biologists estimate this will reduce blacktail populations by 50 to 70 percent on millions
of acres in southeastern Alaska. In parts of Vancouver Island, off the
British Columbia coast, deer harvests declined by 50 percent overall and
up to 75 percent in some watersheds after old-growth forests were cut.

Changes of this magnitude will have serious consequences for people
in small, isolated towns scattered throughout the Tongass National Forest—communities where jobs are scarce, incomes are limited, and nearly
everyone relies to some extent on foods garnered by hunting, fishing, and

gathering. Outside Alaska, there are probably no American communities where residents depend so heavily on venison as a staple food and where deer have such a vital place in household economies.

Among the members of these communities are about 13,000 Tlingit, Haida, and Tsimshian Indians. Many Indian people center their livelihood around traditional subsistence activities, commercial fishing, and whatever jobs they can find. Villagers also hold shares in corporations established under the Alaska Native Land Claims Settlement Act of 1971, and to assure large yearly dividends most of these companies have logged tribal lands as if there were no tomorrow. In fact, the excesses of our U.S. Forest Service look mild when compared to logging by Native corporations in southeast Alaska.

Some Native leaders speak out against clear-cutting on tribal lands and the surrounding National Forest. In a court case related to logging, a Tlingit Eagle Clan elder declared:

> The land, and the plants and animals on it, are our people. . . . We have always tried to take care of the abundant food supply entrusted to us. Others do not share our ideas. Now logging is stripping our land. Everywhere deer live is being cut away.

A chief of the Raven Clan contrasted modern logging to the older traditions of restraint and humility toward nature:

> When we take food from the land we talk to the forest and animals. We thank each of them for their sacrifice to let us live. We are not their masters. We are equals in accordance with our tradition.

It must rend the elders' hearts to see clear-cuts sprawling across the mountainsides, and yet some Tlingit and Haida communities have now destroyed virtually all of their commercially valuable trees.

Since the 1950s, clear-cutting in the Tongass National Forest has been heavily subsidized by the federal government, ostensibly as a way to create employment. According to economist Randal O'Toole, Tongass logging cost U.S. taxpayers about $40 million annually between 1989 and 1992, or $20,000 per year for every timber-related job—including loggers, mill workers, and Forest Service employees. Some have suggested it would be more sensible to simply give workers the money, or use it to retrain them for other jobs, and save the forest from further destruction. If this were done, we could reduce cutting in these ancient forests, giving equal weight to industries like fishing and tourism, which thrive best when trees are left on the mountainsides and in the valleys.

I believe we should redesign the timber industry around scientifically defensible logging practices and local manufacture of finished wood products (rather than shipping raw pulp or lumber elsewhere); this would support the largest number of jobs for the smallest number of trees cut. There is an honorable place for loggers working in the woods; but when loggers have finished, the woods should still remain. Put another way, I am not troubled in the least by a stump in the forest, but few things rend my soul more deeply than a forest of stumps.

The earliest studies that showed how clear-cutting damages deer habitat in the Tongass were done by Olof Wallmo, David Klein, John Schoen, and Matthew Kirchoff. Their conclusions did not rest well with the U.S. Forest Service, apparently because economic and political pressures for large-scale clear-cutting outweighed ecological concerns, and for over a decade government officials tried to prevent these researchers from writing about their conclusions.

Probably no scientist felt more pressure than did John Schoen, a biologist for the Alaska Department of Fish and Game, who figured prominently in these studies. "The Forest Service tried to stop the first publication Wallmo and I did on deer and old-growth forest, because it didn't fit into their management scheme," Schoen told me. "Of course, Wallmo was one of the foremost deer experts in North America, but he received very rough treatment from the Forest Service over this issue. They didn't want us to tell the truth."

For several years, pressure by Forest Service officials also prevented John Schoen and Matt Kirchoff from giving public slide presentations about deer and old-growth forest. "I had several trips to the commissioner's office to talk about my professional career," Schoen recalls. Faced with intimations that his motives were political rather than biological, Schoen found himself defending his scientific integrity. He points out, "As biologists, we were *not* trying to tell people what timber management decisions to make; we were telling them what the *consequences* of those decisions would be." Finally, after destruction of old-growth forests became a national issue, Schoen and his colleagues were allowed to publish and speak freely about their research.

I asked Schoen why he'd risked so much over the issue of deer and logging. "The biggest problem I've had is not how we're going to impact black-tailed deer," he replied. "The reason I stayed with this so long is because it was hard for me to accept that governments working for the people weren't telling the truth." Recently, a bill passed Congress protecting some Tongass lands from logging and requiring more responsible management of timber harvests. But the struggle for responsible logging in the Tongass is far from over.

As Matt Kirchoff and I trudged back to his truck on that winter afternoon, I told him I'd never realized how profoundly clear-cut logging affected the wildlands of southeastern Alaska. Matt smiled knowingly, then acknowledged that biologists might be partly to blame. "Sometimes we've thought we never should have used the word 'clear-cut' in the first place, because it focuses attention on the wrong thing. The greatest impact of clear-cut logging comes *after* the visible scars are gone, when the trees have regenerated to a second-growth stage. That's when deer populations are really going to decline, and they'll stay that way for a long, long time."

Matt described logging methods that might be less harmful to deer and other wildlife—selective cutting of trees or clear-cutting in less productive stands where slower regrowth would delay closure of the canopy. But in the Tongass, timber interests and politicians have nearly always prevailed over concerns about dwindling old-growth, about commercial salmon fishing, about the rapidly expanding tourist industry, about subsistence in small communities, about preserving one of the richest and most exquisite natural communities on earth, and about the key indicator of ecological health in this ancient rain forest—black-tailed deer.

Matt Kirchoff and I stood at the meadow's edge and gazed back toward the upswept mountain walls, now drenched in shadow at the end of a December day. I could still pick out the boundary dividing pristine forest from the 60-year-old clear-cut just below—the young trees distinctly shorter, even topped, more tightly spaced. But from this distance, no one could detect the silence in a forest emptied of birds, and none could see the pure, unbroken snow where deer would seldom leave a track.

EMBATTLED SANCTUARIES

Just as a deer herd lives in mortal fear of wolves, so does a mountain live in mortal fear of its deer. And perhaps with better cause, for while a buck pulled down by wolves can be replaced in two or three years, a range pulled down by too many deer may fail of replacement in as many decades.

—ALDO LEOPOLD

Devouring the Sacred Ground

*I*n the long habitation of this continent by Euro-Americans, we have etched our presence boldly across the land, but we also have shown the wisdom and grace to leave some portions intact. Wildland preserves exist in every state and province, ranging in size from a few acres to thousands of square miles—forests, prairies, marshes, deserts, lakes, rivers, seacoasts, valleys, mountains. I suspect future generations may judge as our greatest single achievement not the cities and monuments we have built, but the places we've spared from our handiwork. We have bequeathed to ourselves a spectacular array of natural treasures, acclaiming the glory of earth itself.

But in the past century we've also learned that protecting wild places is not so simple as putting borders around tracts of land, designating ourselves harmless, and allowing natural processes to go on without interference. We've recognized that most wild communities have been influenced by human activities for thousands of years, that recently exterminated predators like wolves and mountain lions are important to healthy ecosystems, that no landscape exists in isolation from surrounding landscapes, and that no environment—regardless of protected status—exists nowadays without significant human impact. This is clearly illustrated by the case of parkland deer.

Among the original purposes for refuges and preserves was the creation of areas where deer would be saved from extinction and the provision of seed animals for restocking where deer had already vanished. During the 1940s, for example, more than 8,000 whitetails were trapped from the Aransas National Wildlife Refuge in Texas and transplanted elsewhere to augment or reestablish populations. But also by that time, many refuges had become overcrowded with deer, and the animals were malnourished or dying from starvation. Nevertheless, local people often resisted opening these areas to hunting, not because they felt hunting was immoral or unethical, but because they worried that deer might again be threatened with extinction.

Over the past few decades, especially east of the Mississippi, deer overpopulations have become almost pandemic in natural sanctuaries of every size and variety. In the absence of two-legged hunters or four-legged predators that bring deer populations into balance with their habitat, things have gone seriously awry. Overcrowded and hungry, deer have abandoned their normal wildness, depleted vegetation, jeopardized plant and animal species, and faced starvation themselves.

Deer have multiplied until they've brought ecological disarray in one preserve after another—places like Harriman State Park in New York, Bluff Point Coastal Reserve in Connecticut, Everglades National Park in Florida, Ryerson Conservation Area in Illinois, Fontenelle Forest in Nebraska, Yale-Myers Forest in Connecticut, Thousand Hills State Park in Missouri, Boulder Mountain Park in Colorado, Gettysburg National Military Park in Pennsylvania, Rondeau Provincial Park in Ontario, around the Quabbin Reservoir in Massachusetts, and hundreds more.

Where they have created disorder in the parks, they've also caused disagreement among land managers, biologists, agency officials, politicians, conservationists, animal rights activists, and millions of visitors taken with a dream of wild serenity that becomes ever more elusive in the late twentieth century. Inevitably, when a natural preserve is overrun by deer, there are proposals to bring deer numbers down, usually by hunting or

culling; then comes a public furor over the ethics, practicality, or appro-
priateness of killing sanctuary animals. Next, people usually suggest or
try alternate approaches—trap-and-transfer, capture-and-euthanasia, or
sterilization—but these rarely work unless the deer are limited to a very
small area. Most often, hunting emerges as the only practical way to balance free-ranging deer with their environment; either this, or people disagree so fervently that resolution is impossible.

Time and again, the same problems have erupted in natural preserves,
bringing the same debates, creating the same political pressures, inspir-
ing the same experiments—regardless of what already has been learned
somewhere else. When it comes to coping with deer overpopulations, we
seem eternally reluctant to acknowledge the basic laws of biology and
perpetually committed to reinventing the wheel.

To understand the problems of deer in parklands, and to learn how
people have tried to solve them, I visited natural preserves on opposite
sides of the continent. Angel Island State Park is a one-square-mile shoulder of rock, grassland, and forest hard by the shore of San Francisco Bay;
Fire Island National Seashore is a wisp of scrubby woods and dunes
stretched along New York's Atlantic coast. The two islands differ profoundly in natural environment and human use, yet they have nearly
identical deer problems, which have caused years of conflict. Angel Island's deer have been restored to balance and the ecosystem is healthy
again, while on Fire Island, deer are still overabundant, the environment
is being abused, and strife continues. How do we account for these differences and what can we learn from them?

Angel Island and Fire Island stand like parentheses at either side of a
nation, embracing the whole array of stories in between and epitomizing
the struggle to find ecological harmony in our parklands. We have cultivated the wildness in these preserves, as much as we've simply let it be.
Given this fact, are we willing to protect these preserves by maintaining
a balance among their inhabitants? Must we—or should we—keep wild
nature from turning inward to devour itself?

Angel of the Bay

At the city of Richmond, the Richmond–San Rafael Bridge crosses San
Francisco Bay, linking the paved geometric sprawls of Alameda and Con-
tra Costa counties with the greenwood opulence of Marin. Lee Swenson
stretched an arm into the wind as we topped the bridge. "Look way over
there, just off the long peninsula—that's Angel Island." It rose like a flint

egg in an enormous blue nest, closely backed by faded ocher hills. Although only a narrow strait separated it from the mainland, the island looked strikingly apart, as if it were situated far out to sea. Then I realized why, noticing the suburbs laced along nearby slopes, crowded down against the shore, stitched tightly around the bay. Angel Island was isolated by its wildness, a tiny natural enclave surrounded by sprawling expanses of humanity.

A short while later, we grabbed backpacks and binoculars, ran for the dock, and just made the day's only ferry to Angel Island. Hikers, bicyclists, and picnickers jostled aboard the stout passenger boat, along with a whirling batch of adolescent boys and their shepherding adults. Just a quarter mile away, rising from the glitter of Raccoon Strait, was Angel Island's stony hulk. It looked like you could swim across, but you'd have to overcome frigid water and tidal currents that slicked the surface like a river in flood.

After a 15-minute crossing we nudged against the dock at Ayala Cove, facing its lovely sand beach and steep, wooded hills. Lee and I strolled across a shady lawn with picnic tables and barbecues backed by the stately old houses that served as park headquarters. I'd seen pictures, in a magazine published 10 years earlier, of black-tailed deer a few feet from these very tables, begging picnickers for handouts. Today I was torn between my ardent wish to see a deer and my relief that none was visible—evidence of the latest chapter in Angel Island's contentious deer history.

The switchback trail leading from Ayala Cove toward Angel Island's interior went through a storybook forest of sharply bent trunks and interlacing branches. It was deliciously cool and humid, the air saturated with rich earthy smells, the forest floor cloaked in vibrant green herbage brought forth by winter rains. "These are miner's lettuce," instructed Lee, kneeling in a patch of smallish plants with delicate ivory flowers. "They're good eating," he added, munching a disk-shaped leaf and picking another for me. It was crisp and tasty.

We also found hoofprints in the damp soil, conspicuous deer trails threading along the slope, and freshly nipped stems in another patch of miner's lettuce. The fact that we'd browsed the same food as Angel Island's deer brought on a subtle feeling of intimacy, a sense of physical connection with the makers of those tracks.

"It won't be long before all these plants dry up," said Lee, "because we're past Easter and it might not rain again until fall." For California's deer, the yearly cycle of abundance and scarcity is opposite from that in most other parts of North America. Mild, rainy weather generally makes winter an easy time, but summer brings months of drought and stress, sometimes even starvation.

As we approached Angel Island's elevated central plateau, an enormous owl startled from an overhanging limb, swept silently away, and landed in another tree, vanishing as if it had soaked into the bark and leaves. We hiked out across a grassy ridge and hunkered on an overlook, scanning the slopes through binoculars, scrutinizing thickets and shady places beneath copses of trees. But we saw no shape of ear or antler, no silhouetted haunch, no switching tail.

Perhaps the Spanish explorer Ayala had better luck when he first landed here in 1775. Records indicate the island was heavily wooded, offering good cover not only for deer but also for elk and wandering grizzly bears that swam across the strait. The ship's priest, Father Vicente, noted in his journal that deer "were most numerous on the island," and he inferred from the presence of Indian shelters that hunting parties visited regularly. Later on, the island was denuded by woodcutters from passing vessels and grazed by Spanish livestock, then gradually revegetated with oak, chaparral, and exotic species like Australian eucalyptus.

Fort McDowell was established on the island in 1851 to provide respite for soldiers on leave from the Indian wars. It's safe to assume the men regularly hunted deer for mess-hall stewpots. But by 1900, hunting, deforestation, and overgrazing had emptied Angel Island of deer. Fifteen years later the military transplanted about a dozen blacktails from Sonoma County, and boaters' reports of deer swimming toward the island suggest others arrived on their own.

Meanwhile, the government used Angel Island as a point of entry for immigrants, a quarantine station for patients with contagious diseases, a medical exam facility for soldiers during World War II, and later a Nike missile site. Through it all, the blacktails persisted and there was enough hunting to keep their numbers in check. But the situation changed in 1955, when California's Department of Parks and Recreation took over the island and prohibited all hunting.

Sweating under midday sun, Lee and I trekked a ridgeline toward Mount Livermore, the island's high point at 741 feet above sea level. From its rounded top we took in a panoramic view including Alcatraz Island a few miles south, and the scarlet pylons of the Golden Gate Bridge visible to the west. Farther south rose San Francisco's futuristic glass-and-steel skyline, dominated by the Transamerica Building's angled pirouette. And wrapped around the bay's prodigious waist was a great urban mass looped together with boulevard ribbons. Even for a country pilgrim, it had a powerful, trembling, electric beauty—like a glittering dragon splayed over the mountainsides, nostrils aflare, eyes spilling fountains of light.

Down off the summit, we followed a trail through butterfly meadows and pine glades that gave us a sense for Angel Island's scrambled geography of hills, steep-sided ravines, and vertiginous cliffs. Measured on a map the island totals just one square mile, but measured on foot—clambering around its crenelated surface and peering into the dense scrub thickets—it seems at least 10 times that. From the omnipresent tracks, I felt sure we were seldom far from deer and suspected that funneled ears picked up every word we spoke, but we caught no glimpse of the animals themselves. Deer have a gift for tangible but invisible presence.

"This looks like a paradise for deer," I thought aloud. But I knew that over the past 40 years, Angel Island had been a tenuous paradise indeed, dangerously susceptible to the deer's reproductive virtuosity. When the island was closed to hunting in 1955, biological processes almost as certain as gravity were set in motion. Eleven years later, in 1966, the deer population had grown to an estimated 300—a blacktail for every 2.5 acres of land.

No one doubted this was far too many. Even casual visitors complained of emaciated deer trailing them around the picnic grounds, mooching food. Rangers noted that the island's vegetation was heavily browsed from the ground to about five feet, the highest reach of adult animals. Edible plants had vanished from the forest floor and there were no seedlings of oak, manzanita, or other native species to replace older trees when they died. Deprived of stabilizing roots and sheltering undergrowth, the friable soil washed away during winter storms and gullies yawned in the soft bedrock. Overabundant deer had ravaged Angel Island's ecosystem.

Park officials knew something had to be done, so in November of 1966 they issued a public notice and then shot about 50 deer, but the culling abruptly stopped amid a torrent of public disapproval, and over the following months deer starved to death while people argued. When the dust settled, about 100 animals had survived, and many folks thought the problem had conveniently solved itself.

Biologists quietly predicted otherwise, and they were right. As the island's vegetation recovered, so did the deer population, reaching about 225 animals by 1975. Browse lines appeared, raw gullies widened, and a bony congregation of 25 to 50 deer worked the picnic grounds for peanut butter sandwiches. A state proposal to forestall ecological calamity by culling all but 50 deer brought another cloudburst of public opposition. The San Francisco Society for Prevention of Cruelty to Animals (SPCA) went to court against the plan, then got approval to start an artificial feeding program. Biologists sensibly argued that feeding would encourage more growth of deer numbers and perpetuate the environmental problems, but by this time another crash was under way, ending with at least another 100 animals dead from starvation.

The latest crisis was over, but not for long. "By 1980, the deer were so hungry, it was like they were catching acorns in midair," recalled Tom Lindberg, Angel Island's supervising ranger at the time. "The browse line was so heavy, it looked like everything had been pruned professionally. And because the vegetation was getting hammered, other wildlife suffered—there weren't many birds, squirrels, rabbits, or other small mammals.

"The deer were eating candy bars," Tom added. "They were skinny, scrawny, ravaged with internal problems and parasites. But they were the object of everybody's camera, and people loved having a chance to touch deer." Officials worried about the close encounters. Not long before, in Yosemite National Park, a man and his five-year-old son had been feeding popcorn to a spike-antlered buck. When the boy pulled his offering away, the deer jerked its head up and one antler pierced the boy's heart, killing him instantly. The same ominous possibility existed on Angel Island, where a cadre of heavy-racked bucks mingled freely with visitors.

On a summer day in 1980, Dale R. McCullough, a biologist and faculty member at the University of California's Berkeley campus, came to Angel Island for a family picnic. "I hadn't been aware of a problem on the island," he remembered when we talked in his Berkeley office. "But I saw these deer around the picnic grounds, and they were skin and bones. I was sort of appalled that here I was in the midst of a crash about to happen." Professor McCullough was well qualified to understand the situation. His studies of deer population dynamics in Michigan's George Reserve are regarded as classics in the field, and he developed principles of wildlife management used all over the world.

McCullough discussed the problem with park rangers and officials from California's Department of Fish and Game, who asked for his help in resolving the island's deer problems—a project far more complex than anyone could have anticipated, not because of the biological issues involved but because of public sensitivities. What Dale McCullough would later describe in writing as "the Angel Island fiasco" revealed as much about people as it did about deer.

Since it wasn't politically possible to reduce the deer population by shooting, McCullough came up with an innovative suggestion that might fit better with people's attitudes about "natural" control. He proposed releasing six wild coyotes on Angel Island, all sterilized to ensure that their numbers wouldn't increase, and all fitted with radio collars so they could be captured if problems arose. Because coyotes are not very proficient deer predators, they would limit the blacktail population by taking mainly old and sick animals and a portion of the young.

A spasm of sensationalized reporting stymied McCullough's efforts to build support for his idea in advance of public hearings. "Nevertheless, I'd expected a different response"—McCullough smiled faintly—"after all the years that had passed since Earth Day, and all the years of environmental education, all the television programs about predators. But there was a big crowd and the majority were there to argue against the coyote proposal."

Many who testified at the hearing conjured images of coyotes as ravenous killers, and some even worried that their children would be attacked in the midst of cowering bystanders. Others envisaged coyotes slaughtering deer on the lawn at Ayala Cove amid horrified picnickers. "These people intensely believed what they were saying, but it was so far removed from facts that you could only shake your head," McCullough told me. "The need to deal with the deer population and the merits of using predators as a control were never really discussed."

In a recent article, McCullough reflected on the turmoil over his coyote plan: "My sanity and ancestry were much debated in newspaper letters to the editor and columns and on radio talk shows." For a man with impeccable academic credentials and international stature in his field, a man trying to reconcile human sentiments with ecological realities, it was all profoundly unsettling. But to his enduring credit, McCullough did not turn away from Angel Island's troubled deer population.

Months later, yielding to threats of legal action from the San Francisco SPCA, state agencies decided to trap deer on the island and relocate them. Professor McCullough and other biologists warned that many transplanted animals would die, but once the decision was settled, everyone tried his best to make the plan work. The SPCA supported McCullough and a graduate student, Mary O'Bryan, who would do a follow-up study on the transplanted animals. McCullough saw this project as a chance to learn, and he knew that conclusions about its success or failure depended on reliable scientific data.

The next fall state biologists, park personnel, and SPCA volunteers started live-trapping deer and transporting them by helicopter to a new home. Delicate work under the best of circumstances, this was even more difficult because the animals were weak from starvation. At least 275 deer inhabited Angel Island when the project started. Of these, 203 were captured and then released in the Cow Mountain Recreation Area, 100 miles north of San Francisco. Twelve others—a commendably small number—died in the process of capture.

Every relocated animal had identifying ear tags, and 15 wore radio collars so Mary O'Bryan could track their progress. Several died within two weeks, probably of malnutrition, and over the next few months many others succumbed to dogs, wild predators, car accidents, and poachers (bucks had had their antlers removed so they could not be legally hunted). One man found a radio collar along the road, presumably after its wearer was killed by a poacher, and he tossed the collar into his truck. Unsuspecting biologists charted the pickup's neighborhood travels for over a month, and when signals indicated the collar wasn't moving anymore they found it lying in the man's backyard. Only two of the radio-collared deer survived: one in a retirement community and the other on the grounds of a Buddhist monastery.

O'Bryan's study revealed that most transplanted animals survived less than four months, and 85 percent were dead within a year. McCullough and O'Bryan issued their results without judgment, but media reports criticized the San Francisco SPCA for insisting on relocation despite biologists' warnings. The SPCA asserted that relocation had been a success but never advocated trying it again. One reporter concluded, "They didn't bring coyotes to the deer; they took the deer to the coyotes."

A major problem with relocated deer, McCullough points out, is that they seldom stay put. "It's as if you picked up people and dropped them in the middle of the Amazon Basin—they'd start looking for a home or for help. They don't know where they are." Animals from preserves are especially vulnerable because they often lack experience with cars, dogs, predators, or hunters. Even if they're released in a protected area, they'll probably leave or be driven off by resident deer, who don't easily accept newcomers.

Moving Angel Island's deer was also very expensive. The direct cost totaled $87,568—$431 per animal, or $2,876 for each one that survived the first year. Afterward, a drive census on the island came across 16 carcasses and 45 living deer. These survivors were the lucky ones. Relieved of competition for food, they grew fat and healthy, and as one biologist put it, "The does started pumping out twins." Within two years the population was increasing rapidly, a pattern McCullough knew well from his studies on the fenced, 1.5-square-mile George Reserve, where a deer population reduced to 10 animals had grown to more than 200 in five years.

In 1983, confronted by another surge in Angel Island's deer numbers, the SPCA offered a new proposal. This time they would trap and sterilize the deer. Again, Dale McCullough recognized the odds against success, but he urged state approval, confident that he'd do everything possible to make sterilization work. As a scientist, he doubtless understood that experiment carries far greater weight than inference, that practical experience is the foundation on which true authority stands. One of his graduate students, Gene Fowler, would help with a deer census and teach volunteers to safely trap and handle the animals.

The project, begun in 1984, involved SPCA volunteers along with veterinarians and veterinary students, Gene Fowler explained when I met him at the University of Washington, where he was continuing graduate studies in zoology. "We all lived in the same house," he added, "and even the folks at Fish and Game who were most opposed to sterilization got along well with folks in charge from the SPCA." Gene is a tall, athletic-looking man, widely experienced in the outdoors, with a quick mind and a friendly, easygoing nature; he seemed ideal for this situation. The fact that he's also a deer hunter proved that people with very different viewpoints can work effectively together. And in this case, everyone agreed that reducing the deer herd was essential to protect Angel Island's natural environment.

The crew used deer traps made of nylon net stretched over a pipe frame, baited with tempting foods like green alfalfa, apple pulp, and molasses-flavored grain. Whenever they trapped a doe who hadn't been caught before, the veterinarian sedated her, made a small incision in her neck, and inserted beneath her skin a capsule of malengestrol acetate, a drug that suppresses ovulation for as long as several years.

Everyone involved realized their success depended on sterilizing 80 to 90 percent of the does on Angel Island. Like Dale McCullough, Gene was committed to the project, but he acknowledged: "We probably didn't have a snowball's chance in hell. I thought we might be able to capture seventy percent, but that last fifteen to twenty percent would be next to impossible. You're fishing for a rare species, basically, at that point."

During the earlier relocation project, starving animals came easily to the traps, but now, with a lower though rapidly expanding population, deer tended to overlook baits because they had enough natural browse. As a result, captures were very low. Situations like this create an unresolvable paradox, wrote Fred Botti in an article about the project. When deer numbers are small enough so that infertility drugs might stabilize the population, it's impossible to catch enough animals. And when numbers are so high that starving deer will enter traps, it's neither possible nor desirable to stabilize the population.

"Here's what happened," said Gene Fowler. "They spent three months and caught thirty does—that's only about twenty-five percent of the females on the island. Everyone tried pretty hard and I have to give them credit. But they realized that not only were the difficulties of catching animals exactly as expected, but they were worse than anyone's most pessimistic prediction. In the end, the SPCA folks realized they just couldn't do it."

Alternate capture methods such as drives, nets, or helicopter darting would not be effective on Angel Island's rugged, brushy terrain, despite the very small area involved. Biologists also rejected a suggestion to shoot deer with hard projectiles containing implants, because it would risk injuring or killing animals and because the deer were too elusive.

There are other problems with contraception besides the unlikelihood of capturing enough animals. Dale McCullough pointed out that although sterilizing limits reproduction, it leaves the same number of deer to keep on damaging the environment. This means waiting until animals die of old age—which may be 5 to 15 years in a protected area—before the population starts to decline.

Culling, on the other hand, immediately reduces the number of animals, while it also shrinks the breeding pool. Because of this, instead of capturing and treating 80 to 90 percent of the deer, it's only necessary to cull about 20 percent. Sterilized deer may also need to be treated again, a problem that doesn't exist with culling. Furthermore, Gene says that even if 90 percent of the does were treated, there would still be a nucleus of fertile deer to start the next go-round. Again, this brings to mind the explosive multiplication of whitetails inside the George Reserve.

Despite volunteer help and other cost-saving measures, the San Francisco SPCA put about $30,000 into this project, or $1,000 per sterilized deer. Dale McCullough concluded: "When the Society for the Prevention of Cruelty to Animals threw in the towel, they never told the media.

Also, we never told the media. But after this effort was finished, Angel Island's deer population was still zooming upward."

When sterilization failed, the San Francisco SPCA ended its involvement with Angel Island, but the problem of overabundant deer hadn't gone away. The state held public hearings to explain everything that had been tried and, once again, to propose culling. At last, there was public support for the idea, including endorsements from organizations like the Audubon Society and the Marin Conservation League. Tom Lindberg was Angel Island's brand-new supervising ranger. "I'd never hunted deer—ever," he recalled. "But when I was told to develop a program for shooting deer, that's what I did."

Lindberg is outgoing and articulate, with an obvious talent for solving problems, and it's easy to see why he was chosen at this critical time. "All of us were rangers," he emphasized. "We hadn't signed on to be hunters, we had signed on to be interpreters—to talk to kids, to tell people about parks. So we explained this program to people as a distasteful one for those who were doing it, but necessary, and the end result would be beneficial to the animals."

Dale McCullough devised a plan to monitor the island's blacktails and cull as few as possible while holding their numbers within an optimal range, based on ecological concerns along with human interests. For example, if the population dropped as low as 50, people wouldn't often see deer, but if it approached 300, there would be severe starvation, so an ideal figure for Angel Island might be 100 to 150 animals. Culling began about a year after the sterilization attempt. Park rangers trained as marksmen did all the shooting, but since none had ever hunted, Gene Fowler came along to select the animals, give hunting instructions, and show how animals are dressed out.

For maximum safety, shooting was done late at night using spotlights, and the island was closed to all visitors. "This is nothing like sport hunting," McCullough explained. "It's just hard, nasty work that the rangers don't like." Tom Lindberg told a newspaper reporter, "We're trained to protect wildlife, not kill it." But he emphasized that rangers were required to safeguard the park from damage by excessive numbers of deer.

A month after culling started, Cleveland Amory learned of it and headed for California. The high-profile president of the Fund for Animals, a national animal rights organization based in New York, Amory got the full attention of state officials in Sacramento, where he stated his preference for capture and sterilization. But according to a memo summarizing the conference, after park personnel detailed their previous efforts, Amory "seemed to understand that all reasonable methods had been tried and that cull shooting was the only viable solution."

The culling program has continued since 1985, allowing up to six hunts annually during the winter off-season, with a goal of 3 deer per hunt and a maximum total of 18. During years with low deer populations, little or no culling is needed. After a kill, rangers weigh and measure the animal, check its overall condition, and take samples (such as body fat and lower jaws) for biological studies. In recent times the deer have consistently been healthy and well nourished.

The culled animals are taken from Angel Island and nothing ends up in a landfill. Even the internal organs and other unusable parts go to a rendering plant. Antlers, hides, and hooves are donated to school programs, Native American ceremonial groups, and California museums or parks, where they're used for interpretive exhibits. Most important, meat from all animals goes to a nearby dining room for homeless people.

"For the press, it ended up being kind of a dull story," said Tom Lindberg, leafing through a batch of articles he'd clipped. "Everything was very businesslike: we had taken the safety precautions, the studies had been done, and the history was clearly outlined. Also, rangers could look anybody in the eye and say, 'We haven't eaten one bite of these deer.' After about a year and a half the media really weren't interested anymore."

Tom Lindberg took a deep breath and smiled. I sensed the relief he'd felt when public controversy faded and park rangers could again focus on teaching visitors about the natural world. "People would still say, 'Where are the deer? We miss seeing them.' So we'd work it into our interpretive programs and hikes. We'd point out that deer are supposed to be seen at early morning and evening, not in midday as it was before. And we'd show people that the browse line had come down, that erosion on the hillsides was decreasing, that deer were getting healthier instead of being sick. Public acceptance of this program was as important as improving the health of the deer herd."

There was one other thing, Lindberg added, handing me a single-page summary of Angel Island's deer history. It pointed out that culling, the only population control method that had proved effective, was also the least costly: compared with $431 per relocation and $1,000 per sterilization, culling amounted to $74 per animal.

· · ·

Late that afternoon, Lee and I headed back to catch the ferry. From a hillside overlook, I imagined Spanish ships anchored on the diamond waters of Ayala Cove, and the wild, unfettered land that stretched away into the continent's measureless depths. Angel Island was both a surviving remnant of that wildness and a reminder of what has been lost. I peered into the mottled shade beneath oak trees, still hoping to glimpse the animal that had brought me here, but it was enough to know that somewhere nearby a deer's heart drummed.

Back at park headquarters we visited with ranger Floyd Lemley until the ferry arrived. "Most people come here from the city," he observed, "and for them it's a delightful surprise to see any wild animal. We've got about eighty deer on the island right now, which is down a bit because several animals died last summer. There was a severe drought and they might have eaten poisonous soap root bulbs." Then he added, "Last year we culled six deer, but this year we won't need to remove any. Instead we'll make an accurate census." Ranger Lemley's account was simple and straightforward, as it should be once ecological balance is restored.

A short while later, Lee and I sat on the ferry resting tired legs, watching the island slip away behind us. At first it looked immense, unassailable, a bastion of rock and forest secure beyond its tidal moat. But as we approached Tiburon, Angel Island became small against the enormousness of San Francisco Bay, precarious amid the trembling intensity of an urban metropolis, vulnerable to the storms of politics and public sentiment. It seemed strange that a place so lovely and tranquil could have been awhirl with conflict for almost 20 years—torn by a tense interplay of science, human emotion, and moral values centered around a wild creature and its environment. But although solutions were slow in coming, much had been learned along the way.

When I spoke with Dale McCullough, he summarized the lessons gained from Angel Island and from a distinguished career in wildlife research. "The advice I give to people dealing with deer overpopulations is, first try to get public agreement on a maximum number of animals compatible with other uses of the area. Then try to control the population by means other than shooting, but you agree beforehand that any excess beyond this number will be removed by shooting. And if all else fails, you shoot.

"I have no personal stake in shooting as a solution. I have a stake in whatever program is chosen—that it works, and that it protects the quality of the deer and the quality of the environment. But so often, controversy drags on and on, and you lose the things you're trying to protect: the deer die, or the habitat is destroyed."

Results of the Angel Island studies are directly applicable in dozens—perhaps hundreds—of other areas where deer overpopulations jeopardize natural habitats and the animals who live in them. But it's worth remembering that Dale McCullough had predicted the failure of relocation and sterilization programs long before they began, and that he was certain a culling program would succeed. "Our history in this business is that people aren't going to take the biologists' word for it. The only way I achieved credibility was by being right in the end."

McCullough points out, however, that one question was left unanswered: Could deer numbers have been stabilized, as he originally suggested, by introducing sterile coyotes?

A short while later, Lee and I joined rush-hour traffic on the freeway, cars lined up like beads on a string as far as we could see in either direction. When we leveled out atop the Richmond–San Rafael Bridge, he pointed south: "There it is . . . one last look." Glassy waters mirrored a tangerine sky deepening overhead to fuchsia and purple, a few stars glimmering in the heights. And beneath the smooth-edged California hills we could still pick out Angel Island, brooding in its own shadows, awaiting night's descent.

The Wild and the Tame

"Hey, come quick—here they are!" Susan Bergholz whispered urgently through the screen door, and I hurried out to peer from the deck of her Fire Island home. Less than 15 feet away stood a whitetail doe with her ears erect, staring at us, as if her curiosity were no different from our own. Accustomed to the stocky build of coastal blacktails, I was impressed by her slenderness, her willowy legs, her long neck and narrow face, her satiny elegance.

Then I saw another deer just beyond the doe—a thick-bodied, muscular buck with six-point antlers, switching his tail back and forth. Like the doe, he appeared a bit lean for early fall, when deer should be in peak condition with broad, fat backs.

Rather than slipping off as we eased down the outdoor stairway, the doe ambled gracefully toward us. After tucking trouser cuffs inside my socks—a precaution against Lyme disease–carrying ticks—I moved away from the house and hunkered on a mat of crispy leaves. The buck approached to within five feet, then shied back while the doe came closer. She stepped gingerly, pausing, leaning forward until she was near enough to reach out and lick my hand. Her tongue felt dense, firmly muscled, surprisingly warm. She sniffed my legs, my belly, my shoulder, my cheek. A gray fleck the size of a rolled oat drifted on the silky wetness of her eye, then vanished when she blinked.

After a few minutes she followed the buck toward a nearby house, as if the two of them had a definite purpose in mind. "The people over there feed deer," reported Susan, and it didn't take long before the animals' strategy paid off. I talked with the neighbor while he cut and tossed chunks of apple. "My mother comes on weekends and she loves to feed the deer," he disclosed. "So I feel like I should give them a little every day, since I'm here all summer." After finishing their snacks, the whitetails nibbled tender forbs and shrubs in the nearby woods, then bedded down a few yards apart. The buck lay chewing his cud, eyes half closed, 50 feet from a man pounding nails on the back wall of his house.

Earlier that morning, Susan and I had taken the ferry across Great South Bay to Fire Island. Sagging, ashen clouds drifted overhead, and the air felt damp and chill, as you might expect on the Atlantic coast of New York in mid-October. Along the seaward horizon, Fire Island spread out like a rumpled cloth, dwindling to a thin line off our port and starboard quarters, then vanishing in the hazy distance. Although we were 3,000 miles from Angel Island, I had an irrepressible sense of déjà vu: another boat ride to another nature preserve where conflict had erupted over deer. In this case, however, the debate was far from settled.

Our ferry was a beamy steel-hulled launch about 50 feet long, with rows of passenger seats on the upper and lower decks. During summer it would be crammed with beachgoers, Susan pointed out, but on this autumn weekday there weren't more than 20 people aboard. Susan is a literary agent, and her husband, Bert Snyder, is a publishing executive; they live and work in New York City. Except during the winter months, when ferries stop running, they spend most weekends and holidays on Fire Island, where they own a small home.

Great South Bay isn't very wide, but it extends about 25 miles along Long Island's southern shore, connecting with several similar bays, all formed by barrier islands. During our 5-mile crossing, Fire Island's profile gradually lifted from the horizon, revealing mounded dunes and scrubby deciduous forest. From the boat's upper deck, Susan pointed to houses bunched along a half mile of wooded shoreline—the paired hamlets of Davis Park and Ocean Ridge.

Fire Island is little more than a ribbon of sand, 32 miles long and a few hundred yards across, with wider bulges here and there. Much of the land belongs to Fire Island National Seashore, but there are 17 small villages on its western half, totaling about 4,000 houses. Davis Park and Ocean Ridge, with some 250 houses in aggregate, are the easternmost communities, situated near the island's midpoint. Many Fire Island homes are rented to vacationers for a few days or weeks at a time, even the entire summer. Only about 400 families live year-round on the island, most of these near the western end, where access is by bridge as well as ferries. Another bridge is located near the eastern end, where there are no settlements at all. The number of people on Fire Island fluctuates tremendously, from a few thousand or fewer during off-season weekdays to perhaps 40,000 on a summer weekend.

Few vehicles are allowed on the island's sparse network of sand roads, so Susan and I finished our journey on foot, taking the main boardwalk into Davis Park. On either side, houses snuggled as closely as in a suburban neighborhood, but dense trees created a sense of seclusion, and the absence of cars made for a soothing rural atmosphere.

Most of the homes were small, cottage-sized affairs, although we saw a few elaborate, multistoried places, especially atop thinly vegetated dunes overlooking the Atlantic. These seaside houses are Fire Island's premier real estate, but every few years some topple into the surf when storms tear huge chunks from the shore. Susan and Bert's house was on safer ground back off the beach—a single-story place perched on head-high pilings, nested in a shady glade.

Later, we took a stroll down the middle of Davis Park, past a half dozen intersecting walks that led toward Atlantic beaches on one side and Great South Bay on the other. After crossing a wide stretch of open ground we entered the sandy, shrubby neighborhoods of Ocean Ridge. Idling in front of a house were three whitetails—a doe with two half-grown fawns. Two young women sat on the front porch, oblivious of the deer, much as people in other neighborhoods might ignore robins or squirrels.

Farther on, we came across one of the most impressive bucks I'd ever seen. He carried a sprawling rack, its bases as thick as my wrists and festooned with burly protuberances. The main beams formed a broad arc bearing 10 asymmetrical tines and an assortment of smaller points that curved and flexed like tongues of flame. A masterpiece of libertine genetics arose from this animal's brow—nature flaunting her limitless imagination in a sculpture of bone.

Such a great buck should have been a phantom, dismissed as rumor by all except the few who claimed they'd glimpsed him before he pounded off. Instead, as we approached, he strolled to the boardwalk and waited for us, then licked our hands and sniffed our pockets for treats. I crouched on the walkway, almost nose to nose with the deer, shadows of his labyrinthian antlers etched across my chest.

This animal had the quintessential bearing of a white-tailed deer, yet there was no hint of the wildness that should inflame every nerve in his body. I was awed and grateful to be near him, but the encounter also heightened my admiration for truly wild deer, whose power and intensity are whittled to perfection by the keen blade of mountain lion, wolf, and human hunter. What is a deer without secretiveness, without electrified vigilance, without the impulse to bound off in a whirl of leaves?

A while later, Susan and I stopped at the small community center and fire station, where we met Garrett Anger, a house builder who works mainly on Fire Island. When Susan described our encounter with the buck, Garrett shook his head knowingly. "It's *criminal,* what we've done, and I admit I'm one of them that's to blame. After Hurricane Bob awhile back, we started feeding the deer, and now look what's happened—there's nothing wild left in them. Really, this is not right."

I heard similar opinions later that afternoon, while chatting with people along the boardwalks. "When I first came here some years back," said an older woman, "it was rare that you saw a deer except in the National Seashore areas where no one lived. If they did come around the houses, the minute they saw a person they'd follow their normal instincts to get away. That's been totally reversed."

"The deer population really began to mushroom a few years back," her husband added. "People started feeding them and little fawns would come out from the natural areas when they still had spots—so they never learned any fear at all. Now they're like community pets; people consider them entertainment." He gestured toward a group of deer we'd all stopped to watch. "There's just too many of them. They're everywhere."

Fire Island is a haven for people hoping to escape the urban world, as close as many will ever come to witnessing unspoiled nature. Yet by our own presence—our conflicting impulses to preserve, but experience, and to manage, but leave alone—we have pitched the island's natural community out of balance. The deer, perhaps more than anything else, symbolize our image of wildness and epitomize the ways it has been transformed. By causing fundamental changes in deer behavior, unchecked population growth, and the resulting habitat degradation, we have jeopardized the wild nature we so fervently crave.

Toward evening I trekked along the border between Fire Island National Seashore and Davis Park, and there I met another heavy-antlered buck. He reached under a bush to snuffle the dry, weedy vegetation, and then I realized he was gnawing pulp from a broken pumpkin. Lifting his head to look at me, he tore loose a slender branch, which became a delicate, leafy garland draped through the tines of both antlers. Suddenly I forgot what he'd been eating, forgot the nearby houses and boardwalks. Instead, I had a vivid picture of Yaqui Indian hunters performing deer dances, with bright ribbon garlands dangling on the antlers of their headdresses. And when they dance, it is said, their whole being is inundated by the wild deer's spirit.

The next morning, I took a ferry to Patchogue, on the neighboring Long Island shore, to meet with Mark Lowery, a senior wildlife biologist for New York's Department of Environmental Conservation. We found a bench in full sunshine beside the water, ate bag lunches, and discussed his work on Fire Island. One of the most accessible, articulate, and knowledgeable agency biologists I'd ever met, Mark was in charge of deer research and management for all of Long Island, an area where people and whitetails share common ground. When the inevitable conflicts arose, he explained, it wasn't his job to solve these problems but to help communities understand the options and choose their own solutions.

Mark brought a map and a bundle of research reports on Fire Island and its deer. His map showed that between most of the settlements there are wildlands ranging from a few hundred yards to a couple miles long, stretching between the two shores like bands on a raccoon's tail. Each of these wildland sections is part of Fire Island National Seashore. There is also a designated Wilderness Area belonging to the National Seashore that begins at Ocean Ridge and runs eastward for seven miles.

The island's natural vegetation includes maritime forests with specially adapted trees like holly and shadbush, as well as open pine savannas, scrub thickets, thinly vegetated sand dunes, and salt marshes. One area, called the Sunken Forest, is a rare and globally endangered plant community dominated by trees like holly, sassafras, shadbush, and oak.

According to National Park Service researchers Allan O'Connell and Mark Sayre, Fire Island's deer benefit from the diverse natural vegetation, mild winters with little snow, and absence of four-legged predators. Hunting is prohibited and nowadays there's little poaching. Mark said whitetails are found everywhere on the island, but interestingly, they're most abundant near the west end, where virtually all of the people live. Apparently, deer divide their time between National Seashore lands and settlements—where they find nutritious ornamental plantings, succulent garden vegetables, artificial shelter among or beneath houses, and generous backyard feedings.

Although most biologists concur on these basic facts, they also have major points of disagreement. For example, according to Mark Lowery, censuses in the early 1990s indicated a population of 500 to 600 whitetails on the island. The highest number actually counted by helicopter survey was 434 after a fresh snowfall in the winter of 1993–94. Park Service researchers who made this census contend they saw most of the island's whitetails, but Lowery points out that aerial counts always miss a percentage of deer—ones hidden in dense conifer stands, under elevated boardwalks, and beneath houses—so this is a minimum figure.

Mark Lowery believes Fire Island's deer are overabundant and seriously damaging wild plant communities. The most critical threat is loss of dune grasses that stabilize the island against erosion by Atlantic storms. Park Service specialists admit that whitetail numbers are high and probably increasing, but they've tended to minimize the problem. Critics suggest the Park Service position is less scientific than political, to steer away from the divisive issue of shooting or other lethal controls.

Fire Island's deer are "owned" by the state, which has long used hunting as a tool to manage wildlife populations, but no shooting can be done without approval from the National Park Service. In 1968, Interior Secretary Stewart Udall set a policy that allows hunting in national parklands to control overabundant or destructive wildlife, but no matter how it's justified, killing animals in a place like Fire Island is bound to stir controversy.

Back in 1964, when Fire Island National Seashore was established, deer were anything but a problem—in fact they'd become either rare or extinct. It's safe to assume whitetails had lived here originally, but sometime after Europeans settled the island (around 1650), deer numbers dropped near the vanishing point. In most northeastern states, populations decimated by overhunting and habitat loss began recovering after the turn of the century, but Fire Islanders didn't start encountering deer until the 1970s. Perhaps a few had survived all along, or else migrants crossed from Long Island—swimming the bay, walking on winter ice, or even trekking the bridges at night.

In any case, the change from scarcity to abundance came quickly. Aerial survey estimates increased from 250 deer in 1983 to 450 in 1988, and Lowery is certain the upward trend has continued. "You now have at least sixty-five or seventy deer per square mile on Fire Island. We figure the best agricultural habitats in upstate New York could support thirty-five to forty per square mile without serious problems, and here, in a much less productive environment, we've got twice that density." Lowery suggests that 15 deer per square mile—or about 100 deer on Fire Island's seven square miles of land—would be ideal, if the environment were in prime condition.

"But understand," he cautions, "that Fire Island's habitat has been severely damaged. The deer have eaten vegetation that's accumulated over centuries and they've cut into its productivity. Because of this, you might even reduce the deer to fifty if that were possible. Afterward, the carrying capacity would improve as vegetation recovered." Some other biologists, while agreeing that present numbers are much too high, have suggested the island could support as many as 200 to 300 deer. Again, the National Park Service has suggested they need more studies before taking a position.

"On the eastern half of the island there is no serious issue," a Park Service specialist told me. "You can see a browse line in the Wilderness Area, but that's natural with this many deer." He admitted there are excessive numbers of deer in the western half, especially around settlements. "But that's because of people," he asserted. "On the boats, they're bringing pallets loaded with fifty-pound bags of goat and horse feed for the deer. If we had a heavy winter and they'd stop feeding, the deer would die back and the vegetation would have a chance to regenerate."

The fact is, many of Fire Island's native plants have declined because of whitetails, some to the point of alarming scarcity. Of particular concern is the Sunken Forest, where species like beadruby, aralia, and starflower have vanished everywhere except in briar thickets impenetrable to deer. Mark Lowery believes the forest itself is threatened. "Every spring you get a flush of tree seedlings," he explains, "and the Park Service suggests this means deer are not having an impact. But they overlook the fact that no seedlings survive more than two years, because every one that comes up is browsed until it dies." So there is no young generation of trees to replace the older ones.

Although he didn't specifically agree with Lowery's position, a Park Service naturalist told me fences may be put up to exclude deer from a few areas inside the Sunken Forest. In effect, this would create tiny islands protecting plant species from extinction and preserving "seed banks" for the future. "If the deer population drops, you can take the fences down and the plants will work their way out, which would keep Fire Island having a semblance of the natural processes when it comes to vegetation." To me, this sounded like an acknowledgment that Mark Lowery was right.

Studies in many parts of the country show that when heavy deer browsing depletes the forest understory, other wild animal species decline. Birds that nest or feed on the ground are much affected, along with small mammals, reptiles, amphibians, and invertebrates dependent on understory plants for food and cover. When researcher William McShea excluded whitetails from fenced areas in Virginia, he found that populations of squirrels, chipmunks, flying squirrels, and other small mammals increased by as much as 90 percent compared with surrounding tracts. Biologist David DeCalestra, working in Pennsylvania, discovered that songbirds like the indigo bunting, least flycatcher, eastern wood-peewee, yellow-billed cuckoo, and cerulean warbler completely disappeared from plots when deer numbers exceeded eight per square kilometer.

In other words, because people favor deer, creatures that are less charismatic but equally interesting and equally important to the natural community may become rare or locally extinct. This could well be the situation on Fire Island, where deer jeopardize biological diversity that the National Seashore was designated to preserve.

Why has the National Park Service chosen not to reduce or control Fire Island's whitetail population? Perhaps they're convinced that deer are not a serious problem or that a natural die-off will eventually reestablish balance. But they might also wish to avoid a controversy like the one some years back. In 1981, responding to landowner complaints about deer damage and to state biologists' recommendations, the Park Service scheduled a public hunt on Fire Island. For safety reasons, only 25 people were allowed to hunt, using archery equipment and being strictly limited to wild areas. They took just four whitetails, all in poor condition.

Afterward, deer numbers kept on growing, the animals were obviously malnourished, residents still complained, and concerns deepened about ecological damage. In 1988, a Fire Island landowner group requested that hunting be tried again, and the Park Service agreed. They decided to allow separate archery and firearms hunts for "research" purposes—requiring examination of all carcasses for nutritional condition, reproductive history, and presence of Lyme disease antibodies. But public notice of the hunt was like putting sparks to a fuse. People objected to killing deer, they worried about their own safety, and they garnered support from humane organizations, especially a group called Legal Action for Animals. "I think the animal rights people viewed this as a highly publicizable test case, very close to New York City with its big television and radio stations," said Mark Lowery.

Legal action by the animal rights organizations successfully shortened the archery hunt, so just 6 deer were killed; but firearms hunting went ahead as planned, adding 54 whitetails to the tally. From study of the carcasses, state biologists concluded that Fire Island's deer were in "extremely poor condition," and recommended taking at least 200 animals, possibly up to 300, to restore ecological balance. But there has never been another hunt on Fire Island and the deer population remains at or near an all-time high.

Mark acknowledged that before hunting was proposed more should have been done to educate people about deer populations, habitat damage, effective methods of control, and the safety of hunting near habitations. "People really have a lot of fears about hunters," said Lowery. "They're not so much *antihunting* as they are *antihunter,* meaning they're afraid of people carrying a bow or shotgun and wearing camouflage or blaze orange.

"There are no documented cases of a nonhunter being injured by a bow-and-arrow hunter in North America," he continued. "And even in areas as small as ten acres, we know from experience on Long Island that it's safe to hunt with shotguns. We've done that here in Suffolk County for twenty-three years, involving tens of thousands of hunters, and the one fatality we've had was self-inflicted." Mark Lowery believes hunting can be done safely on Fire Island, not just in wild areas but also near communities. Nevertheless, he makes clear that people themselves must decide what, if anything, they want to do about the deer situation.

After finishing our lunches, Mark and I relaxed on the seawall, comfortable in short sleeves, soaking up sunshine reflected from the waters of Great South Bay. A gleaming yacht paraded through the harbor entrance while gulls clucked and circled above. Although it felt like summer, our discussion turned toward the colder months ahead. Even during mild winters many whitetails die on Fire Island, Mark said. "In the sample areas we've surveyed, we've often found twenty-five or thirty-five carcasses. That gives us estimates of a hundred to a hundred fifty deer— twenty percent of the herd—starving to death or dying of nutrition-related causes each year."

The actual number may be higher. A woman told me that she and her husband counted 52 deer carcasses around and under houses in Davis Park and Ocean Ridge the previous spring. Starvation is unavoidable on Fire Island, where deer subsist through winter on poor browse like hardwood twigs and pitch pine needles. "In the literature, it's almost impossible to find references to deer eating pitch pine," Lowery declared, "yet this is a significant portion of the deer's diet on Fire Island. Pitch pine is a useless food with no nutritional value for deer—it would be like humans trying to live by eating cotton."

His analogy clanged like a bell inside my head. It had more impact than scientific data about malnutrition, winter mortality, threatened plant species, or habitat damage. Suddenly I realized how it might feel to be a starving deer. I kept thinking about it as Mark and I walked toward the ferry dock, on a bright October day that made winter and its hardships seem like an illusion.

The next morning, Bert Snyder and I talked about deer with some of his Fire Island neighbors. "There are so many of them," one man complained, "that you can't even eat a peanut butter sandwich on the deck because they all show up. But pruning the herd is just a sop for the hunting interests; I think scientists should be able to come up with a better solution."

A woman in her mid-twenties, who had summered here since childhood, felt otherwise. "A lot of folks come out from the city and it's the greatest thing in the world for them to see a deer. But you can't just pretend this problem will go away by itself, because it won't. That's why I absolutely favor hunting."

Almost everyone agreed that deer had become a serious problem, an impression confirmed in a 1990 survey conducted by Bob Spencer of Davis Park. Of approximately 1,500 seasonal and full-time residents who responded, 76 percent believed there was a deer problem, but 86 percent would have preferred to control it by nonlethal means, and 34 percent strongly opposed hunting. Only 24 percent of the residents strongly supported hunting, but 54 percent said they would support hunting if it were the only feasible way to reduce deer numbers.

Jim Pianta, a retired Texas oil company executive, had given the question a lot of thought. "I'd just as soon have deer in the wilderness area but not in the community," he said. "They ought to issue tags and shoot enough to thin them out."

The previous year, Jim had put cylindrical fences around small trees near his house to protect them from deer, and this summer he found crowds of holly seedlings—as many as six or eight per square foot—growing inside the enclosures, while not one seedling survived anywhere else. "There's no question that deer are eating all the young holly trees," he concluded. Jim pointed out some bigger trees killed when bucks tore away the bark by rubbing their antlers during the rut. Without protective fences, no seedlings could grow up to replace these lost trees, and of course it isn't feasible to install millions of little fences all over Fire Island. So right in Davis Park we found support for Mark Lowery's conclusion that deer browsing jeopardized the National Seashore's forests.

Although most people we visited were acutely aware of damage to their gardens and potted flowers, few seemed aware that whitetails seriously damage natural habitat outside the communities and that stripping of seashore vegetation might threaten the island itself. Signs of trouble could be seen everywhere—browse lines, severely hedged cedars, sparse understory plants, tree seedlings that survived only inside fences—but it took an attentive person like Jim to notice these cues and realize what they meant.

Slipping out early the next morning, I spotted seven does and a hefty 10-point buck, all within the first five minutes. Then I happened upon a very tame doe and noticed she had tiny bumps on both flanks. Eventually she allowed me close enough to gently touch her fur, and by parting the hairs I discovered each lump was the soft, distended body of an engorged tick with its head burrowed into the deer's hide. Most were common dog ticks swollen to the size of pinto beans, but a few were deer ticks not much larger than BB pellets after they filled up with blood. This doe carried at least 15 obvious ticks and perhaps many more hidden in her fur.

If any creature stirs greater attention than whitetails on Fire Island, it's the deer tick, *Ixodes scapularis*. This little crawler harbors a microscopic spirochete called *Borrelia burgdorferi*—the cause of Lyme disease in humans and some animals, especially dogs. Studies show that large populations of *Ixodes* ticks correlate with high numbers of deer, but interestingly, deer do not carry Lyme disease or suffer from it themselves, because the spirochete apparently cannot survive in their bodies. Lyme spirochetes thrive in the blood of wild rodents like the white-footed mouse, and they might also be carried by birds. Ticks in the nymph stage (when they're about the size of poppy seeds) acquire *Borrelia* spirochetes from the blood of small animals; then adult ticks pass the spirochetes along to larger mammals like ourselves. Deer are an important link in this chain, not as disease carriers but as hosts that feed ticks and carry them from one place to another.

Discussions of Lyme disease led me to Pat Sacco, a longtime Davis Park resident—friendly and talkative, with an energetic nature that made her age both indefinable and irrelevant. Pat looked strong and alert, but she had a distinctly uneven gait—the only visible evidence of a 15-year ordeal. "I have chronic Lyme disease that I got here on the island in 1976," she told me. "That was very early, before the doctors knew much about it."

The first warning of Lyme disease is a roughly circular "bull's-eye" rash that develops around the bite after a tick drops off (this symptom does not appear in about 30 percent of Lyme patients). After this, an infected person can develop a variety of symptoms, including fever, headache, malaise, and profound tiredness. Antibiotics are usually successful in these early stages, but they become less effective as time passes. In stubborn or untreated cases, the spirochete can spread throughout a person's body, causing all sorts of problems—meningitis, encephalitis, Bell's palsy, hearing loss, impaired vision, cardiac abnormalities, numb extremities, memory loss, and severe fatigue. Nowadays, early diagnosis and proper treatment keep most people from reaching the chronic stage, but even under the best circumstances, not everyone responds well to antibiotics.

Hers being among the earliest cases, Pat Sacco was thoroughly infected by the time of her diagnosis by a Lyme disease research team at nearby Stony Brook. She admitted it's not easy for her to discuss the subject anymore, and I understood why as she recounted years of struggle with the disease. "I remembered having a bull's-eye rash under my arm, but that wasn't diagnosed. When they finally knew what I had, the doctors did all they could; but still, I was a guinea pig and the wrong medicines were given to me."

Pat's case illustrated the twisted genius for masquerade that often leads to misdiagnosis of Lyme disease. "I've had about every symptom you can get, and they're recurrent," she said, describing episodes of pneumonia and virulent flu that she was less able to fight off because of her afflicted immune system. "There were lots of neurological problems. I used to be good with numbers, but now I invert them—even simple things like telephone numbers. I've also had short-term memory loss, and my eyes became very sensitive to brightness." Pat went through severe withdrawal after long-term massive doses of antibiotics intended to rid her body of the spirochete. "I passed out; my heart raced; I had a critical ambulance run to the hospital. It took six or seven months before I could straighten out and live my life again.

"When I was on the antibiotics everything was good—physically and psychologically. I almost didn't want to give it up, because when you do, suddenly your neck hurts, your elbows, your hands. These are all parts of the disease. With my ankle, the screaming pain would keep me up all night. Doctors didn't know what it was." Finally Pat had ankle surgery, but she spent 18 months on crutches because the surgery refused to heal. Continuing Lyme disease eroded the bone and formed calcium deposits that essentially fused her ankle joint.

From time to time in our discussion, Pat mentioned the nearly unbearable stress that accumulated during her struggle, yet there was no hint of pathos in her voice. A tough, earthy, no-nonsense woman, she seemed to be venting frustration with an invisible microbe that had wrought havoc in her life. For some years now, she'd kept things under control, mostly by the force of will and determination. She was "off" antibiotics, a concept I'd usually associated with alcohol or other dangerous drugs. And she no longer attended the Lyme disease support group that had helped to keep her going in earlier years.

Of course, Pat still worries about ticks and takes precautions to avoid another infection. "Each night I check myself in the shower or in front of a mirror, to make sure there's no ticks or bites. My neighbor across the boardwalk, she had a tick bite. When I told her she'd better get herself over to the doctor, she said she'd never taken a pill in her life. I just said, 'Well, you'd better take it now.'"

I wondered how Pat, after what she'd been through, felt about the deer. "You know, I don't love them like a lot of people do," she replied. For a long moment she stared out the window. "But if worst came to worst and they were starving, I suppose I'd put food out for them."

At dawn the following day, I saw a shadowy figure near the edge of Davis Park. Someone else taking an early stroll, I thought, but then I recognized the shape—a white-tailed buck, his antlers silhouetted against pallid sky. Foggy coos of a mourning dove sifted through the stillness as the deer walked casually toward me, ignoring the age-old rules of encounter between human and deer.

Then he stopped in front of the first house, and in a clatter most unbecoming of his kind, nimbly capsized the garbage can and nuzzled its contents. I moved toward him, pausing when he raised his head to watch, abiding my instinct—or perhaps my desire—that he'd recover his wildness and slip away. Eventually I came within 15 feet, near enough to identify his menu of sliced zucchini, baked potato, and buttered French bread flecked with garlic.

"It happens every morning." I jerked involuntarily, startling the deer and perhaps the hoarse-throated woman as well. Cup in hand, wearing a quilted robe, she leaned on the rail of a porch stilted six feet above the ground. "They know exactly where people are going to put out garbage and how to get at it."

The buck drifted toward her backyard. "A few years ago they'd take off if you whistled or banged pots," the woman observed. "But now you've got to throw a stick or rock at them, and still they won't go far. I feel sorry for the deer, and I don't like to think about them being hungry, yet it's not a good idea to feed them. Some deer are probably going to starve to death in the winter, but that's the balance of nature—when times get rough, the animals die."

I'd heard the same thing from one of the National Seashore's resource specialists, who suggested starvation would bring deer numbers down next time a severe winter came along. Many people seemed to share his view—that starvation is a normal and even benign fact of life in the wild. Let "nature" eliminate a problem that we helped to create but haven't the will, heart, or conscience to solve. And because it happens, conveniently, during winter, people are spared witnessing the protracted, inexorable brutality of starvation.

Some other islanders brought up an age-old "solution" for the deer problem—providing food through the winter months. This is altogether different from recreational feeding by summer folks hoping to entice deer within close range or keep them around the yard. One woman, who shared handfuls of grapes with a deer as we talked, suggested tapping Fire Island's tourism revenue to supply artificial feed. This was not a common opinion, however, apparently because people realize large-scale feeding is prohibitively expensive, can have lethal effects on deer's digestion, and perpetuates or worsens overpopulation problems rather than solving them.

Some residents suggested introducing predatory animals to control the herd "naturally." Fire Island's only predator, the red fox, is much too small to prey on deer. Adding a different twist to the debate, a New York City law professor had proposed release on the island of 60 mountain lions—just short of 10 per square mile or about 1 lion for every 10 deer. Although cougars are masterful predators, especially on deer, they aren't always safe around the neighborhood. In recent years, mountain lion predation on dogs and cats has become almost commonplace in some western states, and humans have been fatally attacked in California and Colorado. Whether or not this affected people's response, the mountain lion proposal found a swift and well-deserved oblivion.

I was intrigued that so many people considered four-legged predators and starvation "natural" and therefore acceptable ways to control deer numbers, but they judged human predation "unnatural" and therefore unacceptable. Perhaps this reflects a tendency to separate ourselves from the rest of nature, as if we were exempt from the biological processes that sustain our fellow creatures. These processes most vitally include death, the means by which life passes from one organism to another, creating the intricate web of connections among all creatures. Of course, this includes ourselves—whether the deaths that keep us alive are carried out by our own hand, or by the gardener's, the farmer's, the rancher's, the fisherman's, the hunter's.

Humans are not merely observers of the Fire Island ecosystem; we stand among its dominant, participating members. And whether deer on the island die from starvation, predation, or some other means, including hunting—people will play a role in those deaths. If this is "unnatural," it's also an inescapable condition of our existence, as certain as sunrise. I can't help wondering why a relatively slow death by predation or an even slower demise by starving is easier for many of us to accept than a far quicker death at human hands. People might feel differently if they came to Fire Island in late winter to see deer become emaciated, lose the strength to walk, and die with opened eyes among the houses.

Another suggestion I often heard from Fire Islanders is to trap the whitetails and release them somewhere else. But even if most survived the trauma of relocation, it's virtually impossible to find new homes for them in the eastern United States. In Ipswich, Massachusetts, for example, officials at the Crane Memorial Reservation and Crane Wildlife Refuge carefully considered relocation as a way to reduce a severe whitetail overpopulation, but they learned that there are legal obstacles to moving deer across state lines, the logistics are expensive and difficult, and the few places with room for more deer are not interested in taking animals known to carry ticks that transmit Lyme disease.

Perhaps Fire Island's excess deer could be trapped and humanely euthanized. But even if people accepted this approach, it's very expensive, injecting deadly chemicals is dangerous for people, and meat from the animals would be toxic to humans and wildlife. There are also questions of conscience, because captured deer inevitably experience terror before they die. In this context, Dale McCullough has written, "We know that in the hands of an expert, a high-powered rifle shot to the brain or upper neck is instantly fatal. We must have the moral and ethical courage to look beyond our own psychological preferences, and squarely confront which method is in fact most humane to the animal."

In some places, professional shooters have been hired to reduce over-abundant deer. On the 1,200-acre University of Wisconsin Arboretum in Madison, for example, marksmen using bait and shooting from elevated stands remove 25 to 35 whitetails each year. This program has weathered objections from animal rights activists and from anonymous opponents who threatened to cut down one living tree for each deer killed in the arboretum. In fact, several rare and valuable trees were destroyed, but despite these problems, shooters have kept the arboretum's deer population in check.

If Fire Island's whitetails were ever to be culled, it's likely that Park Service marksmen—not ordinary licensed hunters—would do the shooting. However, animals become wary and hard to find once they're hunted, so it could take months for a small number of sharpshooters to remove enough animals from the herd, making this approach logistically difficult and costly. By contrast, public hunting concentrates many shooters on the land for a very short time, so it generally brings high success at little cost.

Closely regulated public hunting has been used to control deer in many wildland preserves around the United States. A good example is the program operated since 1970 in Millbrook, New York, at the Mary Flagler Cary Arboretum and its research branch, the Institute for Ecosystems Studies. The arboretum's 2,000 acres of forest, meadows, and horticultural gardens are dedicated to environmental research and education. Raymond Winchcombe, who directs the hunting program, explained that biologists monitor whitetail numbers and habitat to decide how many deer should be taken each year. A limited number of permits are issued to hunters who first pass a shooting proficiency test, agree to follow the rules, always maintain high ethical standards, and have reasonable success in taking deer. Deer population control hinges on the number of females, so Winchcombe emphasizes that hunters must take does as well as bucks. He also makes clear that ecological management—not providing subsistence or recreation—is the sole reason that hunting is allowed on the Cary Arboretum.

Before 1970 the arboretum was severely overbrowsed and deer were dying of starvation, but since that time hunters have taken 65 to 85 deer from the reserve each fall. As a result, whitetails now cause little habitat damage even in severe winters, the natural environment is diverse and thriving, and deer examined at the hunter check-in stations are in good to excellent condition.

"To control the deer population in a place like this," Winchcombe explained, "you have to remove a certain number of animals each and every year. Say you've got one hundred deer in a specific area. After fawns are born it's up around a hundred fifty, and that's about what you'll have in November. If you're going to stabilize that population you need to remove fifty deer, bringing it back down to one hundred animals. Next fall you'll have one hundred fifty again, and the process starts over. In biological terms, recruitment and mortality must balance.

"So when I talk about deer problems I ask people, how do you want to do it? Do you want to have the deer run over by cars? Do you want to kill them with poison? Do you want to put them in boxes and send them someplace else? Or do you want to hunt them? Those are your choices. Pick a method and then find out what it costs. If you're serious about controlling the deer population, that's what has to happen." Ray Winchcombe is convinced that closely managed public hunting is the most practical way to keep deer in balance with their habitat, and often it's the only way that works.

Biologists are developing an overall strategy for deer management in national park areas throughout the eastern United States, and this could affect Fire Island National Seashore. But no matter what choice is made, it's probably going to stir up conflict. However, new information could change people's attitudes and allow them to see that something must be done, especially if they recognize the potential impact of deer eating shoreline vegetation. Without a protective cloak of grasses, shrubs, and trees, Fire Island becomes increasingly vulnerable to storm swells that undercut the shore and tumble houses into the surf, swells that could breach the island itself, opening new channels to Great South Bay and threatening the barrier that protects Long Island's shore.

On Fire Island, I had noticed carefully tended plantings of grass in front of shoreside houses, where people were trying to stabilize the sandy slopes. I had also trekked in natural woodlands and meadows along wave-cut banks, and here I saw mats of densely interwoven roots that looked like threads holding this delicate ribbon of sand together. Overcrowded deer will eat almost anything to keep themselves alive, and in the process they can seriously damage the island's fragile but essential plant cover. I can't imagine a more powerful illustration of the intricate balance between a wild animal and its habitat.

Nowadays, when other possibilities for limiting deer populations have either failed or been rejected, birth control is sure to come up, as it did time and again during my visit to Fire Island. If contraception ever succeeded, it would preserve the lives of individual animals while eventually reducing the overall deer population. It also has the allure of an experimental method, giving hope of success where everything else has failed. Furthermore, regulating deer populations with chemical birth control could be the proverbial and elusive "better mousetrap."

The abandoned sterilization project on Angel Island had required capturing and anesthetizing deer, then surgically implanting a contraceptive that would last several years. On Fire Island, beginning in 1993, a volunteer team led by Dr. Jay Kirkpatrick and assisted by the National Park Service undertook a different approach to sterilization, using a newly developed immunocontraceptive drug called Porcine Zona Pellucida. This study's only purpose was to learn if deer could be sterilized without capture or restraint; it was *not* billed as an effort to bring the whitetail population under control. Blowguns were used to shoot hypodermic darts into docile animals from a distance of 5 or 10 feet, and a darting rifle with slightly longer range was used to inject a few skittish deer.

According to researchers, 95 percent of the wild horses treated with this drug in Assateague Island National Seashore (off the Maryland and Virginia coast), were successfully sterilized, and tests on captive deer were similarly promising. But the contraceptive takes full effect only when animals have been injected twice, several weeks apart, so it's necessary to find and identify each deer for the second treatment. On Fire Island, neighborhood volunteers knew the deer well enough to identify them — a very rare situation. In most places, treated animals would have to be tagged, which adds the major step of catching or immobilizing them.

Infertility lasts about a year after the two injections of Porcine Zona Pellucida, then requires annual booster shots, so it's only practical for deer tame enough to let people come very close. Also, treated does will come into estrus three or four times each fall, compared to once or twice in untreated animals. This could greatly prolong the rut, extending to several months the period when bucks fast and deplete themselves, diminishing their chances to survive winter.

Newspaper reports about the Fire Island project have been enthusiastic and many of the treated animals have not given birth to fawns. But wildlife officials caution that final results won't be available for years. "Less than twenty-five percent of the does on Fire Island have been treated so far," Mark Lowery told me, "which means three quarters are still fertile, and presumably most of those will produce fawns each year. Also, even if you did reduce the population in one area, other deer might come in to replace them, especially with the severe food pressure they're under. Dr. Kirkpatrick hasn't claimed that they're going to control the deer population on Fire Island, but people believe this is what's happening."

It's one thing to show that a contraceptive works on individual animals, but it's quite another to control an entire deer population. The ambitious, well-organized Angel Island sterilization project failed because workers could not capture and treat enough animals—this on an isolated patch of land measuring just one square mile. The method being tried on Fire Island doesn't involve trapping, but it requires multiple injections and annual boosters given at very close range. And the daunting problem of overall population control remains the same.

Also, if most of the does on Fire Island could be sterilized, deer numbers would decline very slowly, bringing no immediate relief for depleted plant and wildlife species. On Assateague Island, said Mark Lowery, the horse population remained excessively high after sterilization, and damage to natural vegetation continued. Because of this, Mark wondered if the Assateague project could legitimately be called a success.

Many people on Fire Island consider Lyme disease the most important reason to control deer numbers. Here again, it's essential to remember the delayed effects of contraception. "Assuming you could sterilize about eighty percent of the doe population every year," Mark explained, "it would take five or six years before natural attrition even began to reduce the deer. And research indicates that *after* you get the deer population to a relatively low level, it takes several more years before the tick population starts to decline. So with deer contraception, it would take a decade or two before you'd see a reduction in ticks that carry Lyme disease."

Mark Lowery points out that the best way to make sterilization work is to reduce the deer population first. In fact, he'd recently heard a humane organization official recommend using "lethal methods" to bring deer numbers down before starting with contraceptives. This suggests that people with different viewpoints are coming closer to agreement.

If Fire Island's whitetail population were brought under control by contraception, it would gain wide notice among people struggling with deer problems in similar situations all over North America. On the other hand, if sterilization fails, this news would get little attention, meaning the same experiment would be tried again, and yet again. And the search for a miracle would continue.

Fire Island's residents have a powerful influence on management of the National Seashore. Ideally, people who care about the island would make an effort to learn how deer are damaging its environment and would base their opinions about population control on knowledge, as well as ethical judgment and emotional sensibility. Few Americans are this closely involved with deer and few are in a better position than Fire Islanders to become educated about them—whitetails haunt natural areas surrounding the settlements, browse outside living-room windows, eat from people's hands, give birth and mate and die in plain sight of passersby. Furthermore, deer overpopulation and alternatives for dealing with it have been simmering issues here for over a decade. Yet the answer remains elusive on Fire Island, as in so many other places.

Sitting alone, my jacket pulled tight against the October chill, I watched Fire Island recede over the ferry's churning wake, and I reflected on dozens of encounters with the island's companionable whitetails, savoring the rare gift of nearness to a wild creature. And yet, while these deer move freely across the borders between forest and village, they have not become like cats and dogs who share our intimate lives. As far as I could tell, the deer were drawn to people only by hunger—a hunger we've helped to create by changing their natural surroundings, by exterminating animals like wolves and cougars, and by eliminating ourselves as predators, allowing their population to stress the ecological limits.

Fire Island's whitetails have come to us, but on their own terms. I remembered a day earlier, when I'd eased close to a hefty eight-point buck and thoughtlessly put my hand on his back. Taking it as a challenge, the deer raked his gleaming tines across my belly, then did it once more for emphasis. This whitetail could have punctured my hide like a sheet of paper, and if it had been the height of November's rut he might have done just that. I also recalled a group of does and fawns on a road in the National Seashore, bursting away with their flag-tails high, clouds of sand flinging from their hooves. As they vanished, I realized that although we share a world, we share it in separate ways.

As we approached Patchogue, Fire Island sank down to a thin line, dissipating like a fog bank at the far edge of Great South Bay. I remembered the last deer I'd seen that morning, a doe with her fawn bedded in a grove of holly and sassafras trees within the National Seashore. When I came slowly toward them, the fawn shied away, but the doe munched on a leafy shrub as if I were irrelevant. I moved slowly closer, knelt within an arm's reach, listened to the sound of her breaths, and gazed into her lovely obsidian eyes.

During those moments, I knew that wildness simmered at the root of her mind, pooled in her belly, ran through her like the blood inside her veins. And I realized this: when it comes to deer, wildness is the greatest truth. And tameness is a tender, innocent lie.

FIVE

THE BACKYARD WILDERNESS

In my opinion they are rats with antlers, roaches with split hooves, denizens of the dark primeval suburbs. Deer intensely suggest New Jersey. . . . I once saw a buck with a big eight-point rocking-chair rack looking magnificent as he stood between two tractor-trailers in the Frito-Lay parking lot in New Brunswick, New Jersey.

—JOHN McPHEE

The Gentle Invasion

Few events in the history of North American wildlife have been so remarkable, so unexpected, and so provocative of conflict as the rise of suburban deer. In some places, as city waistlines spread into the countryside, deer have held their own instead of fleeing to rural lands that are already overcrowded with their own kind. And in other places, deer from the outlands have gradually colonized our neighborhoods, their trails weaving like veins of wildness through the geometry of backyards, greenways, and roads.

Nowadays, deer have taken up residence in scores, perhaps hundreds, of towns and cities around the United States and Canada—places like Eugene, Oregon; Orinda, California; Austin, Texas; Madison, Wisconsin; Columbus, Ohio; Minneapolis, Minnesota; Chicago, Illinois; Portland,

Maine; Rochester, New York; Missoula, Montana; Greenwich, Connecticut; Princeton, New Jersey; Orcas Island, Washington; Philadelphia, Pennsylvania; Savannah, Georgia; Washington, D.C.

In much of the Northeast, farmlands abandoned over the past century have transformed into unbroken, regenerating forest that shades out the understory vegetation deer rely on for food. Surprisingly, new home building helps compensate for this loss by creating thousands of openings with rich undergrowth around their edges, not to mention the enticements of nutritious flowers, ornamental shrubs, and vegetable gardens. In this way, settlement at the urban edge diversifies habitat, allowing higher deer populations than a uniform, second-growth forest could sustain. To take advantage of the situation, deer must change only one thing—their fear of humans. And as millions of residents can attest, they've certainly done that.

The common pattern of deer gradually "invading" suburban neighborhoods begins when wild or rural areas outside the city become densely populated with deer, a situation widely prevalent east of the Mississippi. According to William Ishmael, a wildlife biologist with the Wisconsin Department of Natural Resources, a few pioneer animals from the countryside enter the suburban fringe. Often these are year-old deer driven away by their mothers who are getting ready to have this year's fawns. In eastern and midwestern states, the newly independent youngsters roam especially during May and June, looking for groups willing to accept them.

Some of these drifters choose the only habitat not already occupied by deer—along the city's margin. Impelled by boldness, hunger, or naïveté, they ease in among the houses, often following river courses, park strips, railroads, or other wooded corridors, and sometimes retreating every day to nearby farmlands or woodlots. Every year, young animals ousted by their mothers move deeper into the humanized environment, founding resident herds and creating what Ishmael calls an "urban deer tradition." For the first 20, 30, or even 40 years, the deer slowly increase—as happens whenever an animal moves into vacant habitat—but at some point the population grows large enough to trigger a highly accelerated growth rate.

Urban deer in North America reflect the simultaneous population explosions of two species: theirs and ours. The transformation of natural landscapes into lawns and parks, streets and buildings, has created a tough choice for deer, who must either face overcrowded habitats outside of town or infiltrate the foreign and frenetic sphere of humankind. The outcome is a remarkable and still-unfolding chapter in our continent's wildlife history. Consider that by 1991 an estimated 1,500 whitetails lived within the city limits of Philadelphia. This is more than the total number of deer inhabiting the entire state of Pennsylvania in 1900.

Although deer are gaining urban survival skills, they're less than perfectly adapted to the new surroundings, as city dwellers have sometimes discovered in startling ways. For example, in Colonie, New York, a whitetail smashed through the window of a clothing store, dashed around the aisles and among the customers, then plunged through another window, hurdled a car on nearby Route 7, and vanished into the woods. A couple in Fitchburg, Wisconsin, awoke face-to-face with an 80-pound doe who had just crashed through their apartment's bedroom window. After a tumultuous hour-and-a-half stalemate, humane officers tranquilized and killed the badly lacerated animal. Two years before this, a whitetail had turned up inside the central rotunda of Wisconsin's state capitol building located in the concrete heart of Madison.

Deer also have a terribly flawed comprehension of motor vehicles, leading to a deadly epidemic of collisions in many American cities. In Westchester County, New York, a woman told me: "We've got deer everywhere and you never know when they'll dash out in front of you. People don't realize how big a deer is until it's coming over the hood of their car." In fact, a driver had been killed nearby when a heavy-antlered buck crashed through her windshield.

Even more perilous are encounters between deer and commercial jets. As of 1991, for instance, eight whitetails had been struck by planes at Dulles International Airport in Washington, D.C. Confronted with similar troubles, officials in Baltimore and Philadelphia have used sharpshooters to keep deer off the runways. Marksmen also came in after a jet hit a whitetail buck during takeoff from Chicago's O'Hare Airport in 1982, but when people objected to shooting deer, O'Hare started trapping animals and releasing them out of harm's way.

Conflicts with deer around human settlements are not entirely new. Almost 200 years ago, George Washington wrote from his Mount Vernon home:

> The gardener complains heavily of the injury which he sustained from my halfwit, halftame deer; and I do not well know what course to take with them. . . . Two methods have occurred, one or both combined, may, possibly, keep them out of the gardens & lawns; namely, to get a couple of rounds & whenever they are seen in, or near those places, to

fire at them with a shot of a small kind that would make them smart, but neither kill or maim them. If this will not keep them at a distance, I must kill them in good earnest, as the lesser evil of the two.

Nowadays, we apply the full virtuosity of human imagination to repelling deer or excluding them from valuable, delicate, and otherwise sanctified areas around our homes. Garden plants and ornamentals are festooned with all manner of repellents ranging from human hair to rotten eggs, from lion dung to chemical decoctions. There are fences of every imaginable style: netting draped over flower beds, wire cylinders around bushes and saplings, tall metal fences enclosing gardens or whole yards, electrically charged wire strands arranged in geometric configurations, opaque wooden walls that look like fortifications, and combinations of these designed for every preference or need.

Other discouragements include planting garden species unpalatable to deer (in many areas, lists are available from local agencies), using scarecrow devices like shiny floating balloons, and furtively deploying slingshots or pellet guns from opened windows. Roadways have inspired another assortment of remedies including signs, fences, underpasses, and special reflectors, as well as car attachments like warning whistles and elaborate protective bumpers.

If these and additional measures fall short—as they generally do—the next step is to control or reduce the deer population. This brings hunting into the discussion, which usually incites passionate arguments and, more often than not, cracks the fragile shell of civility. Many a neighborhood friendship has ended in arguments about the deer frequenting people's yards or differences of opinion about hunting as a way to solve the problem. Leaving philosophical differences aside, public hunting can work very well to control numbers of deer in the urban fringe or the woodsy commuter outlands. By far the most effective approach is to open a firearms season, restricted for safety purposes to limited-range shotguns. Allowing only bow-and-arrow hunting is the least effective approach because there aren't enough archers and their success rate is very low.

In New York's Westchester County, for example, hunting limited to archery equipment has failed to contain the growing and increasingly troublesome whitetail population, despite very liberal regulations meant to encourage as much hunting as possible. Even though Westchester lies within easy commuting distance of Manhattan, most of the county offers excellent habitat for deer, and one very important element of this habitat is the security offered by private tracts of land, ranging from huge parks and estates down to small wooded lots. A good share of these lands are strictly posted against hunting, which creates literally thousands of de facto refuges scattered throughout the county. And as any wildlife biologist will tell you, deer are smart enough to use them when the season opens.

Some communities, especially those densely settled with people as well as deer, have hired professional sharpshooters, who can situate themselves in carefully selected spots, hunt only during specified times of the day or night, and shoot from elevated stands over bait stations. However safe and effective this method is, it may not assuage public resistance to the whole idea of killing familiar animals of the streetside and backyard.

Seeking compromise and harmony, people in neighborhoods with deer problems tend to hang their hopes on sterilization, which has yet to become practical, or on the persistent myth that urban deer can be successfully relocated. As a noted wildlife ecologist from the University of California told me, "Nowadays, the nonlethal approaches are 'politically correct,' and biological realities have little to do with it."

Trapping overabundant urban deer and releasing them in the countryside is largely, though not entirely, a recent practice. In the 1950s, close to a hundred deer were captured in Griffith Park, near the center of Los Angeles, and taken to a more suitable rural home. The cost of $59 per head was judged impractically high at the time; and biologists concluded that most of California was already filled to capacity with deer, leaving few suitable places to release urban deportees.

Forty years later, in 1992, officials faced an overpopulation of blacktailed deer in Ardenwood Historic Farm, a 200-acre suburban park at the south end of San Francisco Bay. After the usual debates over culling and sterilization, state biologists yielded to public pressure and agreed to transplant animals to the nearby Ohlone wilderness, but only if the deer were closely monitored to evaluate their adjustment. Experienced technicians captured 29 deer; two died of stress during the 20-mile trailer ride and the others were released wearing radio collars. Tracking their daily movements, researchers discovered one carcass after another, and within six weeks most of the animals were dead.

Accustomed to urban surroundings and unfamiliar with the new landscape, some relocated deer got in the way of trains or had other fatal accidents, and many fell prey to mountain lions. A biologist from California's Department of Fish and Game speculated that a single lion, or perhaps a mother with cubs, could have taken most of the animals. "It was probably a benefit to the resident deer," he suggested. "With those newcomers around, a predator wouldn't have to rely on catching wilder, smarter animals—not until the supply of tame deer ran out." Which it did soon enough. Not one of the relocated blacktails survived.

As this study revealed, efforts to deal humanely with urban deer often fail or cause unexpected suffering. Of course, many people would rather we just leave deer alone, but as their numbers multiply, so do the problems they create, and eventually people's tolerance wavers. Mark Ellingwood, a New Hampshire wildlife biologist widely experienced with urban deer, summarized the decay of attitudes: "People tend to love the deer when they're scarce, like them when they're common, and hate them when they're overabundant."

After trying for years to deal with rural and suburban whitetail populations, Glen Cole, a regional wildlife manager for the state of New York, suggested it might be time to consider a radical solution: round up large numbers of deer, confine them on licensed game farms, and use them commercially for venison as well as other products. Cole had serious ethical reservations about fencing wild animals and selling their meat, and he noted that taking whitetails for commercial use is prohibited by New York law (although deer farming is allowed if the animals are born and raised in captivity). Yet he concluded, "If the deer population keeps increasing, if antihunting sentiment grows, if there are continuing problems with damage, and if people's health or safety are jeopardized, this might be our only way of dealing with it."

A Movable Beast

River Hills, Wisconsin, is a quintessential American "woodburb"—fine homes on expansive forested lots, country-style mailboxes atop painted wooden posts, and long private driveways. The bucolic surroundings create an illusion of distance from all things urban or sullied, despite the fact that downtown Milwaukee is just 20 minutes away. Measuring a bit over five square miles, with about 1,500 citizens, it's officially known as the Village of River Hills—a title carrying psychological as well as administrative weight. To preserve the community's spaciousness and sense of privacy, zoning on about 75 percent of the land requires a five-acre minimum lot size.

And if you drive around in the morning or evening, you're almost sure to encounter the community's leading cause of social and political strife—white-tailed deer. The guide on my first tour was Beverly Bryant, a University of Wisconsin graduate student writing her master's thesis on River Hills deer.

Back in the mid-1980s, Bev recalled, villagers started complaining about deer problems, so a committee was established to look for solutions. Unlike many towns, River Hills could afford whatever choice the residents preferred, and they had enough political clout to assure sympathetic attention from government agencies. In 1987, the village started trapping deer each winter and releasing them out in the country. To compare the movements and survival of transplanted deer against those remaining in River Hills, biologists fitted about a dozen whitetails with radio collars and simply turned them loose where they'd been caught. Beverly Bryant had tracked these animals around the village for a year and a half while she also documented the fate of deportees.

Bev and I rode in her mid-sixties American sedan, ambulance white, a push-button automatic shift on the dash—potentially a classic but conspicuous in the company of BMWs, Jaguars, and Mercedes. "It was worse during the study," she explained. "I had this weird antenna on the roof that I used for locating radio-collared deer, and I'd be creeping along the roads, which meant everyone had to pass. People definitely wondered what I was up to."

Bev's work thoroughly acquainted her with the village's gridwork of narrow roads and with every stretch of woods, every yard and meadow, even the favorite haunts of individual deer. Nevertheless, she wasn't sure we'd find any whitetails at midday during the greenest time of year, when animals are very hard to see. Whatever happened, I would at least get a sense for the community.

Houses, when we could see them at all, were distinguished by their hulking dimensions. Most evident were the newer dwellings, especially those built in open fields like monoliths looming above the Wisconsin flatlands. These places—many of them owned by freshly affluent younger people—had an overbearingly prosperous ambience, crisp and polished and thinly gilded, like a pretentious wine of very recent vintage. We ventured up private drives to peer at older homes cloistered on huge wooded tracts. These, of course, belonged to people with deeply rooted wealth, who could afford stately houses valued, in some cases, at well over a million dollars.

Whitetails couldn't hope to find a better combination of wooded and open habitats than we saw in River Hills, plus they had complete protection from hunting and an absence of four-legged predators. "These animals don't move around much," said Bev, "especially the does. Some will stay on four or five residents' property all year round, probably for years on end." Although it's against a village ordinance, there were home owners who set up elaborate deer feeders or enticed the animals with food supposedly put out for birds. This might explain why the deer seem to have abnormally small home ranges and an artificially high population.

According to state biologists, River Hills could support a healthy population of 15 to 20 deer per square mile—a total of about 75 animals—without damaging the natural vegetation or straining people's tolerance. But in fact there have been 250 or more deer at times over the past decade, and they would increase if nothing were done to keep them in check.

Southern Wisconsin has a tremendous natural carrying capacity for deer, with densities of 50 to 100 per square mile not only possible but inevitable without strict control. Despite intensive hunting, the state's whitetail population hit a record 1.5 million animals in 1995, and it's still growing. Deer have begun spilling like floodwaters into every accessible niche, and cities are the equivalent of high ground, barely out of reach. Such places as River Hills, a bit lower on the flanks, couldn't levee themselves against the influx even if they wanted to.

In 1988, a year after live trapping began, the village board approved a plan to have professional marksmen shoot whitetails from elevated platforms situated above bait stations, an approach that's been used safely and effectively in other areas. However, a coalition of residents and animal rights groups erupted in protest. "In my opinion, the so-called marksmen are doing nothing more than murdering a magnificent animal," one activist lamented. "What's next?" asked another. "The geese? Raccoons? Should we shoot everything that isn't perfect?"

Articles and editorials jammed the newspapers, bringing attention to the controversy from all quarters, even from distant states. There were plenty of advocates for culling—folks who either saw it as the most practical approach or who didn't care what was done as long as it got deer out of their yards and roadways. Among the letters that poured into village offices were several hundred from people volunteering their services as sharpshooters. One River Hills citizen, who perhaps took things into his own hands or could not resist temptation, was charged with shooting a buck in his own yard that weighed 205 pounds after field dressing and carried an extraordinary 20-point rack measuring almost 27 inches across. Although it was described by an official of the Boone and Crockett Club as a "world-class animal," clouded circumstances would keep this one out of the record books.

Across the battlefield stood folks who advocated continuing relocation, experimenting with birth control, or trying assorted miracle cures.
One letter suggested that sprinkling urine from captive lions, tigers, and
wolves around the village would permanently frighten deer out into the
countryside. Another proposed: "Let them pipe to the deer with enchanting music and let them walk away peacefully to their haunts in the
wild where there are no drunken drivers and where God still adjusts the
balance of nature." Many also urged electing a new village board or using
whatever means possible to get rid of the present one. Curiously, some
folks who advocated nonviolence toward deer suggested the opposite toward village board members.

In the end, plans for a shooting program were dropped, ostensibly because of liability insurance problems, not because of ethics or elections.

Meanwhile, in an attempt to control the rapidly multiplying herd,
River Hills kept on transplanting. During the winters of 1988–89 and
1989–90, workers moved about 120 animals to state wildlife areas. Overall, the deer fared poorly, beginning with a death rate of about 20 percent
from capture trauma (which can kill deer a week or more after they're released). Every transplanted animal had an ear tag with an identifying
number, and 24 of them wore radio collars. Closely tracking the collared
animals, Beverly Bryant and her colleague William Ishmael found that
83 percent were dead within a year—killed mainly by hunters and car accidents (average survival was 185 days). By comparison, whitetails back in
River Hills died at a rate of 17 percent per year.

"You have to wonder," Bev mused. "Why continue to relocate deer if
they're just going to be hit by a car or shot by a hunter? Those might not
be easy deaths, whereas animals shot from a stand will die instantly. It
just seems to me that they're casting the blood on someone else's hand."

The deer's urban habits also caused problems after they'd been moved.
"The Department of Natural Resources immediately started getting calls
from people around the release sites," Bev remembered. "They'd say: 'I've
got this deer with a red tag in its ear, eating my shrubs.' One doe was
hanging out in people's gardens and standing around on the highway.
The warden wanted to shoot her because of the hazard and complaints,
but a bow hunter got her instead. Another deer ended up in West Bend,
living in a city park surrounded by houses, until she got hit by a car."

State biologists took a dim view of releasing dispossessed animals in
rural areas that already had dense whitetail populations. Perhaps this is
why, in 1991, the village decided to trap deer, deliver them to a slaughter-
house, and donate the meat to needy people. But after reporters learned

that 10 captured animals had been killed with blows to the head, activists held a pre-Christmas candlelight vigil and aroused a major public outcry. "The village board backed down immediately," Bev remembered. "No more shooting stations, no more euthanasia."

Just then Bev hit the brakes and pointed: "There's a deer right now, up in that yard." Like many biologists who spend months or years studying deer, she had a very sharp eye. At last I saw the animal, a willowy doe standing under a tree surrounded by undulating velvet lawn. Bev immediately recognized the deer and said this one had raised fawns during the past two summers, although none seemed to be around today. The animal stared suspiciously, flipping her tail back and forth, stamping one forefoot, ready to bolt if we stepped from the car. "They're not completely tame," Bev noted, "just habituated to being around people and activity." Finally the doe lowered her head to snuffle in the grass for acorns, and we left her to feed in peace.

As we eased away, I thought of my home on the North Pacific coast, where blacktail deer drift like mist through the wildlands, alert for hunters stalking the muskegs and for brown bears lurking in the forest—the world as it has been for millennia. What a contrast to these suburban whitetails, thriving amid hedges and lawn chairs and artfully arranged trees, where automobiles were the only predators.

A few minutes later we drove a stretch of Brown Deer Road, six busy lanes cutting through River Hills. "Every year, twenty-five or thirty deer get killed in the village, mostly along this road and another like it," said Bev. "The highest year, I think, was thirty-nine; but probably a lot more than that are hit." A police officer in adjacent Mequon had gone to the hospital with a broken nose and facial lacerations after a deer he struck careened through the squad car's windshield. The vehicle—equipped with a high-pitched whistle that's supposed to warn deer or frighten them away—was a total loss.

Studies by the Wisconsin Department of Natural Resources show that the popular "deer whistles" don't seem to work, because whitetails pay little attention to the sound even at close range. The best way to avoid hitting deer, experts say, is to drive slowly especially around dusk and dawn, and always keep a sharp watch for movement or eye-shines along the roadside.

In River Hills and throughout Wisconsin, collisions are among the most obvious indicators of high deer populations. Back in 1961, when deer were scarce by present standards, official reports counted fewer than 400 deer killed by cars on the state's roads. Just 30 years later, in the

1990s, the number had soared to between 35,000 and 50,000 whitetails killed annually, and the actual figure could be much higher, since injured deer often get away from the highway before dying. By the mid-1990s, about 15 percent of all Wisconsin car accidents involved deer, injuring almost 800 people each year. Luckily, these mishaps seldom caused human fatalities. According to the Wisconsin insurance industry, claims for vehicle damage alone average $1,500 for each deer collision, and the total amount claimed for property damage and personal injury now approaches $100 million annually. It even costs the state of Wisconsin about $200,000 every year just to pick up deer carcasses along the highways and haul them to dumps.

Aside from danger on the roads, River Hills home owners complain that browsing whitetails ruin thousands of dollars' worth of ornamental shrubs and flowers, and many have demanded that something be done. They also worry that congregations of deer could be harming wildflowers, forests, and other natural plant communities on large tracts of private land in the village. Some residents have cited Lyme disease as another reason to bring deer numbers down; but in fact, very few cases have been reported around Milwaukee or eastern Wisconsin, although the disease is a serious problem a couple hundred miles away in the western parts of the state.

Beverly Bryant summarized community attitudes this way: "Some people are very set on having certain plants in their yard, or maybe they've hit a deer, or they've got some other concern—and they're saying, 'Let's quit all this fiddle-faddling around and shoot the deer.' But other people really have no problem with deer and they just want the animals left alone. I also think there's people who really aren't troubled about the deer, but they're getting very tired of the controversy and publicity."

As Bev and I continued our tour, we found ourselves talking about people as much as deer. Biologists studying animals in wild or rural areas usually told me that folks made them feel welcome and somehow learned what their research was about, so I wondered how it had gone for Bev, working in an affluent suburban community.

"Deer would be easy to observe here," she replied, "because they're used to being near people. That's why I'd hoped to follow them and study their behavior, then compare it with behavior patterns among deer living in more natural environments. But I had to drop that because most people didn't like the idea of someone traipsing around on their property; and the village didn't want me wandering off, leaving this car beside the road.

"I got acquainted with the policemen, and they'd say, 'Yeah, we know whenever you're out because we get calls—suspicious white car.' People must have thought I was casing out the area for a robbery or something."

Bev swung off onto a bumpy dirt road that dead-ended among scrubby trees and sumac thickets. Here we found one of the deer traps—a large, unpainted plywood box with vertical doors that slid shut if a deer was tempted inside by the bait. When the relocation crew came along, they would transfer the deer to a smaller crate, fasten an identifying tag on the animal's ear, and truck it to a release site an hour or so from River Hills.

Whatever its virtues, this approach is neither simple nor inexpensive. The price for exiling whitetails from River Hills varied from about $18,000 in 1987–88 to just under $38,000 in 1990, and the annual number of resettled deer ranged from fewer than 50 to about 120, translating into $300 to $400 per animal. It's much more costly than "shooting over bait," the cheapest method of deer control—but expense is not a prime consideration in River Hills. Residents have also accepted the likelihood that transplanted whitetails will not survive for long and will die less humanely than if they were culled by marksmen.

In a survey of deer relocation projects around the country, biologists Jon Jones and James Witham found that survival was often poor, especially in release areas open to hunting. Some examples: Farmington, New Mexico—58 percent died; Crab Orchard, Illinois—68 percent died; Freer, Texas—52 percent died; Cook County, Illinois—44 percent died; Florida Everglades—67 percent died. Animals taken to unhunted areas fared better: Ballard County, Kentucky—25 percent died; Riverwoods, Illinois—33 percent died. Overall, hunting was the main cause of death for bucks moved from suburbs to the countryside, while car accidents killed the largest number of does.

Near the end of our tour, Bev told me a story that illustrated how, in the mercurial and unpredictable urban world, deer who cast their fate with our own sometimes face dispossession of another sort. The densely settled neighboring community of Brown Deer has few whitetails—despite its name—but a group of nine took up residence in a small woodlot beside a factory. Workers who "adopted" the animals brought daily offerings of cracked corn, apples by the bushel, and whatever else the deer would eat. Although the woodlot was terribly overbrowsed, generous feeding helped to keep the whitetails big, fat, and healthy.

"Workers really enjoyed looking out their windows and seeing those deer," said Bev. "They knew them all by name, they had pictures of each one, and they'd tell me how the does would bring their new fawns every spring."

But then came the inevitable plan for an office complex that would devour the woodlot. "People showed me pictures of the deer eating apples with a bulldozer behind them. Every day, more trees came down and more construction folks were there, so eventually the deer had to leave. The big buck moved into River Hills and stayed there, but the younger buck was killed by a car up in Mequon, and a couple of the does got hit when they tried to cross Brown Deer Road. I don't know what happened to the rest. Everybody was really upset."

I asked Bev what the River Hills experience had taught her about people and deer. "First of all, I think we need a lot more education in urban areas," she replied. "Even in a place like this, many people haven't learned how to protect their shrubbery, they don't know the facts about Lyme disease, and they haven't accepted that if you want natural scenery, the wildlife is going to be there, too. Some need to be more tolerant about the negative effects of deer, and others need to be more realistic about when there are just too many."

Bev looked out over a broad meadow with a few houses tucked along its edges. "You know, a lot of people think the ultimate issue is shooting or not shooting deer. But actually, it's the fact that everybody wants to live on five acres of beautiful land and there's no place else for the deer to go. If this means we have to do something we think is unpleasant, then for their well-being and ours, we should do it. It's better than having them damage the natural vegetation, or watching them get creamed on the roads and maybe taking human lives as well, or letting their population get to where it's driving everybody crazy.

"This isn't a natural system anymore," she concluded. "We created this environment, the deer are living here, and we have to take responsibility for it."

Long after my visit to River Hills, I spoke with Tom Isaacs, a biologist for the Wisconsin Department of Environmental Conservation, who gave me an update. Every year since 1987, he noted, deer have been transplanted from River Hills, but each summer, new fawns and a few migrants fill the ecological vacancies. Although transplanting has stabilized the whitetail population, overwintering numbers generally remain above the state biologists' goal of 75 animals. For example, approximately 180 deer lived in River Hills at the beginning of 1994, and about 75 were relocated during that winter. This left over 100 animals behind—

a breeding nucleus that could bring the population right back up the following summer.

When I asked if River Hills deer were still being released in wild areas, Isaacs said things had changed. Whitetails captured in the village were now taken to a private, fenced deer farm about 30 miles away, one of many licensed "game preserves" in Wisconsin. The village paid trapping and transportation costs, and farm operators paid the state (which "owns" all wildlife) $25 for each animal. By limiting hunter access and managing their herds, game preserves like this produce large bucks with trophy racks; then, for a fee, they allow hunters access during the regular season.

This was the fate of some animals taken from River Hills—especially prime bucks. The remaining deer were shipped to game farms outside Wisconsin, to be hunted for a fee or slaughtered for meat. (Commercial sale of venison from wild-caught deer is against the law in Wisconsin, but it's legal in some neighboring states.)

Like Glen Cole, the biologist from New York, Isaacs had ethical questions about private purchase and sale of wild deer, which are considered a publicly owned resource. "We would prefer to have the animals killed in River Hills and donated to soup kitchens," he acknowledged. "But once the deer go to a game farm, it's basically out of our control."

However we try to solve deer problems, nothing can evade the biological imperatives of life and death. Whether the animals are hunted in village neighborhoods, relocated to the countryside, or transferred to a game farm, the outcome is little different. It only means, as one newspaper article concluded, that the people of River Hills are "rich enough to make their deer die somewhere else."

On the day after my visit with Beverly Bryant, I drove through River Hills, comfortably lost on a maze of narrow roads, hoping to see deer. I found myself thinking about the excessive, unregulated hunting that had once brought whitetails to the edge of extinction. Nowadays, although we have serious problems with deer, at least we are trying to behave responsibly toward wild animals and to maintain ecological balance rather than exploiting and dominating all of nature. For this I was grateful. Far from despairing about the difficult relationship between people and deer in River Hills, I found it a source of hope. Better this, certainly, than to find the hills and valleys, the forests and meadows emptied of deer.

A short while later I noticed the statue of an elegant buck beside a flower bed in someone's front lawn. A modern American icon, I thought.

Then, as I drove slowly by, he leaned down to pluck a bright red blossom.

The Lions of Eden

On a mid-November morning, six inches of fresh snow blanketed the sidewalks along Kohler Drive, at the western edge of Boulder, Colorado. A few late commuters eased down the sloping, unplowed street and disappeared into the fog below. The neighborhood had an unmistakable tinge of prosperity, though it lacked the spaciousness of River Hills. Windows faced windows over intervening strips of grass, short walkways fronted on the streetside commons, and there were few barricading fences or hedges. Houses looked typical for an upscale western suburb, ranging from medium-sized ranch styles to larger, more extravagant places, some in classic designs and others modernistic—obtuse angles and crannies, floor-to-ceiling glass, wood siding finished in earth tones. On a car parked in the driveway of a place that must have taken half a lumberyard to build, I saw a bumper sticker urging protection of old-growth forests.

Sure as fish live in water, the American professional class had found a habitat here. I sensed also a correlation between higher income and higher elevation—houses became larger toward the upper end of Kohler Drive, the quality of views improved, and landscapes were more elaborately fashioned. The farther up I trekked, the more dense and diverse were the ornamental shrubs, tall conifers, and leafy deciduous trees. On this extraordinary day, every branch, twig, and needle sparkled with pure white snow.

As the sun rose higher, blue holes gaped overhead and the fog gradually dissipated, revealing a broad shrubby wildland that fell away beyond the houses and then steepened abruptly into a vertiginous mass of rock and canyon called the Flatirons. I stood there looking up like a bumpkin amid the skyscrapers of Manhattan, astounded by the glory of those peaks. They seemed almost to lean out over the ridgetop houses—great, shining, smooth-faced strata thrust up at hard angles against the sky, clothed in blinding white powder, wreathed by tatters of cloud, with ribbons of windblown snow purling off their summits. It was enough to shake a person's trust in his own senses, giving the place an almost imaginary quality, as if these suburban yards had been transported to a lost valley in the Alaska Range.

Before long, I encountered the deer—more precisely, Rocky Mountain mule deer—who roamed among these houses and roadways as placidly as their counterparts wandered among pine glades and meadows in the Colorado wilds. Toward the high end of Kohler Drive, I came upon a scramble of hoofprints cutting across the sidewalk, and when I looked in the direction their makers had gone I saw a tight bunch of deer—three does, two half-grown fawns, and an eight-point buck—all strikingly dark against the glitter of snow. They paid slight attention as I eased toward them.

For their part, the deer seemed urgently preoccupied, nipping leaves from a Russian olive tree, its branches bent down under the weight of snow. Perhaps the animals had noticed soggy white clumps falling as the temperature warmed and knew their tasty browse would soon lift beyond reach. I sidled closer, loitering between each step to let the deer settle down, until I'd come within 10 feet. As I had noticed in other places, the fawns seemed more jittery than their elders. From this, I inferred that wildness is spun into the roots of a deer's brain and only diminishes after close contact with that peculiar variety of humankind who simply watch or go indifferently about their business. How odd it must seem, after a prolonged evolution as prey, to find that your keenest predators have suddenly retrogressed into sightseers.

Farther up the street I found three deer bedded under a sheltering spruce a few steps off the sidewalk. I was astounded at the bulk and muscularity of these animals, which dwarfed most deer I'd seen before and reminded me of their larger relative, the elk. Two other deer idled farther back in the yard, not more than 30 feet from a man shoveling snow off his driveway. Neither seemed at all interested in the other, nor did the resting animals take much notice when a woman passed on the sidewalk almost within touching distance.

The shoveler seemed grateful for a chance to rest when I asked about deer. "Oh, they're around here almost all the time," he puffed. "You could count the days on one hand that you don't see them, and that's probably because you didn't pass at the right time. When we built here years ago, we'd see ten, fifteen at once, but lately we've had twenty-five to thirty. Sometimes it gets to be a bit much, especially if you want flowers and stuff."

A short while later, I watched a doe and her two fawns meander across an open lot, then jump an iron fence closely surrounding a modest stone house. Their leaps were so graceful, carried them in such perfect arcs over the drift-laden earth, that I waited nearby in hopes they would exit the same way. In fact, they did . . . but not as I'd expected. Suddenly a middle-aged man charged out the door, waving his arms and yelling, "Hey! You get out of here!" One behind the other, all three deer vaulted to safety, ears back, white rump patches flared, snow flinging from their hooves. But to my surprise, instead of dashing off they halted by a patch of shrubs just outside the fence and went back to browsing. The man glared after them but abandoned pursuit, circled around to the front porch, and vented his anger by sweeping snow. It looked as though all the players had rehearsed this little drama many times before.

"Do they cause a lot of trouble?" I asked sympathetically, with a nod toward the offending trio.

"The damned deer are around here all the time," he seethed. "I mean, they *live* in the yard and they eat everything in sight. The city does absolutely nothing about it."

The man stepped closer, his eyes narrowing. "You know, we used to have a big old dog. For six years she would lazily run after the deer and they'd jump over the fence. Then one day a doe turned around, kicked our dog in the head and killed her. I don't know what in hell's going to be done, but I'll guarantee you, in the next ten years some kid is going to get killed. Even a little doe could do it." He glanced over at the deer, then looked back at me. After a quick but penetrating appraisal, as if he'd determined that my sympathies fell with the enemy, he shook his head and went back to work.

The next day I met Brian Peck, a ranger for Boulder's 7,000-acre Mountain Parks system, which extends from the edge of town up into the Flatirons, including the open lands behind Kohler Drive. A lean and fit man, Peck cut quite a figure in his ranger's uniform. He was also outgoing and quick witted, while he lived up to his reputation as an expert on local deer.

There had always been a few deer in Boulder, he explained, but some winters back, probably around 1980, things had abruptly changed. "That year we got a lot of snow and our theory is that the deer, in order to survive, moved into town. They figured, 'Look at all this great food and it's not buried.' "

Instead of leaving when spring came, some deer stuck with the neighborhoods. Apparently they knew a good thing when they'd found it: grassy lawns with plenty of irrigated trees and shrubs providing better cover and more nutritious foods than the wild vegetation outside of town. "My fertilized junipers have twenty percent protein," explained Peck. "But the ones out there on the mountains only have nine percent. Why should a deer wade around in deep snow for that?"

Later on, people began seeing gangly, spotted fawns—born right around their houses. Peck shrugged and spread his hands. "Where did those fawns spend the first months of their lives? On the 2100 block of Kohler Drive. And the following year—with or without Mom—they'd come back to the same place. A lot of people were putting out salt licks; of course, there was no hunting; and if a dog chased after deer, someone was sure to step out and holler at the dog.

"The city became a high-quality food source and a protective environment for deer, so there was a real advantage to spending much of the year here. These canyons coming out of the mountains are seasonal migration corridors that lead right into subdivisions like the one on Kohler Drive. Animals have been coming down this way ever since there were canyons and deer. Essentially, they've recolonized an area that used to be part of their habitat anyway."

A study commissioned by the city concluded that parts of Boulder are, in effect, deer preserves—and they've become increasingly attractive as trees and shrubs have matured, turning many yards into what Peck called "dense little jungles." Also, along the city's western edge, mountain parkland offers a more arid but rich natural environment of patchy forest, scrub thickets, and prairies. Despite the fact that residents suffer damage to ornamentals and gardens, from an ecological standpoint there is little evidence that deer have significantly overbrowsed either wild or suburban habitats.

During the past decade, biologists tagged, censused, and tracked deer in a 17-square-mile area from Boulder's densely settled westside neighborhoods out to the mountaintops (about 60 percent of this land is park and 40 percent urban). The mule deer population in this area ranged from about 780 in 1983, up to approximately 1,100 in 1986, and back down to an estimated 750 in 1993 (without any human control). This translates into fairly high densities of 44 to 63 deer per square mile. Interestingly, about two thirds of the deer never came into town at all, while the other third spent at least half their time in neighborhoods—so there's a real distinction between Boulder's metropolitan deer and those living in wild areas just outside town.

That morning, I had spotted a big-antlered buck who looked in prime condition but hobbled painfully—doubtless one of the many deer hit by cars each year in Boulder. Along certain stretches of road the city has installed special "Swareflex" reflectors, which mirror headlights back into yards, fields, and thickets, making a "light fence" intended to freeze deer in their tracks until a car goes by. This system is most effective at night and less so around dusk and dawn, when deer are very active. As of 1991, the reflectors cost about $7,500 per mile on two-lane roads, twice that on four-lane highways, and in some areas they've been a good investment. For example, along selected roadways in Minnesota and Washington studies showed 60 to 90 percent reductions in deer collisions after reflectors were installed; but in some other cases they've had little or no effect.

The number of deer killed by cars in Boulder varies from 120 to more than 200 each year, and an equal number (if not more) are injured or straggle off to die in the brushland. Deer accidents increase during winter, midsummer, and especially the fall rut. An animal control officer told me, "We'll pick up two or three dead deer every day in rutting season, plus usually one more that's injured so badly it has to be euthanized." Improved record keeping in 1996 indicates that it's likely that at least one deer is killed or injured on Boulder's roads every day throughout the year. Researchers found that collisions killed between 16 and 19 percent of Boulder's deer in a single year (1983–84), which means that reducing car "predation" could bring a population increase, causing more problems in neighborhoods where some people think the animals are already too abundant.

After watching the half-crippled buck, I chatted with a friendly man while he polished the car in his driveway. "I've had some close calls myself," he told me. "And not just on the road. You know, suddenly this animal pops out while you're running along a sidewalk and you almost have a deer-person collision!

"But overall, the deer have been pretty good to us," he judged. "They haven't caused much damage around our yard and the kids love seeing them. Out on the back patio, they'll be right there at your window in the morning." He admitted, with a self-conscious chuckle, "I always talk to them."

A neighbor woman on her evening stroll joined our conversation. "You have to adjust to them," she said. "Like putting net over the top of flowers or else planting mums, pansies, or the few other kinds of flowers they won't eat. If you want a garden, you'll need a high fence. Also, to start trees you have to fence the saplings until they're mature, otherwise they'll get eaten right to the ground. Deer droppings are a nuisance, too—they're everywhere and they cause burned places in the lawn."

Some people get very angry, she affirmed, but most have come to accept the deer or at least tolerate them. She suggested, however, that friendly attitudes might quickly dissipate if local deer caused more serious trouble—something like Lyme disease. An epidemiologist had told me that, for unknown reasons, the disease is not a serious problem in Rocky Mountain states like Colorado, or in the plains and deserts. Focal areas for Lyme disease include the East Coast, the upper Midwest, California, and to some extent the other West Coast states.

In the middle of our discussion, a doe came out between two houses across the street with a large buck following literally on her tail. He kept his body in a strained half crouch, muscles tensed to the point of trembling, while he stretched his neck toward the doe and savored what must have been an irresistible scent drifting in her wake. You didn't have to be a biologist to recognize the glandular urgency in his pursuit or to deduce that rutting season was under way.

"Everything that's part of a deer's life, you see it right around your house," the man noted with mild embarrassment. "A woman up the street, she watched a fawn being born in her yard. And in winter, when it's real cold or the snow gets heavy, they'll bed under our trees for two, three days. It's good shelter for them in here among the houses. You know, the deer have integrated themselves into the neighborhood."

I realized, of course, that deer had caused a multitude of problems here, yet they also brought an enchanting presence. Most residents I'd talked with mainly appreciated the deer for their simple visual beauty. And some, who observed them more closely, took pleasure in learning about their yearly cycle, their ecology, their interactions with other animals.

One man told me, for example, that deer often gathered in a copse of ponderosa pines up the slope from his house. "I guess the place is a cleaning station," he surmised. "A bunch of magpies come out and they'll sit right on the deer, pecking at them. Sometimes they'll pull up bunches of hair and spit them out, and then sometimes they'll grab after something down in the fur. They must be pulling off parasites and stuff. They'll even sit on a deer's head and stick their long beak down inside the ears. Every once in a while a deer shakes its head so the bird flies off, but then it comes right back. Otherwise, the deer sit very patiently while this goes on."

Although I met only a couple of people who either didn't like deer or wouldn't tolerate the inconveniences they caused, everyone assured me neighborhood critics weren't hard to find. I heard of a woman who became irate over droppings in her yard and believed the deer threatened her children, so finally she shot one with a pellet gun to scare it away—and the animal died. She paid a couple hundred dollars for breaking the law, and for offending public sensibilities she was blistered in letters to the editor.

This happened some years back, when Boulder rumbled with conflicts over what to do about the deer. City officials commissioned studies, consulted biologists, and debated methods of controlling deer or limiting their population. Of course, a flash point for controversy was the suggestion to reduce deer numbers by shooting or other lethal means. Brian Peck told me, "If you did a survey of attitudes toward hunting, I'll bet Boulder would rival some of the capitals of antihunting sentiment anywhere in the world." I heard one resident describe Boulder as a "suburb of California," in contrast to traditional Rocky Mountain communities, where ranching and hunting weave into the local subculture.

People who follow rural, agrarian lifestyles generally understand what it means to draw a livelihood directly from the land. By contrast, most city dwellers tend to perceive mountains, forests, prairies, waterways, and wildlife only as a scenic backdrop, a recreational playground, something to be admired as natural artistry but having little to do with sustaining their own lives. The urban view, in other words, is predominantly aesthetic rather than utilitarian.

People like ranchers and farmers, whose earthbound labors feed the neighboring city folk, often share a similar love for the land's beauty, but they also work on it, use what it provides, and live in direct physical reciprocity with it. Because of this, I believe, they often have a fuller sense of connection to the surrounding environment, not just as scenery but as their own living source, a world that includes and wholly engages them. (Of course, there's wide variation within both groups, and each deserves both praise and criticism when it comes to environmental attitudes.)

Many biologists and wildlife managers—who not only study animals but work directly with urban and rural people—try to find a balance between the aesthetic and pragmatic views. This seemed true of Brian Peck, whose stand on controlling Boulder's deer population was based mainly on science and practicality rather than politics and emotion. "If someone could show me that besides everything else that's going on, these deer were destroying the habitat, then I'd say all right, load up the rifles and take twenty percent of the herd. But there's no proof at all for that."

In recent years, people have softened their attitudes toward deer, Peck contended, and hunting has essentially become a nonissue. "I get four or five complaints in a winter, and often it's just people asking how they can keep deer out of their yard or garden, not how we can get rid of them. We also had an opinion survey showing that most people want nothing done to the deer; no bow and arrows, no professional shooters, no trap-and-move. They only want us to provide information and public education about deer, and that's what the city has done."

Boulder has produced brochures explaining how to build deer-proof fences, evaluating commercial repellents, and listing plants that deer seldom eat. To keep suburban attractions at a minimum, people are allowed to install electric fences, and they're prohibited from feeding deer or putting out salt blocks. Rejected as impractical are proposals like sterilization, fencing off neighborhoods, or improving out-of-town environments to heighten their appeal for deer (providing water or planting artificial browse, for instance). As things now stand, people with deer troubles must engineer their own solutions within legal limits, and experts like Brian Peck are available for anyone to call.

Boulder has achieved a strained but fairly harmonious relationship with its deer, as few other communities have done. In no small way this is because (for unknown reasons) deer numbers have remained fairly stable—a contrast to the growing deer populations in most urban areas, especially east of the Mississippi. But this city has another problem, intimately connected with its mule deer, a problem that brings to people's voices a mix of fear, awe, and exhilaration.

The mountain lion.

Most of us wouldn't imagine that a creature so elusive as this, so mysterious, so brilliantly predatory, would exist anywhere near a metropolis of almost 100,000 people. But remember the Flatiron Range, that convoluted mass of hogbacks and sheer-walled canyons pitched up like the city's furrowed brow. And remember the expansive wildland parks, within a short hike of lawns where kids play on swing sets and mowers brattle during warm afternoons. Like mule deer, mountain lions have penetrated this border of the human world.

Allen Anderson, a biologist with Colorado's Division of Wildlife, explained: "It's not unusual for people to be driving up one of the canyons near Boulder, and a little ways off the road they'll see a mountain lion watching cars go by. And something that commonly happens, right in the backyards, is that lions eat dogs and cats. This is all within the last ten or fifteen years; before that it was practically unheard of."

Adult mountain lions, or cougars, weigh between 90 and 150 pounds and reach lengths of seven to eight feet, including the long, ropy tail. They are without equal as a predator on deer, and many people, including some biologists, believe that Boulder's thriving mule deer population goes far toward explaining why mountain lions have become common near town. According to Brian Peck, they're also attracted by pet food left on back porches and by small creatures like raccoons and skunks drawn to the same bowls of kibble. For the most part, however, cougars elude human eyes, moving like phantoms through the darkened yards and open country nearby.

Of the cougars sighted in town or tranquilized and moved to wilder surroundings, many have been young animals searching for a new home range after their mothers drove them off. These adolescents often roam for a year or more, traveling up to 100 miles from their birthplace; and because they're less fearful of strange environments than are savvy elders, some end up on the streets. In Boulder, they find the extra advantage of good habitat and a protective sanctuary right next to town.

"We've had people snarled at and we've had people approached very closely," recalled Brian Peck. "There was also a woman who was followed by two lions in Four Mile Canyon, and when she climbed a tree one of them came up after her. People say she was attacked, yet all she got was a scratch on her leg. They would have found her *bones* if she'd been attacked. The lions were curious; they followed her when she turned her back and retreated—both of which you should not do. She ended up literally kicking that lion out of the tree; it backed down and left with the other one."

Mountain lions seem especially interested in hikers with dogs, Peck noted. "People say, 'Well, my dog is a lot of protection, right?' I say, 'No, your dog is lunch.' I don't care if your dog's a pit bull, it's history; it's like opening a can of tuna."

People should be watchful especially from dusk until dawn, Peck advised, and keep the kids close, because most cougar attacks are on smaller people. But remember that adult humans are about the same size as full-grown deer—the lion's main prey. There have been several fatal attacks in western states over the past decade, including a woman jogger on a backwoods path in California, a five-year-old Montana boy riding his tricycle, and a high-school boy running on a trail about 20 miles from Boulder.

These tragedies show that mountain lion attacks are a genuine possibility—but just barely. Over the past century in all of North America, cougars have killed about a dozen people. Our own dogs are infinitely more dangerous, to say nothing of our fellow humans. Nevertheless, some people in Boulder—especially families with small children—are understandably nervous about cougars in their neighborhoods. "If we start to get more sightings," one resident told me, "I think it'll change how many of us feel not only about mountain lions but also about deer."

People often suggest that predators like cougars and wolves are the ethically correct way to control expanding deer populations. But in most parts of this country, using wild predators to manage deer numbers is just slightly more plausible than establishing herds of rhinoceroses. If wolves and lions could be maintained in the numbers required to stabilize deer—something they haven't been called upon to do since Native American hunters settled this continent in ancient times—they would almost certainly cause havoc among dairy farmers and livestock growers, not to mention the problems they'd cause for rural folks and suburbanites.

I have lived in small Alaskan communities where brown bears occasionally roam in among the houses, and I've seen how parents react— with their children playing outside, walking home from school, exploring crannies at the town's edge. The outcome is as predictable as sunrise: a bear that lingers in the neighborhood more than a few hours ends up dead. I suspect that, even in the most enlightened communities, the same might be true for any mountain lion or wolf that made itself too conspicuous, ate too many pets, or preyed too openly on backyard deer.

The idea that we could have large predators in sufficient numbers to control deer populations like those of the eastern United States—and that such predators could live without fatal disharmony near our homes, in our heavily used nature preserves, or around our farms—is a venture into dreamland. After the recent attack on a California woman, for example, there was immediate agitation to rescind the state's law that prohibits mountain lion hunting. There's bound to be more controversy about this subject in years to come, as cougars increase in the West and reinhabit their ancestral territories farther east.

Predators like the mountain lion, wolf, and brown bear are legally hunted in most places where their populations remain healthy and viable. Even those of us who would never kill such animals (except in self-defense) should remember that hunting creates and sustains wildness. And we might agree that something vital, mysterious, and powerful is lost when a formerly wild creature adopts a tamed life in the city, not to mention the accompanying conflicts and dangers this creates for people and animals alike. Hunting is what keeps both predators and prey elusive, untamed, haunting their own world beyond the city's edge, in the freedom of forest or prairie or desert, where even a fleeting glimpse elevates our spirit.

My last day in Boulder arose clear and calm, wet snow gleaming like polished ivory under blue skies. At the upper end of Kohler Drive I found six does bedded on an open slope behind the houses, their heads and bellies mounding like dark stones above the drift. Just beyond, I saw a buck of extraordinary size, resting in full sunshine beside one of the neighborhood's most imposing and beautifully designed homes.

I trudged across the yard for a closer look at the buck, from 50 feet, then 30, then 15. At this point he stood, regarded me for a moment, and ambled along the hillside, framed against the looming mass of the Flatirons and the fathomless immensity of Colorado sky. Then he headed up toward the does and lay down again, now well above the surrounding housetops, as if to gain a commanding view of the neighborhood. None of the animals showed any interest when a car pulled into the driveway and a woman stepped out cradling grocery bags under each arm, oblivious to the little gathering behind her home.

After sitting for a while, I moved toward the buck, stepping carefully and waiting at intervals to ease the forwardness of my intrusion. He seemed to regard me with a mix of interest and disdain, but not a trace of fear. At six feet I stopped, having reached the limit of my own boldness, and hunkered down on the snow directly in front of him. I was conscious of heartbeats thumping in my temples.

The buck must have weighed 250 or 300 pounds; his chest was brawny and deep; his back seemed wide enough for a saddle; and his neck, distended with the rut, had almost the girth of my waist. He carried a tremendous rack of antlers, their bases thicker than my wrists and their beams longer than my arms, crowned with asymmetrical tines that splayed off at irregular angles and a single "drop tine" pointed toward the ground. Except in the sanctuary of a city or park, or in a wildland outside the range of most hunters, few bucks would survive long enough to achieve such dimensions.

The big deer fixed his impassive eyes on me, and only occasionally glanced at the does. I kept a close watch for hints of his intentions, but could fathom nothing, as if he were staring out from the depths of a glacier. He could have reached me within two or three seconds, and I didn't care to imagine what even a casual poke from those tines could do. Nevertheless, during those moments it seemed a risk worth taking.

Shortly the does sauntered away and the buck followed. One doe in particular drew his attention, perhaps because she carried the scent of estrus. He came toward her and turned sidelong, as if to display his full masculine grandeur, then lifted his head and curled his upper lip for a long moment, half-opened eyes appearing glazed and sightless, as if he'd lost consciousness. The doe never looked his way, though she seemed keenly aware of being stalked.

Moments later, she ran off a short distance and started plucking leaves from small bushes. You couldn't mistake the buck's dissipating hopes, as his tense body slackened, but after standing quietly for a few minutes he set off on her tracks again. I don't know how many times they went through this ritual of approach and rejection before I left them alone.

Sunshine poured from a cloudless sky as I trekked away, following a deer trail that led down between two houses.

SIX

THE DEER CAPITAL OF TEXAS

Our ranch supports both cattle and tremendous deer populations. If you plowed ranch lands to plant crops, then you wouldn't see all these deer; and you wouldn't see the turkeys or the quail or the other wild animals we've got now. To grow broccoli for the vegetarians, you'd end up eliminating all of this wildlife.

—BART GILLAN, RANCHER

The Deer Factory

A pallid November dawn on Slator Ranch, in the Hill Country of central Texas. Crawling from my tent, I scanned the surrounding terrain, a broad meadow patched with thickets and trees. Almost immediately, something twitched in the distance, and there stood a couple of does beside the dusty, two-track road. They peered intently for a moment, then seeped back into the underbrush, cryptic as mist on the morning breeze. I wondered if I'd really seen them, but a scatter of hoofprints led away through the brittle, tangled shrubs, and I knew those Texas whitetails stood somewhere nearby, listening to my footsteps, listening to my hurried breaths.

Farther down the road, I stood atop a knoll overlooking an expanse of ridges and vales covered with parklike savanna—grassland mixed with scrubby oak, cedar, mesquite, and prickly-pear cactus. A loose bunch of cattle dozed along the nearby slope, like red bricks strewn amid hoary granite outcrops and straw-colored turf. There was something almost poignantly familiar about this landscape, as if it were a lost place from my childhood. Then I realized: Here was the archetypal backdrop for a western movie, as if cowboys and longhorns might appear at any moment in the gully below.

Early descriptions of the Hill Country, also known as the Edwards Plateau, reveal a frontier terrain quite different from the one before me now. Periodic Indian fires created oceanic expanses of grass with trees narrowly confined to river courses. During seasonal migrations, immense herds of buffalo spilled down over the horizon, grazed the prairies to stubble, pounded and fertilized the earth, then moved on. Pronghorn antelopes also abounded on the grasslands, but white-tailed deer stayed mainly in the sheltering riverine forests and patchy upland cedar brakes. Indians hunted all the wild ungulates, as did wolves, bears, mountain lions, and coyotes.

Between 1850 and 1900, Euro-Americans annihilated the buffalo and colonized the newly vacated land with millions of cattle, a close relative and ecological counterpart to those disappearing hordes. Intense, confined, uninterrupted grazing by cows, as well as sheep and goats, degraded the native prairies. This, coupled with the end of Indian burning, encouraged growth of trees and shrubs, giving rise to the modern savanna; at the same time, any predators large enough to kill livestock were systematically exterminated. By 1900, overhunting also brought deer to the edge of extinction, but remnant populations survived, thanks to the timely demise of market hunting and the establishment of game regulations, which began in 1903. All it took was a measure of protection. During the first few decades of the twentieth century, whitetails multiplied explosively in the brushland habitats that had replaced open prairie, and they have flourished ever since.

Today, Texas has almost 3.5 million whitetails, more than any other state, and if one region epitomizes the ascendance of deer in modern Texas, it's a cluster of counties including Llano county, where whitetail numbers range as high as 160 to 180 per square mile. According to wildlife biologist James Teer, this is probably the highest regional population density of whitetails anywhere in North America.

Although Texas is a huge state, it's split into 254 smallish counties. And from just three counties in the Hill Country—Llano, Mason, and Gillespie—hunters every year take 35,000 to 55,000 deer, far exceeding the total yearly harvest in many states. "I mean, it's a deer *factory* in that area!" said Donnie Harmel, another Texas biologist and whitetail expert.

For folks who live in the Hill Country, deer are much more than an abundant wild animal, much more than a lovely creature gracing their countryside, much more than a source of venison for local hunters. Over the years most Hill Country ranchers have also come to regard whitetails as an important commercial "crop." Some have also learned to manage livestock grazing, manipulate habitat, and regulate hunting in ways that produce the highest-quality deer—large, healthy does and heavy-racked bucks. Their motive? Principally economic.

More than 50 years ago, hunters began paying ranch owners for access to their lands, and today hunting leases rival livestock as ranchers' prime source of income. To the traditional lifeway of cattle and cowboys, they've added this "harvest" of deer, carried out by thousands of hunters who come each year from other parts of Texas and from all over the continent. While harkening to the frontier tradition, these deer hunts are also very much an element of the New American West.

Hunters, local and outsider alike, have become a major influence on Hill Country subculture. The annual influx of hunters into Texas is something of a pilgrimage—to the Great Outdoors and to the homeland of white-tailed deer. Principal objects of this quest, according to sociologists and hunters alike, include escaping from "civilization," getting closer to nature, spending social time with relatives or friends, seeking what might be called a primal engagement with the chase, and bringing home the year's supply of venison. Some hunters also have a particular zeal for trophy antlers, which are found only on prime, heavy-bodied bucks—the wildest and most elusive members of their species.

I was drawn to the Texas Hill Country because of curiosity about these subjects, and because there may be no other place in the world where deer are of such paramount and pervasive importance. A series of telephone conversations with local biologists had led me to Bart Gillan and Debbie Slator Gillan, who own a sizable ranch near the town of Llano. They had suggested I come and learn firsthand about managing habitat for deer and cattle, about hunting as part of the modern ranch business, and about their most select class of hunters, whose goal is the trophy whitetail.

Slator Ranch

When I arrived a few days earlier, I had taken the straight-line highway out of Llano (population 3,000, self-proclaimed "Deer Capital of Texas," whose courthouse lawn is graced by a gigantic leaping deer perched atop a high pole—a local icon analogous to St. Louis's arch or San Francisco's bridge). A few miles west of town I stopped to gawk at a bull the size of a small van, separated from the road by a few strands of wire, the sort of creature who brings on an instinctive urge to lock the car doors. Not far beyond was a gravel drive leading back to a stately old home surrounded by trees and outbuildings. At the driveway's entrance stood a monolithic granite arch, its spandrel inscribed: "Slator/Granite Cliff Ranch."

Across the road, at a small hut that served as headquarters for the Slator Ranch deer hunting business, I was greeted with Debbie Gillan's easy grin and firm handshake. Without being told about Debbie's years of ranching experience and degree in veterinary medicine, I sensed this compact, brown-haired woman knew exactly where she was, what needed to be done, and how to go about it.

Shortly, Bart Gillan arrived in a dusty pickup. He seemed the classic image of a cowboy: tallish and fit, attenuated handlebar mustache, topped by an oversized white western hat that came down near his ears and eyebrows. Bart had grown up in Houston, majored in geology, and learned about cattle right here on the ranch Debbie had inherited from her father and uncle.

To an outlander, Debbie and Bart had the bearing of a traditional ranch couple, perhaps a bit old-fashioned for people just into their forties, but from the biologists who'd recommended them, I knew they were innovators in the practice of ecologically based range management and were doing it extraordinarily well. Rather than privately hoard the formula behind their success, they did everything possible to spread the word—giving speeches around the state, talking it up with neighbors, offering explanations to anyone willing to listen.

It didn't take Bart long to recognize that I was among the willing. "Our ranch used to look like most of the others around here. We've got 10,750 acres, and the whole thing was in bad shape because we had too many deer—they'd done a lot of damage to the habitat. Also, the animals themselves were really small and you'd never see a trophy-sized buck."

Back in 1984, Fielding Harwell, a biologist with the Texas Parks and Wildlife Department's Kerrville office, had helped the Gillans develop a program for managing deer. "Fielding showed us how to do census counts and take measurements on deer our hunters brought in. We found out that on this ranch there were more than three does for every buck. That's a terrible ratio. And due to the overpopulation we also had poor fawn survival."

Because people hunted mainly for bucks, this left the ranch with far too many does, who produced large numbers of fawns each year, leading to an extremely high deer population and chronically overbrowsed habitat. To Harwell's dismay, most landowners were not interested in reducing their deer populations, apparently figuring more deer equals more income, regardless of the animals' size and condition. However, the few bucks they had were small and young and not many survived long enough to grow trophy antlers. For this reason, most landowners couldn't charge anything like the premium lease prices that hunters would gladly pay for a good chance at trophy deer.

From Harwell, Debbie and Bart learned how well-managed hunting could bring the Slator Ranch deer population into ecological balance and how this would improve the animals' health while restoring their depleted environment. As long as they don't breach state regulations (4 whitetails per hunter, not more than 2 being bucks), Texas ranchers can set their own hunting restrictions as a condition for access to private land. During that first season, Slator Ranch allowed an extremely liberal harvest—almost 400 whitetails—leading some neighbors to suggest the Gillans had taken leave of their senses. But hunters could take only does or bucks with small, spike antlers, while larger bucks, the most economically valuable animals, were strictly protected.

Results showed in the next year's census. A lower deer population meant nursing does had better access to food, gave more milk, and raised healthier fawns. About half of the deer born each year are bucks, so by improving fawn survival—and by taking out more does—sex ratios among Slator Ranch whitetails started to shift. After the first year of Harwell's management plan there were only two does for every buck, and since then the number of does and bucks has drawn almost even. With less competition for browse, Slator Ranch deer also grow larger, and because strict hunting limits allow the bucks to live longer, they've produced more impressive racks.

I had no trouble understanding that the Gillans wanted to balance deer numbers with their habitat, but why all this emphasis on big deer, bucks, and antlers? Most hunters are primarily after venison, and from this standpoint, big, healthy deer of either sex should be equally desirable. But the fact is, many hunters favor bucks. I also learned that some will pay considerably more for access to land frequented by large bucks, especially if records show a consistent harvest of animals with trophy antlers. On certain Texas ranches, trophy whitetail leases can run as high as $2,000 to $5,000 for a week or less of hunting. By contrast, on the typical ranch—with overabundant deer and few trophy animals—leasing for the whole season might cost $600 to $800. So there's a good economic incentive to keep whitetail numbers in balance with their habitat.

In recent years, the success of its hunters brought Slator Ranch a growing reputation for trophy bucks. "We typically book between fifty and fifty-five buck hunters during our November trophy season," Bart explained. "For fourteen hundred dollars they hunt five days and we allow them to take only one trophy buck—with eight points or more. If they want, they can also take up to three does; and we'll let them take a smaller buck toward the end of their hunt if they haven't gotten a trophy deer."

By comparison, the ranch opens in December for does only: three-day leases with a limit of four animals per hunter at a cost of $340. "There's plenty of guys who can afford that," said Bart. "And if they get their deer it's a lot of venison for the price." Bow hunters, who take very few animals of any sort, come to the ranch in October. At $130 per day, they can try for does, spike bucks, and bucks with eight points or more, but not for the intermediate-sized bucks destined to become trophy animals as they grow older. In all, about 400 hunters pay for leases on Slator Ranch each year. So far, the Gillans have limited this access to hunters, but some other ranchers use the same approach for activities like camping, fishing, hiking, and wildlife watching.

I had come in November during one of the trophy hunts, armed with a notebook and a quiver of pencils. The first hunters pulled in as Bart and I talked—about a half dozen men between the ages of 30 and 50, close buddies from a rural area south of Llano County. They busied themselves setting up a trailer camp in the open field near headquarters, complete with a Texas-sized barbecue on wheels towed behind one of their trucks. "That's Dickie White's group," Bart observed. "They've been here before, like most of our hunters, so they know all of our rules."

Among these rules: No alcoholic beverages outside the camp area; every deer must be officially measured for the ranch's monitoring program; bag limits set by the ranch are strictly observed; and all state laws must be obeyed, such as the prohibition against hunting after dark. Also, trophy hunters are allowed only one branch-antlered buck, and they're urged to take an animal with at least eight points. According to the lease agreement, anyone who exceeds the single trophy buck limit will pay a minimum $2,000 fine and will not be allowed to hunt on the ranch again.

By late afternoon, a small assembly of camps had sprung up on the field near headquarters. Men dressed in earth-colored gear stood in little clusters and the air was astir with hunting talk. Bart waved me over to the truck. "If y'all want to come along, I'm gonna show Bob and Jackie their hunting stands." To keep everyone widely and safely separated, he explained, each party is assigned a specific area within the ranch.

We hadn't gone a half mile when Bart suddenly pumped the brakes and shook his finger toward our left. "Hey, there's a nice buck!" His voice went up a pitch or two, hardly like a man who came across critters like this every day. At last I glimpsed the deer, sprinting full tilt, flashing between thickets, flag-tail waving, head high, antlers gleaming in the sun.

"Looks like an eight-point," Bart declared. "I'd say his spread's about eighteen inches." I was astonished that he'd seen the animal at all, much less caught the number of tines and judged the span of its antlers. When he spotted another buck farther on, he not only called out points and spread, but said it was a two-and-a-half-year-old. Over the coming days, I'd learn these were no idle guesses—Bart Gillan had an eye for deer and an amazing ability to interpret what he saw.

The bumpy two-track road took us through seemingly directionless oak-and-grass parklands. I was totally lost, but inside Bart Gillan's mind was a map detailing every fenced pasture, every patch of trees, every mound of bedrock, every creek, and every hill on Slator Ranch.

"Hey, Bob and Jackie, there's one of your stands now." Bart nodded toward a heavy-limbed oak with cross-pieces nailed on the trunk, laddering up to a wooden platform. "Even sitting up there, you've got to keep totally quiet," Bart advised. "And once a deer's in sight, if you move too fast or bump your rifle against something—it's gone."

Like most of the hunters, Bob and Jackie planned to spend the morning and evening hours sequestered in stands, but instead of taking the usual midday break, they'd stalk quietly around their designated area. Bart admired their ambition and guessed the strategy might work because not all deer spent the brightest hours bedded in thickets.

The road took us past several towers, 15 to 20 feet high, with either an open chair or a boxy wooden blind perched on top. Like the tree stand we'd seen earlier, these offered clear views of terrain favored by deer. There were about 70 stands on the ranch, and near each was a feeder, consisting of a bucket suspended from a low tree limb with a mechanism that dispensed occasional trickles of corn. I wondered about hunting near feeders that attracted deer, because it wasn't something I could imagine doing myself.

"For most of our folks, these five days are the only time they've got to hunt during the year," said Bart. "And very few of them would get a deer if they didn't use stands near feeders. You saw how those bucks ran from the truck, and they're a lot worse if they see a man."

He added proudly: "These are *wild* deer. And that's how deer are supposed to be."

It's hunting, Bart emphasized, that inflames the wariness of Slator Ranch whitetails, and wariness, in turn, makes the animals challenging to pursue. For Bart, wildness is an element of the "quality" inherent in a properly managed deer herd. As he spoke, I remembered a doe we'd seen earlier bolting across a sorrel meadow, then leaping over one fallen tree trunk after another, etching arcs against the sky.

"There's another reason for the feeders," Bart continued. "If it's a trophy hunter, you want him to have a good look at several animals so he can pick out the mature one—with at least eight points—not a younger one that'll grow bigger next year. And aside from trophy hunting, we need to take out the excess does and spikes every year to manage the population size and its makeup. How can you be sure of removing the surplus animals and taking only the right ones? You do it by putting the hunters near feeders.

"And one more thing. When the deer are standing at a feeder, there's less chance of somebody wounding an animal. That hunter's going to make a quick, clean kill, which is what you want."

Hunting on closely managed ranchlands, Bart pointed out, is not the same as hunting in pristine wilderness. Without feeders, he contended, hunters could not reliably take enough animals of a certain age and sex from the population each year, and if that happened, habitat condition and herd vitality would decline. Although the ranch is a beautiful place, not altogether different from a wildland preserve, it's also an intensively utilized landscape, managed to produce two principal crops: cattle and deer. In this situation, there must be a balance among practical, aesthetic, ethical, and ecological considerations.

I still felt ambivalent about the issue of wildness. As individual animals these Hill Country whitetails seemed pervasively wild, but their population as a whole was intensely controlled. Is it possible to minimize human influences on deer in such a place as this, or is it essential to manipulate their overall environment and ecology? The aesthetic and romantic parts of me believed something vital about nature had been lost here. But the realist, acknowledging that compromises are unavoidable nowadays, was impressed by the ways Bart and Debbie Gillan had balanced these many considerations.

Back at headquarters, we had a visit with Bart's friend and adviser, Fielding Harwell. Except for a baseball cap bearing the Texas Parks and Wildlife logo, he looked pure ranch: lanky and sinewy, sun-weathered face, faded bluejeans and western shirt. As a well-known expert on Texas deer, he's helped more than 100 ranchers manage their deer herds. When I asked if he enjoyed his work, Fielding gazed across the sweep of land and smiled. "This is my hobby!"

I wondered how deer management on Slator Ranch differed from that on other places around the area. Most owners, Fielding explained, allowed their hunters open access for the whole two-month season—nothing at all like Slator Ranch's closely monitored one-day, three-day, and five-day leases. Also, most simply followed state regulations, which allow each hunter four deer, including up to two bucks of any size. Few bothered to record the harvest or census whitetail numbers, which of course meant far less work than the Gillans' complex management scheme, but a laissez-faire approach also caused serious problems.

"This part of the state is noted for producing horrendous numbers of deer," Fielding declared. "In some areas, there's a deer to every two and a half acres—that's about 256 deer per square mile! During droughts, they'll get huge losses of animals from starvation." Bart pitched in, "As you can imagine, deer on those places look like little balls of hair; they weight about fifty pounds."

Slator Ranch, by contrast, averaged a deer to every 10 acres, or about 64 per square mile—high compared to almost anywhere else in North America, but low by Hill Country standards. Fewer animals meant less competition for food. "We're seeing some exceptionally nice deer coming from this ranch now," observed Fielding Harwell. "If the trend continues, some of these bucks are going to be well up there on the Boone and Crockett scoring system." This system is widely used for measuring trophy antlers and keeping track of the biggest deer taken in a given area or state, or in the whole country.

Every time a noteworthy buck came off Slator Ranch the word got around, and folks couldn't miss the simple correlation between good management, quality deer, and higher lease income. Obviously, Fielding delighted in Bart and Debbie's success, but he had more reasons than just whitetails. "In Texas, where people pay for access to hunt on someone's land, it puts wildlife up front in the owners' minds. This gives them an incentive to improve the quality of the habitat and take better care of the whole ecosystem, which means every plant and wildlife species benefits."

. . .

That evening I wandered down a sand road, past a herd of cows grazing serenely beneath scattered oaks. Raspy bird voices sparked from the thickets, and dove wings winnowed on the breeze. Scrawled in the dust at intervals were tracks of deer, feral pigs, coyotes, and small critters whose signatures I couldn't identify. The sky deepened from fuchsia to mauve; early stars flickered in gaps between clouds. I'd nearly given up on seeing deer, turning my attention to the scenery and to the tranquillity of an approaching Texas night.

Then, suddenly, I heard a clamor of rattling branches and crispy leaves. Seconds later a whitetail doe burst from a patch of shrubs as if she'd been charged by a mountain lion—her body low, her neck outstretched, her bent legs recoiling like a bow setting an arrow aflight. She sprinted out over the grassy flat and leaned through a glorious, sweeping turn, as if she were running purely to revel in her own speed.

I stood there, awed by the unveiling of her power and swiftness as she cleaved the dry, chill air. She crossed a gentle ridge, angling away and then gradually descending beneath its rim, but I still saw the reach and rebounding of her head, the rise and fall of her back, the bend and flex of her tail—all visible after her legs sank down out of view. For a moment it seemed that the air crackled, closing back against itself in the roil and turbulence of her wake. And then she vanished, as if a hawk's wings had closed down over her.

Long after dark, I joined Bart and several hunters inside the headquarters shed, poring over a book of snapshots from previous years: proud hunters squatting beside hefty bucks, clutching the polished bone of racks. Propped on the ground in each photo was a hand-lettered sign listing the animal's Boone and Crockett score, a combined measure of beam, tine, and spread. "That's the one-twenty-seven that came in a couple years ago," one of the hunters remarked. "When I first saw it, I figured it's an easy one-forty, I guess because of those long tines."

His finger slid across the page. "I like that one, too. See, he's got a lot of mass in his horns. I don't really care that much about the spread, as long as it's a heavy rack, not thin like a pencil. One of my favorites was that buck a couple years ago. You guys remember? He had twelve points, twenty-two-inch spread, and plenty of mass, with a drop tine. Now that was a real trophy deer."

Bart shuffled through a batch of pictures, offering quick glimpses of each deer. "Look here, some antlers go up real high and some go real wide. They can have thick beams or thin ones. There's differences in the length and shape of their tines, plus they can be symmetrical or asymmetrical, and some have drop tines. If you looked at the antlers of a hundred mature bucks, there's not one of them'll even be close to the others. That's why I like to say whitetail racks are like snowflakes: every one is different."

Some hunters develop a fascination with deer antlers—especially racks distinguished by impressive size, exceptional beauty, or unique form. They regard antlers as masterpieces of natural art, crowning emblems of the whitetail deer, symbols of glory days spent in wild places, and tokens of hunting skill or blind, bountiful luck. The quest for these trophies adds another motivation to their long list of reasons for hunting.

Because I've never been a trophy hunter and have misgivings about it, I couldn't fully comprehend what it meant to these folks, but I wanted to learn about this fascinating part of the Euro-American hunting tradition. Also, as a fellow hunter, I knew most of us were on common ground in our emphasis on bringing home venison, our fascination with deer, and our intense appreciation of the outdoors.

For many Slator Ranch hunters, trophy bucks were the object of a nearly sacrosanct pursuit. But for Bart and Debbie Gillan, these animals represented more than beautiful, elusive quarry; they were a result of properly regulated deer numbers and carefully directed harvesting. And hunters on the ranch were not only guests, not only a source of income, but also the means of implementing biological management. To serve the purpose most effectively, they needed training.

"We get 'em Slatorized," Bart was fond of saying, "so they'll know how to tell a good deer when they see one. That's a benefit to them and a benefit to us."

Earlier that day, I'd been Slatorized along with several hunters new to the place this year. Squeezed into the tiny headquarters, we watched slides of deer while Debbie offered advice on selecting the "right" deer. She urged hunters to leave the young four- to seven-point bucks alone, for example, because they'd become more valuable with age. On the other hand, she encouraged them to take bucks whose antlers remain permanently in velvet due to low testosterone levels. These sterile animals, known locally as "stags," use as much browse as any other deer, but they can neither reproduce nor become trophies. Biologists speculate that an unknown species of browse plant may cause this condition, which is rarely seen outside the Hill Country.

Debbie flashed a superb trophy buck onto the screen. "You're looking for ones like this, four and a half years or older, with at least eight points—meaning four tines on each side. That's a prime deer for harvest. Some three-and-a-half-year-olds also have eight points, but their rack's going to be a lot smaller. If a buck's antlers don't stick out beyond his ears, he's a little one. We try to let the younger deer grow up, and since you'll probably come back, you'll want that big one to be around."

Among those big ones was a fabled, shadowy beast known as the "Minnesota Buck," named for the Midwest hunters who'd first spotted him on the ranch some years ago. Others claimed sightings over the next few seasons, but the deer never fell to a hunter and was now presumed dead of old age.

That night, billions of stars dusted the Texas sky, shedding a scant and heatless glow on the tent walls. I lay awake with eyes closed, snug in the downy billows of my sleeping bag, and imagined all the constellations re-arranged to form a single, horizon-spanning deer, moonlight beaming in his eyes, antlers shaped by curtains of opal-green aurora, meteors fling-ing from his hooves. I sagged away toward sleep, and while the earth re-volved, the great buck pinwheeled slowly overhead, surrounded by wind and thunder and darkness.

Around five the next morning I was awakened by pickups easing past my tent—hunters entering Slator Ranch's network of dirt tracks. A couple hours later, I opened my eyes to a silver sun hulking above the horizon, savanna grass glittering with frost so thick it looked like snow. I thought of the hunters in their stands, squinting against shards of refracted light, struggling to keep quiet while their bodies trembled with cold. And I imagined the heat of excitement surging through them each time a deer stepped into view.

Since dawn I'd heard rifle shots at intervals from the surrounding ranch lands, and occasionally three or four in quick succession indi-cated someone shooting at a distant or running animal. To me, this was unethical behavior because it greatly increased the risk of wounding. Most were single reports, however, indicating either clean misses or in-stant kills, probably by hunters who waited for close shots at standing animals.

Around midmorning, hunters trickled in from their stands to convene at the hut. Nearly all had seen does or small-racked bucks, and some re-ported spotting feral pigs—the only other large game animal regularly taken on the ranch. But no one on Slator Ranch had fired a shot. Big bucks always come in last, the experts advised, and that might not happen for a day or more. At this stage it was important to move quietly, sit still, and cause the least possible disturbance.

Midday was a time to nap or socialize. None of the hunters had arrived alone, and it was clear that being here with friends or family members was no less important than the hunting itself. I talked with a man who came with his two sons-in-law, another who brought his nephew, and a father accompanied by his adult son. The younger of this pair told me, his voice softening with unconcealed emotion: "I really can't explain how special it is for me, being able to do this with my dad."

That afternoon I rode with Bart to a Llano feed store, which advertised the shelled corn Bart used in his feeders, as well as nutrient-rich "deer blocks" specially formulated for Llano County whitetails. After picking up a few supplies, Bart asked the proprietors how much of each year's business came from deer feed. They figured sales of deer corn alone totaled five million to six million pounds, and returns for all wildlife feed—which means primarily deer but includes turkey and quail—accounted for 30 to 35 percent of the store's annual income.

A self-satisfied grin spread across Bart's face. These figures supported his own judgments about the importance of whitetails to Llano businesses. For the ranchers themselves, he added, deer hunting amounts to a crucial 25 to 40 percent of annual income, which can make the difference between sustainability and failure. Livestock prices fell during the economic downturn of the 1980s, but there was little if any decline in hunting. While a rancher's income from whitetails may not equal that from cattle, hunting is more stable and reliable over the long run.

Jackie Hatfield, office manager at the Llano Chamber of Commerce, added another perspective. "For the average merchant, I'd guess at least a third of their annual income is from deer hunting. And it's probably more than that for the grocery stores and restaurants. There's no business that isn't touched by it. Even the little gift shop across the street—deer season is the only time she stays open on Sundays. And the fact is, some hunters come at all times of the year, to investigate possible leases, set up their blinds, or just bring their families for vacation."

When I asked if local people felt invaded or became annoyed with the yearly influx of hunters, she shook her head. "I've never, ever heard anybody say anything derogatory about them being here. Texans by nature are friendly and we try to make people feel welcome. Also, everybody around here is bright enough to know it's the butter on our bread. Without hunting, a lot of our businesses wouldn't survive." I'd already seen figures attributed to the county Agricultural Extension Service indicating that whitetail hunting brings about five million dollars into Llano's economy each year—an impressive amount for a town this size, and coming at a slow season for everything else.

Down in south Texas, deer hunting is second only to oil and gas as the most important source of income, according to the *San Antonio Light*. And here again, hunting is more stable than the boom-or-bust petroleum industry. Much of this stability can be attributed to the animals themselves, because while it's easy to deplete some resources, deer populations are almost too resilient. The truth is, many parts of Texas would benefit ecologically if *more* people came to hunt the overabundant deer. It's no surprise, then, that income from deer hunting has steadily increased over the years and will likely continue to grow.

Nor is it surprising that among all the states, Texas receives the greatest economic benefit from deer hunting. During the 1994 season, one study concluded, this hunt supported more than 11,000 jobs statewide, accounted for retail spending of about $516 million, and had a total economic impact of more than $1 billion annually.

When Bart and I returned to the ranch that afternoon, everyone had gone back out to wait for deer emerging from their daytime seclusion. "You want to get settled in your stand and be completely still before the deer start moving around," Bart pointed out. "The last half hour before dark is your best chance to see 'em." He drove me out several miles to an unoccupied stand on the summit of a low ridge. Up in the tower I found a pivoting chair allowing open views in every direction and equipped with rests for bracing a rifle. There I sat with my paper, pencil, and binoculars—a tourist in a hunter's world.

I was soon taken by the peace of solitude among lovely surroundings—oak and mesquite copses intricately laced over a tawny carpet of grass, sunset kindling the horizon, the breeze ebbing, silence soaking down over the land. But sudden, agitated scuffles jarred my contemplations, something loud enough to be a deer or coyote directly under my stand. Peering down, I saw instead a gray creature the size of a gallon milk jug, with four stubby legs and a narrow, tapering, almost cylindrical head—an armadillo, rattling around as if its spring had been wound too tight.

The animal so absorbed my attention that I forgot all about deer—until I heard the *whump* of a distant rifle shot. Scrutinizing the area afterward, I caught a tremor of movement beside a nearby thicket, then saw a whitetail stepping quietly into the open. From the animal's bulky size I knew it was neither a doe nor a fawn. For 10 minutes he stood there, motionless as a rock, watching the familiar terrain for any hint of movement, appraising every tick and murmur in the mosaic of sounds. Finally he eased out onto the meadow's broad reach like a leaf drifting on a stream. At intervals he paused, twitched his tail, and lifted his nose to the invisible currents of air. His patience was impeccable, as if he knew the entire night lay ahead, giving him plenty of time to browse in the secure embrace of darkness.

Eventually, the shelled corn Bart had scattered beneath a huge oak enticed him closer. And now I saw that he was no ordinary buck, but one of the infertile "stags" Debbie had described earlier. Not only was his rack in velvet (normal bucks had shed their velvet long before), but his antlers were also peculiarly shaped—long and tall, standing almost vertical, one twisted forward and the other twisted back, making a strange but graceful corkscrew.

Although the buck's maleness was compromised, he lacked nothing in hot-wire reflexes. Twice he approached the scatter of corn, then bolted off at full tilt. The third time he appeared with a small-bodied doe whose caution almost equaled his own, but she held her ground when he burst away again. Reassured by her boldness, he came back more quickly, and then, as if they'd made a decision, the pair strolled over to the big oak and fed eagerly on corn.

The armadillo never stopped rustling, yet neither deer paid it much attention. On the other hand, human sounds would instantly have set them aflight. Deer are alarmed not simply by the noise our feet make, but by the steady, unpausing *rhythm* of our steps, which is altogether different from the irregular hops and scrambles of small animals or the four-legged hoofbeats and long hesitations of larger wildlings like deer. These whitetails could distinguish between armadillo and human sound patterns as surely as I could hear the difference between a piano and a drum.

Ghostly under the oak's low boughs, the stag and doe busied themselves snuffling corn. Hoping to see one of those elusive, mysterious bucks, I stayed on until dark. All the talk back in camp—the "Minnesota Buck" stories, the fervor that brought everyone else to this place—I had to admit was contagious even for someone who came only to watch. What I saw instead was the fluttering back and forth of birds, a sliver of moon adrift in the luminous wake of sunset, and the stars accumulating like snowflakes on the black dome of sky.

When I aimed my flashlight toward the shadowy outline of the oak, it revealed four shimmering eyes that seemed to float in space, wavering back and forth as the whitetails peered toward me, curious yet unafraid. But as I started climbing down, they vanished like a sigh into the immense and waiting night.

"It was Dickie White that got 'im," someone sang out as I approached the headquarters hut. Squeezing into the tight circle, I saw Bart Gillan and Mike Green, one of the hunters, bent over a deer's sleek, gray shape. Then I noticed its head, its opened eye, and its rack—the elegantly curved beams, thick and burled and reddened at their bases, and the array of 11 long, vertical tines, each point polished smooth and bright.

Bart and Mike stretched a tape across the deer's rack to measure its inside spread. Next they measured the length and circumference of each main beam, then did the same for every tine, all to the nearest eighth inch. Whenever they paused to write down the numbers, Mike stood back, shook his head, and proclaimed: "Damn, that's one beautiful deer!"

By contrast, Dickie White looked on quietly from the side. "I watched him fifteen minutes before I decided," he confessed. "It was a hundred-twenty-yard shot—he went right down and never moved. I didn't know he was that big until I walked up to him." If the other hunters felt twinges of envy, Dickie's good luck also nurtured their own hopes and fired their excitement about the days ahead.

Bart took each measurement carefully, conservatively, and honestly. When they finished, Mike Green stood beside the animal and praised it yet again. "That's a helluva deer, Dickie. I guaran-damn-tee ya, there's no way I'd have waited fifteen minutes."

Next came the scale. "A hundred twenty pounds, dressed weight," Bart reported. Then everyone jammed inside the hut to watch as he figured totals—adding together the measurements for each antler, plus the inside spread, then deducting the amount each measurement on one antler differed from its complementary measurement on the opposite side. For the highest Boone and Crockett score, both antlers should be as nearly identical as possible.

Bart ran through the numbers once, then twice, creating an almost unbearable suspense. Finally, he turned to the group, smiling mightily: "We've got one-forty-seven and six eighths." Mike blurted out the final score again, as if someone in that tiny hutch might not have heard. Dickie grinned self-consciously while Mike grabbed his hand, pumping it up and down. Everyone spilled outside to admire the deer again, amid talk of entering this one in the "Bull-of-the-Woods" contest for champion buck of Llano County, with a $400 prize.

"That's the biggest buck we've had this year," Bart declared, savoring yet another affirmation of all that he and Debbie had worked for.

"Pretty soon, somebody'll get a buck on this place that'll make the Boone and Crockett record book," one of the hunters predicted. "And after that happens, they'll be able to charge a price guys like me can't afford."

Afterward, beside a crackling mesquite campfire, I asked two hunters, Larry and Buddy, how people got interested in trophy deer. They said most beginners are primarily after venison, but as their skills improve, some start looking for larger, more challenging bucks. This in turn requires learning more about deer behavior and advanced hunting techniques. "One of the true values in hunting is learning to appreciate your craft," Larry remarked.

"I also know a lot of guys who've hunted for a long time and still do it only for the meat," he added. "One of my hunting partners, when I get too serious about trying for a big buck, he'll laugh and tease me, saying, 'You can't eat the horns.' But of course, I hunt for the meat, too, not just trophies. We've got four in our family and probably eighty percent of our meat is wild game."

Larry and Buddy agreed that getting a deer isn't the only reason for hunting, or even the most important one. A main benefit of sitting for hours in a stand, they said, is to watch the squirrels play, the quail come in for corn, the turkeys strut around, pecking at each other and dusting off. "Once, about a half mile from Harper's stand I saw two mountain lions cross the creek," Larry recalled. "That's a big part of the enjoyment—being out there and watching the wildlife."

"What's your highest goal as a deer hunter?" I asked Larry.

"Well, I'd like to take a Boone and Crockett deer," he replied. "But it's not just that. After you do something for a long time, you get to where you enjoy the work more than you do the actual goal. I guess what I really want is to do this with friends, and tell stories, and listen to stories, and watch other people enjoy their hunts. That's when it's the best."

We all sat quietly under a starry sky, watching the flames and embers, grateful in our own ways to be here.

The New Buffalo

An enchanted, otherworldly dawn: every twig and blade and blossom thickly mantled with frost, a billion sunrises dazzling in the diamond trees and crystal grasses. As I stepped from the tent, I picked out something dark and alive just beyond the fence. Then I realized it was a white-tail buck, raking his many-pronged antlers against a bush, tearing and shredding branches. I smiled a bit, thinking of the hunters crouched in distant blinds while the object of their yearnings displayed his virility beside the camp they'd left an hour before.

When the buck caught me taking a single step for a clearer view, it triggered a lightning bolt inside his brain. He dashed away through the mazework of shrubs and trees, shaking down curtains of glittering frost, his body cloaked in cold fire. And within seconds he was gone.

Later on, I had an altogether different experience with the other large herbivorous animal for which Slator Ranch is known. This, of course, was *Bos taurus*—the cow, more specifically the rusty-colored Herefords, often known as beef cattle. Instead of bounding away like deer, these critters rumbled along behind Bart's pickup while he drove in loops and circles around their pasture, honking the horn. It wasn't a special enthusiasm for trucks or horns or Bart that motivated their galloping pursuit. Hitched behind the truck was a two-wheeled device that spewed out feed pellets, like lollipops tossed to kids at a parade. The little brown nuggets, Bart explained, are a supplement to the herd's grassy diet.

But why not simply fill a trough and let the cows eat, in deference to their phlegmatic nature? The explanation, it turned out, was far from simple.

Bart reminded me that the vegetation native to this place had co-evolved along with buffalo—millions upon millions of buffalo, in massive herds that swarmed over the land, grazed and stomped for a while, and then moved on. After they'd gone, the natural community didn't languish and it didn't simply regenerate—it flourished. For one thing, after being fractured and pulverized by buffalo hooves, the ground absorbed rainfall more quickly, diminishing losses to evaporation and runoff. For another, deposits of urine and droppings fertilized the soil. Also, the plants grew back more vigorously after being pruned because a long process of evolution had adapted them to being grazed. In short, buffalo herds enriched and sustained the vegetation that nourished them and in this way played a vital role in their own ecosystem.

From a biological standpoint, Bart contended, there isn't much difference between buffalo and cattle. The two species are evolutionary siblings, fairly close in size and behavior, with similar digestive systems and much the same way of grazing. Also, he asserted that the total number of cattle in America today—about 110 million—pales in comparison to the magnitude of the several buffalo herds, which numbered 40 million to 70 million each. (Others have estimated the total bison population at 30 million to 70 million animals, and the number of cattle in America's grassland region today at about 45 million.) Bart did acknowledge one very important difference, however. Buffalo herds moved freely over vast areas of land, so their impact on any particular locale was intense but intermittent, while the impact of permanently confined cattle herds is dispersed but continuous.

Bart glanced in his side mirror at the clomping bovine crowd. Amid the honking and mooing and the Pied Piper cavalcade, he broke into a canny smile. "We're making these cows run around like buffalo, so their hooves crack the ground. Also, we've been dividing the ranch into a bunch of fairly small, fenced pastures so we can shift our cows from one to the other. We'll put them in a pasture for a short time, let them pound up the earth, let them eat the grass all the way down, let them urinate and dung on the soil. Then we'll take them out of that pasture and give it a complete rest so everything can grow back, just like when the buffalo were around."

Bart credited this approach to range ecologist Alan Savory, whose concepts of "holistic resource management" have attracted growing, if sometimes controversial, interest throughout the American West. "Savory tells us this land was *meant* to be grazed," Bart declared. "Some people nowadays say we should get rid of cattle, but taking away livestock is the most damaging thing you could ever do to this environment and to all the wildlife that lives here. These plants evolved for thousands of years with millions of buffalo and other grazing animals eating them and stomping the ground."

Bart waved his arm out the truck window. "Look at that cow eating grass over there; she's a modern-day buffalo. That's all she is." You wouldn't mistake Bart Gillan for a man of flimsy conviction. Whatever anyone else might think about these brawny and graceless creatures, Bart knew they had an important role to play in the ecological management of Slator Ranch.

The reason many western lands have been damaged is not grazing per se, he asserted, but maladaptive and destructive patterns of grazing, and he is convinced that range degradation can be corrected without reducing livestock numbers. It's not hard to find ecologists and environmentalists who flinch at this sort of optimism. For one thing, western environments are so diverse—running the gamut from tallgrass prairie to scorching desert—that a single solution isn't likely to encompass them all. Nevertheless, some ranchers, including Bart and Debbie Gillan, had seen abundant evidence for recovery on their own property: long-extinct

springs flowing again, vanished native grasses reappearing, whole plant
and wildlife communities being resurrected. All this while the land is
being grazed.

But how do whitetails fit into the picture? Cows mainly eat grass, Bart
explained, but deer concentrate on woody browse and broad-leaf weeds.
Because of their different diets, cattle and deer complement rather than
compete with each other, so they do well on the same land. By contrast,
sheep and goats vie against whitetails for the same foods, so they don't
make a good combination.

For another opinion on these issues, I visited William "Bill" Armstrong,
a biologist at the state-operated Kerr Wildlife Management Area, a research facility sprawled across 6,500 acres of rangeland near Kerrville,
about 60 miles southwest of Llano. Over the past 40 years, Kerr researchers have investigated ways to manage ranches for healthy populations of both deer and livestock. Results of their studies are applied all
over Texas—passed along by state biologists like Fielding Harwell and by
scores of independent biologists who advise landowners.

Bill Armstrong's chronicle of deer and cattle programs on the Kerr
Wildlife Management Area, delivered in a melodic Texas accent, echoed
much that I'd heard about Slator Ranch. "In the 1950s, our deer were
small and stunted, and every few years we'd have a major die-off," Bill recalled as we jolted around the Kerr Area in a pickup truck. "So we started
by using hunters to bring down our deer population, which reduced
pressure on the habitat and built health back into the herd.

"There were large stands of cedar here, but we found that cedar wasn't
eaten by deer, or by cows, goats, or sheep. So we used fire to open up
those stands, leaving strips for deer cover. We discovered that in our
burned pastures we got improved plant growth and more species diversity, and the cows grew larger." Here was another case of modern scientists resurrecting the Native American tradition of intentional burning to
enrich habitat and increase wildlife populations.

"We also experimented with different grazing systems. We've got
twenty-eight pastures now, and we'll put our entire herd of cattle in a pasture for three to five days, then move them to the next one. After they
graze off a place, you've opened up the mat of grass so more light gets to
the ground, and when it recovers you find a greater variety of plants growing back. Also, for a few weeks after burning and grazing, deer can eat the
fresh, regrowing grass. This whole system adds more plants to their diet
and increases the carrying capacity, so you get bigger, healthier deer."

Hunting, burning, grazing. Bill Armstrong described a way to closely integrate human uses with the environment, allowing both people and nature to thrive. While he spoke, a loose mob of cattle ambled off the road ahead. "Basically, we're re-creating the old-time ecosystem," Bill contended. "We're using cows as a tool to manage the habitat—making them work like the buffalo herd used to. We don't need *no* grazing, we need *proper* grazing, at moderate levels. This benefits not only deer and cattle, but everything else, like frogs, lizards, snakes, songbirds, and other animals."

When Bill mentioned other kinds of wildlife, I remembered spotting some unusual creatures along the highway between Llano and Kerrville—deer that looked like elk, wild sheep bearing great crescent horns, and heavy-bodied antelopes with striking black-and-white faces. They seemed quite at home on the Texas ranch lands, yet looked like escapees from a zoo.

"Exotics . . . ," Bill sighed. As far back as the 1930s, some Texans began releasing wildlife from other parts of the world onto their land, then charging premium rates to hunters who wanted a different sort of experience. By the 1980s, there were 56 exotic species in Texas, numbering almost 170,000 animals, and as you traveled the state's outlands you might see anything from a gazelle to an ibex, a giraffe to a rhinoceros. Today the most common exotic species include axis deer, blackbuck antelope, and nilgai antelope—all from India; aoudad sheep from North Africa; fallow deer from Europe; and sika deer from Asia. Although none of these exotics interbreed with native deer, they are a serious concern, Bill Armstrong warned, because they eat a wider variety of foods than native deer and generally outcompete them. Although landowners build high fences to prevent escapes, their efforts are bound to fail, so there are now wild, free-ranging populations of exotics in many parts of Texas. And like starlings or house sparrows, they'll almost certainly spread outside the state.

Scientists at the Kerr facility put six whitetails and six sika deer in a 96-acre pasture surrounded by deer-proof fence, with no livestock inside and no hunting permitted. Both species increased to roughly 16 apiece before edible plants began running short. Over the next five years, sika deer multiplied while not a single whitetail fawn survived to adulthood. When the project ended after nine years, there were 62 sika deer inside the enclosure and no whitetails. In a simultaneous study, whitetails also succumbed to competition from axis deer. Researchers concluded that Eurasian deer are "severe competitors" with whitetails, presenting "a real threat to the management, well-being, and survival of this native species."

Fielding Harwell noted that exotic game species are illegal in many states, and he recommended keeping it that way. "It doesn't look like we'll ever get rid of them in Texas, because they're too deeply ingrained," he admitted. "But there's no closed season or bag limit on exotics, so a rancher who wants to eliminate them can do it at any time." On Slator Ranch, Bart and Debbie encourage hunters to kill any exotic animal wandering onto the property.

Harwell acknowledged that exotics give ranchers a source of income without seasonal restrictions. Also, there is a growing commercial demand for game meat. Wholesalers like the Texas Wild Game Cooperative in Kerrville sell venison from exotics to upscale supermarkets and restaurants all over the country, and they ship live animals for breeding stock to growers nationwide. An overwhelming majority of North American wildlife biologists oppose this spread of exotic game animals. "Our ecological niches are filled by species that evolved here," a Texas researcher told me, "so there's no room for introduced animals." Bart Gillan put it differently: "I doubt that man can come up with anything better than what God already put here."

Valerius Geist, the Canadian biologist, points out that in New Zealand and Europe, introduced white-tailed deer have fared poorly because of competition from Asian and European species. He also cites the example of Assateague Island National Seashore, where sika deer introduced in 1916 have gradually displaced native whitetails. And he warns that exotics may transmit potentially devastating diseases to native wildlife.

Despite these perils, commercial farming of exotics is spreading in North America, and animals constantly escape into the wild. Bill Armstrong noted that domestic livestock species are also exotics, but with a crucial difference: they're much easier to control. If we're going to raise animals for meat, he says, we should minimize the threats to native wildlife by sticking with traditional domestic species.

What about the broader issue of commercializing *any* use of wildlife? Valerius Geist, like many of his colleagues, believes the whole concept of "Texas-style game management"—including not only production and sale of wild animals but also paying fees to hunt on private land—should be prohibited everywhere in North America. Furthermore, he asserts that game ranching makes wildlife into someone's private property, undermining our public sense of responsibility for wildlife management and conservation. Just as important, opening the market for wild game encourages professional poaching.

"Very slowly, paid hunting concentrates access to wildlife in favor of a smaller and smaller segment of increasingly affluent, politically powerful people," Geist contends. This limits the number of citizens who can benefit from wildlife, fosters resentment toward privileged landowners and hunters, and increases trespassing as well as poaching.

There's truth in these arguments, and in the simple fact that most hunters prefer free access on both private and public lands. But Delwin Benson, an expert on fee hunting, notes that only one third of the land in the United States is publicly owned, much of that in the West. Most states east of the Mississippi are like Texas, where about 95 percent of the land is held privately. This is a simple, unalterable fact, and it presents major problems for people who hunt.

Millions of owners stake out their boundaries with "No Hunting" signs. For example, about 50 percent of the private lands in upstate New York and 79 percent in Colorado were posted by 1980. These landholders obviously find more reasons to exclude or limit hunters than to admit them, and among their reasons is lack of financial return. Despite the limitations, most of America's 12 million deer hunters use private land, writes Benson; and although only a small percentage (6 percent in one survey) now pay for access, more than half say they'd accept a modest fee in exchange for the outdoors experience and the possibility of bringing home valuable meat. This is clear enough in Texas, with about 550,000 licensed hunters providing landowners with a strong motive to allow access.

According to Benson, hunting fees can also bring a very important ecological payoff. Consider what's been happening to America's private lands: every year literally millions of acres are brought under cultivation, drained, filled, clear-cut, dammed, paved, mined, industrialized, and subdivided. The record of private owners nurturing and protecting wildlands is absolutely dismal—because there's money to be made by destroying natural habitat. If Benson is right, fee hunting gives property holders a financial incentive to keep their land in a natural condition, to carefully manage game populations, and to become stewards of wildlife habitat.

"Hey, how'd you like to use one of our stands this evening?" It was Larry, poking his head out the window of his big-cabbed pickup. I grabbed my jacket and binoculars, then squeezed in with Larry and his hunting partner, Buddy. As we drove toward their designated area on the ranch's far side, I realized the invitation wasn't entirely philanthropic. Larry and

Buddy planned to use two widely separated stands, and they wondered what was happening near a third. "If you spot a good buck," Buddy requested, "be sure to count his points and check the width of his rack. One of us could go there tomorrow."

My stand was a plank seat nailed in the fork of a massive oak tree. During the first hour nothing moved except branches shaking in a cool breeze and a mockingbird who perched just out of reach, cocking her tail and blinking her bright eyes. Moments after she flicked away, I spotted a deer loping across a meadow and through binoculars discovered it was a brawny buck with almost preternaturally tall antlers, the sort Bart called a "basket rack."

As the deer slipped away beyond hatchwork scrub, I again felt a twinge of the trophy hunter's yearning, and I realized it sprang from that nearly universal human desire to find or pursue or possess something exceptional. For some who love deer hunting, big bucks are the paragon, the metaphor, and the embodiment of excellence. Fascination with hefty-antlered whitetails probably began with the first European settlers, if not long before, but the custom of displaying racks might have come later. One settler reported that in 1851 he'd seen racks nailed on every woodshed along Main Street in Portville, Pennsylvania, and he suggested each hunter was trying to outdo the others. Today most people have little sympathy for the impulse to bag or exhibit trophy antlers, and historian Robert Wegner estimates that less than 5 percent of American hunters are specifically after trophies.

Like any other passion, this one can become twisted and hypertrophied. "There are two kinds of trophy hunters," a seasoned Texas biologist told me. "One I call the 'book hunters,' whose whole objective is to get a deer that ranks as high as possible in the Boone and Crockett record book for firearms hunting, or the Pope and Young for archery. They tend to be wealthy people, because it costs money to go seriously after trophy animals: it takes guides, it takes private land, it takes lots of time, and it takes hunting in lots of different areas."

There is also a cadre of book hunters so driven by perverse desire and ego that they operate illegally—violating closed seasons, using spotlights at night, hunting in parks or preserves. And there are outlaw guides who specialize in closed-season hunts, charging as much as $10,000 for an exceptional trophy. Even more bizarre, people have been known to buy trophy racks or mounts from professional poachers, then claim the glory for themselves.

"The other kind of trophy hunters are ethical people who mainly want the experience but are also looking for trophy animals," the biologist continued. "More than likely, these hunters aren't going specifically for the book." In fact, I was told that most record-book deer are taken fortuitously, by people who haven't gone out with a trophy animal in mind but happen to be in the right place at the right time. I suspect the great majority of hunters interested in trophy racks are typified by the sort I met on Slator Ranch—ordinary law-abiding folks whose quest for antlers is serious and ardent, but not their main reason for going afield.

Half an hour after the first buck's passage, another ambled across the same meadow, nose to the ground, as if he were drawn by the scent of a doe in estrus. He was a fine deer: lean bodied, with long legs, smooth tan coat, and gracile six-point rack—the sort of animal Bart regarded as biological and economic capital. Left alone by selective hunters, living in uncrowded habitat, spared the trials of drought or disease, he could become a prime trophy whitetail. This deer might also contribute his genetic prowess toward the vigor and continuity of future generations on this patch of Hill Country. But if he'd been born on another ranch, where habitat quality and herd management carried little weight, he probably wouldn't have survived to this age, wouldn't have grown so large in a few years' time, and wouldn't have developed this beautiful crown of antlers.

Rosy afterglow simmered at the sky's western edge while the east deepened to ash and purple. I glassed the shadowy face of an adjoining ridge, the scramble of grass and thicket surrounding my stand, the unattended feeder 50 yards away. Everything seemed empty, and yet I knew there were deer all around, watching from the thicket's edge, testing for scents on the slow current of air, savoring the chill and silence, feeling no urgency to show themselves. Headlights traced a road beyond the distant fenceline as night eased across the Texas savanna.

Soon as I climbed back into the truck, Buddy reported seeing lots of does and a few smallish bucks but no sign of a trophy animal. Then, after a modest pause, Larry reported that he'd taken a 12-point buck and would need help loading it into the pickup. As we drove toward his stand, a solitary doe bounded onto the road, froze momentarily in the glare of our lights, and leapt away, vanishing like a stone pitched into black water.

Back at headquarters a dozen hunters jammed close while Bart weighed Larry's buck: at 124 pounds, it was good sized for a southern whitetail. "His rack's not as tall as Dickie's, but he's got *twelve points*!" marveled Mike Green, fingering each tine, shaking his head like a zealot before the Grail.

"A typical twelve-point's a rare deer," Bart offered. "This is only the second one we've had on the ranch." Racks with this many tines are generally the sort called nontypical, meaning the two antlers are asymmetrical and often oddly shaped. These peculiarities can range from small differences in the shape and number of tines to wildly erratic embellishments—drop tines, kicker (extra) tines, off-kilter bends, mooselike flares, extraordinary thickness and burliness in the beams. A big, asymmetrical rack is like fire shaped into bone. Some hunters prefer such antlers, drawn either to their extravagant beauty or their masculine unruliness. But Larry said he'd always preferred typical antlers, so this was his lucky night.

Bart peered at the buck's teeth and ran his fingers over them, judging age by the amount of cusp wear. When it came to aging deer, even experienced biologists like Fielding Harwell deferred to Bart, who over the past decade had perfected his skills by assessing literally thousands of animals. To Bart's amazement, the buck was only four and a half years old, meaning it had reached exceptional size and antler development for such a young animal.

"Think what he could have been if he'd lived a couple more years," said Larry, his voice flagging slightly. Bart had a way of making his clients into disciples.

"I've been coming here seven or eight years," Larry added, "and I've only taken four bucks, because I just keep waitin' for the biggest ones. You see more nice deer in a day on this ranch than you'll see in a week anyplace else. It's the chance of a lifetime, hunting out here."

Larry's deer totaled just over 127 inches, so his dreams of a Boone and Crockett buck hadn't been realized, but he quietly admired the animal and mentioned that he'd like to have a taxidermist preserve the trophy as a head mount. Everyone praised the deer's beauty—after all, a 12-point would be exceptional anywhere on this continent, even though the world record is 23 points for a typical whitetail rack and 49 points for a nontypical rack.

"This deer is a rare gem," Bart declared, as willing hands hefted it into the cooler. "You can't just go out anywhere and expect to see a buck like that. More and more hunters are realizing that trophy bucks are a *product*—brought about by taking proper care of the deer herd and the land. If the ecosystem wasn't healthy, you wouldn't get a deer like this."

A Taste of the Hill Country

I didn't have much trouble locating Miiller's Meats in Llano. Once I got to the general neighborhood, I followed a maroon pickup with an open tailgate and two deer inside. It pulled into the parking lot of a large, whitish building, blank faced except for a single glass door that looked tiny and out of place. The small anteroom contained just one display case offering a selection of fresh cuts and "Award Winning Smoked Meats." Work space and cold storage took up virtually all of the building; this was a processing plant, not a retail store.

I explained my interests to the owner, Bryan Miiller, while he worked at a machine stuffing seasoned venison into a flaccid, translucent casing. An endless, mottled python of sausage lay in coils and snarls on a steel table beside him. Miiller was as friendly as you could expect from a hurried man at the peak of his busiest season. "If you want to see how we handle deer, you're welcome to talk with Chad, our plant supervisor." At the end of a long corridor I entered a spacious room with concrete floor and high ceiling, a perfect echo chamber for the radio's fervent country music serenade.

Three men, aprons stained livid crimson, clustered around a bulky, T-shaped wooden table with a deer carcass on top. The person evidently in charge—thirtyish, thickset, black hair, stubble beard—gave me a quick glance, scarcely missing a stroke with his slender-bladed knife. He worked at a furious pace, slicing through meat and cartilage, severing joints, dissecting the animal at a speed I never would have imagined possible. Each time he cleaved off a part—foreleg, hind leg, neck, rib cage, pelvis—he'd slide it to his assistants, who almost as quickly pared every bit of meat from the bones.

Between knife strokes they flicked venison into a flattish cardboard box, bones and fat into a scrap drum. Both helpers were in their twenties, long-haired and wiry, and like the boss they seemed comfortable in T-shirts while I shrugged deeper into my jacket. The first deer vanished in about five minutes; they hoisted another onto the cutting table and blades flew again. No one said a word to me but I could tell they sensed my appreciation and were showing their stuff.

As soon as the second deer was boxed and gone the head guy looked up, smiling faintly: "Can I do somethin' for ya?" His voice was serious, but the Texas cordiality shone through. I explained myself while he lifted another deer onto the table. "I'm Chad Parker," he nodded. "Go ahead and ask any questions you got."

"Ever cut yourselves?"

Parker flashed a heavily bandaged finger. "Oh yeah, all the time." Then, perhaps to make clear that even the best can slip, he added: "I've been butchering deer my whole life. Shot my first one when I was six years old and my dad made me do it all."

After the crew disarticulated a couple more deer, Parker offered to show me around. On the room's opposite side, he heaved open the door of an enormous cooler with about 10 deer inside, their hind legs snagged on metal hooks that ran along a ceiling track so workers could easily pull animals into the cutting room. I noticed each deer was tagged with the hunter's name.

"We keep them in here until we're ready to skin a bunch," Parker explained. "Might as well show you how it's done." He pulled a deer from the cooler, made long cuts down its legs and from belly to chin, and then—with help from an electric winch—peeled its hide cleanly off, much as you might remove a sock. In three minutes, he'd done what could take half an hour for an expert with a skinning knife. Most hides were left with the processor, who sold them to a tannery.

Each cardboard box stacked near the butchering table contained the meat from a single deer with specific processing instructions. For a basic charge of $45, hunters could order their own selection of roasts, tenderloins, ribs, and burger. Specialties like chili, sausage, or jerky were available at additional cost.

"From the time a deer comes in, we can have it skinned, butchered, wrapped, and boxed in about twenty minutes," Parker estimated, with no scarcity of pride. "We can butcher up to seventy deer in a day and skin as many as two hundred. We've had four hundred seventy-five come in over the past week and we've already finished about four hundred of them. Last year we did thirteen hundred total. That's way more than anybody else in Llano County, but down in San Antonio there's plants that do three, four thousand deer every year."

Outside the building Parker showed me a large bin piled high with scraps. "What goes in here is bones, hooves, tendons, and fat. They'll pick it up later for the rendering plant, and it's made into stuff like fertilizer. Nothing's wasted."

Watching Chad Parker team up with his assistants on another deer, I was reminded that amid all the public discourse and debate over hunting, the most remarkable fact is that *food* is rarely mentioned. American hunters take about 4.5 million deer each year, which are processed into roughly 130 million pounds of meat. In every city, town, and hamlet there are people who love the rich, wild taste of venison, value its symbolic importance as food harvested from the land, cling to it as a remnant of self-sufficiency in a largely synthetic world, and treasure it as a deeply ingrained tradition.

Venison is prepared much like beef and has an equal range of possibilities. Anyone who hasn't inherited recipes penned on slips of paper can buy wild-game cookbooks to stimulate the culinary imagination. Besides excellent flavor, venison has less fat and more protein (but somewhat higher cholesterol levels) than beef. Also, in areas like the Texas rangelands, where deer feed on natural vegetation rather than eating crops treated with fertilizers and pesticides, the meat is "organically grown" and free of chemical additives or hormones.

Many successful hunters divide their take with partners who aren't so lucky, and they pass venison along to friends, neighbors, or relatives. In recent years—with growing deer populations and liberal bag limits—hunters have also begun donating some of their venison to charities, soup kitchens, homeless shelters, orphanages, and needy families. One of the organizations set up for this purpose is Hunters for the Hungry, which has branches all over Texas. In Llano County, hunters bring field-dressed whitetails to the chamber of commerce for distribution to people who have put their names on a list. Recipients do their own processing and there's no charge to anyone.

"Most of our processing is done for out-of-town hunters, because they've got the money for it," Brian Miiller told me during a break from the sausage machine. "Local people generally take care of their own deer." I asked how much of his business depended on hunting. "About fifty percent of our annual gross income is from deer processing," he calculated. "Without it, we couldn't stay in business."

This reminded Miiller of his anxious customers waiting for their deer. "I generally put in a hundred hours a week for the two months of deer season," he sighed. "I like to hunt, too—but there's no time for it."

On my way out I picked up a business card for Miiller's Meats, its emblem proclaiming: "Our Taste of the Hill Country." To sample that taste I bought some hard sausage and sliced off a big chunk before I left the parking lot. It was delicious . . . and spicy enough to make tears run down a midwesterner's cheeks.

Late that afternoon, everyone took notice when Rich, the young doctor, pulled up beside headquarters. In the back of his truck was a large buck carrying a 10-point rack, heavy beamed, with stout, blunt tines. "Now there's a really old deer," said Bart at a glance. Onlookers crowded close as he pried open its jaws to check tooth wear. "Sure enough," he nodded. "Eight and a half years!" Then, as he so often did, Bart gave his hunters an ecology lesson.

"Boy, am I glad you got him. He would have laid down and died this winter, because pretty soon he wouldn't be able to eat. Come on, you guys; take a look." One by one, Bart's apprentices peered at the buck's lower teeth—worn almost to the gumline by years of grinding. "An old deer gets to where he can't chew his food anymore," said Bart. "So finally he'll starve."

As patriarchal bucks decline, their antlers also change, retaining mass but becoming shorter and producing fewer tines. Several of the men leaning against Rich's truck conjectured about the enormous rack his deer must have carried a few years earlier. "You know, think about it . . . ," Bart mused. "This might just be the Minnesota Buck!" What pleasure he seemed to find, nurturing such dreams among his friends and hearing them chew on the idea while he stretched his measuring tape from beam to beam. The rack's final tally didn't challenge Dickie White's buck, nor did it have the symmetry of Larry's, but Rich seemed happy. He said he'd probably grind the meat for sausage, because venison from old animals can be as tough as cactus.

About this time, Bob and Jackie arrived with a handsome, long-beamed six-pointer. "This one's Jackie's," Bob reported. "It's the first buck she's ever taken." A flurry of accolades followed, although Jackie's pride was mixed with some abashedness over the buck's modest proportions, and she wondered aloud if she should have waited in case a larger animal had come along. Not just a novice, but a woman in a stereotypically male domain, she wanted to represent herself well. Women hunters numbered about 1.5 million in 1985, according to a U.S. Department of the Interior survey. This translates into 9 percent of the total hunting population, up from only 6 percent in 1965.

Bob had taken her picture with the deer out by their stands, said Jackie, explaining her neatly combed hair and fresh ruby lipstick. "Chipped my nail polish working the rifle bolt," she added with a sly smile, gently flaunting the graces she'd brought to this shaggy assemblage. From comments I heard, in Jackie's presence and away from it, the men seemed pleased with her success and impressed by her determination. If any felt threatened or uneasy about her presence, they kept it to themselves. Of course, Jackie wasn't the only woman hunter present—everyone knew Debbie Gillan could hold her own with the best of them.

Still, it would have been interesting to see the reaction had Jackie brought in a monster whitetail.

Wildlands Within Fences

On the hunt's final day, sunshine and warmth poured down over Texas, and glory blossomed on every hill. In the pasture near my tent, meadowlarks sang, cattle mooed and bawled. I heard more shots than on any other morning and soon realized why: almost everyone had already taken a buck, so they were hunting does "for the freezer." This suited Bart, because it would help to improve the ratio of bucks to does, keep deer numbers down, decrease competition for winter browse, and improve fawn survival the next summer.

Bart suggested driving to a part of the ranch where no one was hunting, and it was clear he wanted to show me something important. We jostled for miles along rutted tracks, cresting rocky hills and wallowing across dry, sandy creek bottoms. At intervals he'd stop to point out features of the landscape—a granite outcrop with straight-edged cuts from past quarrying and native plant species returning to abundance as a result of well-managed cattle and deer populations. Whether he intended it or not, Bart was giving me a tour of his personal geography, drawing from knowledge gained by long, intimate working experience with this land. Here was the nexus of Bart Gillan's mind and heart, on a terrain he was learning to nurture, as it nurtured him in turn.

Finally, we intersected a deer-proof fence—about eight feet high, the lower part heavy mesh and the upper part tightly strung barbed wire—that ran straight as a surveyor's line along one edge of the property. Because whitetails and livestock on most adjoining places were not managed like those on Slator Ranch, the ranch had become an island of habitat far superior to that on surrounding lands. It was crucial to protect this environment from the crowds of undersized, hungry deer outside and to prevent the big, healthy animals inside from wandering off. "We're building this fence to keep bucks from our land in here and does from other people's land out there."

Farther down the road, Bart stopped and gestured out the window. "Now what do you think of that?" Across the fence stood a cluster of buildings surrounded by land so heavily browsed and grazed that nothing remained except bare earth and a few scraggly bushes—a stark contrast to the lush vegetation on our own side. In the near distance was another homestead on another little tract, less ravaged than the one

beside us but again lacking the richness of Slator Ranch. And beyond
that place I could see more rooftops on other parcels of land.

"Subdivision," Bart intoned. "It's happening all over, because a lot of
ranches can't make it financially." I knew cattle markets were in decline,
partly because of the changing American diet, and I realized the ranch
business was under pressure because of growing concerns over abusive
grazing on public lands and destruction of predators, ostensibly to safeguard livestock. Bart also explained that some ranchers are being pressured out of business by inheritance taxes based not on the land's worth
as agricultural property but on its far higher potential value as real estate.
For example, because Debbie had inherited Slator Ranch, she and Bart
would spend the rest of their lives in debt to the federal government,
working to pay off a seven-figure tax liability.

"So what's happening to ranches like ours? Everywhere in Texas, people
are subdividing their land into these little five-acre or ten-acre places," said
Bart. In fact, driving up from San Antonio the previous week I had marveled at the number of signs advertising "ranchettes" for sale. The same
process is taking place all over the American West, fragmenting large
ranches into smaller and smaller parcels. "For a lot of ranchers, selling these
pieces is the only way they can afford to hang on to some of their land,"
Bart contended.

Breaking up expansive private holdings like Slator Ranch has major
environmental consequences. What we saw along this edge of the property was a swarm of smaller, subdivided tracts, each with its own buildings and fences, its own land uses. This created a checkerboard pattern
of intensive habitation, profoundly altering the natural habitat and in-
terfering with the lives of wild animals. In fact, the fence was now a dividing line between two completely different environments.

"What happens to the deer over there?" Bart asked. "And what about
the coyotes? The wild pigs? The mountain lions? Even the smaller animals and birds?"

I'd never imagined that such changes were taking place around the
American West, nor had I thought about their implications for habitat
and wildlife. Even when they're poorly managed—as far too many of
them are—the expansive, privately owned western ranch lands constitute
de facto wild preserves, their condition fundamentally natural despite a
century of intensive use. In many places, to be sure, mismanagement of
livestock has damaged the environment and severely depressed wild animal populations. (The same thing has happened, Bart pointed out,

where deer and other wild ungulates have been allowed to increase beyond their habitat's carrying capacity.)

But even on overgrazed ranch lands there are still whitetails, mule deer, pronghorn antelope, elk, coyotes, black bears, mountain lions, badgers, gray foxes, and a whole array of smaller creatures from jackrabbits and prairie dogs to kestrels and scissor-tailed flycatchers. As long as big tracts of grazing land remain—regardless of their present condition—the potential exists for restoring their full richness.

On some things Bart and I could not agree. He's an ardent advocate for private land ownership, whereas I believe that as much of North America as possible should be publicly owned, and I would support public acquisition of private lands at every opportunity. Yet I think Bart is right about keeping these large, private ranches intact. From a conservation standpoint most people would likely prefer to see the American West sprawling with cattle ranches than to have these wildlands splintered and developed. Properly managed, private ranches can contribute on a massive scale to our national environmental heritage as well as our economy.

According to environmental writer George Wuerthner, just 8 percent of the ranchers in 16 western and Great Plains states use public lands for grazing. The other 92 percent forage their livestock entirely on private land. If their cattle operations failed, it's unlikely that these ranchers— who own countless millions of acres—would just let their lands go fallow, nor could the government afford to buy them and create a virtual subcontinent of national parks. Probably, as we now witness throughout the West, the ranches would be subdivided for weekend retreats, country homes, or suburban growth. Others would be parceled into fields, plowed down to bare earth, and planted with monotype agricultural crops.

Does it make sense, I wondered, to drive such people off their land? Or are there good reasons to help them stay here? A true ecological wisdom, it seemed to me, is one that keeps people and land together in the business of producing food while they develop a more balanced and sustainable relationship with the natural environment.

Back at headquarters we found a hive of activity—some hunters unloading freshly taken deer and others removing animals from the cooler. Over by the fence, members of a couple of groups hung their deer from horizontal poles, then skinned and quartered each animal, experts showing beginners how it's done. Impressive quantities of venison went into boxes and ice chests, and I felt among these people a satisfaction that's become increasingly rare in the modern world—that of providing their own food from the land. But I also noticed that difficult, bony parts like necks and ribs were generally put aside and hauled to a dumping spot frequented by night scavengers. It contrasted with the butcher shop, where every bit of meat was used.

During this final ritual I sensed most clearly the satisfaction each of these people found through hunting, and the pleasures they gained by coming here with friends. There was a strong camaraderie within each group, a feeling of shared experience, and a general lament that things were coming to a close. No one, it seemed, felt more pleased with it all than did Bart Gillan, who mingled, laughed, swapped tales, made final pronouncements on hunting techniques and deer management, talked about next year's season, and clasped hands extended from pickup windows.

That evening I walked to a stand in an oak grove not far from the Gillans' house. I had just settled into the high perch when two does slipped from the underbrush and made their way to a feeder hanging under a tree nearby. Their wariness was something to behold. Every few seconds one or the other would jerk to attention, peer into the tangle-work of trees and thickets, listen for incongruous sounds, then lean down to nuzzle corn kernels.

Eventually they wandered off, but half an hour later five whitetails tentatively approached the stand, screening themselves behind broken thickets. They hesitated for a long while, unwilling to show themselves, blending almost invisibly into the sere, shadowy background. I began doubting their existence, as if these misty shapes might be rocks or leafy branches, but I kept as still and silent as they did. Then, without apparent reason, they scattered off in separate directions. I wondered if the evening breeze had curled my scent their way or if they had sensed a danger beyond my reckoning. Dusk nestled down over the silent, emptied land.

Well past dark, as I trekked back toward camp, a minor commotion led me to an armadillo rooting frenetically among clumps of crackly grass. He looked like a tiny armored knight and seemed oblivious to my intrusion, but every time I got closer than six feet he'd scuttle off into the void. When I tracked him down again he would stare questioningly into the flashlight's beam, raising his tubular snout and shifting his outsized ears back and forth. Although I found him utterly endearing, his gaze seemed to judge me otherwise. At last, tiring of my company, he skittered away and stopped so far off that I gave up, leaving him to the night's urgent business.

I switched off my flashlight and walked along a narrow path, navigating by the faint glow of stars and crescent moon, stopping at intervals to savor the comforts of darkness and the voiceless amity of trees. In the middle of a long pause, there came a sharp, explosive snort, so close by that I gasped aloud and my heart banged like a fist against my ribs. At this same instant I caught the sound of hoofbeats, magnified in the still, cool air, so loud that I conjured an angry bull rushing at me. But instead, the animal pounded away, its chain of thumps dwindling and muffling until no sound remained.

It was a deer, and yet—in my unraveled condition—I thought it must be no ordinary whitetail. I concluded this was a prodigious buck, one of Bart and Debbie's carefully nurtured elders, majestic in girth and weight and bearing, his head graced with a monumental trellis of bone. And so clever, so vigilant, so impeccably wild, that he'd never been glimpsed, except at great distance and in the last flicker of sunset.

Then I found myself wondering if I, in the black belly of this Texas night, had encountered the legendary Minnesota Buck.

SEVEN

OPENING WEEKEND

It is here that we
seek—and still find—
our meat from God.

—ALDO LEOPOLD

Dawn

Opening *Weekend.* In Wisconsin the very phrase carries an aura of sanctity and consequence. The state's firearms deer season was about to begin—as dictated by law and tradition—with the first light on the Saturday before Thanksgiving. And on this particular Opening Weekend, an estimated 650,000 hunters would take to the forests and farmlands.

For Jim Mlsna, it was the dawning of heaven's own day. "Our dad taught my brothers and me how to hunt, right here on this farm," he told me. "Back then you weren't allowed to hunt deer until you were sixteen years old. But when we got to be twelve or thirteen, Dad brought us along on drives he made through the woods with our neighbors. Us boys would carry a stick and hit the brush with it to make noise and push the deer out from cover. As we got older, they had us carry a bigger stick so we'd learn to go through the woods with a gun in the crook of our arm. Finally, around 1959, I started hunting deer with a gun. I went every year after that, but I didn't get my first deer until Opening Day of 1982—a six-point buck.

"So I hunted for the first twenty years and never got a deer; either I didn't see any or else I missed them. Obviously, I'm doing it not so much for the game, but because I enjoy hunting, and the camaraderie that goes with it, and the challenge, and the venison, if we get any. But the biggest part of all is just being out there, the sheer pleasure of sitting in the woods, me and nature together."

Jim was about 50, just under middle height, built like a fullback. In the flashlight's circle, I could make out his round face, thick glasses, graying beard, and self-conscious smile. His quilted jacket, canvas pants, and hat were all blaze orange—easily exceeding Wisconsin's hunter safety requirement for at least 50 percent blaze above the waist. Needless to say, this color doesn't shriek to a deer's eyes the way it does to our own.

Jim leaned into the back of his truck, pulled a shotgun from its case, and slipped into his pocket a box of 20-gauge shells that fired heavy lead slugs. Then we trekked across strips of mown hay and corn stubble, toward a line of trees faintly visible on the slope below. A few minutes earlier, Jim's hunting partners, Dan and John, had gone into the woods a short ways down the valley.

One of every three Wisconsin males over the age of 12 hunts deer, and 46 percent of the state's households report at least one hunter in residence. But these figures, however impressive, give little sense of the cultural and emotional weight of deer hunting among Wisconsin's people. Schools in many towns avoid rampant truancy by officially dismissing students when deer season begins. For the same reason, factories, stores, construction projects, and a whole range of other businesses close their doors, and despite fanaticism over football in these parts, games scheduled during hunting season are often played before half-empty stands.

Over the previous days it seemed that no one could be unaware of the approaching hunt. News stories offered background and analyses, predicted the deer harvest, ventured editorial opinions, and advertised everything from ammunition to venison processing. Officials with the Department of Natural Resources (or "DNR," which has become part of the vocabulary for anyone speaking the regional dialect) had reported 698,500 licenses purchased for the coming firearms season and 217,000 for the separate archery hunt. They had also estimated this year's statewide deer population at 1.3 million, an increase of 150,000 from the previous year. Around Wisconsin, this figure was almost as well known as the name of the Green Bay Packers' quarterback.

Everyone also knew of the problems caused by high whitetail numbers—car accidents, suburban deer conflicts, agricultural damage, overbrowsed habitats—and about the DNR's perennial effort to "get the deer population under control." Because hunting is the only way this can be accomplished, deer season has tremendous ecological importance, along with its prominent role in Wisconsin's social and economic life.

Hunkered down on the frozen hay field, I watched the sky's edge, smoldering with shades of lavender and apricot, while relentless cold prickled against my cheeks, seeped through my clothes, set my toes throbbing. Growing light revealed that I was cupped in a shallow swale, one of the valley's upper tributaries, with dense forest along the contour 50 yards below. From here, even if I couldn't see Jim and his partners, I'd spot any whitetail that left cover. A few hundred yards to my right, half visible through tall, lacy trees, was the farmstead where Jim had grown up, now operated by his brother Mark. Toward the north and west, beyond the widening valley, twinkled lights from other farms and from the tiny hamlet of Middle Ridge. The emerging scene was quintessentially midwestern, a mix of deciduous forest and cultivated fields that made some of the richest deer habitat in North America.

Because I was accustomed to the wild expanses around my home on the Northwest Pacific coast, it seemed strange that people would hunt so near houses, villages, roads, and fence lines. Although I'd been raised in suburban Wisconsin, hunting had no place in our family; in fact, I grew up considering the whole business atavistic, arrogant, and immoral. In this sense my background was completely the opposite of Jim Mlsna's. Only later, when I lived with Eskimo and Indian people in Alaska, did I become a hunter myself. Now, back on my original home grounds, I wanted to close the circle: to experience a part of life I had missed earlier. Above all, I'd come to discover what role deer hunting plays in modern life here, and to learn how hunting captivates the human mind and soul, regardless of the culture or community in which it takes place.

Jim Mlsna epitomized the zeal and commitment millions of people bring to hunting. His sentiments grew from lifelong experience, from a passion rooted deep in his heart, and from (or perhaps in spite of) rigorous childhood training. "When I was fourteen or fifteen," Jim recollected, "some people around here said they'd seen a huge buck. He was twice the size of the does and had a minimum of twelve points on his rack. One evening around dusk, my dad and I spotted him by the edge of the cornfield. He stopped and we both piled out of the truck, but I made a big mistake. Before Dad could shoot I slammed the door . . . and that buck took off like a shot.

"My dad turned around and he said, 'If you weren't my son, I'd . . .' Then he told me, 'You walk over and put your cap down in the snow by that track.'

"At seven the next morning I had to go there and start following that deer. They had about eight guys waiting at stands in case he came by ahead of me. I followed him all day, and when I got done that night I laid my cap down by his tracks so I could start again the next morning. Eventually I tracked him all the way to Coon Valley and then all the way back to where he started. For three days I followed that deer, but we never did see him—not until a month or so later, after the season closed.

"When I scared that buck away, it was the only time I ever came close to getting hung out to dry by my dad."

I thought about the memories swarming through Jim Mlsna's mind as he awaited dawn, beginning another year on his deer stand. For me, shivering now and anxious to feel the sun's warming touch, this day couldn't begin soon enough.

At 6:15 a.m., a hound dog broke the frozen stillness, moaning and baying on a neighbor's farm. Gazing at the horizon I imagined earth's great, curved rim rolling ponderously down to meet the hidden sun. Three minutes later, at 6:18 a.m., there came a single, muffled thud far off toward the southeast. Who could see well enough to shoot? I puzzled. And who, in the midst of so many hunters, would jump the legal starting time by 15 minutes?

Showing the Blaze

The previous afternoon, I'd left my parents' home in the southern Wisconsin town of Stoughton, found my way to Interstate 90, and pointed the dashboard compass northwest. It was a pure blue day, farmlands sprawling gloriously over rounded hills, black soil in neatly plowed rows, gray branches shaking in the wind, but almost everything else a variation on brown: light tan meadow grasses, bleached-bone cornfields, sandy-buff hay stubble, silvery-beige sedges and cattails, auburn leaves stubbornly clinging to the oaks. So often I'd heard this part of the country described as ordinary, austere, unspectacular. Did you have to grow up here, I wondered, to sense the beauty in this land?

The interstate was jammed and frenetic, so I relaxed into the slow lane, watched the passing traffic, and soon realized it was dominated by hunters. I saw many camper vehicles, as well as cars and trucks packed with outdoor gear, but overwhelmingly, in scores of vehicles, the give-away was hunter orange. It couldn't be a coincidence that so many bright vests, jackets, hats, and coveralls had been conspicuously placed—hanging in windows, draped atop piles of gear, laid over seat backs, or perched on dashboards and rear ledges. Soon I was convinced: these hunters, streaming toward the Wisconsin outback, were showing the blaze.

Why? Perhaps it was an urge to fly their flag of allegiance. Or to broadcast their association with a group, like putting a Green Bay Packers sticker on the car window. Or possibly members of this largely male congregation took pride in displaying an emblem of their status and pride, as a football player might wear his letter jacket.

Countless thousands of vehicles had crowded onto the Wisconsin highways, a northbound procession filled with people anticipating tomorrow's dawn—the renewal of tradition, the pleasures of being outdoors, the ritual and promise of hunting itself, the companionship of friends and family. Even I, more a bystander than a participant, felt the almost hypnotic enticement of a mass human event, the allure of being part of something very, very big.

Although Wisconsin license plates dominated, I saw a few hunters coming from Illinois, one from Michigan, even a car from Georgia with a blaze coat in the window. You didn't need a formal census to know state residents make up the overwhelming majority of Wisconsin deer hunters, but statistics bear it out. Among 674,422 gun licenses sold back in 1991, for example, only 26,877 went to nonresidents.

The interstate angled west into a corrugated landscape of tightly spaced hills with farmlands in the narrow valleys and along bisected ridgetops. By late afternoon I reached the town of Sparta, 20 miles from the Mississippi River and the Minnesota border. Here I figured to make an important purchase. Although most shops had sold out everything luminous, at the Big Bear variety store I found one blaze sweatshirt big enough to wear over my heavy coat. The clerks, both deer hunters, had time on their hands.

"Well, I think I'm ready," said the older one, who looked to be in his forties. "The last five nights I've been out shinin' deer, just lookin' at 'em, so I'll know where to go on Opening Day." The other man, about 30, said he'd just put a bunch of "No Trespassing" signs around his grandmother's farm. "Me and my brother, we've got the whole ninety-four

acres to ourselves," he grinned, "unless somebody trespasses." That's a
bad idea in Wisconsin, where venturing onto posted land without permission can bring as much as a $1,000 fine even if you're trailing a
wounded deer. "Ask first!" warns the state regulation booklet, while sug-
gesting that most owners will allow considerate people onto their land.

The older man didn't say where he intended to hunt but revealed it
was along a border separating two "management units." Wisconsin has
about 120 of these units, each comprising an area of similar deer habitat
and land uses, bounded by designated roads. This way the DNR can lo-
calize regulations—limiting the hunt to bucks in some areas, for example, while opening others for deer of either sex, or allowing hunters to
use rifles versus restricting them to shotguns (which have a shorter effective range, making them safer in populated areas). As part of their strategy, hunters can shift between management units, the clerk explained.
"If we don't get a buck with rifles in the unit where we start, we'll cross
the road where it's legal with shotguns for either does or bucks."

The whole town of Sparta was geared up for hunting season, he observed. "All the businesses cater to it. The gas stations and restaurants,
they'll be open at four or four-thirty tomorrow morning. And if you
come here in the afternoon, you'll see the guys that already got their deer,
and they're lined up at the registration station. Later on, some will get together at the taverns and restaurants. Yeah, things are always pretty busy
this time of year."

Of course, it wasn't just Sparta. In towns and cities all over Wisconsin,
deer hunting occupies a substantial economic niche. State hunters spend
about $380 each per season (on lodging, food, transportation, equipment,
licenses, land leased or owned for hunting), totaling an estimated $255 mil-
lion per year and supporting an equivalent of 8,000 jobs. Figured this way,
if hunting were a single business it would rank among Wisconsin's 15 most
profitable companies. Most of the rewards garnered by hunters themselves
are beyond calculating—but venison and deer hides, at least, can be measured in cash equivalents. If each deer averaged 50 pounds of meat, conservatively valued at $2 per pound, a harvest of 380,000 deer (modest by
recent standards) would be worth another $38 million, plus $1.6 million
for the hides.

Hunting also contributes to the public treasury. In the United States
as a whole, fees paid by hunters and fishermen cover more than 75 percent of the cost for all wildlife management. Deer license fees bring
almost $15 million annually to the state of Wisconsin, vital revenue to
cover the cost of deer management as well as other wildlife, fish, and

endangered species programs. Taxes on firearms and ammunition bring in another $3 million per year, money that's been used to purchase about 85 percent of Wisconsin's public wildlife lands, to fund wildlife research, and to support nature education programs.

Someone calculated the monetary worth of Wisconsin hunters' "enjoyment" at $32 per day, totaling $157 million annually statewide; but I seriously doubt that people like Jim Mlsna would give up hunting for such a modest sum, nor do I believe you can compute the real value of a cherished tradition. Try to imagine judging the importance of Christmas to an American family on the basis of only the dollar value of gifts, food, and travel, or asking people to give up Christmas in exchange for that much cash. I choose this example deliberately because for many who take part, deer hunting is no less important than Christmas. For example, 60 percent of Wisconsin hunters in one survey reported they would miss deer hunting more than most or all other activities in their lives.

It's often suggested—tongue in cheek—that some folks approach deer hunting as if it were a religious experience. This came to mind in a town south of Sparta where I'd passed a large, modern Catholic church with a billboard out front announcing: DEER HUNTERS MASS—4:30 A.M. I had seen newspaper photos of such a Mass held at St. Gregory's Church near Sheboygan: hunters in blaze jackets taking communion, guns arrayed by the altar for the priest's blessing, a man clutching between folded hands the deer antlers he'd rattle in the woods to attract bucks. I wondered if the priest might read from Deuteronomy 14:4–6:

> These are the beasts which ye shall eat: the ox, the sheep, and the goat, the hart, and the roebuck, and the fallow deer, and the wild goat, and the pygarg, and the wild ox, and the chamois. And every beast that parteth the hoof, and cleaveth the cleft into two claws, and cheweth the cud among the beasts, that ye shall eat.

Most local folks around Sparta hunted principally for meat, the older clerk told me as I headed for the door. "With the cost of food now, people want venison—they'll use everything from their deer—and lots of them butcher it themselves to save money. People with families, the wife buys a license and gets her own deer tags so they can bring home as much as possible." His sidekick listened, nodded, and wished me luck. I didn't have the spunk to confess I only planned to watch.

Shortly after sunset I passed two cars along the shoulder of a country road a few miles out of Sparta. One had just struck and killed a doe, her soft brown shape sprawled in the headlights while three men huddled over her. When I came by later, both cars and the deer were gone. In Wisconsin, drivers can keep road-killed deer or give them to someone else if the carcass is first tagged by a police officer or game warden. Far better this, I thought, than leaving animals to decay along the highways.

Thunder in the Hills

Back on the hillside daylight gained momentum after that first illicit shot. At 6:22 a.m. I glimpsed a meteor flaring across the northern horizon—a chalky streak that vanished the same instant it was drawn. Several minutes later, there was a flurry of distant, rumbling shots, and as daylight came on, the frequency of shooting increased, at times rising to a bedlam of reports from all quarters, near and far, like popcorn crackling in a hot pan.

I clamped a pencil between numb fingers and tried to tally the shots, but it was hopeless. I could only estimate that I'd heard between 200 and 300 rounds in the opening half hour. From my experience on this tiny patch of countryside I tried to imagine the whole state of Wisconsin with 650,000 hunters afield, the air sheathed in an unbroken cacophony of sound, as if a gale had shattered the brittle atmosphere into billions of fragments.

Of course, the noise would not have been evenly distributed. According to sociologists Thomas Heberlein and Bruce Laybourne, about 70 percent of Wisconsin's deer hunting is concentrated in the state's agricultural southern half, where the Mlsna farm is located. Hunter densities commonly range between 25 and 35 per square mile in southern areas, and peaks of 70 to 80 per square mile have been recorded. The forested northern half averages only 5 to 15 hunters per square mile.

Not surprisingly, hunters congregate in southern Wisconsin because that's where deer are most abundant. State wildlife managers say they're hard-pressed to hold whitetail populations in this region as low as 25 per square mile, despite yearly harvests averaging about 10 deer per square mile (statewide). If the take lags for a few years in a given area, numbers of deer soar, with a corresponding increase in crop damage, car accidents, and landowner complaints. Up north, by contrast, deer populations generally range from 10 to 25 per square mile, held in check not so much by hunting but by natural factors like severe winters, low habitat productivity in continuous forest, and scarcity of nutritious croplands.

It's also harder to find deer in the northwoods, where extensive forest conceals the deer, sparseness of roads limits access, and there aren't so many hunters pushing deer from cover. In more crowded places like Middle Ridge, only the craftiest old bucks know enough to stay in deep thickets and impenetrable marshes—and such creatures are rare indeed. In northern Wisconsin, a buck radio-collared by biologist Orrin Rongstad lived to be at least nine and a half years old, but Rongstad told a newspaper reporter he doubted there was a buck that old in the state's entire southern half.

Over 90 percent of Wisconsin's deer hunters take to the field on Opening Day. It isn't just that they're anxious to get out hunting or that social plans revolve around this particular weekend, although both play a role. Equally important, each hunter tramping through the countryside increases the other's chances because crowding keeps deer on the move. This helps to explain why about 60 percent of all the deer harvested during Wisconsin's nine-day firearms season are taken on Opening Weekend. Not surprisingly, hunters admit having mixed attitudes toward their compatriots, but overall, at least in Wisconsin, they're very tolerant of high numbers. Evidence for this tolerance is available to anyone who goes abroad on Opening Weekend . . . and simply listens.

After seven a.m. on my morning watch there came longer silences broken by shots and sporadic volleys averaging about five reports per minute. Amber sunlight tingled in a line of trees atop the next ridge, then finally spilled out over the distant highlands. At seven-fifteen a.m. I heard seven rhythmic *whumps* from one direction, then nine more from another, and in two minutes' time I figured there were 25 gunbursts. Afterward a prolonged hush fell over the countryside just as the sun's edge burst out above the neighboring farm and poured silver light across my chilly hillside.

In the lengthening intervals between gunshots I heard blue jays calling, a faraway dog barking, cars whining along a distant road, faint breezes rustling in the cornstalks. Then, just after eleven a.m., a single, ear-splitting shot detonated in the valley below me and pealed away over the land. There were no clues in the stillness that followed, so I guessed that Jim or one of his partners had missed a deer.

Twenty minutes later I happened to glance up the slope directly behind me and saw four heavy-bodied does galloping shoulder to shoulder across open cropland, their hoofbeats raising clouds of frost and dust. Still tightly bunched, they veered down toward the woods where Jim waited, but then held short. About 50 yards away, the does stood in a tight line, staring anxiously into the trees, huffing misty breath. The watcher inside me was taken by their pure, electrified beauty; the animal lover inside me felt empathy and compassion; the hunter inside me desired them as prime, enticing prey.

Then came a shot from the adjacent ridge. It had nothing to do with these deer, but their bodies drew up tight as fists, their legs bent like drawn bows, and they whirled away, tails flared, heads outstretched, hooves flying, like caribou sprinting across open tundra. In seconds they vanished over the crest. I stared after them, expecting gunfire from that direction, but heard none.

At lunchtime I tromped back up the hill, shed a few layers of clothes, and waited for Jim. Just after I arrived, an aging sedan bumped down the dusty lane crammed with five friendly guys, all in their twenties and garbed in blaze. One identified himself as Jim's nephew. "We've been hunting since early this morning. Sat for a while, but you know, that gets old pretty fast." I leaned against the car, squinting through furls and strata of cigarette smoke. "So we split up into drivers and standers, made a couple drives in the woods, and got one nice doe." He gestured toward the trunk, which was cracked open so the animal's legs angled out, clearly visible, as state law requires until each deer is registered at an official check station.

"We figured to try a drive here if nobody's around," he explained, pointing toward the valley. My reply came as a disappointment—it wasn't good manners to disturb a place with hunters already on stands. They were astonished that Jim and his partners intended to stay put all day. "We'd *never* do that!" exclaimed a voice from the backseat. "It's too boring." Then off they went.

In Wisconsin, about one quarter of all deer hunters are under 25 years old, according to Heberlein and Laybourne, and the average hunter is 36 (compared with the national average of 42). A great majority of Wisconsin hunters (71 percent) are married with children, about 30 percent have graduated from college, and most work at nonprofessional or nontechnical jobs. Interestingly, almost half of all United States hunters have attended college, which exceeds the percentage with college experience in our population as a whole.

The number of American hunters grew from 4.3 million in 1923—just under 6 percent of the country's population—to something over 15 million today, or 10 percent of our total population. Presently there are about 12 million deer hunters in the United States. Heberlein's studies reveal that most grew up in rural areas and were taught by their fathers. The relatively few women who learn to hunt at an early age are often firstborn or only children of fathers who are avid hunters. Women who become hunters as adults frequently do it to share the experience with a boyfriend or husband who serves as their teacher; and in some states, there are special training programs for women who want to learn hunting skills.

The United States has gone from a rural nation, where more than half of the people lived on farms, to one in which almost everyone lives in cities, suburbs, or towns. This helps to explain why the number of hunters has declined nationwide in recent years, a trend that's probably destined to reach even strongholds like Wisconsin. Many urbanites regard wildlife as a part of the scenery, to be used only for viewing pleasure, not for food or the other rewards of hunting. These "nonconsumptive" values, sociologists predict, will increasingly displace "consumptive" wildlife uses.

Should hunting decrease significantly, biologists would confront a snarl of environmental and societal problems caused by the resultant explosion of deer numbers. On the other hand, attitudes about hunting could take an unexpected turn, given the trend toward greater ecological awareness, along with heightened interest in Native American and pioneer traditions, practical outdoors skills, wild-foods harvesting, and self-sufficient home economics.

For Jim Mlsna, hunting required no resurrection of lost knowledge or abandoned values, no intellectual or philosophical calisthenics. It was deeply rooted in his own heritage, something wholly unaffected and spontaneous yet complex and vital. In this, his good fortune abounded, I thought, as he came trudging up from the woods. He stopped a few feet away, took a deep breath, and puffed: "Well, I saw a six-point buck a little while ago! Couldn't get a clear shot . . . but then Dan got him." This explained the single, startling boom. "Dan and I cleaned the deer together and dragged it down to the valley bottom so he can pick it up with a truck this evening."

When Jim finished his news I commented on all the shooting just after dawn. "That really wasn't much at all," he remarked. "I think the temperature had something to do with it. Soon as they get cold, hunters usually leave their stands and move around looking for deer, or they'll start making drives." Jim leaned his shotgun against a fence post. "This morning it got warm pretty quick, so most of them sat tight. There weren't many guys out pushing the deer around, so you had less shooting than usual."

The two of us perched on the tailgate eating sandwiches and getting better acquainted. We'd first met a few days earlier in Sheboygan, where

Jim works as a nurse anesthetist at a local hospital. It was a lifelong friend of mine, anesthesiologist Dr. Donald Harvey, who brought us together. "Jim would be perfect to show you Wisconsin deer hunting," Don had surmised. "Some of our anesthetists moonlight to earn extra income, but not Jim, because it would interfere with the things he really wants to do. All Jim Mlsna asks in life is that he can hunt and fish."

Jim pointed toward the cluster of farm buildings about a quarter mile up the lane. "This place has been in our family for over a hundred years. My mother's grandfather was Bohemian; he came over from Czechoslovakia and homesteaded this entire section. They always hunted right here, same as we're doing it now, except back when deer were scarce in this part of Wisconsin."

As a kid, Jim helped process deer even before his dad let him tag along with the hunters. "Of course, we grew up having venison, so I always enjoy it. I married a city slicker, but she's learned to eat venison, especially the sausage, butterfly chops, other parts that taste close to beef; and our kids mostly eat the steaks.

"Dan, John, and I share whatever we get. We usually limit ourselves to two deer because we don't need any more meat than that."

Tradition, family, and place shaped the foundation of Jim's hunting. "I've hunted this valley—we call it a coulee—every year since 1979. Same spot. Same guys. I tried other parts of the state, but here I know the area and I know the people. Also, my brother Mark farms this place, so he knows where the deer are. We park ourselves in the coulee, which is a natural funnel the deer tend to move through. I like this type of hunting because you can wait until the animal stops moving. That way you get a sure shot. And here you're shooting down into the coulee, which means your bullet doesn't travel far, so it's safe."

After lunch, Jim and I tramped down through the deep, crunchy leaves past stumps of big trees cut years before, now replaced by leaner second-growth oaks. Jim assigned me a lookout midway down the slope, then went another 30 yards toward the bottom of the narrowing cleft. All around was a maze of lanky tree trunks and scant undergrowth offering cover for deer yet open enough to allow good visibility for the hunters. Now I understood why Jim and his partners liked this spot.

I brushed the leaves off a small patch of ground so there'd be no noise if I moved a bit, then settled in to wait. Gunfire continued sporadically as it had all day, heightening my sense that a deer could show up at any moment. Down here in the sheltered coulee I also felt more alert, watchful, and expectant as the first hour passed. Tree shadows crawled across the forest floor while Jim sat motionless, braced against the far side of his chosen trunk. Except for a few chickadees and juncos the place seemed empty. Eventually I lapsed into daydreams.

Then, glancing off through the fretwork of trees, I noticed something on the move. A whitetail, I knew immediately . . . and from its head-down posture I guessed perhaps a buck following a doe's scent trail. Moments later I caught the bony glint of antlers. The deer stopped for a long while, nearly invisible against a tawny backdrop of tree trunks and leaf litter, then angled down into a ravine just to my right. I felt sure he was coming my way but couldn't suppress doubt as the minutes slipped by.

At last I heard a faint jostle of leaves and in that capricious, unexpected, phantasmal way of deer, a buck emerged from the gully not more than 30 yards off. Deliberately picking each step, he came along the slope scenting first the air and then the ground, until he stood so close I thought he'd hear my eyes blink. There he paused, broadside and crosswind, his attention focused away from me. The deer's sturdy-beamed antlers, arching symmetrically from burnt ocher bases to polished gray tips, carried a total of six points. Not a legendary buck, but an immaculate whitetail—the sort that had brought Jim Mlsna to this hillside every year for decades.

Few hunters would deny that they're captivated by the beauty, the stature, the wariness, the challenge of a prime buck. With high deer populations in most areas today, there's no ethical or ecological justification for emphasizing bucks and leaving does alone, but hunters do it anyway. Things were different back in 1915, when Wisconsin first started protecting antlerless deer, hoping to save whitetails from extinction. Strict hunting laws brought a spectacular recovery. By 1944, Aldo Leopold said, Wisconsin's deer population, estimated at 500,000, was too high and should be reduced. Hunting for antlerless deer was allowed intermittently during the 1940s, but not until 1951—after massive winter starvation in northern areas—did the legal hunt for antlerless whitetails really become established.

Even so, when I was a high school student in the fifties, we slandered as a "Bambi killer" anyone who brought in an antlerless deer. "It's taken a long time for hunters to change their attitudes," conceded William Ishmael, a leading deer biologist with the Wisconsin DNR. Only in recent years have antlerless whitetails made up more than half the annual harvest. Nevertheless, few bucks make it past their second year in southern Wisconsin, and virtually none reaches the age of five.

The buck standing so close to me now must be at least two years old,

I figured. And he was a very lucky deer, having come within a few yards of the only unarmed person in these woods. I fairly ached from keeping still and figured I could shift a bit without frightening him as long as I did it slowly. But when I moved—I mean that very *instant*—the buck detonated into a full dash, not the stuttering gait of a mule deer but a flat-out sprint, straight along the slope, his body arching and flexing, neck reaching out for speed, hooves rebounding like a drum roll over the taut skin of land, on and on without slowing or hesitating, until the sound of his panicked flight faded in the distance.

I listened breathlessly in the quiet that followed, wondering if a hunter would spot him down the way. Sure enough, a shot . . . silence . . . and then another shot. This troubled me because the animal was probably sprinting full tilt and shots at moving deer are very difficult to make accurately. Nevertheless, judging by the multiple reports I'd heard all day, few hunters shared Jim Mlsna's reluctance to fire at a deer on the run. In fact, with so many people in the woods you weren't likely to see a white-tail standing still.

Loss of wounded game is a serious problem in hunting today, as it has been since the first humans learned to pitch a spear, and, indeed, since predatory animals came into existence. In modern times, however, with sophisticated firearms and no specter of starvation for hunters who come home without game, wounding of animals *should* be extremely rare. In my opinion, a skilled and ethically responsible hunter will never fire without taking rock-steady aim at a clearly visible animal that is standing motionless within close and certain range, and after making absolutely sure no one is in the background.

The buck's appearance put an exclamation point in the middle of an otherwise tranquil and uneventful afternoon. Gauzy overcast drew gradually across the sky, softening the light, assuring an early dusk. Jim and the others left their stands shortly before sunset and convened along a dirt lane that followed the valley bottom. When I mentioned the buck, Dan and John said they had both fired at him but missed cleanly. They heard no shots afterward, so apparently the deer got away unscathed.

After loading Dan's whitetail in the truck, we drove to nearby Portland for supper at the home of Jim's mother, Janet Mlsna. Before anything else, we hung the deer from a tree in her backyard and Dan rinsed out all traces of blood or dirt. "When we get back to Sheboygan," Jim explained, "the three of us skin our animals and do our own butchering." This approach has become old-fashioned in Wisconsin, where nowadays most hunters pay to have professionals butcher their deer, process the meat, and prepare venison specialties like breakfast sausage, bologna, and bratwurst—the regional favorite.

Janet Mlsna had prepared a hunters' feast for us: platters heaped with meat, potatoes, and vegetables. We sat around the big dining room table, adrift in Lawrence Welk melodies, surrounded by family pictures and knickknacks. Everybody hurried through dessert so they could get to Saturday night Mass—a convenience for hunters who would otherwise have to attend at an ungodly hour before tomorrow's dawn.

Meanwhile, I took a drive to West Salem, a small town about 10 miles from the Mississippi River, where the most popular spot this evening was Karl's gas station, grocery, and sporting goods store. A line of cars, trucks, and vans snaked from the busy main road into Karl's parking lot, and if you looked closely you'd see evidence of deer in, or on, most of them. This was one of Wisconsin's 475 deer registration stations, where successful hunters are required to log in their whitetails. If you want to look at deer, talk to hunters, or find out how the season's going locally, you check out a place like this.

I immediately saw a knot of men in blaze outfits traipsing from one vehicle to another, led by a fellow in dark-green coveralls with a headlamp strapped over his knit cap. When the group surrounded a pickup truck with a hefty doe on board, I squeezed in for a look. A young woman recorded numbers from a tag fastened to the animal's ear and matched them with numbers on a bright-green "back tag" pinned (as law requires) conspicuously on the hunter's jacket. Then the fellow in coveralls asked: "Would it be okay if we checked your deer to see how old it is?" Everyone pressed closer to watch.

The examiner was John Olson, a DNR biologist—bearded, in his thirties, with a pleasant, soft-spoken manner well suited to the human relations side of his job. Olson pried open the deer's mouth and beamed his light inside. "One and a half years old," he concluded, running his finger along the teeth. "See here, the milk incisors have been replaced, so it's not a fawn, and the adult premolars are just coming in, which means she was born the summer before last." Olson's assistant also noted the animal's sex and the area where it had been taken, while the hunter seemed pleased by all the attention focused on his deer.

"By registering deer we get a harvest total and we can profile the structure of deer populations both locally and statewide," Olson explained. This system, in place since 1953, has produced the longest continuous body of information on North American whitetails, and it's the cornerstone for deer management in Wisconsin. Biologists use registration data to estimate the number of bucks in each area, the ratio of males to females, and the ratio of does to fawns. Also each year they assess hunting pressure, use weather data and census counts to evaluate survival during the previous winter, and estimate summer fawning success.

From this information, DNR experts figure the state's total deer population entering fall, then establish a goal for each season's harvest, based on how many deer can survive winter without causing habitat damage or other problems. The statewide harvest goal is broken down into regulations for each deer management unit, such as limiting the harvest to bucks as a way to encourage population growth, versus harvesting deer of either sex or giving out "bonus tags" for does only to reduce, stabilize, or maintain the population. But the process doesn't end here. Each year wildlife managers' recommendations are scrutinized by the general public and by a sequence of committees and boards, most important, the Wisconsin Conservation Congress, a lay advisory group for the DNR, largely made up of hunters and fishermen, known for its willingness to disagree with biologists' conclusions.

John Olson peered inside a station wagon at a whitetail that couldn't have weighed more than 60 pounds. "This deer was born last summer," he concluded. "There's no need to check the teeth." In rich farm country some deer can grow as large as yearlings in just six months, he said. But others—especially those born late in the season—are small enough to be obvious at a glance. "This one's also a buck," he added, running his fingers across the forehead. "Go ahead, try it." I felt the bony, fur-covered "buttons," or pedicles, that in subsequent years would have grown into antlers.

Olson moved from vehicle to vehicle, record sheets in hand, neon-orange crowd milling alongside. He examined a brawny six-point buck like the one I'd seen this afternoon, and to my amazement declared it was just a yearling, more precisely, one and a half years old. Most deer taken by hunters around here belong to this age group, he added. Given the "right genetics," plus high-quality food like corn and other nutritious crops, farmland deer can grow at an incredible rate. Although only a few bucks survive beyond two years, these lucky or elusive older animals have much to do with the agricultural Midwest's reputation for producing huge whitetails.

Proof that such creatures actually exist came when a flatbed truck pulled into the lot with a proverbial "swamp buck," quickly drawing a crowd. When I finally got close enough to take a look, I saw a deer of tremendous brawn and girth carrying antlers like roots of an upturned tree—broad and thick, festooned with 13 asymmetrical points, a couple of them snapped off in rutting battles. Olson figured the buck's age at four and a half years, a veritable ancient in this neck of the woods.

Word flashed around the parking lot and it wasn't long before Karl himself emerged from the store, tape in hand, to measure the rack for this year's Big Buck Contest. The crowd fell silent when Karl stepped back, shining his flashlight along the buck's substantial flank. "He's got a nineteen-and-a-half-inch spread—an awful nice deer—but we've had a couple bigger ones in here already."

Next came the bloodstained platform scale. This hunter, like most of his comrades, expected his deer to weigh about twice what it actually did—just under 170 pounds. A bit short of the heaviest so far, which had scaled 187 pounds, Karl reported, and well below the station's all-time record of 230 pounds. With an audible sigh the hunter concluded there was no point entering the contest, but this did nothing to inhibit the crowd's enthusiastic gawking and admiring. Even splayed lifeless in the back of a truck, it was a creature of extraordinary beauty and proportion.

"In northern Wisconsin you come across a lot more bucks with eight points or better because of low hunting pressure," John Olson told me. "We're trying to get people to redistribute, but they don't want to go up north because they like having other hunters around to move the deer." While such folks are in the clear majority, many others—like Olson himself—feel that bringing home a deer is less important than having a good experience in the woods. "When I think back on my early hunts," he recalled, "there weren't many deer around. I mean, we'd be elated to get one about every third year. Still, that was excellent hunting. Some of us feel that a quality hunt means not seeing other people even though having more hunters around makes the success rate higher."

John Olson hadn't reached middle age, yet he remembered a time when deer were scarce by today's standards because they were still recovering from the excesses of an earlier era. Back in 1922 the state's Game Commission reported, "Deer are destined sooner or later to cease to be a game animal in Wisconsin." In Iowa County, down toward the state's southwest corner, it was big news around the 1890s if someone came across a single deer track. The county was closed to whitetail hunting in 1907, and it wasn't until 1942 that another season opened. Deer numbers grew, aided by closely managed hunting, heightened pressure against poachers, regrowth of forests and thickets, and mild winter conditions. Eventually Iowa County's whitetail population reached a "critical mass" and erupted. By the early 1980s, biologists tallied prehunt densities of 80

deer per square mile in the county. Faced with complaints about extensive crop damage, the state encouraged doe hunting, liberalized seasonal
quotas, and attracted more hunters to the area. In the early 1950s, not
more than 50 to 60 deer were taken annually from Iowa County, but by
1980 the seasonal harvest reached a phenomenal 13,000! Continued
hunting eventually lowered deer numbers to about 30 per square mile,
and they've been held near that level ever since.

Wisconsin's whitetail population stands at an all-time high, exceeding
biologists' population goals in most areas despite DNR efforts to keep it
down. Weather is an important factor, especially in northern forested
areas, according to biologist William Ishmael. In the past, thousands of
animals starved to death during frequent severe winters, but there hasn't
been a heavy winter kill for the last 10 to 15 years. Many Wisconsin
hunters don't believe deer populations are as high as DNR researchers
contend, and they wouldn't want to bring the numbers down anyway.
After all, more deer in the woods means each hunter has a better chance
of success. But tough winters will come eventually, experts warn, and the
inevitable mass starvation may convince hunters that biologists have
been right all along.

When it comes to deer management, Wisconsin hunters are bedrock
conservatives and staid traditionalists. For example, pressure from hunters
restricted deer seasons to the same nine days for 45 years, despite the fact
that whitetail numbers tripled over the same period, from 500,000 back
around 1950 to 1.5 million in 1995. Finally, in 1996, hunters yielded to an
additional four-day special opening, held before the regular season, limited to does only, and restricted to areas with extremely high deer populations. In many states, longer seasons than Wisconsin's are the norm: for
example, 16 days in Minnesota, 28 days in Maine, 44 days in New York,
and as long as two and a half months in Georgia.

In the parking lot at Karl's that night I didn't find it hard to understand the old-guard sentiment. Regardless of the economic and ecological problems caused by high deer populations, hunters had never been
better off. Droves of them gathered here to swap tales and bask in their
collective satisfaction. While John Olson examined a fork-horned buck,
I chatted with the man who had taken it. "My son and I had a perfect
day," he mused. "We hunted together and both of us did pretty good. As
far as deer hunting in Wisconsin goes, you know what they say: 'If it ain't
broke, don't try to fix it.' "

I thought too about Jim Mlsna, who had spotted only two deer and
hadn't fired a shot, yet he seemed happy as a kid on his birthday. For Jim,

hunting was a time to be outdoors; to savor the company of friends and family; to talk about land, about hunting strategies, about whitetails and turkeys and pheasants; and to help his partners dress and clean their game. All of these things—not just dragging a deer from the woods—shaped his hunting life.

If you look at studies of hunter motivation and satisfaction, Jim Mlsna comes closer to the majority than does someone whose singular purpose is bringing home venison. Consider that more than half a million hunters take to the Wisconsin wildlands each year, but only 40 percent come home with a deer. By national standards, incidentally, this is a high success rate. It follows that people hunt for many reasons besides killing and eating animals—a fact abundantly supported by sociological research.

It's important to remember that hunters *are* after something that cannot be gained simply by hiking in the woods, looking at animals, or taking pictures of wildlife. Something deeper and more powerful in the human psyche, founded on the quest for direct, primal, physical engagement with the natural world. Something related to the stakes involved, the braiding together of human and animal, of flesh and blood and soul. Something that eludes the grasp of language and might be comprehensible only to those who actually experience the hunt.

I wonder if hunters answering researchers' questions understate the importance of taking game or at least knowing they've got a chance. Recall those thousands of Wisconsin hunters who crowd into southern areas where deer populations are high, while far fewer choose the northwoods, where solitude abounds but whitetails often do not. On the other hand, most hunters who come home without venison still feel satisfied and grateful for the experience, especially if they've seen deer.

Summing up his Massachusetts research, Thomas More wrote: "I suggest that the pleasure of hunting comes more from the *process* than from the *product*." Or, as one Wisconsin hunter told me, "Getting a deer is not important; going hunting is what's important." To better understand this conclusion, we might remember that people garden for purposes beyond harvesting vegetables, people fish with more in mind than putting filets on the table, and people eat for reasons besides simply filling their stomachs.

The Drive

The next morning, I rode with Mark Mlsna and his 12-year-old son, Ben, to a farm just outside the crossroad hamlet of Newburg Corners. There we joined a bunch of men in blaze jackets and hats, clustered around their trucks discussing where to start their first drive.

Mark is a dairy farmer and inveterate hunter—tall, blond, solid build, with a steady smile and a talker's gift. "Most of us live on farms right around this place," he explained. "We've known each other all our lives and we're practically all related." Mark introduced his brother-in-law Mike, as well as Mike's sons Matthew and Mark, both near Ben's age, and Mike Jr., who looked around 20. The rest of the group included Pete, Stanley, John, and Ken, plus a few sons and nephews. The only ones not hooked into the Mlsna genealogy were Tom, a neighboring farmer, and his adult son. I counted 16 in all, ranging from two in their mid-fifties down to three boys just old enough to hunt.

Everyone turned his attention to a wooded ridge protruding like an enormous thumb into a cornfield across the road. The more knowledgeable and assertive men discussed a hunt strategy, indicating where the "drivers" should start and where the "standers" should position themselves. Afterward, the men crammed into a couple of trucks, and as we jounced along a dirt road Mike explained our task. "We'll get in a line, from the bottom to the top of that ridge, and we'll walk along together all the way to the end." He pointed north toward the ridge's narrowing tip. "Then we'll go right on around to the other side. You'll see, it's a big coulee back there. Try to keep the other guys in sight, above you and below. You might have to holler once in a while to keep track of everybody and stay even with them. We like to move in a straight line."

I was assigned a spot just below Mike Jr., the top man. "Young guys climb highest," someone remarked. I hardly qualified as "young" and couldn't tell if this was flattery or a test of stamina, but after yesterday's protracted sit, it felt good to scramble up the steep, brushy slope, heart drumming, lungs pumping crisp autumn air. "Once the drive gets going, yell out if you see a deer," Mike Jr. instructed. "Then duck down or get behind a tree if you think somebody might shoot even though we all know where it's safe to aim during a drive." Sage advice, I figured.

You'd be hard-pressed to see another person in these woods, even wearing traditional hunter's red, but it's a different story with blaze orange. Each man in the line below us stood out like a fluorescent spotlight against the drab gray of limbs and trunks, the tan and russet of fallen leaves. In fact, before the drive someone had pointed out a hunter standing atop another ridge, like a tiny glowing droplet, plainly visible a mile away.

I found this reassuring, and remembered that, although Wisconsin's hunting population has almost doubled in the past 30 years, shooting accidents have dramatically declined, mainly because of the blaze clothing law and hunter education courses (taken by about 500,000 people since the DNR started classes back in 1967). Wisconsin had 44 fatal shooting accidents in 1909, when a total of 3,985 deer were taken—one hunter death for every 90 deer brought in. During the 1990s, there have been 60 to 70 nonfatal accidents and three or four deaths during most hunting seasons. The four fatalities in 1991 represented one hunter death for every 88,000 deer taken.

With blaze orange requirements and mandatory hunter education in almost every state, accidents have dropped by about half nationally over the past 20 years, but the record still needs improvement. In 1990, 146 hunters died in firearms accidents throughout the United States and Canada. For comparison, during that same year in the United States, 46,300 people died in motor vehicle accidents, 12,400 in falls, 5,200 by drowning, and 4,300 in fires.

Statistics like these demonstrate that hunting is a relatively safe activity, yet most people think it's extremely dangerous. Some have suggested this reflects our psychological response to voluntary versus involuntary risks; in other words, we're less concerned about high risks that we've chosen for ourselves—driving a car, for example—than we are about infinitely smaller risks that we feel are imposed upon us, like being injured by a hunter's bullet. It's worth noting that a great majority of hunting accidents (82 percent in Wisconsin during the 1994 season, for example) involve people either hurting themselves or being hurt by someone in their own group.

Looking down at our line of hunters, I felt lucky to be among experienced men who didn't seem likely to take risks in the heat of the moment. Then I saw Mike give the signal to move ahead, and I quickly realized this wasn't going to be a casual stroll in the woods. The hillside—layered with crisp, smooth oak leaves—was almost as slick as ice, and there were thickets of purple-stemmed blackberry festooned with thorns that snagged clothing and hooked tender flesh. Deer like to hide in these brambles, Mike Jr. had advised, so drivers should either push right through or toss in a stick. After a few briar patches—bloody scrawls adorning my hands and face—I started pitching sticks.

Muddling among bushy thickets, having no idea how fast to move, before long I could neither see nor hear the other guys. Then I heard a chain of hard thumps coming down the slope, and seconds later saw a doe pounding straight toward me. She stopped 30 yards away, stared long enough to twitch her tail a couple times, and then tore on by. "Deer!" I yelled, but nothing came back except the wheezy banter of chickadees.

A while later somebody caught sight of me. "Hey, you better hurry up; they're way out ahead!" I recognized the elder Mike, who had the job of "tailer," staying behind in case a deer slipped through our drive line. On lower ridges there's no need for a tailer, because drivers are so closely spaced they're almost sure to flush every deer. Berating myself, sweating and huffing, I scrambled along the hill to catch up. But as compensation for losing the others I had the pleasure of seeing two more does, both running hell-bent away from the drivers. I listened for a shot from the direction of Mike Sr., but the deer eluded him as well.

After rounding the tip of the long, narrow ridge and heading back along its opposite side, I heard a fusillade of shotgun booms somewhere down the slope. A while later it happened again, louder this time, indicating the drivers weren't far ahead. At last I heard voices and spotted blaze among the trees, but to my disappointment the men were trekking downhill, meaning this drive was over. Following them out of the woods, I entertained a flimsy hope that no one suspected I'd been off hiking by myself.

The hunters converged at the upper end of a grass-covered valley pinched between our wooded ridge and another about 100 yards away. Everyone's attention focused on two whitetails—both fair-sized does—felled by standers when the deer ran from cover. It all worked exactly as planned. One of the deer lay amid a circle of men, like the dark center of a poppy surrounded by flaming orange petals.

"Look here," said Stanley, kneeling beside the animal. "Now that's a fine shot, clean in the shoulder." He spoke to everyone but meant his words as a compliment to young Ben, who had taken the deer. A slender, pleasant-faced lad, he carried his pride quietly. "Yup, now that's good shooting," someone agreed.

The fact soon emerged, largely by my own confession, that I'd fallen behind the drive line. This triggered a round of teasing about a guy from the Alaskan wilderness getting himself lost on a Wisconsin farm. "Well," Mike Sr. consoled, "it happens to us sometimes, too." There was no gain in protesting that I was only separated, not lost. The greenhorn got turned around on a landscape known minutely to those who made it their home. I was honestly pleased to be a mirror reflecting an elegant truth about the rewards of long affiliation with the land, a truth best honored and left undisturbed.

The older men, who had traversed these ridges for decades, decided where we should hunt next: the opposite slope facing our coulee. It stood much lower, covered with leafless oak, birch, and brambles, affording a fairly open view, so from my position near the top I could see the entire brightly garbed phalanx—two above me and six below. As soon as we started I realized how seriously I'd underestimated the tempo of a drive. I could also see the men tossing sticks and rocks into thickets, hear them talking back and forth, and then shouting when a deer burst out. The canny animal dodged away between juniper patches and disappeared unscathed.

There was nothing subtle about the drive: a bunch of men scrabbling along the sidehill, decked out in tangerine-colored outfits, making lots of noise, too busy and preoccupied to contemplate the scenery. It was a far cry from the patient, meditative approach preferred by Jim and his buddies back on the Mlsna farmstead, but as Jim had acknowledged at supper the previous night, "If you really want deer, driving's the way to get them." Actually, some hunters make very slow, quiet drives, stopping at intervals to watch, trying either to force deer from cover or spot them on the move.

In a narrow, forested ravine partway along the ridge I flushed a hen turkey from her treetop roost. She burst away, wings drumming like an unthinkably huge grouse, then fanned her rusty tail feathers and cupped her wings in a long, vanishing glide. I'd never seen wild turkeys while growing up in Wisconsin because they were hunted to extinction during frontier times. However, a seed population established in the mid-1970s quickly took hold, and nowadays turkeys are a common sight in fields and woodlands throughout much of Wisconsin; there's a hunting season each spring, and in some areas the hefty birds are common enough to make themselves a nuisance for farmers.

About an hour into the drive, somebody jumped a deer along the lower slope. A shot thundered . . . then another, and I heard a voice— "Somebody get one?"—followed by a long silence. "I don't know." At the end of the ridge, we followed each other down into a spacious hay field. "There they are," shouted one of the drivers, and as we came closer, "Horns!" Now I saw a large buck with beamy, polished six-point antlers, similar to the one Dan had taken yesterday. "He came out of the woods, really moving, and went into that patch of corn," said the elder Mike, gesturing beside the animal. "That's where I got him."

Everyone looked on while Mike field-dressed his deer—making a long cut down the belly, splitting pelvis and brisket, drawing out the shiny mass of viscera. I noticed that a couple of our standers hadn't returned, and before long a shot thundered from the nearby forest. "They must have found that wounded deer," Ken surmised. "She ran out ahead of Stanley and me, and we followed her blood trail quite a ways in that woods."

Minutes later two men emerged from the line of trees dragging a small-ish doe. "Somebody hit her pretty bad," one reported. "Must have happened earlier this morning." Mike sat back on his heels. "You've got to find a deer if it's been wounded like that," he declared. "You can't just let it go off and die." One of the older men nodded agreement, then added: "In twenty-seven years of hunting I've never lost a wounded deer."

"Who's gonna put their tags on these?" Mark asked. In Wisconsin, every licensed whitetail hunter receives one tag, but it can be used for an animal taken by anyone in the group. In certain areas with high deer populations, license holders can also apply for a "hunter's choice permit," making their buck tag valid for deer of either sex, and there are limited numbers of "bonus permits" allowing one additional antlerless deer.

We've already seen, however, that Wisconsin hunters are likely to rebel against anything that could mean fewer deer in the woods. "Back in the mid-eighties, the DNR wanted more deer killed," Jim recalled, "so we all took bonus tags and we really got a lot of deer. But for the next couple years after that we hardly got any. That's when we decided the DNR doesn't know what they're doing. Everybody decided we're going to regulate our deer herd ourselves, so a lot of guys around this area are turning down the bonus permits and voluntarily passing up does. Deer hunting's a tradition you want to keep going. And maybe you can't keep it going unless you control it yourself."

Needless to say, wildlife biologists take a different view, one based on their yearly counts and the problems caused by high deer populations. "For us, it's a delicate balancing act," the DNR's William Ishmael told me, "between the advantages of having lots of deer and the disadvantages of having too many. In other words, we've got to weigh the *possible* number of whitetails against the *acceptable* number of whitetails."

The men immediately fastened tags on both deer, keeping in mind that Wisconsin's game laws are strictly enforced and fines amount to considerably more than a slap on the wrist. Since 1980, lawbreakers have faced a minimum $1,000 and maximum $2,000 penalty for poaching, which includes possessing an untagged deer as well as hunting out of season or taking deer at night with a spotlight.

Back in the 1970s, when poaching carried fines of no more than $200, Wisconsin's illegal deer kill may have equaled the legal harvest of about 100,000 animals annually, according to DNR official Ralph Christianson. With tighter enforcement and higher fines, poaching cases have dropped from a peak of 1,500 in 1979 to approximately 500 each year now, with about 95 percent of arrests leading to conviction. Increasing whitetail numbers and liberal hunting regulations have undoubtedly lessened the incentive to hunt illegally. At the same time, experts suggest that less poaching could be a factor in the dramatic deer population growth, so each affects the other.

Although game law violations have dropped off, at least in Wisconsin, they're still a problem throughout North America. Poaching keeps deer populations well below their potential in certain parts of the country, especially the West. In Washington State, for example, wildlife agents estimate that about 40,000 deer are taken illegally each year. One of the more creative ways to nab lawbreakers, used in many states, is by setting up fake deer along country roads while officers hide nearby waiting for poachers to shoot them. Other common offenses include hunting out of season, exceeding bag limits, having no license, carrying uncased weapons inside a vehicle, "shining," or "jacklighting," deer at night, trespassing on private land, and transporting illegally killed animals.

Statistical profiles of poachers show that they generally are young (in their twenties or early thirties), single or divorced rather than married, more rural than urban, and likely to hold blue-collar jobs. The southeastern United States leads all other regions in poaching arrests, followed by the Midwest, West, and finally Northeast. People who take game illegally often say they do it for the meat, but many admit they're out for fun or excitement—a kind of vandalism against wildlife. There are also rural folks who assert they have a right to take game out of season, especially deer nourished by crops on their own land.

People mistakenly tend to regard poaching as a minor crime, but research shows that poachers are often intoxicated; they sometimes violently threaten officers; they sabotage wildlife management and jeopardize game populations; they seldom pursue wounded animals; and they trespass on private lands as well as protected areas such as national parks. They also denigrate the majority of hunters who support game laws, obey them to the letter, and abhor poaching.

Late that afternoon, the hunters assembled for their final drive, along a hillside that ended back at the farm. "Watch for the big white barn and come down behind it," Mike Sr. advised. I asked why some of the guys had groaned when they heard about the plan. "Well, this hill's *really* got blackberries," he grimaced, uncasing his shotgun. "If you brought gloves along, you better put 'em on."

"And it's got deer, too!" said Pete. "Last year up in that thick brush, three bucks jumped out right in front of Ben. They ran straight away, then turned around and came back past him. All he had was a stick because he wasn't old enough to carry a gun, but he did just the right thing—yelled so everybody'd know and then ducked down to be safe."

From the start, this drive proved as nasty as its billing—slow, tough, steep, sweaty, and painful—a nearly continuous briar patch that had grown up after logging unshaded the hillside. But the millions of needle-sharp hooks that frayed our clothes and bloodied our hides apparently didn't bother whitetails, to judge by their tracks and droppings. I wondered how many deer lay hidden in this fortress of brambles while drivers passed within a few yards. We did flush a big doe near the start, but no one tried for her, and at the very end another doe jumped out between two of the young hunters. One boy simply let her go; the other fired three times, close enough to make my heart jump. I dropped instantly, figuring to hug the ground, but found myself suspended on a lattice of prickly stalks.

The boy felt sure he'd missed every shot, and a careful search revealed no blood on the ground—the deer had been moving too fast and was half screened by underbrush. A more experienced hunter would have watched her run off, realizing the faint chance for a killing shot. "It takes time to learn when to shoot and when to hold your fire," one of the older men remarked. "At least these boys are with us, so we can talk to them afterward, maybe give them a little advice." I remembered my years with Eskimo and Indian people, who recognized that hunting skill comes only with years of practice under the guidance of elders, and that mistakes are an essential part of learning.

Studies in Wisconsin by the psychologists Robert Jackson and Robert Norton show that young hunters typically are fascinated with weapons, love to test their abilities, aim at all sorts of things, and often lapse into adolescent recklessness. The youngsters in our group seemed different, perhaps because they had the advantages of growing up in farm country, working on the land and in close association with animals, directly experiencing the processes of life and death. Hunting with adults since early childhood, they could learn through apprenticeship the necessary skills and the code of proper behavior followed by their fathers and uncles, friends and neighbors.

These boys were far removed from that ugly minority known as "slob hunters"—people who abuse wildlife and property, who disregard ethics or law or courtesy, and who are terribly estranged from the natural world. Unfortunately, these deviants have infected the public image of "typical"

hunters, so the hunting community must do everything possible to eliminate misconduct and get "slobs" out of the woods. The best way to ac-
complish this, I believe, is by thorough, meticulous, obligatory training,
well beyond what most states now offer in hunter education courses. I'm
also convinced that *every licensed hunter should be required to pass a rigorous
test of skill, knowledge, ethics, and judgment*—much like a driver's license
exam. Some hunters will consider this excessive, but increasing numbers
realize that stringent requirements are crucial for the future of hunting.

Historian and hunting expert Robert Wegner offers Germany's system—developed by hunters themselves—as an example worth following. To earn a license, each hunter takes about 100 hours of classroom
study, followed by a three-hour written exam, a three-hour oral exam,
and a demonstration of shooting skill. Course subjects include wildlife
identification and natural history, game regulations, trespass laws, field
dressing, meat preparation, game management principles, hunting techniques, and hunter ethics.

According to Wegner, German hunters also practice a ritual called "the
last bite," in which they pay respect to a fallen deer or other game animal. This involves putting a small branch in the animal's mouth and then
addressing a prayer to Saint Hubertus, patron saint of the hunt, giving
thanks for the game, the weather, and the comradeship of other hunters.
Making this final salute to the game animal, says Wegner, is a way to acknowledge its status as a fellow being and to symbolize "the return of [its]
soul to our Maker."

I trailed Mike and Pete down through the last bramble patches and
into the barnyard's untangled freedom. The men, looking ragged and
tired, congratulated themselves on another successful day—plenty of
deer encountered and four more added to yesterday's take of seven. "We
share our deer equally among everybody in the group," Mike Sr. told me.
"Last year we only got five deer, so first we butchered them and had
sausage made; then we divided everything among us." This year, with 11
deer on the first weekend and only three tags left to fill over the Thanksgiving holiday, each person would probably end up keeping the deer he'd
tagged. "We hunt together," said Mike, "and as long as we get something,
everybody takes venison home."

Finale

The Middle Ridge Tavern's parking lot overflowed with cars and pickups,
most of them containing deer, reminiscent of Karl's place the previous

night. Here, the tavern owner and his wife shuttled from one vehicle to another checking deer and recording hunters' license numbers. Some of the trucks carried three or four whitetails, and one flatbed, belonging to a large hunting party, arrived with 12, including several burly-racked bucks. On a typical Opening Day, Jim had told me, between 300 and 500 deer are registered at Middle Ridge, and they're all from the immediate area. This is tangible proof of the sustained abundance of deer in Wisconsin's intensely hunted rural countryside.

After touring the lot I wedged my way inside, encountering a sea of orange that looked like a convention for the color-blind. In such quantity, this strident hue is about as relaxing as a jackhammer, but at the Middle Ridge Tavern on Sunday afternoon of Opening Weekend, blaze was the uniform and folks wore it with pride, even if that meant sweltering in a heavy winter coat.

A blaze banner hanging on the wall proclaimed: WELCOME WISCONSIN HUNTERS! BUY THAT SPORTSMAN A MILLER. Whether or not the sign had anything to do with it, I saw a lot of Millers going around, keeping company with Budweiser, Heileman, Busch, and other local favorites. It doesn't take a sociologist to deduce that folks in this part of the world lean toward beer as a social refreshment. I also learned, while squeezing through the crowd, that deer and hunting were virtually the sole topics of discussion . . . except among diehard Packers fans jammed into one corner, hypnotized by the game on a television mounted near the ceiling.

Finally I spotted Jim and Mark Mlsna with a bunch of the other guys, most of them wearing civilian clothes. Jim fairly shouted the news: "Well, we finished the season at eleven this morning—another six-point buck. That deer walked right by Dan. We figured that was all we needed, so we quit and went home to do the butchering."

I wished I'd been around to share in the final hours of their hunt. Now that I'd experienced both styles, I confessed a preference for the meditative quiet of stand hunting. Yet I'd seen that driving offered more rewards than just bringing home game—the pleasures of working outdoors with friends, the fresh air and strenuous exercise, the long days trekking beautiful ridges, and the encounters with all sorts of wildlife along the way. Mark agreed, editorializing that stands are boring and uncomfortable. "Sure, I could sit all day in *this* weather," he added, "but deer season in Wisconsin is usually a whole lot colder. I mean, you freeze out there!"

Compared to Jim, Mark seemed far more single-minded and pragmatic about hunting. Of course, Mark spent his working days outdoors, not confined indoors longing for the countryside, and perhaps his approach reflected the practicality of a farmer whose livelihood centered on efficiently harvesting what the land provides. Besides hunting for whitetails, Mark said he'd usually butcher cows, hogs, and chickens each year for his family's own use. "I love meat," he proclaimed. "I don't care what they say about cholesterol; I'd rather die happy."

Among those gathered around our table were the three youngsters—Ben, Mark, and Matthew—feeling like men, I supposed, yet looking very much like boys. Reflecting on my own suburban childhood, I couldn't help envying these farm lads growing up with their feet on the soil, their hands toughened by hard work, their eyes open to biological realities that people far older than they often overlook. Who would need to remind them that seeding and harvesting, life and death, sustain us all? These boys lived in direct connection with their own ecology, where they could experience (as opposed to reading about or being told) how plants become grain, animals become meat, living organisms become food on the table, and food becomes ourselves. The truth of it was braided through their daily existence, carried on without need for analysis or description.

At the same time, the boys were being initiated into a social and cultural tradition that arose from this land as surely as the crops and the game, into a way of life spanning generations here in Wisconsin and stretching unbroken to their agrarian ancestors in Europe, into a community linking people not only with each other but also with their place on earth.

"Touchdown Green Bay!" somebody yelled, inciting the Middle Ridge crowd into a delirium of hoots and waving arms. Over the next hour a cliffhanger took shape, and everyone's attention fixed on the big, blinking screen. Finally, when the home team scored a winning touchdown with 16 seconds to go, a breathless hush shattered into pandemonium, followed by a general charge toward the bar.

Our own gang had tipped a few brews, with a corresponding increase in the volume and eloquence of discourse. "Whenever we go deer hunting we come here afterward," Jim fairly shouted above the clamor. "But I'll tell you this," he proclaimed. "We don't drink before we hunt, we don't drink in the woods, and we don't drink while we're hunting. It's only after we're done that we get together here."

Most hunters, at least in my experience, vigorously condemn any mix of alcohol and firearms. Yet the image of hunters as malignant drunks remains an accepted "truth" among a huge segment of our society. Somehow, it's believed, thousands of ordinary citizens retrogress into dipsomaniacs for the duration of hunting season, then almost miraculously return to normal when they come home. Hunters need to address this perception by setting impeccable standards in all their behavior, by drumming inebriates out of their ranks, and by insisting on strict law enforcement.

With late afternoon's sagging light, tables began to empty around us. No midnight prowlers, these rural folks. At last, Jim sighed, "Well, I guess that's about it for this year." The day's cold had flushed his cheeks, he looked tired but utterly satisfied, and already there was a tinge of nostalgia in his voice as he glanced around the table at his cadre of friends and partners. "Things couldn't go much better."

When I drove onto the interstate a blizzard of headlights filled the southbound lanes as far as the eye could see—much heavier traffic than I'd encountered on the drive north, doubtless because everyone started for home around the same time. Darkness kept me from spying inside vehicles, but now I had a better way to identify hunters. I saw whitetails in the beds of trucks, fastened on little trailers, tied atop roofs and across the backs of cars, visible in half-closed trunks.

An image came to mind of this year's venison harvest streaming out from the countryside, coalescing along the roadways, filtering into cities and towns, and finally dispersing among thousands of homes throughout the state. Deer season provided sustenance for body and soul, drawn from the forests, fields, meadows, and marshlands of Wisconsin, and it signified a continuing tradition that has linked humankind with whitetails on these lands for thousands of years. On this Opening Weekend, Wisconsin hunters had taken nearly 171,000 deer, and for the entire nine-day season their total would exceed 350,000 animals, not including more than 49,000 whitetails brought in by archers during their separate and longer season. The following years would see increasing takes from a whitetail population that continued growing to all-time highs.

I wondered what thoughts spun through Jim Mlsna's mind as he trucked home from another season on his stand. A couple days earlier he'd told me, "The only reason I work at my job is so I can hunt and fish. You see, I grew up with it. I've always done it and I still enjoy it. This is what's ingrained in me."

"Do you think you'll ever quit?" I asked.

"I might get a little slower," he replied, "but as long as I'm able to do it, I'll keep on."

"Are there any things you dream about or look forward to in your future hunting?"

He gazed off at nothing in particular, a faint smile on his lips. "It's not so much that I have dreams, but sometimes when I'm in the woods I sit and think. I'm in my early fifties and mainly what I'd like is to keep on hunting, keep on doing what I've been doing. And you know, my real hope is to have things stay just like they are now."

EIGHT

IN SEARCH OF EDEN

For that which befalleth the sons of men befalleth beasts; even one thing befalleth them: as the one dieth, so dieth the other; yea, they have all one breath; so that a man hath no preeminence above a beast.

—ECCLESIASTES 3:19

Among all the animals native to this continent, deer probably evoke the tenderest and most protective sentiments. It hardly seems possible that creatures of such grace, loveliness, and innocence could exist at all, much less haunt the edges of our towns, enter our backyards, wander among our parks and farmlands. In an era when people devote enormous energy to preserving every facet of nature's beauty, deer are the paragon of creatures deserving refuge. And as our urban society becomes increasingly detached from its rural foundations—widening the distance between people and their sources of sustenance—we have come increasingly to regard nature as something we should admire but never touch, that we should love but never use, that we should harvest with our senses but never with our hands.

From this perspective, deer may be viewed as sacred icons, wild survivors in an imperiled world. The notion of hunting them for food, as millions of citizens do each year, could be judged a travesty—a perversion of all that is moral and good in our efforts to define a balanced relationship to nature. People who hunt deer find themselves in a tense middle ground between this fundamentally urban worldview and a very different one that celebrates rural traditions and self-sufficiency, that recognizes the need for balancing wildlife populations with habitat, and that embraces a yearly ritual of harvesting the wild.

In recent times, activists promoting an ethic of "animal rights" have voiced strenuous opposition to hunting, even taking to the field as "hunt saboteurs," putting themselves—literally or figuratively—between hunters and game. Some regard these activists as visionaries and heroes; others consider them misguided ideologues and fanatics. The same might be said about hunters, who are admired or accepted in certain quarters, mistrusted or loathed in others. Putting both groups afield in the same place, on the same day, strikes almost anyone as an incendiary, even dangerous combination.

At least this is how I felt when I joined antihunting protesters at dawn on another Opening Day of the whitetail season in rural Wisconsin. I had come to learn firsthand about the animal rights philosophy and to get acquainted with some of its most ardent supporters. The experience led me to reflect on the place of animals in our society today: How has the celebrated tale of Bambi affected our attitudes toward nature and hunting? What is the relationship between animal rights and environmentalism? Is there a moral ground that encompasses both hunting and animal rights? What can we learn about our own lives as animals by considering the ethics of hunting, meat eating, and vegetarianism?

While I talked with animal rights activists, I remembered my own strenuous opposition to hunting as a young man growing up in Wisconsin. Then, living as a cultural anthropologist with Iñupiaq Eskimos and Koyukon Indians in northern Alaska, I had an opportunity, seldom possible in the latter twentieth century, to become an apprentice to traditional Native American hunters. With these hunters, I encountered another view of what might be called animal rights, expressed in a code of moral and spiritual beliefs handed down by generations of elders. In a sense, returning to Wisconsin for an antihunting protest brought my own transformations back to where they had begun.

Stalking the Hunter

"Remember, we don't want any solitary encounters with deer hunters out in the woods, so you *must* stick with your group. Last year we had people who lallygagged behind and read the little nature tips. I got really frustrated with that. This is a paramilitary action. There's going to be a lot of people dying out in the woods this year; let's make sure it's none of the good guys."

Darcy's voice cut sharply into the cloying predawn murk. The little group—I'd counted about 15 besides myself—clustered around her, shoulder touching shoulder. I didn't think people had bunched like this just to hear her words above the wind; rather, I was reminded of musk oxen, shelterless on a tundra plain, gathered for assurance against wolves lurking in the night.

Across the asphalt parking lot, steely blue footlights illuminated the headquarters for Kettle Moraine State Park. Blizzard warnings had been posted throughout Wisconsin, but here at the state's eastern edge, with temperatures still above freezing, the late November storm felt more like an autumn monsoon. On a pole beside the main building an American flag whipped and snapped amid whirling veils of rain. One of the women switched on a flashlight as if to assuage her fears, and in its glow I noticed that several protesters wore crinkly plastic ponchos, blaze orange, with boldly printed messages across the back: BAN THE HUNT. STOP THE SLAUGHTER.

"We're not here to be rude necessarily," Darcy emphasized. "We don't want any verbal harassment of hunters. No physical contact. Do what any officer requests, unless you're willing to be arrested for breaking the hunter harassment law." A few raised their hands when Darcy asked who was prepared for arrest; volunteers were needed so that antihunt activists could test the Wisconsin law in court. "At least one of you should be in each of the small groups," Darcy instructed.

"Okay, be careful. And be polite," she advised. "Remember, humans are animals, too."

As they sorted into smaller groups, everyone heard cars and pickups driving along the nearby road—hunters on their way to spots they'd picked for Opening Day. I presumed the others felt much as I did: tense, apprehensive, charged with nervous excitement. Yet my feelings differed at their very roots. After all, I am a deer hunter, and at home venison is our most important staple food. A year before I had tagged along on a whitetail hunt with Jim Mlsna and his friends at Middle Ridge, just across the state. During that experience, I was comforted by staying on familiar emotional and philosophical ground, but on this November morning, I alone was out of place, a lion in sheep's clothing, ready to join an ambush against my own kind.

"Car coming!" somebody shouted. Approaching headlights stared through dizzying swirls of rain. I stood there, heart pounding, as the sedan pulled in among our vehicles. Then a voice sang out, "It's Channel Six!" The newsmen cracked their window for a brief status report, then started setting up equipment inside their car. Minutes later another vehicle arrived and parked across the lot. More anxious moments until word came around: "Channel Four." Everybody seemed pleased that two Milwaukee television crews had arrived, then disappointed when no others showed up. This meant two out of our four groups would operate without the publicity payoff of cameras and microphones, not to mention the safety in having television people on hand should there be an angry confrontation.

A stranger, and in so many ways an outsider, I found relief in the company of Jodi Kemper, president of the Madison group called Alliance for Animals, and her husband, Bernard "Buzz" Kemper, who had arranged for me to observe this year's hunt intervention. Needless to say, his gesture on my behalf was extremely generous. When we'd first met, I led with the hard fact that I am a hunter, but then emphasized our common ground: my strong objection to the inhumane treatment of animals in laboratory studies, wildlife research, and industrial farming; my interest in environmental ethics; my involvement with conservation activism; and my sincere desire to learn about the antihunting philosophy.

I didn't mention a personal motive for joining the protest: I wanted to meet people whose ideas about hunting differ absolutely from my own, who consider something I greatly value to be unconscionable and invalid, and who advocate its abolishment. The best way to avoid hostility toward people who disagree with you, I believe, is to get acquainted with them, to find that you share many of the same values, to experience firsthand the basic human goodness of your adversaries. I sought this comfort for myself, first of all, but imagined the benefits might even go both ways.

I had immediately liked Buzz and Jodi, and I'd been impressed by the Madison activists' commitment to what they believed was right. "I have a feeling that there's too much violence in the world," Buzz had told me, explaining how he'd become involved with animal rights. "There's too little respect from people of one type toward people of another type, and then from people toward members of other species. If we can get people to have basic respect for a lab rat, a beaver, or a deer, I feel they can't help but have more respect for each other." Buzz spoke with the force of deep conviction, yet there was an abiding gentleness in his voice.

"Any being that has the ability to experience pain or suffering has the right *not* to have pain and suffering inflicted upon it," he continued. "We don't own these animals. We can't say, 'Well, I feel like going on a hunt because it's fun.' Or, 'I hope there'll be a lot of deer this year because I want to get a big buck.' To me that's a skewed idea. I want to make people aware that those creatures have lives; they have a sense of who they are and where they are; and they have goals. They have an idea of what their past was and what the future brings. I think we forget that."

There were few men among the protesters, so Darcy allocated one of us to each of the groups. My companions included Penny and Mary, as well as Darcy, the protest's overall leader, who belonged to a Green Bay organization called Voice for Animals. Darcy instructed everyone to get in their assigned cars, wait for hunters to arrive, then keep out of sight until they uncased their rifles and headed for the woods. If protesters revealed themselves too soon, she warned, the hunters would probably drive somewhere else, spoiling the intervention. As everyone took their places and the watch began, I recognized a familiar sensation inside myself: the intense, heightened anticipation of an encounter with prey.

We four sat in a small station wagon, engine idling and heater on. "People who find hunting morally reprehensible should bear witness," Darcy asserted. "Frankly, I'm more comfortable coming out here—being part of the war and actively dealing with it—than sitting at home going, 'God, I hope a stray bullet doesn't come through my window.' "

Penny shook her head in frustrated agreement. "It just irritates me that someone would go to all this bother to kill something."

"And risk their lives!" Darcy agreed. "I mean, I'd risk my life to *save* something. But risk my life to kill something? We come from two different universes. Hunters are in a perpetual state of war with the universe, instead of just letting it be."

It wasn't hard to see why Darcy had been chosen to head the protest: she was agile and assertive, pouring out words so quickly that their edges blurred, her dark eyes flashing and her emphatic gestures affirming every point. While her compatriots—people like Buzz, Jodi, and Penny—spoke from the heart as well as the mind, I sensed that Darcy's activism was harder edged, leaning more toward the intellectual and the purely political.

Penny wiped the fog from her window, nervously watching for headlights, admitting she hadn't been able to sleep all night. "As I get older I
always try to see the other's perspective, but with hunting I just can't. I
suppose it's because I'm so into being vegetarian."

I glanced at my watch—6:15 a.m.—then at the sky. Dawn light suf-
fused dense, running clouds that dragged their bellies over the treetops.
More cars passed on the road, but still none came into the parking lot.
Darcy wondered if someone might have breached security, then reassured herself that it wasn't possible. Public announcements had revealed
only that a state park somewhere in Wisconsin would be the site for this
year's hunt sabotage, and just a few protest leaders knew beforehand
which park had been chosen. Our group, for example, had driven in tan-
dem from Madison, guided by one person entrusted with knowledge of
our destination. After picking a site, Darcy had called to inquire surrep-
titiously about hunting in this part of Kettle Moraine. "They told me
there'd be cars stacked in here," she recalled, impatient and perplexed.

I asked why the group wanted to protest in a state park as opposed to
anywhere else. "Hunters are only sixteen percent of Wisconsin's population," Darcy replied. "We would hope that state parks, which are one
percent of the land, would be open to the other eighty-four percent of
our population who choose not to hunt. There's a feeling amongst the
hunting community that while they're out perpetrating their war on
wildlife, everybody else darn well better take cover."

For many years, hunting was prohibited in Wisconsin's state parks,
but it's now allowed during the annual firearms season in about 25 of the
72 reserves. According to state officials and biologists, overabundant deer
have harmed natural vegetation in the parks, depleted habitat important
for other wildlife, and damaged crops on adjacent fields, provoking complaints from farmers. There is no way other than hunting, they contend,
to keep deer herds balanced with the ecosystem in and around these
refuge areas.

"Right now we're only asking to get hunting out of the state parks,"
Darcy continued. "But I am an absolutist, and I absolutely want an end
to hunting. Everywhere. That's just not what you ask for publicly.

"Also, deer overpopulation is in the eye of the beholder. It's easy for
the Wisconsin Department of Natural Resources to say there's too many
deer in this area or there's not enough in that other area. But my question is this: Does the DNR really want to bring the deer population
down, or are they managing deer to keep the population high?"

This last point is often emphasized by antihunting activists who place blame for high deer numbers squarely on agencies like the DNR. And historically, at least, they're right. Beginning early this century, not just in Wisconsin but throughout North America, wildlife managers worked hard to reestablish deer and help them increase: instituting closed seasons, limiting harvests, protecting does, and encouraging the creation of favorable habitat (such as second-growth browse that follows logging). The main reason natural resource agencies wanted higher deer populations, critics say, was to provide game for hunters, and it's the hunters, in turn, whose license fees support these agencies. As a consequence, game species and hunters have traditionally gotten higher priority than have nongame animals and folks who simply enjoy watching wildlife or hiking in the woods.

Many wildlife managers admit that government agencies focus on charismatic species like deer, which have a very big public constituency. The best way to correct this imbalance, they explain, is for nonhunters to carry more of the financial burden for wildlands purchases, habitat protection, and the developing but still embryonic nongame programs. They also stress that professional biologists no longer support unrestricted growth of deer populations. "Our primary concern in Wisconsin today is to *reduce* the number of whitetails, not to increase them," a DNR biologist told me. But he acknowledged that hunters have frustrated efforts to bring the whitetail population down—for example, by resisting DNR proposals to lengthen the hunting season.

Before long there was enough light to see the swaying tops of oaks and maples, the flinging saturated leaves, and the shivering autumn grass. But there were no hunters. "What could have gone wrong?" Darcy muttered, her concern deepening. After all, everyone had driven a long way and this was their one chance of the year to confront hunters. The trap was set, television reporters had cameras ready, but not a single hunter appeared. Should the saboteurs stay put or get out on the highway to look for them? With each passing minute I found myself drawn more tightly into the pursuit, wishing somebody would show up and fracture this mounting tension. I felt pulled in every direction. The protesters wanted to spoil an experience many hunters hold virtually sacred—probably the most important day of their year—yet for my own selfish reasons I hoped victims would appear.

Then there was the matter of fear. After all, the activists were not stalking deer, they were stalking keyed-up, determined, poorly rested, well-armed human beings who likely regarded antihunting protesters as naive, offensive pests. Most hunters confronted during previous interventions remained calm, but last year a man lost his temper, waved his gun around like a jousting stick, and shoved a television cameraman hard enough to cut his face. People described other frightening episodes, including telephoned threats against Buzz and Jodi Kemper and bloody animal parts left outside their home. I felt ashamed that anyone would do these things, regardless of the issues involved, and helpless to distance myself from such rude, petty behavior. These tales also led me to understand why the protesters grew edgy as they peered into the dawn's stormy breath. Truthfully, I wondered why I hadn't just stayed home. Couldn't I have learned enough about this by watching tonight's news? Would respect for the law and basic human courtesy keep everyone under control?

Statutes like Wisconsin's hunter harassment law protect activists' rights to hold demonstrations and to publicly express their opinions, but protesters are not allowed to directly interfere with hunters or disturb their property. Convicted violators can be fined up to $1,000, or twice that if they defy an officer's order. Similar laws are on the books in almost every state, and high court rulings affirm that they do not infringe on activists' First Amendment rights to freedom of speech. Nevertheless, some of the protesters believed Wisconsin's law was "too broad and vague" and would eventually be overturned.

Obviously, there wasn't going to be a court case if the group didn't have a protest, and there couldn't be a protest as long as they sat in the parking lot by themselves—so people agreed that a scouting party should check to see what was happening. Everyone watched the scouting party's taillights dwindle and then waited impatiently. Within five minutes they came back, excitedly reporting dozens of vehicles parked along the road. All were empty. "They've gone into the woods!" Darcy lamented, and like everyone else I felt my heart sink.

"Let's get out on the road!" she ordered. Doors slammed, engines revved, and the little squadron swung out onto the highway, television crews close behind. Sure enough, there were cars and trucks scattered along the neatly mown shoulder, their windows vacant and doors locked. By now we had full morning light, enough to see the rain-slicked road curving away through closely impinging forest. For these hunters, now quietly sequestered in their stands, the deer season was well under way.

Before we'd gone a mile, Darcy stabbed her finger against the front window and cheered: "hunters!"

Convergence

The way your life is supposed to pass before your eyes in desperate moments, my brain spun back to the previous night. I had driven with Buzz and Jodi to an older, two-story home in a quiet Madison neighborhood. There we met a dozen or so members of Alliance for Animals, nearly all women, crowded into a small back room around a table arrayed with *Vegetarian Times* magazines. Most said they planned to join the hunt intervention, but a few—who didn't intend to participate—had come to lend moral support. In charge of proceedings was a friendly, strong-looking, fiftyish woman named Lu. One of her 10 cats, an enormous and gloriously rotund tortoiseshell, luxuriated in the abundance of warm laps. Everyone treated me kindly, and were it not for the issue at hand I suspect we'd have found much to agree about.

After a detailed summary of the hunter harassment law, Lu disclosed that she and four others had been arrested the previous year, though not for breaking the statute in question. They'd come across a hunter and walked in circles around his stand as a gesture of protest, not realizing they had wandered onto private land outside the state park—and this fellow was its owner. He was bothered enough to phone the sheriff and charge the group for trespassing. Lu said she didn't care to be arrested again, although she would join the protesters tomorrow. Under no circumstances, she urged, should anyone stand in the way, touch, or verbally assail a hunter—no shouting, no swearing. And to keep things under control, one person should be designated to speak for each group.

When Lu finished giving advice and instructions, she cued up television news videos of last year's protest. The purpose, I assumed, was not just to prepare inexperienced members, but also to hearten and inspire the troops. Prominently featured in each report was the irate hunter I'd heard so much about, fuming in the midst of activists, law officers, and reporters, finally jostling the cameraman so the picture veered wildly. Our group responded with jeers for the bad guys—hunters and officials—and accolades for the good, plus a few suggestions for avoiding trouble this year. Then Lu ushered everyone to the door with a bit of advice: "We'd better get home for a little sleep. The place we're going is a couple hours' drive from Madison, so we'll have to meet again at two a.m." Groans all around.

A few hours later I drove to our rendezvous point, the parking lot of an all-night supermarket. Not a car in sight, and I wondered if I'd been ditched as a possible spy, but within minutes somebody else pulled alongside. When she rolled down her window to say hello, I recognized one of the more outspoken people from last night's gathering.

"Are you the hunter?" she inquired, her voice as chilly as the raindrops prickling my cheeks. I tried to soften the truth, as I had done with Buzz, but to slight avail. We stumbled over a few courtesies, then closed our respective windows and sat there, side by side in our separate vehicles. During the brief but seemingly endless moments before someone else arrived, my gate-crasher paranoia grew almost too heavy to bear.

At last the others showed up, divided themselves among three cars, pulled out onto a nearby highway, and headed northeast toward Lake Winnebago. By a stroke of luck, Jodi Kemper had volunteered to ride with me. For one thing, her companionship would keep me awake, despite just two hours of sleep, and I hoped she'd tell me more about animal rights along the way. In an earlier conversation, I'd been impressed by Jodi's clear and cogent articulation of her beliefs. Of course, I didn't know our destination, and if Jodi did, she wasn't saying, so we sandwiched our vehicle between the others as a guarantee against becoming lost.

My sidekick, who looked to be in her twenties, was an enthusiastic talker—lively, interesting, intense—who responded at length to each of my questions, asked few of her own, but listened closely when I had something to say. She spoke about her love for the outdoors, her dedication to vegetarianism, her interest in occult spirituality, and her background in animal rights activism.

"I've loved animals all my life," Jodi declared, "so I wanted to work with them. There was an ad in the newspaper for an animal caretaker in a laboratory, and I thought, 'Wow, this is cool.'

"Well, it's a consumer product-testing laboratory—acute toxicology—and the studies are very short. I saw rats with giant cancer things on their bodies. I watched little rats being starved until they got so hungry they'd eat baby diapers. That was to find out if a baby were to shred its diaper, would it be toxic to the child. I also saw animals being starved until they died. The cages were up to code, but some of the animals could barely turn around in them. The conditions were horrible!

"Eventually I started having nightmares, so I got another job; and after that I decided to get involved with the animal rights movement."

When it came to the hunt, Jodi expressed a wild mix of emotions, sometimes clear and sometimes hazy, but resolved into straightforward political rhetoric. "I grew up around hunting," she recalled. "I remember my mom saying, 'Try this, it's bear meat. It'll taste just like hamburger.'

"Also, my father hunted deer and they were our food. We had to hunt deer, he said, because if we didn't, the deer would starve to death and that would be horrible. I grew up believing the only way you can save the herd, or save these animals, is to kill them. But now I feel it's a lie, just like the laboratory lied to people."

The matter of hunting and deer population is a sticky one for animal rights activists. When hunters reduce deer numbers it means less competition for food and therefore healthier animals who produce more fawns—so the population comes right back up. Everyone acknowledges that deer populations must stay in a reasonable balance with their environment, but activists like Jodi and Buzz believe hunting is not the right solution.

"That's a very sudden, traumatic, and unnatural way to deal with the problem," said Buzz in an earlier conversation that included Jodi and fellow Madison activist John Barnes. "I think we have to slow down and stop the hunting, and we should get our predator population back to what it ought to be. I know the farmers aren't going to like that idea, but there doesn't seem to be any perfect solution.

"We should just let the population alone," Buzz continued. "Yes, there will be some starvation, but in the natural world starvation is a reality. I think most animals, if they could respond to you, would go ahead and take their chances with that. Nature handles these things better than we can." Here he spoke with deep sincerity, and although I understood the appeal of this argument, my thoughts drifted to the starving deer Barry Lopez and I had seen in Oregon: the dead doe suspended head down in a barbed-wire fence, the little buck with disarticulated hips who had become frozen into the ice, and the withered fawn whose suffering we had ended.

Leaving aside the issue of starvation, if hunting ceased in places like Wisconsin, the deer population would grow explosively, causing severe damage to the natural habitat and affecting not only deer but many other wild creatures. "There's not a simple answer," Jodi replied, "and there's not one answer that's going to be totally humane across the board. But I can't stand to see any animals slaughtered."

John Barnes, a retired veterinarian and widely respected leader for animal rights in Wisconsin, offered a compromise originally proposed by Luke Dommer of the Committee to Abolish Sport Hunting, a national group headquartered in New Jersey. "In order to get back to where we don't have an extreme overpopulation and deer causing a lot of agricultural damage," said Barnes, "hunters should only be allowed to kill does for five years—no bucks at all. After that you leave the deer alone, so they can have some sort of a natural existence."

I asked Buzz and Jodi how they felt about this suggestion. "I have a pretty good idea what would happen if all hunting just stopped," Jodi responded. "You know, the mass numbers that would result, and the severe starvation . . ." Her voice trailed off.

If a concentrated hunting program of this sort drastically reduced the whitetail population, it's hard to imagine what would keep them from increasing again as they did after dropping to the edge of extinction near the turn of this century. In the absence of a clear answer we let the subject go.

After our caravan had been on the road a couple hours, Lu turned off for a pit stop at a combined gas station and grocery store. The clerk, an earthy middle-aged woman, closely scrutinized our group: predominantly female, dressed for the outdoors, traveling through the wee hours on Opening Day. "Well, I suppose you folks are headed someplace for deer hunting," she speculated. In the monstrous silence that followed, it seemed as if every other customer—all of whom appeared to be hunters—listened for the reply. I cringed and held my breath.

Thankfully, someone came up with a vague answer, giving no hint of our true intentions. I wasn't afraid we'd be chastised or verbally assaulted, but I did feel abashed, knowing how most Wisconsin folks would regard a bunch of protesters about to sabotage deer hunters. If my companions felt any of this, it was probably offset by pride in their mission—something I couldn't share.

After we left the store Jodi confessed she'd also been on pins and needles. In fact, when a man dressed in hunting gear stepped through the middle of our group, she'd half expected somebody to start the protest right then and there. "Some of these women are very strong minded," Jodi remarked. "They're way more outspoken than people like Buzz and me. We're moderates in the group." Although Jodi and Buzz took strong positions on issues like treatment of farm livestock, meat eating, use of fur, and laboratory animal experimentation, they did allow some philosophical leeway—at least in discussions with me—when it came to hunting.

"If someone is going to eat meat," Buzz had told me, "I guess I don't have a lot of qualms about that person killing their own animals. I certainly find the subsistence hunter—who hunts with some degree of respect and some realization of his or her part in the ecosystem—less offensive than the typical recreational hunter. But even that's not great.

"Now we're into this mode where you go to the grocery store and buy your meat; then you go somewhere else to kill a deer for fun. I think we've perverted the whole idea of hunting. Also, when it comes down to hanging some part of a deer on your wall, we've really got to question where we are as human beings."

Jodi agreed that hunting might be tolerable under a few circumstances. "I like to think that hunting for food is your last resort, only when you've got to do it to feed your family. But hunters I talk to, it costs them more to go deer hunting than it would to buy the same amount of food at a store.

"The funny thing is, how those people rationalize what they're doing. They honestly believe they go out hunting because they like the woods. For them, it's the whole mystique or tradition that's been built around hunting, and getting together with the guys or whatever. But I think, can't you go out somewhere and bond without your guns?"

"I would just as soon everybody became a vegetarian," Buzz concluded. "It would be better for the animals and for the earth."

Back on the highway, time and miles passed quickly, thanks to Jodi's company and our growing anticipation of what lay ahead. Eventually, we turned onto a narrow country road that straight-lined across cultivated flatlands, passed through oak and maple forests, and then looped into the crowded hills of Kettle Moraine State Park. How fervently I wished I'd come here to wander across saturated autumn meadows, to sit under a tree listening to the storm flail in its branches, or to quietly watch for whitetails along some sheltered ravine. But today I could only hope to glimpse these beauties as the backdrop for a purely human drama, a confrontation over whose definition of right and wrong should prevail at the land's wild edge.

Ambush

With each sweep of the windshield wipers, I glimpsed a powder-blue truck on the roadside just ahead—engine running, two figures visible through foggy windows. At last, here was the moment I had anticipated with unspeakable dread since receiving Buzz Kemper's invitation many weeks earlier. My innards seethed, as if in a foolish moment I had promised to wrestle an alligator . . . and here it was.

"Pull off a little ways in front of them!" Darcy ordered. As we coasted by, the truck's blaze-jacketed driver stepped out, giving us a casual glance. One of the television crews parked just ahead of us, and the other vehicles stopped well behind the victims' truck. Then everyone piled out and stood there peering at the hunters from a safe distance. How strange it must have looked—this congeries of women and men dressed in a mix of hiking gear and city clothes that no hunter could possibly mistake for his own kind. In fact, none of the protesters tried to conceal the anti-hunting messages on their wrinkled ponchos. In this place, on this particular morning, to these people, the interlopers probably seemed as unlikely as a gathering of flamingos.

What the two hunters did next epitomized the exercise of common sense and logic: they hopped back into the truck, slammed both doors, made a quick U-turn, and left us standing in the rain. One of our groups took off after them with a television crew close behind. Meanwhile, Darcy opened her arms, rolled her eyes toward the growling heavens, and reminded us all: "You've got to stay inside your vehicle until the hunters start for the woods!"

She instructed the other two groups to head off on their own, look for more hunters, and carry out the action as planned. To be sure the remaining television crew would record a successful intervention, Darcy told them to stick with us. After all, coercing a few hunters to leave the field would have virtually no impact without media coverage that amplified the event and brought attention to the antihunting cause.

We hadn't gone more than a quarter mile before luck smiled on us, or perhaps it frowned on a pair of hunters who happened to be clambering from their shiny maroon pickup as we came along. This time we parked well up the road and waited—hearts pounding, palms sweating, minds whirling—until the perfect moment for ambush. The men paid us little attention, shouldered their packs, got out their rifles, and then headed up a steep slope toward the woods.

"Let's go!" Darcy hissed.

Almost immediately they had us pegged. Not that our approach would leave much question in anybody's mind: three unarmed women scrambling up the hill, followed by a guy who looked like he wanted to be somewhere else, then two men in brand-new blaze jackets lugging a television camera, recorder, and microphone. Feigning concern for the reporters, I waited while they struggled to climb the briar-snarled embankment. Truth is, I was nearly paralyzed with embarrassed apprehension.

Finally, yielding to a blind sense of duty, I traipsed up to join the others. The hunters stood side by side in a tiny opening surrounded by dense brush. One looked to be around 60, the other perhaps 40, both clean shaven and dressed in fresh-looking, high-quality outdoor gear. With the protesters squeezed around them, both hunters unloaded their rifles, which impressed me as singularly wise. At the same time, speaking quietly and politely, Darcy and Penny asked them if they might consider doing something else today. "Wouldn't it be better just to take pictures or go for a hike instead of killing deer?"

The men didn't respond, didn't look at us, didn't even acknowledge our existence, perhaps hoping we'd give up and leave. I stood there, fairly contorted with empathy, as they peered out across a grassy swale with a serrated wall of forest on its far side, wrapped in the gray gloom of dawn. Pointing one direction and another, talking in hushed tones—as if this were a normal hunt—the two discussed where they might sit to watch for deer.

"I should tell you that whatever you guys decide to do, we'll be coming along," Darcy interjected, making it clear they would disrupt the hunt and frighten off any whitetails that might happen by.

I kept off to one side, as far from the activists as cramped space would allow, on a flimsy notion that someone would correlate physical separation with political separation. The hunters fell into a prolonged silence, contemplating what to do next. At last, the older man suggested they leave and the other agreed, noting pointedly that they could hunt on a nearby farm where anyone who followed would be trespassing. There was a brittle, irritated edge in their voices, yet they didn't utter one angry word or lean even slightly toward confrontation. The two simply turned and marched wordlessly down the hill, as if they only wanted to get away from us and find a place to hunt.

We all followed them to the truck, then stood around while they sat on the tailgate, cased their rifles, and submitted to a brief television interview. The younger man explained that he lived about a mile away, and this was his father, who had driven up from Milwaukee for Opening Weekend.

The reporter suggested, "These people feel that perhaps they've accomplished something by forcing you folks to hunt on private land."

"Well, it's got pros and cons," the younger man responded. "About three times a week you almost hit a deer along here . . . they just bound across. The deer herd is bigger this year than it's been probably for longer than a lot of people can remember. So it's like managing cattle or anything else—there's a way to do it. If you don't manage the deer, they'll die, they'll starve, they'll get diseases. A shooting death is not as cruel; it's faster."

"What do you think of the technique these protesters are using?"

"Oh, they have their rights, too, I guess," said the older man. "It's not a very nice thing for hunters. The hunters invest a lot of money, and so forth, in doing what they like to do. It's like fishermen. If you fish on a lake, you kill fish, too. Something happens, no matter what you do."

After the interview I spent a few minutes alone with the pair, tending to my psyche, explaining that I'd come along only to observe, not to demonstrate. I also thanked them for staying calm. "I wouldn't start any problems or argue with anybody," the younger man replied. "No, it's better if we just go away." Although he still sounded frustrated and peeved, I also suspected—from his faint smile and easy tone—that we'd given him a good story to tell when he got back home.

I hurried off to join the others, immensely relieved, thinking this might not be so bad after all. The protesters had been cordial and even friendly; the hunters were restrained, tolerant, perhaps slightly bemused. I was impressed that such civility could prevail between people at complete odds, in a situation involving potent emotions on both sides. It uplifted my spirits, seeing how strongly decent folks are imbued with the ethic of civility. When I said this back in the car, Darcy attributed the hunters' patience to the unblinking eye of television cameras.

In any case, our jubilant crew declared the encounter a success. "We drove them out of the woods," said Darcy, "and that's what we came here to do. I mean, we're willing to risk our lives, just as they do, but it's for a different purpose. We'll go out and see the beauty as they claim they do, but they kill it. That's the big dividing line."

"I just wonder if it ever dawns on any hunters," Penny mused, "that maybe we're supposed to live with these creatures instead of manipulating them."

Darcy shook her head, frustrated with a system she considered morally and ecologically bankrupt. "What I'd like to see is a laissez-faire, hands-off system of management, starting with the state parks, where you let nature decide if deer are going to go hungry. You allow them to have some starvation; that's better than getting wounded or dying with a bullet in their spine."

She suggested deer populations would eventually control themselves without human intervention. "Animals that go hungry are going to have less fat and they won't have fawns the next spring; that's the key to it. Also, we don't have the other predators anymore, so man is the only one left. Animal protection people, not hunters, are the ones who want to restart wolves."

I asked Darcy if she found any common threads between groups like hers—who believe no one should have the legal right to take an animal's life—and organizations who believe no one should have the legal right to end a human pregnancy. Weren't both groups hoping to make their moral choices apply to everyone? Her response was immediate and unambiguous. "I'd like to think I have nothing in common with pro-lifers!" she laughed. "I'm an adamant feminist."

"I would say I'm pro-abortions for deer," Penny offered. "But in the case of these deer, they're already born; and when hunters want to slaughter them, the deer have no say in the matter."

This reminded me of the earlier conversation I'd had with Buzz, Jodi, and John Barnes. They acknowledged that humans cannot survive without taking the lives of other organisms; nevertheless, they considered it immoral to kill any "sentient being" capable of suffering or feeling pain. "I mean, you can go all the way down the phyla of the animal kingdom," said John Barnes. "They become less and less sensitive as you get into the clams and mollusks. We're concerned about those that can be identified or suspected of having sentience or awareness."

Buzz Kemper expanded on this thought: "I would ask a hunter, 'Why do you feel that we have the right to harm an animal?'—the same way I would ask the lab experimenter or anyone else. The hunters will say, 'Well, they're just deer,' or they'll give you the biblical view that we have dominion over the animals. I'm not a real religious person, but if you believe God put us in charge, that means we're supposed to take care of all this stuff. Just like being given dominion over your children doesn't mean you shoot them for fun."

Once we got back out on the road, it didn't take long to find more hunters. A weary-looking sedan, faded brown, crammed with people, pulled onto the shoulder as we approached from behind. The occupants sat inside for what seemed like forever, perhaps looking out the rearview mirror to see what our group would do. Finally the entire crowd—three men and two women, all dressed in brilliant orange—piled out and opened the trunk. Showing no particular haste, they sorted through rifles, packs, and other gear, then surveyed the terrain as if they weren't sure where to go.

We watched the proceedings intently, silently, almost hypnotically. To my amazement, I felt electrified with the chase, having lost my earlier anxiety. Did my companions recognize, I wondered, the similarity between their pursuit and a hunter stalking prey? Meanwhile, the target group didn't look terribly serious about hunting, given that they'd come so late and acted as if they were preparing for a stroll or a picnic. At last they strung out along a footpath that climbed a grassy hillside toward promising woods a few hundred yards from the road.

Without a word from Darcy, everyone launched out after the hunters. Their leader was a slightly built man, probably in his mid-fifties, accompanied by his two daughters and their respective boyfriends, all in their twenties. Only the three men carried weapons. Taken completely by surprise, they accepted the intrusion with remarkable calm, as if it wasn't altogether welcome but might prove interesting, like an encounter with door-to-door salespeople or survey takers.

As soon as the television camera started rolling, our three women repeated their suggestion that it might be a nice day for some other outdoor activity. This led to a short, now-familiar, and not terribly informative debate with the older man concerning the evils or virtues of what he'd come to do.

"Wouldn't you rather be out here with a camera?"

"Well, it's kind of hard to eat a picture."

"Yeah, but between the three of you guys, you could each legally get five deer. That's fifteen deer altogether. Doesn't that bother you?"

"We'll be lucky if we get one, really," the man responded. He didn't mention that hunters cannot legally take five deer in Wisconsin. A person who worked all the angles, hunting both the firearms and bow seasons and also holding a special bonus permit, could take as many as four in certain management units. Officials say this rarely happens and that most successful hunters take a single deer.

"Don't you worry about the message it gives to younger kids, telling them that hunting is an okay thing to do?"

"What's wrong with that message? Hunting's been going on since the beginning of time."

"Yeah, but I mean slavery went on for a long time, too."

The hunter had a question of his own: "How are you going to deal with the car collisions, the agricultural damage, the urban deer wrecking people's gardens, and other problems from high deer populations?"

"Well, that's very simple," Darcy replied. "Collisions won't happen if people put deer whistles on their cars, and if you've got special reflectors along the highways, and if you mow a certain way along the roadsides. Also, with farms, you just plant a couple extra rows of corn around the field which the deer eat; and then they leave the rest of the corn alone. If deer come in your backyard to eat your red tulips, well, you might find out they don't like yellow tulips. These are cost-effective measures."

Darcy added, "Then you've got the DNR, over the last decade, managing deer populations for more and more and more, trying to get the maximum deer yield per acre. They kill off the bucks every fall, and then you get does having two or three fawns. When you follow a hands-off approach, allowing nature to take her course, the deer population averages out. We just want the deer left alone instead of having atrocities permitted against them."

The elder hunter countered each point with a firmness that equaled Darcy's. He was calm, steadfast, and unfazed, if a bit impatient. For their part, the protesters tempered their strident assertiveness with flawless courtesy. And so it went.

One of the couples kept to the background during all this, but the other pair stayed close, listening intently while casting an occasional glance toward the television camera. At one point the young man sidled over to ask the reporter which station he came from, if we'd all be on the evening news, and if we'd get paid something for this.

At last the father announced, "I respect your right to say your piece and it's been nice talking to you, but we're going hunting." Not without our company, Darcy let him know. "Well, I guess that's fine," he responded, and then all three men unloaded their rifles, slipping the ammunition into their pockets. Judging by the heavy blaze coveralls each of them wore, I figured they wouldn't hike far. The television guys said they'd have to stay behind, keeping their equipment dry inside the car until the protesters returned. Everyone else trekked up the narrow, soggy trail—a single-file procession of flaming orange outfits that looked like a Halloween parade.

When we topped the ridge a quarter mile from the road, the older man called a halt. From here we looked upon an exquisite little valley—broad swaths of auburn meadow, sumac thickets with clinging scarlet leaves, and a surrounding forest dominated by ivory-trunked birch and aspen. The place had an ethereal quality, wreathed as it was in mist and drifting rain, like a romantic painter's vision of paradise. I could hardly imagine a less appropriate venue for political wrangling, yet here we were, ready for a standoff amid the wilds.

I hadn't heard a shot that morning, perhaps because of the noisy gale, but now, somewhere in the distance, a blue jay's call surged and faded on the wind. I longed to see that bird, flinging over the treetops like blue satin torn from the sky's edge. But the bird, having its own desires and the freedom to pursue them, never came within our sight.

"I guess we'll sit right here on this hill," said the elder man. "Looks like

a pretty good place to hunt." The shy couple talked softly for a few minutes, then hiked off to hunt or wait elsewhere, but the other two sat on
the grass beside our circle. They seemed more interested in the debate—
or perhaps the event—than in hunting. While continuing his discourse
with Darcy, Penny, and Mary, the man took a small bottle from his
pocket and dabbed a stick into it.

Instantly the whole area was saturated with dense, lurid skunk scent.
"We use this to mask human odor," he explained. "You know, so deer
won't smell us." Despite his placid, businesslike demeanor, I sensed a little gesture of retaliation here and caught an impish glint in his eyes. But
the saboteurs seemed unperturbed. Perhaps they appreciated this forth-
right and uncomplicated fellow as much as I did—an ordinary man altogether equal to this extraordinary situation. In fact, I was impressed by
every performer in this little melodrama. Of course, given the clatter of
voices, one player certain not to make an appearance was the white-tailed
deer.

Much of the dialogue had become familiar, so I chatted with the
daughter and her mate. Both said they'd hunted before but neither had
yet taken a deer. To assuage my guilt I mentioned that I'd come not to
protest but to watch and report. At this, the young man beamed like a
lottery winner. "Oh, you're a writer! Do you think we'll make it into a
book?"

"Does it make you angry, having these folks interrupt your hunt?" I
asked.

"Heck, no." He smiled, eyes widening. "I want to get on TV!"

About this time, Darcy played another card, warning the father that
we'd stay around until they all abandoned the woods. "That's fine," he
parried. "We'd like to get a deer, but we'll have a nice day outdoors no
matter what happens." The young guy leaned toward me and whispered,
"I figure you're gonna have to leave pretty soon; but I'd rather you didn't,
at least not if the TV guys come out here."

Back in the main arena, Darcy probed for a different nerve. "I wish I
could tap into your brain, to understand how hunting can be fun—
seeing the life go out of a deer's eyes . . ."

"Well, I can't say I don't enjoy hunting," the elder responded. "And I
also love venison. Of course, we're not starving, but we still like to get our
deer for the meat. I'm not after a trophy buck, even though unfortunately all we have this year are buck tags. We sent in for doe permits but
didn't get any."

"You might decide later in life to just look at deer or take up the camera instead," Penny suggested.

"I probably will when I can't manage to walk up the hills or get to the places where we hunt. You know, I love being out here in the woods."

"I could sit here for a week and just watch, and I'd be happy," said Darcy. "We'd probably agree with you on ninety percent of this, but it's just the killing . . ."

After about half an hour Darcy checked her watch, sighed, and threw in the towel. "Time for us to get along," she announced.

"And I guess we'll get on with our hunting," the elder man replied. Everybody swapped amicable good-byes, and then Darcy's crew marched back down the trail, ponchos flailing and slapping in the wind. All three women seemed delighted with the way things had gone.

On our return, the television reporter interviewed Darcy while the two of them strolled side by side down the road. She judged the protest a great success, declaring they had achieved their goal of forcing hunters to leave the woods.

"You're also protesting the fact that parklands should be available for those who want to hike and so forth?" the reporter inquired.

"I think we're showing that there's people who want to use this land for other things besides killing animals, that these people should have some rights in these woods during the fall."

"Some people question your tactics here," he challenged. "They say hunting is only nine days out of the year . . . it's not as though it's a year-round thing."

Instead of responding, Darcy changed the subject. "They can also say [this protest] is illegal according to the hunter harassment law; but as you can tell, today we did not get cited. So what we have on the books is a paper tiger . . . a law that is not going to be enforced. And as we continue to do this, more and more activists are going to come out into the woods, because they know they will not be cited and will not be fined." Apparently she was looking ahead to next year's intervention, hoping to provoke an arrest that would bring the law into court.

"Do you feel you've accomplished anything today?"

"Absolutely," Darcy affirmed. "We've accomplished all our goals. We've protected the deer, we got the hunter harassment law up for debate again, and we educated the public."

When the reporter asked how many protesters had taken to the woods this Opening Day, Darcy hinted at large numbers and implied that other

sabotages were going on all over Wisconsin. This wasn't true, but the actual number of antihunt activists mattered very little, given the media's
power to magnify. Our group of about 15 protesters spent less than two
hours on the hunting grounds and directly confronted 20 or 30 hunters.
On this same day, an estimated 650,000 deer hunters had taken to the
fields and forests, meadows and marshlands of Wisconsin, outnumber-
ing saboteurs by about 32,500 to 1. Yet on tonight's news and in tomorrow's papers the protest would loom large among Opening Day reports.

Of course, animal rights activists represent a much larger constituency
who stayed at home, but the same is true for hunters. Deer hunting is
practically without equal in Wisconsin as a social, economic, and cultural event. Although only 16 percent of the state's residents actually go
afield, the impact extends—in some way or other—to almost everyone.
Boldly leaning against the collective weight of regional culture, the
protest captured attention far beyond its actual magnitude, as if everyone in a crowd became so fascinated by a mouse that they didn't notice
the elephant standing over it.

Around eight-thirty a.m., Darcy's group was the last to arrive back at
park headquarters, where they met an excited knot of activists clustered
in the rain, swapping tales and celebrating. All of the encounters with
hunters had been peaceful, except for one, which everybody wanted to
hear about. Apparently, a man had become angry enough to charge at the
protesters, seething and cursing, telling them to leave him alone. And
that's exactly what the group did.

"The rest of the guys we came across were very polite," a member of
that same bunch told me. "I mean, we met this really great older man
and we stood with him for a while, shooting the bull. Then we went up
to another guy we saw on a hill, and he said, 'I don't want to be rude, but
I don't want to talk to you.' So he just stood there and so did we. Finally
the TV crew ran out of tape, so we all left and the hunter stayed."

Intensifying rain encouraged an early end to the festivities, helped
along by the fact that everyone was tired, wet, cold, emotionally drained,
and anxious to get home. I planned to head off on my own, so it was time
to thank my companions for allowing someone from the opposition to
tag along. In return, I hoped to accurately represent the arguments and
viewpoints they had given me. I had not, of course, abandoned my differing philosophy any more than Jodi or Buzz, for example, had been
swayed by anything I might have said. My hope was that we'd come away
respecting one another and acknowledging that each of our choices—to
hunt or not to hunt—was made after concerted moral introspection.

Before we parted Buzz mentioned there would be a second protest, something lighter, in Madison tomorrow. I said I'd be there.

The Quest for Innocence

Avoiding the interstate, I drove country roads homeward, squinting through sheets of rain thick as a blizzard, steadying the wheel against brawny gusts. At intervals I passed cars parked on the shoulder, their engines running and windows fogged, drenched hunters warming up inside, waiting for partners too tough or stubborn or fanatical to give up.

The radio kept me entertained and awake. "Guys might have deer hunting," blared one commercial, "but gals, you've got a big fashion sale right here in downtown Milwaukee . . ." And the play-by-play announcer for a football game suggested it was deer hunting—not stormy weather—that explained why the stands weren't filled that day.

About 30 miles north of Madison I spotted five men clustered in a hay field, their outfits bright as lightning. Figuring they must be at work on a deer, I mustered the courage to pay them a visit. Aloof at first, they relaxed when I admired the fork-horn buck they'd taken, especially when they learned I was also a hunter. "We're four brothers and a cousin," one explained. "All of us grew up on farms right around this place, and so did those guys over there." He pointed to another bunch alongside the woods a quarter mile off, also field-dressing a deer.

"When you came walking out here we figured you might be one of those animal rights people," he admitted, grinning easily now. I didn't consider—not for a second—trying to explain how I'd spent the morning. Another man chimed in: "You never know when somebody's going to get all upset. There's people, even here in Wisconsin, that see a deer and think, 'Hey look, it's Bambi!' "

I drifted off for a moment, lost in a childhood memory of that most endearing of all fantasy creatures, prancing big-eyed across the screen with Thumper, Friend Owl, Flower the skunk, and dainty Faline. Bambi—the quintessential fawn, the paragon of wild innocence—lives deep down near the root of our psyches. For many Americans, Bambi is virtually synonymous with "deer," and his mother's death by a hunter's bullet affirms a dark view of humankind's bellicosity toward nature.

"It is difficult to identify a film, story, or animal character that has had a greater influence on our vision of wildlife than the hero of Walt Disney's 1942 animated feature," writes environmental historian Ralph H. Lutts. Enduring popularity has made *Bambi* not only a modern folklore classic but also one of the most profitable films ever produced. Many of those who watched the movie as kids have seen it again with their own children, maybe also their grandchildren.

Disney based his film on the 1923 book *Bambi: A Forest Life,* by the Hungarian-born novelist and journalist Felix Salten. After moving to Vienna in the mid-1880s, Salten applied his literary talents to a variety of projects, including plays, translations, criticism, even a pseudonymous pornographic novel. He was both a hunter and an animal lover, who shared his private hunting preserve with aristocratic friends. Salten's portrayal of Bambi's world included, without moralistic judgment, such ecological realities as animals dying from winter starvation and being killed by predators. But humans loomed as complex, frightening, nearly omnipotent beings—known simply as "Him"—who mindlessly devastated forests and slaughtered wild animals.

Walt Disney rendered this story into cinema by simplifying its plot, transforming its characters, and underscoring its theme of human malevolence. When the project began, Disney brought to his California studio a pair of fawns, christened Bambi and Faline, but instead of replicating these models, artists were told to give their fawns childlike human qualities—huge eyes, shortened snouts, rounded heads, expressive faces, comical gestures, captivating personalities. Bambi's head became almost as large as the rest of his body; his countenance featured eyes with permanently dilated pupils and enormous, blinking lashes. Anthropomorphism was the key to Disney's approach. "We have them talking and the minute you have them say a word, you've got that human parallel established," he instructed the film's creators, "so I mean in their mannerisms—in their action—it should all be based on certain human beings."

"He had no intention of making a film about realistic deer living in a forest," recalled the pioneer Disney animators Ollie Johnston and Frank Thomas. "What Walt saw were personalities."

If the characters in Bambi's world are distortions of real animals, the forest they inhabit has almost nothing in common with an actual environment and almost totally lacks a sense for ecological relationships. Rabbits, mice, and grouse live harmoniously with carnivores like skunks, raccoons, and great horned owls. Herbivores take an occasional nibble, but predators never eat.

According to biological anthropologist Matt Cartmill, "The film portrays the natural world as a realm of peace and beauty, saturated with innocent love in all its varieties." Lutts concurs: "Salten's sharp, naturalistic vision of woodland life is degraded into a fantasy of nature cleansed of the traumas and difficulties that may trouble children and that adults prefer to avoid." Except, of course, the traumas caused by humankind.

At the edge of this idyllic world—never visible on-screen yet always lurking somewhere in the background—is the relentlessly evil "Him." Terrifying moments begin early in the film, when the mother of the tiny, helpless, lovable fawn narrowly escapes from hunters. The doe and her child struggle through a bitter and hungry winter, one of the film's rare leanings toward accurate natural history. Finally, with the gentle onset of spring their survival seems assured, but as the two deer eat newly exposed grass, hunters stalk the meadow's edge. Bambi's mother catches their scent, listens, and cries: "The thicket!" Two shots ring out as they dash for cover, and when the little deer makes it safely into the forest, he finds that his mother hasn't escaped.

"One thing Walt realized quite early was that Man killing Bambi's mother would be the most powerful and memorable statement ever made in an animated film," recalled Johnston and Thomas. "No longer philosophical or an important lesson about survival, it spoke directly to the heart." Many of us who saw the film as children recall how passionately we empathized with the little fawn's terror—an orphan alone and unprotected in the great, shadowy forest. It's a moment etched forever not just in our own minds but in the collective memory of our society.

Later on, a pack of vicious hunting dogs chases the panicked Faline, and Bambi comes to her defense, but while he fights off the dogs he's struck by a hunter's bullet. Quickly recovering, he barely manages to escape a raging wildfire started, of course, by the rogue hunters. Scenes of scorched and devastated forest bring to a final crescendo the film's litany of human transgressions. As the story ends, another spring promises healing and rebirth. Bambi—now a magnificent buck—stands on a clifftop watching over his mate, Faline, who nestles in a thicket with two fresh-born fawns. Many of us have forgotten that *Bambi* ended on this note of tranquillity and hope; what we remember are the scenes depicting our own kind as a relentless, murdering scourge.

"It may be that more people have, consciously or unconsciously, based their understanding of deer and woodland life on Walt Disney's *Bambi* than on any other single source," suggests historian Lutts. "Bambi has become one of our most widespread and emotionally powerful national symbols of nature, one that motivates deep concern, and dedicated action to protect wildlife."

Lutts concludes, however, that "Disney's Bambi is an empty symbol, because the concept of nature that his fawn represents is impoverished.

The film motivates, but does not educate. It may stimulate action, but not understanding." While it appeals to our sentiments, this animated epic also misrepresents wild animals as cartoon caricatures of humans. As a result, it does more to widen the distance between ourselves and nature than to bring us closer.

Critics like Cartmill and Lutts agree that *Bambi* nourishes our longing for a simple, uncomplicated, romantic world, and satisfies our desire to find in nature the perfection of Eden. Unfortunately the film gives our children no suggestion that humankind can be anything but a destructive force; it offers no positive direction toward responsible participation in our environment; and it allows us no rightful place in a natural world that we must use if we are to survive. In this sense, the "Bambi syndrome" is one expression of a view of humankind's relationship to the earth as increasingly dysfunctional.

Discovering the Animal Within

Matt Cartmill, writing in *Natural History* magazine, characterizes *Bambi* as "probably the most effective piece of antihunting propaganda ever made." Without question the film has added impetus to antihunting activism over the past 50 years, but interest in animal welfare started much earlier. For example, the American Society for Prevention of Cruelty to Animals was founded in 1866, and the American Anti-Vivisection Society began in 1883. These associations promote the humane treatment of animals in homes, zoos, laboratories, and on farms. Modern animal rights organizations also generally oppose animal experimentation for medical and consumer research, trapping or raising animals for their fur, killing livestock for food or other products, control by lethal means of wild or feral animal populations, and of course, most or all forms of hunting.

Often mentioned as a founding sourcebook for contemporary activists is *Animal Liberation,* by Peter Singer, an Australian philosopher. Singer believes humans are guilty of "speciesism," which he defines as "a prejudice or attitude of bias toward the interests of members of one's own species and against those of members of other species." This view underlies what Singer calls "the tyranny of human beings" who have not extended "the basic principle of equality of consideration to members of other species." Prejudice against nonhuman creatures, he believes, is as objectionable and oppressive as racial or sexual prejudice against our fellow humans.

For Singer and many others, individual animals should be accorded rights, including the right not to be killed by humans. Hunting, therefore, is immoral. Killing plants or "lower" forms of animal life is not wrong, Singer believes, because our moral responsibilities are limited to creatures with a central nervous system. "A stone does not have interests [or rights] because it cannot suffer. Nothing we can do to it could possibly make any difference to its welfare. A mouse, on the other hand, does have an interest in not being kicked along the road, because it will suffer if it is." Following this principle, Singer offers no moral anchorage for people "who eat pieces of slaughtered nonhumans every day."

Animal rights advocates do not judge other creatures by the same moral standards they apply to ourselves. Like most people, for example, they highly esteem predators like wolves and mountain lions, despite their habit of killing and eating nonhumans such as deer. Some activists admit, however, that they're troubled over the suffering caused by nature's tooth-and-claw realities. *Sierra* magazine once asked Cleveland Amory, founder of the Fund for Animals, what actions he would take if granted absolute power to rule the world. He emphasized that humans would no longer be allowed to take animal lives; in fact, people who did so would themselves be shot. And as Amory imagined his perfect kingdom,

> All animals will not only not be shot, they will be protected—not only from people but as much as possible from each other. Prey will be separated from predator, and there will be no overpopulation because all will be controlled by sterilization or implant.

Amory would also eliminate government agencies whose names include "conservation," "wildlife," or "natural resources." This reflects a firmly antiecological bent prevalent among animal rights organizations, which often reject the whole idea of wildlife management. Their primary concern is the well-being of *individual* creatures, not of species, habitats, or environments. For example, in nature preserves throughout North America, animal rights proponents have fought against use of lethal methods to reduce animal overpopulation that threatens natural vegetation and jeopardizes other wildlife. One such case is San Clemente Island, off the California coast, where activists have opposed plans to remove feral goats responsible for wiping out nearly 50 indigenous plant species and endangering some native animal species.

In 1982, heavy rains inundated the Florida Everglades, concentrating white-tailed deer on small areas of dry land where they quickly stripped

the vegetation and trampled the soil until it was bare as a barnyard. The
deer population should be quickly reduced, biologists warned, to prevent
further habitat damage leading to a massive die-off; but shortly after officials authorized a hunt, animal rights organizations made the issue a national controversy.

Michael Hacker, a Miami attorney who filed suit against the hunt,
pointed out that animals had no voice in the issue, suggested human development had caused the flooding, and advocated transplanting or artificial feeding to save the deer. In Hacker's opinion, culling the Everglades
herd

> amounts to a deprivation of the rights of the deer to live freely and
> peacefully on earth, according to nature's order, without man attempt-
> ing to control, mastermind or engineer the destiny of 6,000 innocent,
> helpless, harmless and otherwise happy creatures that have been placed
> on earth by God to be free from the torment of man, and the problems
> induced by man.

After the court challenge failed, hunters took about 700 deer in a designated portion of the Everglades. In areas that were not hunted, up to
1,000 animals (about 67 percent of the herd) died from stress, starvation,
or drowning. Within the hunted zone, biologists found less vegetation
damage and a larger deer herd than would have survived if hunting had
not taken place. Eighteen whitetails were captured alive for relocation,
but 12 died before activist volunteers acknowledged the effort was futile.

It's important to distinguish animal welfare organizations such as the
Fund for Animals or People for the Ethical Treatment of Animals from
environmental organizations like the Audubon Society, Sierra Club, or
National Wildlife Federation. Animal rights activists focus on protecting
individual creatures from harm or suffering; environmental activists
focus on protecting entire animal populations, usually by conserving the
environments they depend on for survival. Most environmental groups
do not oppose hunting, and they share with the hunting community an
overriding concern for habitat preservation.

Of course, many members of environmental organizations oppose
hunting, just as many animal rights advocates consider themselves environmentalists; but it's much harder for hunters and antihunting activists
to find common ground. In a nationwide survey of American attitudes
toward wildlife, Stephen Kellert discovered some fascinating patterns
among these two groups. He categorized hunters into three general
types: "utilitarian hunters" often came from rural backgrounds and

hunted primarily for meat; "dominionistic," or "sport," hunters did not indicate much affection for animals and valued hunting mainly as an expression of prowess, mastery, or masculinity; "nature hunters" expressed strong love for animals and the outdoors, and they saw hunting as a way to achieve intimacy with the natural world.

Antihunters in Kellert's national sample were predominantly female, resided in large cities, and showed no special involvement with animals or the outdoors. While their lack of affinity for animals might be surprising, it does not impugn the strength of their beliefs. Peter Singer, often considered a founder of the modern animal rights movement, replied this way when asked how he and his wife felt about animals:

> We tried to explain that we were interested in the prevention of suffering and misery . . . that we believed animals were ruthlessly and cruelly exploited by humans, and we wanted this changed. Otherwise, we said, we were not especially "interested in" animals. Neither of us had been inordinately fond of dogs, cats, or horses in the way that many people are. We didn't "love" animals. We simply wanted them treated as the independent sentient beings that they are, and not as a means to human ends.

In Kellert's study, opponents of hunting fell into two distinct types. "Humanistic antihunters" stressed their emotional identification with animals, especially pets and large mammals like deer, whom they considered innocent and virtuous. They were concerned about the welfare of individual creatures, not the well-being of entire species. "Moralistic antihunters" emphasized that hunting is an inherently debased and ethically wrong exploitation of the natural world. To exemplify this position, Kellert quotes the venerable nature writer Joseph Wood Krutch:

> Killing for sport is the perfect type of that pure evil for which metaphysicians have sometimes sought. . . . Most wicked deeds are done because the doer proposes some good to himself. The liar lies to gain some end; the swindler and the thief want things which, if honestly got, might be good in themselves. . . . The killer for sport, however, has no such comprehensible motive. He prefers death to life, darkness to light.

"Moralistic antihunters" also lean toward a belief that hunters cannot develop a sense of belonging to nature, but remain aloof, distant, and alienated from it. On the other hand, members of Kellert's "nature hunter" category consider "the prey-predator relationship a basic way for humans to experience a sense of kinship and interaction with the natural world." On questions measuring people's knowledge of animals and nature, groups who scored highest included birdwatchers, trappers, and "nature hunters," in that order. Groups with the lowest knowledge brought together a most unlikely pair: antihunters and dominionistic hunters.

Comparing hunters with nonhunters (a large category that includes hunting opponents), Kellert found intriguing differences: hunters showed more interest in the outdoors, more affection toward and desire to live around wildlife, and greater interest in backpacking, camping, fishing, wilderness areas, and pets. "Thus, despite the somewhat paradoxical fact that hunters killed wild animals for food, recreation, or other purposes, they were characterized by substantially greater affection, interest, and lack of fear of animals than [were] non-hunters."

In the United States, hunters and antihunters make up small percentages of the total population. According to a *USA Today* opinion survey in 1992, 17 percent of Americans believe hunting should be illegal, while 58 percent of nonhunters and 80 percent of all Americans said hunting should remain legal. This brings to mind the New York biologist Mark Lowery, who told me that many more citizens are *antihunter* than are *antihunting*. While they do not oppose hunting, they're troubled by what they've seen or heard about hunters who trespass, damage property, disregard the law, or violate ethical standards.

Studying New Jersey residents, James Applegate found that "people who know hunters generally favor hunting, whereas people who have no hunting acquaintances are generally opposed to hunting." The number of residents who know hunters is declining, which reflects a population movement toward the cities, away from the countryside and from our agrarian roots. Researchers have found time and again that rural experience correlates with a willingness to accept or participate in hunting.

Public opinion also reflects a great concern about hunters' motivations and purposes. Michael Satchell and Joannie Schrof, writing in *U.S. News & World Report,* found that "more than 80 percent of Americans approve of hunting to put game on the table—be it a native Alaskan subsistence hunter or a white-collar suburbanite with a taste for . . . venison." By contrast, 80 percent of the surveyed Americans opposed hunting "for trophy heads to mount on the wall," and about 60 percent disapproved of hunting "merely for sport or recreation."

In short, many people base their judgment of hunting not on what it *is,* but on *why someone does it.* As an old friend once told me: "I don't think there's anything wrong with hunting itself, but nobody should be able to hunt for sport, for the pleasure of killing a wild animal."

The issue is a lot more complex than this simple statement implies, however. Among the abundant sociological and psychological studies of hunters, not one supports the idea that hunters are motivated by a single goal or purpose. It's erroneous to characterize the hunt as "killing for sport" or "killing for recreation," as if participants trekked afield for the singular amusement of causing an animal's death. I believe most hunters would consider this a twisted and perverse aberration. "I no more hunt to kill deer than I garden to kill cabbages," states the Canadian wildlife biologist Valerius Geist.

The hunter I know best—myself—has a very long list of motivations. Like the majority of hunters interviewed or surveyed by researchers, being close to nature and connecting myself intimately with the environment are among the most important of my reasons, along with providing healthy, organic meat for my household, sharing the experience with family and friends, and harvesting food directly from the land. These incentives and rewards cannot be viewed separately; instead, they merge like the colors and patterns and movement on the surface of a river.

This brings to mind my experiences in northern Alaska with Iñupiaq Eskimos, Koyukon Indians, and Gwich'in Indians. Living from the land—hunting, fishing, trapping, and gathering—is not only how these Native American people get their food, it's among their greatest sources of pleasure and joy, a way to fulfill themselves as individuals, and a means of expressing their social relationships. They hunt with a zeal that could never be explained in purely economic terms; it is their work, but it is also their passion and their fundamental being. The most consummate hunters I ever met were Iñupiaq men, and I became convinced that although they hunt to live, they also live to hunt.

At the deepest level, I regard hunting as a biological process that helps to sustain my life as an organism. This touches sensitive ground in our Euro-American culture, which has long emphasized a sharp distinction between ourselves and animals. For some people it's still hard to accept the idea that humans evolved like all other creatures, much less to acknowledge that our biological makeup is identical to theirs, and that a hunter is—among other things—an animal seeking food.

In seventeenth- and eighteenth-century England, according to historian Keith Thomas, philosophers and Christian thinkers dwelled at length on the "total qualitative difference between man and brute." Similarities between ourselves and other animals—as in the case of bodily functions—were concealed, denied, and rationalized. Cotton Mather, the Colonial American Congregationalist, revealed in his diary:

I was once emptying the cistern of nature, and making water at the wall. At the same time, there came a dog, who did so too, before me. Thought I; "What mean and vile things are the children of men. . . . How much do our natural necessities abase us, and place us . . . on the same level with the very dogs!"

But of all biological functions, sexuality is the one identified in Western cultures as most clearly and potently "animal," and therefore most disturbing. Historically, some American religious groups went to the extreme of prohibiting sex entirely, which probably made winning converts as challenging as it was essential. In certain denominations today, sex with the intent to produce children is sanctioned, while sex for pleasure is immoral, although it's hard to imagine how anyone keeps the two entirely separate. This brings us back to the original and elemental purpose of hunting, which is to sustain human life. Hunting is also inherently pleasurable, for an array of biological, social, psychological, economic, and cultural reasons. Here again, judging that it is immoral to hunt "for pleasure" suggests that people can isolate one motive from a whole complex of others, and this simply is not true.

Food is a prime motivation for the hunt, yet eating also evokes questions of right and wrong. Keith Thomas quotes an 1897 letter from Kate Greenaway to her friend Violet Dickenson: "It's so horrible, things having to be killed for us to eat them—it feels so wicked. Yet we have to do it—or die ourselves." Nowadays, we have the luxury of deciding what kind of organisms our conscience allows us to eat. Should we draw the line at plants only? At invertebrates like shrimp and oysters? At cold-blooded vertebrates such as tuna and salmon? At birds like chicken and turkey? At such mammals as cows and deer? Proclamations of absolute right and wrong abound on either side of what might be called the omnivore's dilemma.

"I can hardly wait to eat fresh venison," said a hunter I met after the Opening Day protest, as he field-dressed a whitetail. He reminded me of the satisfaction I feel whenever I do this same work, preparing food our family will enjoy over the following year. Regardless of my Euro-American roots, I believe this sense of fulfillment reflects, more than anything else, the fact that I am an *animal,* and that I am driven by the same hungers that motivate any other creature—the squirrel in the forest, the vole in the meadow, the bear on the mountainside, the deer in the valley.

What could I learn by keeping constantly in mind the fundamental, encompassing fact that I am an animal? And by remembering that I share with every creature on earth the need to sustain my life by eating other organisms? This biological need reveals that I am not just one *of* the earth's living creatures, but also one *with* them. At the deepest level, all forms of life are interchangeable: animals eat plants, and plants are nourished in turn by animals. There is only one kind of life, shared equally, identically, and universally among the earth's organisms. We pass life back and forth—the fire that burns inside us all—creating a spectacular network of interdependence.

Nowhere is our membership in the earth's living community more evident than at mealtime, when our table is arrayed with *organisms.* Listen to their names: corn, wheat, rice, potato, carrot, radish, celery, broccoli, tomato, lettuce, rhubarb, blueberry, banana, pear, strawberry, orange, cherry, apple, salmon, halibut, red snapper, perch, chicken, turkey, duck, cow, pig, sheep, elk, deer. We veil ourselves from them with everyday euphemisms: grain, fruit, vegetable, cereal, herb, condiment, relish, sauce, beverage, poultry, meat, filet. And we conceal them by mixing, dicing, whipping, coloring, leavening, mashing, dressing, dehydrating, stewing, boiling, smoking, roasting, frying, boxing, and wrapping. Yet at every breakfast, lunch, dinner, banquet, picnic, and snack each of us is fed by other lives, passed along to us as our daily bread.

The supermarket is an agent of our forgetfulness.

Organisms we buy in stores and array on the table are our makers, the creators and nurturers of our bodies, until eventually we die and nourish other organisms in turn. As a society, we could benefit enormously by finding ways to remember, acknowledge, and celebrate this process, to accept with gratitude and respect the plants and animals who keep us alive, who weave us into the living tapestry of earth.

During our long drive to the antihunting protest, I had questioned Jodi Kemper about her life and beliefs, especially how she became involved with animal rights. Her answers helped me reflect on the transformations I had gone through, and because she seemed interested, I told her some things about myself. Most important, I wanted to explain how I became a hunter and how I learned about a traditional Native American code of "animal rights."

Since early childhood, I explained, I was enthralled by animals, and had there been antihunting demonstrations when I was a young man in Wisconsin, I would have stood at the forefront. As a university freshman I majored in zoology, planning to shape a career around my love for wildlife and natural history. But I found modern biology a disappointment, with its emphasis on such imponderables as microscopic structures, quantitative ecology, physiological processes, and genetics. There didn't seem to be a place here for animals. And by that time, natural history—the observer afield with binoculars and notebook, senses immersed in the direct experience of nature—was considered old-fashioned, better suited for a hobby than a profession.

While I became disillusioned with zoology, I stumbled onto cultural anthropology. What caught my attention were studies of hunter-gatherers like African Pygmies, Australian Aborigines, North American Indians, and Alaskan Eskimos. I fairly devoured ethnographies describing how these people lived, what they knew about their environments, and how they used this knowledge to wrest a livelihood. Over thousands of years, hunters and gatherers had woven their lives and culture intricately into their surroundings. Paramount among the expressions of this intimacy were traditions of natural history far beyond anything I'd found in the writings of Western scientists. And what they had to teach was exactly what I wanted to learn.

At the age of 22, I went to live with Iñupiaq Eskimos in the village of Wainwright on Alaska's Arctic coast. Under a grant from the U.S. Air Force, my assignment was to record what Iñupiaq people knew about their environment, along with their methods of hunting, travel, and survival—information to be used in manuals for pilots who crashed on the sea ice.

This study was based on an unusual premise. Although Euro-Americans had worked energetically to learn *about* Native American traditions, we had rarely sought to learn *from* them. In other words, we hadn't taken seriously the intellectual achievements of North America's indigenous people. But Frederick Milan, the anthropologist who conceived this project, recognized that Alaskan Eskimos are the foremost authorities on their environment and that their knowledge is valuable for anyone trying to live in high Arctic conditions. My job was to become a student to Iñupiaq hunters and to write down the lessons they taught.

Once I arrived in the village it didn't take long to see that if I wanted to accurately describe the Eskimos' subsistence and survival methods I'd have to learn them for myself—exactly as generations of young Iñupiaq people had done. This meant having clothes made from caribou and sealskin, building a sled and learning to drive my own dog team, making a kayak and other hunting implements, listening to elders' stories about the tundra and sea ice, and finally heading out to become an apprentice hunter. The experiences that unfolded were so compelling, so rich, so vital that they resonated through my soul like nothing I had ever imagined possible.

Under the close and steady watch of Iñupiaq teachers I took to the hunter's lifeway as if I'd been born to it. Over the course of a year I hunted almost constantly, joining anyone who would take me along and often going out alone, once I gained confidence. I reveled in the pleasures of traveling by dog team and skin-covered boat; sleeping in tents and snowhouses amid that immense, almost impossibly wild country; following tracks of polar bear, wolf, and wolverine; encountering caribou, seal, walrus, and whale; and trying to comprehend what the Iñupiaq people told me about animals, land, ice, and weather.

On one of the first hunts my Iñupiaq partner spotted a furtive seal, scratched on the ice to attract the animal within shooting range, then retrieved its floating body with a clever snagging device. When he finished, he pointed to his brow, smiled, and declared: "You see, Eskimo is a scientist." I knew enough by then to realize it was true, and over the year I spent with Iñupiaq people I saw with increasing clarity the depth, sophistication, and accuracy of their knowledge. For example, an old man described how he once stretched prone on the ice and imitated a basking seal, hoping to attract a polar bear he'd seen in the distance. The bear spotted him, swam across a lead of open water, and stalked to within close shooting range. At that point, the hunter transformed himself from phantom prey into the impeccable predator he truly was.

This man possessed such fluent, intimate knowledge of animals that he could predict and manipulate their behavior, as if he had penetrated their minds. Here was a merging of the human genius with the animal genius, in ways that elevated me to awe and sometimes defied my comprehension. The naturalist heroes of my youth paled by comparison.

When snow came in September I traveled with a group of men far inland, where we encountered herds of migrating caribou. I watched my teachers skin and quarter a few animals, then tried for myself, gradually learning each step. A few days later, my sled laden with as much meat as the dogs could pull, I alternately rode and walked the 50 miles home to Wainwright. There, exhausted and famished, I treated myself to a feast of caribou. Never had anything tasted so delicious as this, and suddenly I realized that my pleasure came not just from the meat but from the whole experience. This was the first time I had ever taken full responsibility for the process of feeding myself: finding the animal, hunting it, field-dressing and transporting it, butchering the meat, cooking it, and then eating it. I sat in my tiny house, caribou meat steaming on the plate, and at last I comprehended where my life came from.

This moment is engraved forever on my mind. Yet in retrospect, it's hard to fathom that something so basic and straightforward had not occurred to me until I was 22 years old. My Iñupiaq companions had participated in the making of their own lives since childhood, and what had seemed to me a moment of profound recognition was probably so basic that they would never have put it into words. In this way I learned that people who grew up as I did, in the cities and suburbs, had lost the most elementary comprehension of their own biological roots.

I was so taken with Iñupiaq life that I often imagined making the village my home, yet I craved the familiarity of my own culture and realized where I truly belonged. However, I would take with me the lessons taught by Iñupiaq people and would draw from these lessons to shape my own course. This, I now clearly understood, meant staying close to the land, being in the midst of wild country, and harvesting my own food by hunting, fishing, and gathering.

Jodi listened closely to all this, and despite our very different viewpoints on the subject, she seemed as interested in my recollections as I was in hers. We had an ideal setting for talk of the Alaskan wilds as we drove through the midnight blackness with storm gusts and rain whirling around the car.

After my work on the Arctic coast I spent a total of several years with Koyukon Indians, who live near the Arctic Circle in Alaska's boreal forest. Their lifeway centers around hunting animals like moose, caribou, and bear; trapping marten, beaver, lynx, and other furbearers; fishing for salmon, whitefish, and pike; gathering edible plants and berries. And like the Iñupiaq, they have an extensive, highly refined knowledge of their natural surroundings. But Koyukon people have something more, something vitally important, to teach: a tradition of religious beliefs and practices passed down through generations of elders, showing how to live in balance with the natural world.

"Every animal knows way more than you do," a Koyukon man once told me, as if it were the most important thing a person could know about living successfully as a hunter or, more broadly, as a human being. He explained that all of nature has power, sensitivity, and awareness— the animals and plants, the lakes and rivers, the hills and mountains, the air and sky. In the traditional Koyukon view, stones *can* feel and they do have rights.

For Koyukon people, each living and nonliving thing has a spirit, much as Christianity teaches that each person has a soul. This spirit must be treated with respect and humility, according to an elaborate code of rules and courtesies. A person who violates the rules will have bad luck in hunting, trapping, fishing, or gathering, and for serious offenses the guilty one or a family member might fall sick, possibly even die. In the Koyukon world, no creature is regarded as a lesser or insignificant being, whether it's the moose people depend on for food or the songbird flitting in a thicket. And certain animals—like the wolverine, wolf, otter, and bear—have extremely potent, volatile spirits.

Koyukon people learn hundreds of ways to show respect toward nature. For example, animals are offended and alienated by anyone who brags about his success as a hunter, trapper, or fisherman. "If somebody talks big, he probably won't get anything," the elders warn. A hunter going out after moose—the villagers' most important staple food—shouldn't even speak directly about it, because animals have the power to know what people say. Because of this, I often heard cryptic remarks like "Tomorrow I'll go out and try to find a moose track." Also, to preserve his hunting luck, the person who takes a moose should never waste any useful part of the animal—meat, fat, organs, bones, hide. Creatures like the moose, whose spirits are fairly benign, seldom do more than shun someone who offends them, but with such animals as the bear, an insult could have deadly consequences.

Traveling with Koyukon hunters, I came to understand that no one gets a moose, caribou, bear, or any other game purely by skill or coincidence. Instead, the creature *gives itself* to a person who has honored and respected others of its kind. This can also be true for plants, such as straight-grained spruce or birch trees used to make everything from dogsleds to canoe paddles. "A person that didn't treat them right can walk past a good tree and never see it," I was cautioned. By following this creed, Koyukon people keep themselves in a state of grace or harmony with every living species. "If a person has good luck—catches game—it is because something created the world, and *that* is helping him to get what he needs," a woman explained to me.

Nature's power reveals itself to the hunter in many ways. For example, if a hawk owl flies across someone's trail, it foretells bad hunting luck, but if the owl flies parallel to the trail, it augurs success. A raven rolling topsy-turvy in the sky while making a call that sounds like the Koyukon words "Animal! Animal!" is showing the way toward game. People sometimes ask a raven to give them luck or protect their health. "It's just like talking to God," one of my Koyukon teachers said. "That's why we talk to the raven. He created the world."

Whether at home or afield, Koyukon villagers are mindful that they move in a world filled with power far greater than their own; power that allows no place for arrogance, waste, indifference, or disregard; power to perceive and understand in ways beyond human comprehension; power that must be approached humbly; power that may give or withhold the animals and plants they depend on for survival; power that can affect our own fate and well-being.

Koyukon people follow, along with these beliefs, sophisticated conservation practices based on ecological principles essentially identical to those in modern wildlife management. Villagers are keenly aware that overharvesting can deplete wildlife populations, so they try to regulate themselves and encourage all community members to behave responsibly. They also believe that anyone who is wasteful or improvident will be punished by the spiritual powers of animals or plants. A Koyukon man once told me, "The country knows. If you do wrong things to it, the whole country knows. It feels what's happening to it. I guess everything is connected together somehow under the ground."

Living with Koyukon people, I was constantly struck by the wisdom and sensibility of their ways, and I tried—within the limits of my knowledge—to follow their teachings. Of course, their culture is not my own, nor is their way of seeing nature a part of my inheritance. I will never know if animals and plants have spirits, if the tree I stand beside is aware of my presence, if respectful gestures bring hunting luck and protect my well-being. But I am absolutely certain it is wise and responsible to behave *as if* these things were true.

Without adopting or imitating specific Koyukon customs, any of us can follow the same principles that have guided these people for thousands of years: recognizing that we depend on the environment for every moment of our existence, acknowledging that nature's power is greater than our own, using our environment with harmony and sustainability as paramount considerations, and approaching nature with humility, respect, and restraint. To me, this seems a much wiser and more deeply considered view than the modern animal rights philosophy, and among all of the insights achieved by humankind throughout history, these may be the most universal and most important.

Harvest and Salvation

The next day a chill north wind blustered down over Wisconsin, whipping ribbons of snow across the highway leading into Madison. I followed Buzz Kemper's directions to a shopping center parking lot on the south side of town.

It wasn't hard to pick out the antihunting folks, busy around a dozen or so cars near the lot's main entrance. What first caught my eye were the bumper stickers: FUR IS DEAD. BOYCOTT VEAL—STOP FACTORY FARMING. FUR COATS: NO SKIN OFF *YOUR* BACK. WARNING: I BRAKE FOR ANIMALS.

Buzz had promised that today's protest would be lighthearted, and I saw what he meant. Two women from yesterday's group, wearing headbands decorated with brown paper antlers, hoisted a dummy attired in blue jeans, plaid shirt, and blaze-orange hat onto the roof of a car. On the door, they taped a handwritten sign: THINNING THE HERD.

Other antlered protesters were tying brightly dressed, flaccid mannequins on their roofs or hoods. A poster on one car opposed hunting in state parks, and another declared: THERE'S NOTHING SPORTING ABOUT SPORT HUNTING.

"Using the hunter dummies gets lots of attention," Buzz explained. "It has humor value but also shock value by pointing out that the thing strapped across a hunter's hood is a dead being."

The anxieties that kept everyone serious yesterday had now dissolved into easy smiles and laughter. A man rummaged inside his car for the missing head of his dummy. "That's all right," one of the women quipped, "hunters don't have brains anyway!" I chuckled and feigned indignation, recognizing her as a good-natured soul from yesterday's protest.

Bits of paper skittered around in bone-chilling gusts as the preparations continued, and finally—to everyone's relief—a television crew arrived, assuring widespread publicity for the event. The newsman chatted with a few people beside their cars, filmed the dummies and signs, and then questioned Buzz, the group's official spokesperson.

"We go to the grocery store and get meat that's wrapped in cellophane," the reporter began. "Deer hunters go out to get meat and then put it in their own cellophane. What's the difference? You people eat meat, too, right?"

"Well, no," Buzz responded. "Almost all these people are vegetarian. If you go around and ask, you'll find—"

The correspondent, who had noticed Buzz chatting with me, stepped over and held out his microphone. "Are you vegetarian?" he asked. I backed off, raising my hands in the classic "No comment" gesture, and left poor Buzz to explain.

Quickly recovering, the newsman asked what message Buzz and his compatriots wanted to send out. "We're here to protest the recreational killing of wildlife," he responded. "We just don't recognize the killing of sentient beings as a recreational activity, and we want to point out that it's actually quite cruel. We need to have the DNR listening to the entire public and realizing that the people who want to hunt wildlife are the minority."

Buzz reiterated the animal rights activists' accusation that deer over-population in Wisconsin and elsewhere is perpetrated by wildlife agencies to satisfy hunters. "I would like to make it clear that the Alliance for Animals does not support a high population of deer," he explained. "We believe that if the DNR would be more responsive to the public and not try to create these overpopulations, the deer population would be able to manage itself."

I was shivering like a chihuahua by the time everything was ready—interviews finished, dummies tied in place, signs taped on car doors. Buzz told me they planned a course through Madison, circling the state capitol, honking their horns. I wished him luck and shook his hand, choosing to sit this one out.

Horns blaring, the demonstrators pulled onto the street and turned toward downtown Madison. On one of the last cars a bumper sticker implored: FRIENDS DON'T LET FRIENDS EAT MEAT.

NINE

THE HIDDEN HARVEST

Deer are the same as any pest. They're not beneficial as far as I can see; they just come and eat your
crops. In fact, deer are like the human species:
we'll keep breeding until we ruin the planet, and
deer are going to do the same thing.

—KIM FOSTER, CALIFORNIA ORGANIC FARMER

Innocent Thieves

A sultry August evening in southern Wisconsin: crickets chirping, fireflies blinking, nighthawks rasping and fluttering. To cool off, I drove through the countryside and hiked a dirt lane into a farmer's fields. The viscous, overheated atmosphere clung like spiderwebs to my skin and flooded down into my lungs, bringing on twinges of claustrophobia.

On one side of the road, shrouding the course of Badfish Creek, was a dusky woods, and on the other sprawled a ripening cornfield, the stalks dark green, head high, and tasseled. I walked quietly on the bare dirt, then hesitated where the track made a sharp turn, keeping myself hidden in the bulging rim of corn. Lightning bloomed among distant clouds, and muffled thunder rolled over the flatlands.

In the hush that followed, I picked out a whitetail doe ghosting at the forest's edge, her muzzle toward the breeze, her ears erect. She waited several minutes and then stepped out into the lane, raising each hoof as if she were entering shallow water, bringing it down in a gentle but deliberate stamp, telegraphing a wildness so intense I could imagine her spontaneously bursting into flame. She had the graceful legs, willowy neck, and sylphlike build of a gazelle.

At the middle of the pathway she turned to look over her back, and as if she had summoned them, two half-grown fawns pranced out from the thicket. The first came to her side, leaned forward, and touched its nose against hers; then all three idled to the field's edge and began nuzzling ears of corn. I squatted down and watched through binoculars, elbows braced against my knees. Now I saw the doe plucking silk from an ear of corn, tugging at the long green husks, and nibbling succulent kernels.

Then she looked up and down the lane, flicked her tail, and moved deeper into the corn with her twins close behind. I waited in hopes of seeing them again, but mosquitoes swarmed from the darkening woods and I hurried back to the car. As I drove away I imagined the doe and fawns wading deeper into the field, gorging themselves on tender corn—a bounty richer than anything the nearby forest and meadows could provide.

This same ritual, it occurred to me, was taking place all over North America: deer—incalculable thousands of them—slipping into cultivated fields as summer's evening drew itself across the land. Deer foraging on lettuce in New York, beans in Pennsylvania, peas in Georgia, squash in Ohio, corn in Illinois, wheat in Nebraska, peanuts in Texas, alfalfa in Wyoming, apples in Washington, grapes in California. I wondered if the animals might reasonably imagine that farmers plant their fields each year solely for the benefit of deer.

On the other hand, some farmers may suspect that deer visit their lands solely to wreak havoc and destruction. This is not, after all, an untroubled relationship. For example, throughout much of the Midwest's farm country cultivated plants total between 40 and 60 percent of the food eaten by deer. In Kansas, Nebraska, and Missouri, biologists have found that crops provide about half of the whitetail diet. One Iowa study concluded that farm plants—notably corn, soybeans, and alfalfa—made up almost 80 percent of the food consumed by deer. Other research showed that corn is eaten by more than 84 percent of Iowa deer, accounts for 70 percent of their diet by weight, and ranks first among all plant species they consume.

Crop damage by deer can be very costly, even threatening, to people whose livelihood depends on a healthy and productive harvest. In Pennsylvania, for example, hungry whitetails account for crop losses totaling as much as $100 million per year—a figure so large it's impossible to grasp. But we can all understand what it means when an ordinary farmer loses $30,000 worth of crops in a single growing season. As damage problems spread and increase, so do the conflicts between people with differing interests in deer—farmers, tourists, wildlife watchers, hunters, and game managers. On this subject a Wisconsin state biologist once told me, "We've got to maintain the image of deer as a wild animal, not as an agricultural pest."

Crop damage by deer has a long history. Among the earliest records is this English countryman's lament recorded by William Browne in 1613:

> Is it not lawful that we should chase the deer
> That breaking our enclosures every morn
> Are found at feed upon our crop of corn?

Closer to home, Theodore Rodolf, a Swiss immigrant to the Wisconsin frontier, reported in 1848, "When our cabbages in the garden were nearly full grown, they were almost all eaten up one night by a lot of deer which had jumped the fence, within a hundred feet of our dwelling, and regaled themselves at our expense." Deer damage was reported as early as 1875 in Southern California croplands, and by 1930 a single California county reported losses totaling $90,000. Twenty years later, in 1949, California farmers were allowed to shoot almost 700 deer under special crop protection permits.

Drastic measures like these are employed nowadays in farmlands all over the United States. Shooting, whether by permit or by hunters during regular open seasons, is the most common and effective way to reduce crop damage by deer. Other approaches include every imaginable kind of fencing, an array of homemade or commercial repellents, and scare devices ranging from shiny metallic balloons to automated noisemakers. When these remedies fail, as they often do, growers in some states can apply for compensation payments funded by taxpayers. Despite efforts to find a solution, relationships between farmers and deer are increasingly seasoned with frustration, invective, biological controversy, and political wrangling.

Underlying this trouble is North America's tangled mosaic of wild and agricultural lands—an idyllic mix of habitats for deer. In the fields are dense plantings of well-tended, often fertilized, highly nutritious crops, while the nearby forests and thickets furnish protective cover as well as natural browse. Especially in western states irrigation further enriches the food supply and adds a dependable source of drinking water.

Of course farming isn't always beneficial. Hundreds, if not thousands, of deer and other hoofed animals drown each year in steep-sided irrigation canals lacking the mercy of escape ramps. Extensive clearing for new croplands, which continues today in areas like California and the Southeast, can deprive deer of cover they need to survive. In parts of the American West, expanding cultivation forces mule deer into rugged mountain strongholds while favoring the spread and increase of adaptable whitetails. But on the whole, our continent's burgeoning agriculture favors deer, and growers are doing whatever they feel is necessary to protect their livelihoods from flourishing herds.

The Only Good Deer

"Sometimes we'll shoot ten deer in one night," Bob Stroud told me, in the quiet, matter-of-fact tone you'd expect from a lifelong farmer. "And every month, if we've got bad problems, the New York Department of Environmental Conservation gives us a permit to shoot some more."

Bob leaned against a weathered barn and surveyed a long ridge covered with row upon row of apple trees. "Next day after we shoot deer, we'll call the game warden to come pick them up. He usually lets us keep one deer out of the permit, which I give to my men because they like venison." Animals killed under permits are supposed to be distributed among social agencies and organizations that feed hungry people, but this hasn't always been possible in recent years because of food inspection problems and fears that deer carcasses harbor ticks infected with Lyme disease.

The Stroud farm nests among meadows and wooded hills in northern Westchester County, a place so rural and peaceful you're hard-pressed to imagine that New York City is just an hour's drive away. Beside the complex of sheds, outbuildings, and a venerable three-story home there's an open-sided stand where folks from the surrounding area buy fresh fruit and vegetables in season.

Bob took a break from tractor repairs to chat with me. "One year the deer came in and killed about a hundred young apple trees, waist-high to chest-high—bucks rubbing their velvet broke every one right off. Deer also eat the buds in springtime so you end up with misshapen, dwarfed trees. Then they'll eat our tomatoes, squash, broccoli, and lettuce, and they can clean out a whole field of string beans in one night.

With pumpkins, they'll start by eating the plants and blossoms, then later on they break the pumpkin in half with their hooves and eat all the seeds. There's one field I don't even attempt to use, because they'll wipe out anything I put in there."

Just the day before, another farmer, named John Gellerman, had told me, "For deer, pumpkins are like the peanuts at a bridge party. One year we had expected to harvest five thousand pumpkins but ended up with only three hundred fifty." When the pumpkins were still green, no bigger than grapefruit, whitetails cracked them open. "All they'd leave was the stem, the bottom, and part of the insides. It was quite picturesque when they got done, actually." Gellerman shook his head and smiled grudgingly as he described the thieves' handiwork.

He was luckier than his neighbor, a woman named Jane Wilman, who told me she'd gotten fewer than 100 pumpkins last year from a three-acre field. "They'd just stand there while I was driving the tractor up and down," she complained. "I mean, they could care less. We had cavalcades of people driving along the road at night just to look at the deer. My husband said we should charge admission and at least get some benefit from the situation."

Jane pointed to the fenced area beside a large red barn where dairy cows lounged in the afternoon sun. "Last winter we lost two acres of strawberries over there. Also, a few years ago we planted forty-five hundred Christmas trees along our back edge—Scotch pine, white pine, Douglas fir—and deer hit them so hard that less than fifty survived the first winter. For the strawberries, we invested in a seven-strand electric fence, and that does work, but we had to give up on evergreens because the area's too big to fence. We do let bow hunters come in every fall and that helps somewhat."

Jane mentioned nursery owners with even worse problems than hers—people who raised ornamentals like rhododendron, arborvitae, yew, hemlock, fir, maple. It must be the answer to a deer's dream, I thought, living around a veritable forest of tasty, nutritious, pampered shrubs and saplings. Small wonder that two thirds of the nurseries in a recent New York survey reported significant damage by white-tailed deer. Those with serious problems averaged losses of $6,000 to $43,000 per year, and the worst of them suffered more than $100,000 worth of damage annually. Most growers said they tried to keep deer away with commercial repellents, soap, human hair, and scare devices, and about one quarter of them, people whose acreage was quite small or whose income was high enough to justify the expense, put up deer-proof fencing.

On Bob Stroud's Westchester County orchard and vegetable farm—with about 200 acres of scattered fields—installing fences would be too expensive. Instead, he settled for repellents like bars of soap, or little bags of human hair dangled from fruit tree branches and strategically placed around each field, or he'd put out shiny balloons. Nevertheless, on winter nights it wasn't unusual to see 40 to 50 whitetails on his land.

"Our place could handle twelve or fourteen deer, maybe fifteen, without any trouble," Stroud estimated. "But for safety reasons they only allow bow hunting in this county, and with that we're never going to get the population down. So we depend on shooting permits which allow us to use rifles and to shoot at night with spotlights when it's easy to approach deer. The object is efficiency, not sport. Still, the deer keep increasing, and even if we knock them down for a year or two they come right back up again. My wife and I were saying the other day, our best hope is for a heavy winter that starves a lot of them to death. That would take care of things, at least for a while."

I heard similar tales from Tom Sampson, who operated an orchard and roadside market about 20 miles from the Stroud place—a man who figured deer damage had cost him $75,000 in each of the previous two years. Sampson encouraged people to hunt on his land during the open season; and, like Stroud, he killed whitetails under state permits throughout the year. "Between myself and the farmer next door, we shot over two hundred deer in a single year," he told me. "But unless you've got hunting on the same level throughout the whole area, it doesn't work."

Many Westchester County residents oppose hunting whitetails for any reason, so farmers are often reluctant to talk about it. According to Sampson, long-term residents generally don't object to taking deer under damage permits, because they have a commonsense understanding of rural life. "But you've got so many newcomers that just moved up here from the city. It's easy for them to judge what we're doing, since they've got no idea what it takes to keep a farm going or to grow the food that ends up on their table."

He leaned toward me and lowered his voice. "I hate to tell you this, but I've come to feel that the only good deer is a dead deer. People wonder how I can say that, but if you've worked for something all your life, then somebody comes and steals it, you do what you can to protect it." Sampson said he likes having some whitetails around, but he wants far more taken—by hunters using firearms—to restore a sensible population level.

What would happen, I asked, if he could no longer shoot deer to protect his crops? "I don't think I could keep my operation going," he replied. "Either they'd have to put me in jail for killing deer or I'd have to herd them together and go into the deer business."

Purity and Pragmatism

A few months later on the continent's opposite shore and under strikingly different circumstances, I heard echoes of Bob Stroud and Tom Sampson. In mid-February, while frigid northerlies hardened the snowdrifts in Westchester County, lush green cloaked the mountainsides adjoining Kim Foster's California farm, just off the Pacific Coast Highway north of San Francisco.

Kim Foster, I knew from a mutual friend, was an offspring of the sixties—an activist and creative thinker who left the Bay Area to pioneer commercial organic farming in California. About a mile from the nearest town, Foster Organic Farms occupies a patch of flatland tucked between a saltwater estuary and a hillside covered with mixed eucalyptus forest. The driveway runs beside a sprawling field to a low-slung headquarters building and a huddle of equipment sheds. Emerging from behind his office computer, Kim was in his early fifties, lanky and fit, with keen, bright eyes.

The main field, our first stop, was blanketed with low-growing bell beans and vetch. "We use these cover plants to build humus and increase nitrogen content," he explained, "so they'll be plowed back into the soil. We do this because everything we produce is organic, so of course we can't use any artificial fertilizers."

When I asked about his main crops Kim listed several kinds of lettuce as well as squash, cucumber, garlic, and a variety of specialized herbs, even edible flowers, plus salad greens like arugula, radicchio, borage, mizuna, chervil, and other names I'd never heard before. These he'd sell mainly to restaurants and stores catering to fashionable, health-conscious, generally well-heeled people in and around San Francisco.

Beyond the main field we crossed a tree-shaded creek and entered a smaller, isolated parcel closely surrounded by forest and meadowlands. A perfect haven for deer, I speculated. "Oh yeah, we get quite a few in here." Kim swept his hand toward the far edge, where trees shouldered against plowed land. "We have thirty-five or forty acres in these lower fields and at night deer get all the way out to the middle. Also we have even worse deer problems on twelve acres we lease farther back in the valley. Of course, this whole area is basically surrounded by the Point Reyes

National Seashore, which has a lot of deer, even though some are killed to hold the numbers down."

California is the third-largest state, yet its total estimated deer population (comprising blacktails along the coast and mule deer inland) was only 700,000 in 1991. Dry, stressful summers—along with disease, parasites, land development, and competition with grazing stock—do not favor a population density like that of whitetails in the eastern United States. On the other hand, much of California's agriculture focuses on high-value crops like Kim Foster's organic vegetables, so it doesn't take many animals to create a very expensive problem.

In California orchards, for example, deer eat everything from ordinary apples and pears to exotic avocados and almonds. They also snap branches with their forelegs while reaching up to browse or pluck fruit, and although they don't usually eat citrus fruits like oranges or lemons, rutting bucks damage the valuable trees with their antlers.

According to Sonke Mastrup, a biologist with the California Department of Fish and Game, "Deer get into just about every vegetable and grain crop that's grown here, especially near the end of our summer drought and in spring when the new shoots start coming up. They'll eat pretty much any plant that's green. In the fall when deer migrate out of the mountains there's also a big impact on alfalfa, a crop that's used mainly for horse and cattle feed."

Damage problems are greatest near the hills and in small valleys where deer move easily from natural cover to croplands. These areas also happen to be ideal for California's most famous crop, grapes for table use and wine making. "We have a serious problem of deer damage to the vineyards," Mastrup told me. "It's also increasing, because over the last five to ten years the acreage in vineyards has doubled and much of this is in prime deer habitat. You plunk a vineyard down among the coastal mountains or Sierra foothills, where grapes do really well, and you've got a deer problem just through physical proximity."

Deer enter vineyards early in the season to browse developing buds and young leaves, then turn up their noses as the leaves mature. But when harvest time approaches, they share with the rest of us a fondness for tasty, succulent grapes. "Some growers don't mind deer taking a few bushels of their grapes," said Mastrup, "but others just come unglued even if deer only eat a few grapes now and then. So there's a tremendous range of tolerance."

Most vineyard owners put up fences if they can bear the cost, Mastrup explained. "Some of the big ones fence their entire property and then kill all the deer inside, which pretty much solves their problem. Those who don't want a fence or can't afford it will get depredation permits after Fish and Game inspects the damage and establishes that the problem warrants it. This allows growers to shoot deer when they're causing problems." Needless to say, vineyard owners aren't scrambling to publicize their struggles with deer, nor are they eager to burden connoisseurs with the entire story behind that glass of Beaujolais, Pinot Noir, or Chenin Blanc.

Back at the Foster place, Kim led the way to a series of long, low-roofed structures with open sides sheltering rows of tiny herbs and salad specialties like totsoi and mizuna. "They'll come right in here for this stuff," he said, plucking a leaf from a plant I couldn't identify and suspected most of us commoners would never find in our evening salad. "This is chervil. It's real sweet, with kind of a licorice taste." It was delicious, and gaps in the row indicated that some wild creature—probably a deer or rabbit—also enjoyed the taste.

"Deer are terrible on squash because they'll walk down the row and take a teeny nibble off every one, which means all those squash are unmarketable. A few deer can ruin the entire field in just one night. They'll even dig up potatoes and eat them. Once they discover that, they're pretty good at it."

As we trekked back toward headquarters, Foster mentioned that he didn't have much trouble in the rainy winter season, when deer found plenty to eat back among the hills. During summer, on the other hand, they'd hang out in nearby woods and come into the fields at nightfall. Even then, it was unusual to see more than about eight blacktails around the place at once—but it was enough to cause trouble.

"We'll go out and shine lights to scare them off," he explained. "And the dogs help to keep them away, too. In fact, there's no better deer fence than a dog. Also, I've made a soluble repellent spray out of bloodmeal, which sticks to the leaves. Plants love it because bloodmeal is a great fertilizer, and the smell really helps to keep deer away. The other thing I should do is show you our fence."

We drove a couple miles of crooked road, then followed a dirt track into a beautiful pocket of land surrounded by forest and scrub. "We've been leasing this five-acre field for some years," said Kim, "but the only thing we could grow in here was broccoli, because deer usually wouldn't bother that. For a number of reasons, broccoli is no longer profitable for us, so last year, in order to plant our leafy green crops, we had to put this fence up." The square mesh fence, made of heavy wire, was about seven

feet tall, supported at close intervals by wooden posts, and it was as expensive as it was impenetrable.

"When we have damage problems, the guy from Fish and Game says,
'Well, you'll just have to put up a deer fence here.' But on most of our
land that's too costly, and it's not practical because we need to get in and
out all the time with our equipment. So we've gotten depredation permits and we have taken deer—usually not more than five a year and some
years none at all. If we start counting a half dozen or more deer in the
field and we see that they're doing a lot of damage, then we have to think,
'Maybe we should do something about it.' "

There was a tinge of regret as Kim spoke of killing deer, and he emphasized he'd do everything possible to avoid it. Besides, shooting didn't
rest well with the neighbors: "*BOOM* in the middle of the night, and
they call you to find out what's going on." But farming was Kim's livelihood, and like the other farmers I'd met he made it clear, in an unapolo-
getic and matter-of-fact way, that he was determined to protect his
harvest.

"One thing that's pretty unattractive—but I've found it really works
without having to shoot a lot of deer—is you only take one and you cut
it open so there's plenty of blood. Then you drag the body behind the
tractor so it leaves a blood trail all the way around the field, and this
frightens the others away. Deer really do not like blood."

Fingers hooked over the thick wire strands, Kim gazed at a part of the
land he'd worked for the past 20 years, doing things as he believed they
should be done for the betterment of earth and humankind. But regardless of principles, farming sometimes involves difficult choices. In upscale restaurants and groceries, organic vegetables raised by farmers like
Kim Foster carry ethical and ecological distinction—as indeed they
should. But few people recognize the hard, practical necessities that help
to bring this elegant food to their table.

"I know you're supposed to say we're all here to share," Kim reflected.
"But the fact is, you can't convince the deer to just share. Deer are like
rodents. They're in competition with us—that's what it comes down to.
And who is going to deal with this problem if we don't do it ourselves?"

Corn Rats

"Check out how the cornstalks are smaller, darker, and skinnier in these
outer rows. And even from a distance you can see those bare, reddish
cobs." Dan Hirchert led me along the edge of a Wisconsin cornfield,

then stopped and plucked what had once been a healthy ear. The papery husks had been pulled apart and only a few bright yellow kernels remained; human fingers couldn't have shucked it more neatly. "This is one kind of damage: where deer eat the fully developed corn."

Then he pointed out swaths of stunted, bedraggled, knee-high stalks with tiny cobs or none at all. "That's another kind of damage, where deer clipped the plants when they were young, which leaves nothing for the farmer to harvest." Deeper into the field, corn plants stood six to eight feet tall with bright gray stalks and large, healthy cobs. "None of that's been touched, because deer haven't gone in that far—at least not yet."

Dense oak and maple forest hugged the field's margin, making a perfect setup for whitetails, who could stay hidden during the day and easily raid the crop at night. "In this field last year, deer ate most of the corn in the outer ten to twenty rows, so the farmer had a pretty significant loss, probably a few thousand dollars. They haven't hit it so hard this year, maybe because there's an unusual abundance of acorns, which deer love to eat."

Dan Hirchert was in his mid-twenties—tall and blondish, a husky guy with a gentle, friendly disposition. For much of the year Dan's work appraising and helping prevent crop damage kept him right where he wanted to be: trekking the fields, meadows, and woodlands of southern Wisconsin. Qualifications he brought to his job with the U.S. Department of Agriculture's Animal Damage Control (ADC) agency included a rural background, college studies in biology, and a knack for getting along with farmers even when he became a target for their aggravation about deer problems.

"We'll have guys when they really get frustrated saying, 'Look, your deer are destroying my corn!' like we own the animals or we're in charge of them. We just have to be patient with it."

Our first stop on a sunny October morning was this carefully tended farm near Mazomanie. The owner—a round-faced man, thickset, wearing striped coveralls—finished welding a broken piece from his combine before leading us out into the fields. More businesslike than sociable, he seemed to regard us as emissaries from an eternally suspect and habitually blundering government.

"We've had a lot of deer coming out of the park," he informed Dan, referring to a small state preserve nearby. "I figure there were probably eighty deer in this cornfield one day last winter, and around that same time a couple hunters said they saw over a hundred right in here. It's no wonder we lost so much corn last fall." Dan shook his head, listening sympathetically. His personable style and familiarity with agrarian ways thawed the farmer a bit.

Leaving him to his work, Dan and I headed for the field's back edge, then trekked the weedy seam between corn and forest until we found a sizable damaged area. Here, Dan measured out a small "sample plot" from which we picked all the ears, shucked the kernels into a bucket, and weighed the result: 8 pounds. A comparison sample we harvested from the nearest undisturbed rows scaled 16 pounds, showing that 50 percent of the corn was gone from our damaged plot. Two other samples yielded similar results. Finally, Dan walked around the field to estimate the total damaged acres and then calculated the amount of corn this farmer had lost.

"The Department of Natural Resources will pay a farmer up to five thousand dollars compensation for deer damage," Dan explained, "but first there's a two-hundred-fifty-dollar deductible they have to meet, just like insurance. So if somebody's got a four-hundred-fifty-dollar loss, he'll get two hundred dollars' compensation from the state. But in this field, it looks like his loss won't exceed the deductible, and not all the damage was caused by deer."

During our inspection we'd found several patches of broken-down cornstalks, their dry husks tattered and cobs roughly chewed. "Raccoons," observed Dan. "Deer don't have to knock over the stalks and they never shred the husks like that." Nearby was a raccoon trail, which looked just like a deer path but slipped under the 12-inch space between a woven wire fence and the ground. "There's no compensation for raccoon damage, so I always like to show people how it looks different from damage caused by deer."

The farmer, who had his combine up and running by the time we finished, listened skeptically to Dan's report. "Well, anybody can tell where deer came just now and ate the corn," he argued. "But some other damage—like the bare spots where they took all the newly sprouted corn plants last spring—a person can easily miss seeing that."

Dan had already shown me several places where this might have occurred or else the corn had simply failed to sprout. Too much time had passed for anyone to know for sure, which is why farmers must have damage examined within two weeks if they want compensation. The man shrugged and sighed—a subtle but unambiguous comment on government regulations—then he thanked us and got back to work.

As we headed toward the truck a red-tailed hawk drifted overhead with two pugnacious blackbirds diving like warplanes at its back. "Another reason we like farmers to call us early in the growing season when they first notice damage is so we can recommend an abatement technique," Dan remarked. "If the methods we try don't stop the problems, we'll come back a couple weeks before harvest and appraise the loss for compensation."

Back in 1931, Wisconsin passed its first law authorizing compensation for crop damage and allocated $12,000 to cover the costs. Nowadays, with tremendous increases in deer numbers, that amount wouldn't keep the operation going for a day, so the program has shifted toward preventing damage before it happens. One approach is to supply farmers with fences, repellents, and scare devices like noisy "cannons" that fire at intervals. The other is to remove some deer under agricultural damage permits. Farmers with more than $1,000 damage in one year can apply for a permit to shoot deer on their land at any time of year provided they also allow public hunting during the regular season.

The money used to pay for crop damage—more than $1.5 million in 1994—comes from a one-dollar surcharge on Wisconsin hunting licenses and from "bonus tag" fees also paid by deer hunters. About 90 percent of the compensated damage is caused by whitetails; black bears and Canada geese account for the rest.

The state DNR administers this program in partnership with the Animal Damage Control agency that employs Dan. In Wisconsin, anyone who knows how farmers struggle with deer damage is likely to praise the ADC, but in other parts of the country—especially out West—the agency gets mixed reviews, mainly because of its battle against predators. Under a federal law passed in 1931, ADC's mission includes the "eradication, suppression, or bringing under control . . . of mountain lions, wolves, coyotes, bobcats, ground squirrels, rabbits, and other animals injurious to agriculture . . . and to conduct campaigns for the destruction or control of such animals."

This is a far cry from the job wildlife damage specialists like Dan Hirchert are doing in the fields of Wisconsin with their scales, notebooks, and official forms. Also, the ethics aren't so cloudy in a state where, according to the last survey in 1984, more than half of the state's 86,000 farmers reported deer damage. Estimated losses in that year tallied $36.7 million, with corn and hay taking a major share of the hit. Most Wisconsin farmers have only a few hundred dollars' worth of deer damage each year, but claims in some "hot spots" averaged more than $9,000 in 1990, far above the $5,000 payment limit. A few growers, especially those raising specialty crops like snap beans, apples, and

Christmas trees, suffer as much as $40,000 worth of damage in a single year.

The impact of deer on crops has increased tremendously in Wisconsin over the past few decades. Because of intense hunting pressure, most whitetails inhabiting these agricultural lands survive just a year or two, but the enriched diet allows them to reach extraordinary size. Also, farmland deer breed so fast—many does producing twins or even triplets—that the population keeps increasing despite Wisconsin's yearly harvest of 350,000 to 400,000 animals. "When you think about all this," a DNR biologist told me, "it's not hard to understand why people's attitudes toward whitetails are changing, even getting antagonistic, and why deer have gotten the nickname 'corn rats.' "

An hour later, Dan and I passed a soybean field down along the Wisconsin River, and he explained that many farmers are planting soybeans because they're worth about three times as much as corn. Deer have their own reasons for loving this crop—high nutritional value being the most obvious—and they'd rather browse through a soybean field than do almost anything else. In some areas Wisconsin growers have used shooting permits and public hunting to reduce damage problems, but in the worst hot spots, unless they've put up a deer-proof fence, farmers have simply gone back to their old crops.

Dan had much to say about the white-tailed deer's eclectic taste for cultivated plants. For example, they often damage ginseng, even though it's grown underneath low-slung shade canopies where you'd never expect a deer to go. He also knew of a cranberry farmer who found it virtually impossible to keep whitetails out of his cultivated bogs. "They'd get in there and just think it was candy." This man tried every possible remedy and finally saved his business by installing an electrified fence.

"Then there's the muck farmers who grow carrots in peat soils. On a place over by Portage they killed forty-three deer in one year under shooting permits, but even that didn't work. Sometimes shooting deer to protect crops is like pulling dry sand out of a hole—as soon as you remove some animals from your farm, other ones fill in from the surrounding land. On that carrot farm, they finally put an eight-foot electrified fence around the whole place. It cost about twenty thousand dollars, but that's worthwhile when you've got a high-profit operation."

In certain cases, when a farmer has damage to a high-value crop growing in a fairly small field, Dan provides an electrified Visible Grazing Systems (VGS) fence. The fencing itself looks like bright-yellow tape, about a half inch wide, made from interwoven plastic fibers and wire, and is capable of delivering a feisty 3,000- to 7,000-volt electric charge. All it generally takes is a single strand at about waist height, clipped onto slender fiberglass rods. This easily installed fence, developed by livestock growers in New Zealand, is often very effective for keeping deer away from crops.

Since whitetails can jump a six-foot fence, why wouldn't they just hop over this little yellow ribbon? First of all, the highly visible material catches a deer's attention, and then you make it more attractive by rubbing peanut butter into the woven strand. A deer comes up to the fence, picks up its rich peanut scent, can't resist taking a sniff, touches it with her bare, moist nose, and gets a harmless but hopefully unforgettable jolt. "The idea is conditioning," Dan explained. "They learn not to come near that fence and usually don't try to jump over it, even though they could."

You have to keep the battery charged and cut weeds so the fence doesn't ground out, he added. Also there can be problems during winter, because a deer standing on snow or well-frozen earth isn't likely to get a strong shock. But the fence usually does an adequate job, and it's far less expensive than installing an elaborate multistrand electric wire fence or a woven wire fence seven or eight feet high.

Any farmer who gets fencing through Dan's program must allow hunters on his land throughout the deer season, and lists of participating farms are published each year so the hunters know where to go. This ensures that farmers who take compensation payments or fencing or other damage assistance also do everything possible to reduce deer numbers. The practicality of fencing depends on a crop's value, how many acres are involved, local deer abundance, and the farmer's tolerance for losses. In truth, most of Wisconsin's fields are very large and major crops like corn or alfalfa are not valuable enough per acre to make fencing economical. And fencing never solves the overall problem, because it simply concentrates more deer onto everybody else's land. You cannot fence an entire state.

Dan also described a new strategy for protecting crops, called "invisible fencing," which uses dogs to chase deer away. Each dog wears a special collar that gives a harmless electric shock if the dog tries to cross a cable buried around the field's perimeter. This means the dogs are free to wander and patrol, but not to leave. "On a hundred-ten-acre, three-parcel apple orchard in New York, the system reduced damage by eighty or ninety percent, using a total of six or seven dogs," said Dan. Apparently it costs much less to install than putting up deer-proof fences, especially when large tracts are involved; but of course there are ongoing expenses for the dogs.

Late in the day, Dan and I stopped at a nursery over in Sauk County, where browsing deer had killed hundreds of small Christmas trees and disfigured many others, so they looked stunted or lopsided. Under his damage permit, the grower legally allowed hunters to take antlerless deer in the summertime, but this had brought a storm of complaints from his neighbors. Dan said it was a familiar story, recalling a strawberry grower with a damage permit who got punched after mentioning he killed deer out of season. "There's a lot of hostility sometimes, and yet if your goal is to bring the deer population down, you should shoot when the does are pregnant or in summer when they've got fawns. A lot of guys with permits have decided to shoot deer only during the regular hunting season—just to keep the peace."

As Dan and I headed back toward Madison I mentioned that none of the farmers we'd met seemed really angry at deer. "Ninety-nine percent of them will tell you they like deer and enjoy seeing them around," he observed, "but they don't want so many as we've got nowadays. Of course, younger farmers have never known anything else, but the older guys remember when they didn't have deer problems, and some of them get pretty upset."

Dan recalled an elderly farmer, partly disabled, who had called to complain that deer were taking over his place: ruining the shrubs in his yard, damaging his corn and soybeans, and cleaning out his hay fields. As if this wasn't enough, they'd even started "living in the machine shed" and he couldn't close its oversized doors to keep them out. This last tale sounded a bit farfetched, Dan thought, but he decided to have a look.

The first thing Dan saw when he arrived was a deer standing between a couple of buildings and whitetail tracks all over the ground. Maybe this fellow wasn't imagining things after all. "When I met the guy, I said, 'Boy, I just saw a deer over there, right in the middle of the day!' And he goes: 'Only one?' "

The farmer told Dan that after they'd talked on the phone a few days earlier he managed to close the door on his equipment shed. No sooner had he finished when something started clattering around inside, and when he wrestled the door back open several deer came bursting out.

"Well, he took me to see that shed," Dan recalled, "and sure enough, the hay stored inside was all pawed down, the dirt floor was full of tracks, there were deer droppings everywhere, and you could even see where deer had bedded down in there."

The farmer told Dan he used to leave hay bales in the field for white-tails to eat during winter. "He kept telling me, 'Would I do that if I was a mean guy? I'm not a gangster!' First he'd be calm, and then he'd cuss me out and tell me to get my deer out of his land. Basically, he's frustrated and fed up, and he wants the deer off his farm."

Later on I talked with the farmer myself. "I'm very antagonistic to-ward the DNR," he told me. "They say the deer belong to them and I can't touch them. Then why don't they come and feed them in the win-tertime, so these deer will leave me alone? If they said the deer on my farm belong to me, I'd take care of them quick, you can be sure of that! I'd thin them out, and my neighbors would do the same."

The Tightening Bind

A cold north wind pouring down over the Wisconsin flatlands can make April feel a bit like December. On such a day, Wade Owens and I headed into the countryside near Waupun, about 50 miles northeast of Madison. Wade, like his friend Dan Hirchert, covered a southern Wisconsin terri-tory for ADC, assessing damaged fields and helping farmers protect their crops. He's a wiry guy, sharp featured, early thirties, with a lingering Mis-souri twang.

On our way to the Carl Burton farm we drove two-lane roads laid out in the square-mile geometry of townships, passing woodlots and marshes, pastures and cultivated fields. Carl greeted us with an indiffer-ent hello, then slipped into heavy brown coveralls that smelled formida-bly of the barn. Everything about his place hinted of agrarian prosperity: the comfortable home, the spanking array of outbuildings, the cluster of blue metallic silos, the fleet of specialized equipment. Despite shyness as impenetrable as fog, Carl allowed that his operation ranked "near the top in this area for production and profit."

Dwindling hair and wire-rimmed glasses made him appear bookish, though his vocabulary suggested otherwise, and after Wade introduced me as a writer I took his flaccid handshake as a commentary. We should look at the alfalfa, he announced, leading us to the shed where he kept a mud-spattered four-wheeler that looked like a miniature tractor. To my amazement, Carl stacked all three of us aboard: he himself on the driver's seat, Wade perched tenuously over the front wheel, and I clutching a metal carrier on the back.

Then off we sped into the frigid gusts down a bumpy lane and across a rutted field, death-grips turning our knuckles white while Carl chattered at Wade as if this were a casual summer ride. At last he stopped near the edge of a woodlot bordering one of his alfalfa fields—obviously an attractive spot for deer. "I had a shooting permit last winter," Carl declared as we rubbed grit from our eyes. "A bunch of whitetails would come out here and I could see them from up by the shed, so I'd get my rifle and sneak down along the back side. That put me pretty close and I'd just shoot from there."

He knelt down and ran his fingers through a straggling patch of alfalfa. The plants looked like clover with multiple clusters of triple leaves branching off the main stem, now less than half grown at six to ten inches tall. "You see how all these have been clipped?" He tipped back his cap, revealing a sharp tan line across his forehead, and peered up at Wade. "Now look, there's deer tracks all over." It was easy to pick out hoofprints in places like this, where most of the plants had been grazed off by whitetails. In other spots alfalfa grew thick and deep green, more like an aggressive weed than a cultivated species.

Unlike most crops, which die back and need replanting each year, alfalfa survives winter and can grow for up to five years from a single seeding. Also, rather than yielding just one harvest, it's usually cut several times each summer. But there is a delicate side to alfalfa. Burton pointed out, for example, that a hard freeze in September makes the plants brittle, so they're easily broken and trampled by deer. Later on, whitetails do further damage by scuffling and compacting the snow, not to mention eating alfalfa all winter long. Of course, losses are greatest in summer when deer thrive on the succulent new growth.

"Deer mainly clip off the tops," Carl Burton observed. "That's the most nutritious part—best for deer and best for cows, too. After deer get in the field, you might cut the same tonnage but you're not bringing in the same quality feed." Although Carl addressed his comments to me, they were obviously intended for Wade, who would determine the size of his compensation payments.

Although Carl was stretching every angle for sympathy, he was also telling the truth, at least in this case. Alfalfa is a highly nutritious, palatable, mineral-rich food for both livestock and deer. Most important, it averages about 20 percent protein, but the percentage drops by about half when deer browse off the tops—and that's a substantial loss for the farmer. Thinned and damaged alfalfa stands are also invaded by weeds, again lowering the crop's value for cash or livestock feed.

In the United States, alfalfa covers more than 30 million acres, the largest harvests coming from states like Wisconsin, California, Minnesota, Iowa, and Nebraska. Like corn, alfalfa has become a major element in the ecology of deer and the economics of farming in North America today. Biologists working in southern Wisconsin found that alfalfa made up one quarter to three quarters of the whitetail diet from April through December, and a Pennsylvania survey showed that deer consumed about 20 percent of that state's entire alfalfa crop.

"When you get down to the individual farm, it's pretty hard to accurately figure a damage claim on alfalfa," Wade acknowledged. Monetary judgments are all the harder to make because many farmers rarely sell alfalfa, but dry and bale it as hay to feed their own livestock. In fact, for Carl Burton and thousands of other dairymen, milk products are the ultimate source of earnings derived from alfalfa. "If you don't have enough hay because of deer damage, then you've got to buy it from somebody else, so that's coming out of your pocket as a cost of producing milk," Carl explained. "Alfalfa is my hardest-hit crop, my biggest dollar loss. A year's growth is worth five hundred dollars per acre, and the other crops—like corn—are worth maybe half that."

Back on the four-wheeler, we pummeled across a washboard cornfield littered with cobs stripped clean by last winter's deer. I felt sorry for Wade, stuck up front like a tick on a bull's nose, but our indefatigable host kept right on talking in Wade's ear. "The deer damage," I heard him say, "it's like an unfair tax on me. And people that buy milk aren't paying it—I am." To judge by his fervent solicitations, Carl saw our visit as a chance to milk something other than cows.

"I've also had deer problems in the sweet corn and soybeans, and in the feed corn I use along with hay for the cows," he shouted over the engine's blare. Many farmers harvest corn to feed their dairy herds, Wade pointed out, so in this case—as with alfalfa—deer damage ultimately affects production of beef, milk, and other dairy products. Corn is the most important food for pigs, chickens, turkeys, ducks, and geese, which means whitetail problems carry over to pork, poultry, and eggs.

"Deer also get into this winter wheat I'm going to show you," said Burton, as Wade and I stumbled from our perches. All along the woods bordering this field Wade found a scramble of fresh tracks and signs of extensive browsing. "I can't really assess damage here until later in the season," he advised, "after the wheat's had more time to grow and we can see what the deer have done to it." Like an attorney confronting unexpected evidence, our host was visibly disappointed but didn't stop presenting his case.

"We get some real concentrations of deer in the winter. They like to hang out back here because it's pretty far from the road and hunters won't see 'em. You know, right before hunting season a lot of people come out spotlighting to see where the deer are. Plenty of times, when I myself have been spotlighting back in these fields, I've counted two hundred deer on this place. The most I ever saw in one night was about three hundred." A claim large enough to nourish skepticism, I thought, yet it seemed plausible since the farm bordered an enormous tract of forest and marshland.

Back at the Burton house, Wade and I had admired a pair of impressive 10-point whitetail racks, and Carl's only moment of unrestrained pleasure during our visit came when he described taking the biggest of them. As a hunter he couldn't fully suppress his enthusiasm about the abundance of deer around his place, but as a landowner plying the government's man for cash he maintained a somber and businesslike tone.

"You know, farmers are the ones who support these animals on our land; we're the ones who end up feeding deer for everybody else; and we're also the ones who get all the damage." On this point, Carl would find plenty of support among his fellow Wisconsin crop growers, who consider themselves unfairly burdened with the cost of sustaining wildlife that legally "belongs" to all of the state's citizens.

As we walked back to the dreaded four-wheeler, Carl Burton summarized: "With all the losses we've had from deer, it's like working overtime and not getting paid for it. If your farm operation is doing well, you'll probably get by in spite of the damage. But if you're just barely making a go of it—well, then the deer situation might be what puts you out of business." Here again, many farmers around the country would wholeheartedly agree.

From Wade's earlier remarks, Carl understood there would be no payments following this visit because he didn't yet have enough damage, but the growing season had just begun, and Carl knew the system required that he establish a record of losses as summer passed. Eventually, I had no doubt, he would find a state check in the mailbox.

Before we left, Burton took us to a patch of weedy, uncultivated ground beside a dirt lane. "I wanted to show you guys something I found the other day," he remarked, pointing into the thicket. "She must have got hit on the road a couple weeks ago and dragged herself down here." Half hidden in deep grass lay the carcass of a whitetail doe, stringers of dried meat and cartilage clinging to an ivory cagework of bones, bits of rumpled hide strewn around by scavengers.

We stood quietly for a moment and then Carl sighed. "Well, there's one deer that won't be eating any alfalfa this summer."

Late that afternoon, Wade and I visited another farmer, Bill Mackinnon, who had damage much more severe and costly than Carl Burton's and who depended on reducing deer numbers to deal with the problem. I asked Bill how it would affect him if deer were completely protected. "I'm not a hunter," he explained, "but you've *got* to have hunting—there's no question about it. If we had no hunting these deer would multiply so fast that we'd be out of the farm business in three to five years."

Interestingly, a farmer in an adjacent county had said almost the same thing. "I believe they're right," Wade concurred. "Without hunting, there could be a couple hundred whitetails per square mile in these areas—nobody really knows how high the numbers would go—and then you just can't imagine the damage that would occur. Farms like these probably couldn't operate."

Later on, I posed the same question to a state biologist widely regarded as a leading expert on Wisconsin whitetails. "Deer are already causing huge amounts of damage," he told me. "But if that herd was allowed to grow statewide without hunting as a control means, I would agree with those farmers, and I'd say the farming economy in Wisconsin could be virtually eliminated, probably within three to five years."

If unrestrained growth of deer populations could devastate Wisconsin agriculture, it could almost certainly do the same in much of the eastern United States and in parts of the West. Needless to say, this is a matter of concern not just to individual farmers whose livelihoods depend on the harvest; it's an important issue not just for community, state, and regional economies; it's personally significant to all of us who rely on agriculture for the food we eat.

Repast

Crops damaged by deer range from the exotic to the mundane: almonds and apricots, beets and black-eyed peas, cherries and chard, green beans and lima beans, pears and peppers, plums and popcorn, squash and scallions, and dozens of other grains, vegetables, fruits, herbs, and livestock feeds. In fact, I heard many farmers and biologists recite the same mantra: "Deer will eat just about anything you can plant."

In modern America much of our food comes from areas where agricultural damage is a prime factor in the management of deer populations. For example, southern Wisconsin's farm country is probably capable of sustaining about 100 healthy whitetails per square mile of land over the long run. But wildlife managers have learned that when deer come anywhere near this abundance they severely damage almost every cultivated crop.

In southern Wisconsin, 25 to 30 deer per square mile is about the highest overwintering density farmers can tolerate. In other words, the environment's biological carrying capacity for deer is much higher than its social carrying capacity; and nowadays hunting is the only means by which deer populations can be kept near an acceptable level. Therefore, in Wisconsin and many other parts of the United States today, hunting is no less important to farmers than is the plow.

Tracing our connections to deer can reveal disquieting realities and unexpected dilemmas. Soybeans, for example, provide such nutritionally meritorious foods as tofu, soy milk, soy sauce, soy hot dogs, and soy burgers, as well as the soy ink widely used in printing and publishing. Writer Pagan Kennedy calls soy "the most politically correct legume" and "the saintly bean." But deer also love soybeans, and for this reason, hunting is an essential part of soybean cultivation.

In public and private forests, high deer populations often overbrowse saplings, preventing or suppressing regrowth after a timber harvest or wildfire. Hunting keeps the number of deer in balance with these forest habitats, protecting trees that supply wood for our houses, the furniture inside, and millions of other items we use, not to mention the paper in our books, magazines, and newspapers, as well as the manicured evergreens we bring into our homes at Christmas.

Whenever any of us sit down for breakfast, lunch, dinner, or a snack, it's likely that deer were killed to protect some of the food we eat and the beverages we drink. This is true for everyone: city dwellers and suburbanites; men, women, and children; omnivores and vegetarians; hunters, nonhunters, and antihunters. Wherever we live and whatever we do, as long as it includes subsisting on groceries from our continent's farmlands, writer Wendell Berry reminds us that "eating is an agricultural act. Eating ends the annual drama of the food economy that begins with planting and birth." And, we might remember, a food economy that also depends on hunting.

Deer are not merely a part of the scenery, not just works of natural artistry carrying on lives remote and disconnected from our own. We are bound together with deer in an intricate biological relationship centered around cultivated crops. As a consequence, everyone in modern North America who lives each day on agricultural foods belongs to an ecological network that necessarily involves deer hunting. White-tailed deer, mule deer, and black-tailed deer are a fundamental part of our personal ecology. In this sense, the blood of deer runs through our veins as surely as we take bread and wine at our table.

Next morning I drove out to the farm where I'd seen the doe and her twin fawns on that August evening a couple months before. It looked entirely different now—the woods spangled with russet, gold, and amber leaves, the harvested cornfield a milewide expanse of stubble, the gray earth inscribed with geometric furrows. A swarm of blackbirds flung skyward at the field's distant edge, pitched and veered in unison, then spilled down like a fistful of tossed seed. Dried milkweed shook in the breeze, silky parasols drifting from half-opened husks.

Scrawled on the dirt path was a footprint listing of the local fauna: raccoon, skunk, red fox, opossum, squirrel, chipmunk, vole. And I came across fresh prints of several white-tailed deer, following the lane and crossing between woods and field. Even now, with the corn thicket gone, scattered cobs and kernels attracted deer each night to glean their final share of the harvest. I knelt beside a deep, wide hoofprint, imagining it was that doe's buck fawn, grown to 100 pounds or more in these few months, now carrying a slender rack of antlers.

Down near Badfish Creek I noticed a hunter's stand, weathered boards nailed in the crook of an oak like a kid's treehouse, strategically placed to overlook corn on one side, alfalfa on the other. Between the two fields stood a thicket of sumacs, where I found three conspicuous deer trails winding beneath scarlet clouds of leaves. Bow hunting season was already open, and fresh boot tracks revealed a hunter had used the stand that same morning.

Oak leaves rattled in the breeze, and I thought of all the plants, all the animals, all the people living on the American earth—so beautifully intertwined.

TEN

HEART OF THE HUNTER

The secret.
and the secret hidden deep in that.

—GARY SNYDER

The deer's hoofprints, keen edged in wet, black sand, couldn't be more than a couple hours old, but the brown bear's tracks look even fresher. Deeply dished indentations of its hind feet, 12 inches from splayed heel to scimitar claws, obliterate several of the deer's imprints, proving the bear came afterward. Pushing her muzzle into each depression, Keta savors a feral scent as dense and pungent for her as burned toast would be for me.

I unshoulder the rifle and kneel down to put my nose beside hers, but detect nothing except the salty tang of kelp and tide. Then, hunkered shoulder to shoulder with the dog, I carefully scrutinize the way ahead, a lazy curve of beach ending in a bedrock point heaped at its edges with seaweed. But I see no trace of shaggy flank, no furred hillock of shoulder and back, no glint or blink of eye—only a batch of crows above the tide's reach, pecking and flapping and gabbling.

The long windrow of seaweed, 5 feet deep and 30 feet wide, washed ashore in massive swells kicked up by our latest North Pacific storm. Clambering onto it, I find a series of broad pits dug into the snarl of composting eel grass and kelp, with the posthole depressions of bear's feet leading from one excavation to the next. Beside the last and biggest crater is a mound of droppings the diameter of a medium pizza, bright tan, moist, and gleaming. It looks something like dog scat, but appropriately scaled for a creature weighing 600 to 800 pounds.

I make no claim to fastidiousness or refinement, having occasionally eaten things most people from my own culture wouldn't touch with a long stick, yet when I lean close to inspect these droppings, their feculent, curdling aroma takes the breath right out of me. The odor, which outclasses anything of this sort I've ever encountered, does eloquent justice to an immense, churning digestive tract. Its contents include a goulash of plant seeds, grass, and seaweed, along with bits of gravel and shell—evidence of the bear's shoreline foraging.

To find out if this scat is as fresh as it looks, I poke two fingers far down into the glutinous melange. And sure enough, from the surface to the very core, there's not a hint of cooling. In fact, a thermometer inserted where I've stuck my fingers would probably register close to a brown bear's normal body temperature. Information like this should never be taken lightly. I fasten my eyes on the shoreside forest just beyond a batch of driftwood logs about 40 feet away—the direction in which Keta is presently sniffing and peering. I suspect the animal saw us coming, hesitated just long enough to deposit this organic calling card, and then took off at a dead run. On the other hand, it's only prudent to assume the bear is lurking back among those shadows deciding what to do about us.

Perhaps we should get out of here, but I choose instead to follow Keta up toward the trees, pausing for long intervals to watch and listen, trying to ignore the heartbeats thrumming in my ears. This is not blind foolishness, however, because I trust Keta's judgment. If she sensed the bear nearby, she'd fix a burning border collie stare on one spot in the underbrush and her whole body would tremble excitedly. But now, although on full alert, she acts like the place has been abandoned.

As we ease into the forest, I can't stop thinking of what we found in this same place a few months back. Beneath an enormous spruce, in a game trail worn raw by the previous winter's deer traffic, lay a bloodstained shoulderblade neatly punctured with a single tooth hole. Not far away we found a patch of matted grass and trampled earth 10 feet in diameter thickly strewn with gray-brown hair plucked from a deer's hide. Then we discovered the four scattered legs, their bones still articulated, hide and meat stripped away, tendons shredded, hooves intact. A wafting smell of decay indicated several days had passed since the blacktail—a full-grown adult—had been killed or scavenged by a brown bear.

I imagined the deer feeding just outside the woods, and the bear stalking meticulously into the wind, hunching behind bedrock mounds much the same color as its fur, lifting its head to watch when the deer leaned down to nibble seaweed, then cringing back when she snapped to alertness; and the bear drawing shallow breaths, neurons flaring in the maelstrom of its brain, muscles coiling and hardening; and the bear, unleashed like a boulder on a steep slope, pitching against the deer's late flight; and the collision of muscle and bone, the shearing of flesh, the two animals twisting together and becoming still; the unraveling violence lapsing to serene quiet, broken by the bear's heaving chest; and fog bursting from the bear's nostrils, warm blood rivering down its tongue; and the deer's body yielding and relaxing, its heartbeats subsiding, its eyes staring absently into the sky as night came down and down.

I trust these imaginings because I've stalked deer in this same place and watched them with the same predatory intent, drawing from the part of my mind that is purely and passionately a hunter. In this sense, the bear and I differ little from each other, or from our fellow island predators—flicker and robin, mink and shrew, marten and river otter, great blue heron and bald eagle. We all have the gifts of canniness and guile, we share a common hunger, and our bodies are made from the flesh that feeds us.

And here, on this wild island at the continent's far northwestern edge, a human hunter must accept the possibility of also being hunted.

When I found those deer remains I was keenly aware that a brown bear, after killing its prey and eating until satiated, often buries the leftovers under dirt and brush, beds down nearby, and keeps watch. Anybody who stumbles onto a cache risks unleashing the big animal's protective fury, so rather than dawdle around, I motioned Keta to my side and we quietly deserted the place.

But today's situation is clearly different. Although the bear couldn't be far off, there is no sign of a kill and no indication the animal hung around to protest our arrival. Most important, Keta now seems more interested in a winter wren scolding from a thicket than she is in the bear's cooling scent. Of course, bears are always somewhere nearby on this Alaskan island and they must occasionally watch us without letting themselves be seen, so, except for the fresh reminder, this day is no different from any other.

The morning's events remind me of what a Tlingit Indian man once told me about bear country etiquette. "The elders taught us," he recalled, "that if we didn't bother bears then bears wouldn't make trouble for us either. And if we come upon a brown bear, we should talk to it like this: 'My grandfather, forgive me for trespassing on your land. I'm just a poor man hunting for my food, the same as you are.' According to the old people, if you do this, bears will leave you alone."

During my years as an apprentice hunter in Koyukon Indian villages, I heard much the same thing. Elders advised that someone who comes across an aggressive bear should act unthreatening and say in an easy voice: "I'm not bothering you, so you might as well go away." A woman can shame and quiet the animal by uncovering what is most female about her while saying, "My husband, it's me." This harks back, I believe, to the ancient story of a woman who married a bear and had his children, a history that links our two species and still affects the ways Koyukon people behave toward bears. In Koyukon tradition there is a powerful feeling of affinity between humans and other animals, and one of the most important moral virtues is avoiding arrogance toward any part of nature.

With these lessons in mind I motion Keta to my side and head on past the spot where we found the punctured scapula last spring. I've walked this path hundreds of times over the years and have a pretty good mental map of the surrounding terrain, with its puzzlework of forest and muskeg, stream and pond, hillock and swale. Of course, blacktails and brown bears have also used this path, perhaps for centuries, and they know the landscape far more intricately than I do. Nevertheless, I've poured my heart into this island, I have a strong sense of belonging here, and I think of myself as a member of its living community. In common with the other animals, I take food from this place to nourish my body, and I come here to nurture my spirit as well. The trail, inscribed with tracks from last night's deer, leads me back into a familiar and beloved world.

Taking a few steps, then hesitating for long minutes to watch and listen, Keta and I move at a pace only slightly faster than no pace at all. My senses become increasingly engaged, warming up like a runner's muscles. Beside the trail I notice that most of the dainty twigs on a huckleberry bush are pruned to nubs—evidence of deer browsing during last winter's heavy snows. Faint chitters reveal a mob of white-winged crossbills among the boughs high overhead, prying seeds from spruce cones and unleashing a shower of flaky brown scales.

Today's excursion started at first light when I stashed camping gear and enough food for several days into the skiff, eased away from our home shore on Anchor Bay, and set a course across Haida Strait. I felt a bit lonely going off without Nita, my partner and usual hunting companion. Although she doesn't carry a weapon, Nita has an impeccably sharp eye for deer, loves being outdoors in the patient and meditative way of "still hunting," and enjoys participating in the work that provides our staple foods—most important, venison, as well as salmon, halibut, lingcod, rockfish, berries, and other edible plants.

Given her penchant for seasickness, Nita was lucky to miss this morning's boat ride. Like an afterthought from the 50-knot storm two days ago, a hefty swell ran in from the ocean, setting up a fracas on Haida Strait. Here in the North Pacific, October's burly gales and constant rain are just occasionally interrupted by a day like this, when the beast of autumn sleeps. As I approached the island, a gap widened among crumbling colonnades of cloud, spilling out the first sunshine I'd seen all month. Blue water sparkled like shattering glass and the island stood out in crisp detail: driftwood logs stark as bones on black rock, the land sweeping away in long ridges serrated with trees, and above it all the chasmed face of Kluksa Mountain—enormous, snow covered, and ethereal—half hidden amid gauzy webs of fog.

I felt as if the island were imbued with a pervading, indecipherable power that both frightened and compelled me. Then I gazed out over the Pacific stretching off to the horizon's brink, and I recognized how minute and vulnerable I was, alone on this remote shore. But I willingly accept the risks, and regardless of consequences, I'd rather be here than anywhere else on earth. Many times I've yearned to own some part of this island, although it's public land that rightfully belongs to everyone, and this morning I realized the equation is in fact reversed, that the island owns *me*. To this I freely yielded myself as I anchored the skiff in a cove sheltered by reefs and islets.

Partway through the woods, Keta abruptly halts and stares ahead as if she's spotted a deer—or is it something bigger? Momentarily I realize the object of her interest is a red squirrel about the size of a kitten, perched on a fallen tree trunk six feet away. The squirrel should dash off like a lizard on a rock, but she hesitates, acting almost tame, then crabs awkwardly along the mossy bark, her body strangely crooked. Easing closer, I notice the fur on her right shoulder is creased and soiled. Perhaps she fell off a high branch, but more likely the squirrel escaped from an eagle, marten, or mink. In any case, wobbling gait and dazed behavior make her an easy mark and I doubt she'll survive for long out here. Nature is not fed by mercy, after all.

Daylight glimmering between mazy tree trunks reveals the muskeg just ahead. We inch past a saturated swale crowded with enormous skunk cabbage that look like they belong in a tropical forest, their broad, spatulate leaves standing as high as my waist. Hungry blacktails have scalloped some leaves to about half their normal width, and several others have been torn right out of the ground, their stems eaten and their roots excavated. Bear work, probably earlier today.

I stop at the muskeg's edge, half hidden by the trunk of a cedar tree, and hold my open palm toward Keta—our hand signal to sit. She folds back her ears, obeys, then pricks them up and watches as I kneel quietly beside the cedar for a long look at the surrounding landscape.

Back in August, Keta and I came to this same place to watch just as we're doing now, and she picked up a strong scent indicating a deer close by. We began moving slowly upwind, stepping noiselessly on wet grass, concealing ourselves behind a copse of shore pines. During our approach, I never once glimpsed the deer, but from Keta's growing excitement I knew it wasn't far off. Bucks, except when they're addled by the rut, have an almost preternatural sense for danger, a mind entirely different from the less cautious does and adolescents. This thought came to me as I heard a sudden thump of hooves. And then I saw him—a buck with sprawling antlers, their beams almost as thick as ax handles. He bolted across the muskeg, never once hesitating or stopping to glance back as blacktails often do, and within seconds he vanished into the far woods. Although I'm not interested in trophy hunting, I'll admit keeping a sharp eye out for that deer ever since.

The same boggy meadow stretches before us now: autumn-sere grass patched with stunted pines and brushy junipers, a few small ponds and streamlets, and Kluksa Mountain's timbered flank rising steeply behind. The broad sweep of land looks inviting and fecund, as if it should be alive with animals like the Serengeti plains. But the island has only two large mammal species, brown bear and blacktails, and our deer usually take shelter in the woods during full daylight.

This muskeg is separated from another by a narrow isthmus of pines, but there's a short break where you can see into both—an ideal spot to try the deer call. Because we've had weeks of constant rain, the moss and duff squish loudly underfoot, but I pick each step carefully and reach the opening in about 10 minutes. There, I lean the rifle against a pine, gesture for Keta to sit, and give the call a few short blows. Its thin, reedy sound, similar to blowing on a grass blade pinched between your thumbs, makes a fair imitation of a bleating deer, or a fawn's voice if it's pitched very high. Bears may also come rumbling toward a call, apparently hoping to find easy prey, so the prudent hunter carries a powerful rifle and uses the call near a good climbing tree.

Knowing a bear is around, I keep a close watch both on the muskeg and the inscrutable radar dog. A few minutes later, Keta locks her ears and eyes on the woods about 50 yards away. Crouching down, rifle braced against the tree trunk, I strain to pick out any movement. It seems as if there's nothing . . . until I spot a doe well out into the muskeg, as if she'd somehow materialized there. The deer comes deliberately toward us, moving in the stiff, mechanical way that telegraphs her anxiety, switching her tail, reaching out for a scent, leaning from side to side, honing her ears in our direction. Keta stays put, although she can't help quivering with desire.

The doe stops 40 feet away, facing in our direction, more inquisitive than afraid, and for several minutes there's a petrified stillness, as if we were all snared in an unbreakable gaze.

Koyukon people say animals offer themselves to those who have shown respect toward all members of their species, and there is no shame or guilt in taking what is given, so long as it is done properly, never in excess, and used without waste. I haven't forgotten that I am here to hunt. This island has a healthy population of blacktails, does are legal game, and I am not unwilling to take female deer. Of course, a buck would be in prime condition now and probably heavier than a doe, but this female looks very large and very fat. What constrains me is the possibility that last summer's fawn, although well past nursing and fully capable of living independently, could be tagging along somewhere nearby, still learning from its mother. Part of me urges doing what I came for, but another part is tangled with ambivalence, wondering if a fawn might eventually appear.

While I'm knotted by indecision, a raven soars out from the woods, circles overhead, and lands in a dead tree not more than 30 feet away. The hawk-sized bird clutches a bare, whitened branch, tilts down his head, and unleashes a clamor of gurgling, sonorous croaks. Shading my eyes against the corona of sun, I watch his beak open and close, the feathers on his throat ruffle and flatten. He looks like a midnight phantom etched on a screen of molten light.

I remember sitting on a bluff in northern Alaska with Grandpa William, a Koyukon elder, while he scanned the valley below for moose. A raven appeared, gliding low enough so he could have heard our whispers. Grandpa William watched for a moment, then spoke earnestly to the bird, as if he were imploring divine help in our search for game, which indeed he was: "*Tseek'aath,* Old Grandfather, I wish the animals would come our way easily." The raven drifted on without giving a sign—no aerial somersault to "drop his packsack full of meat for us" and no yodeled *Ggaagga!* (the Koyukon word for "Animal!") to assure us of luck and show the way toward game. A few days later we went back to the village empty-handed.

Above me now, the raven inflates his body, bends his spindly black legs, turns his shining beak this way and that, and spills his convoluted chant into the forest. It was the Great Raven who created our world, Koyukon elders say, and his living descendants still have extraordinary powers that can benefit people. For example, the raven will sometimes lead hunters to game, although it isn't simply out of goodness, because he knows he'll get scraps from the kill.

Still, I can't help wondering why a raven has appeared at this moment. Is he laughing at this man, so distant from his earthly roots that he's paralyzed with indecision when a deer presents herself? For generations beyond reckoning, our ancestors lived free from such dilemmas, accepting what was given in the hunt, moving in the embrace of an inspirited natural community, surrounded by wild creatures who listened and understood. But in modern societies, the old order has lapsed and we're beset with moral confusion about our dependence on the living world.

So here I stand, befuddled, the raven's voice echoing in my ears, the doe looking on. She comes nearer until she finds an eddy in the breeze laden with scents of man and dog. At this she flinches back, raises her head and flags her tail, then struts off. Near the center of the muskeg she stops behind a juniper bush and looks back for a long minute, as if she's presenting herself one more time. But I have lowered the rifle and watch as she melts off into the woods.

Grateful for Keta's partnership and patience, I stroke her silky black fur and whisper, "Good girl!" in her ear. The deer's exit has triggered Keta's roundup instinct and she's all afire, looking eagerly into my eyes, begging me just this once to let her chase. When we first started training a few years ago, I used to pick her up and aim her snout in the direction of a deer because otherwise she'd never see it. I also tied a light cord about 20 feet long onto her collar, and if she charged after an animal I'd yank back when she reached the end. Startled and amazed, she quickly learned to stay put.

These lessons had another important purpose: in wild country an uncontrolled dog is liable to chase after a bear, harass and anger it, then come running back to you with the enraged bruin on its heels.

Over the next few hours Keta and I track through a series of boggy muskegs separated by strips of forest—lofty Sitka spruce, western hemlock, and yellow cedar growing mostly along stream courses and steep-sided ravines. The sharply whetted concentration of hunting brings on a relaxed, almost hypnotic state that I've never experienced any other way, even while stalking animals with a camera. It's as if the primal mind becomes wholly engaged and nothing matters except this footstep, this tanglework of brush and trees, this muddy track or nibbled leaf, this moment's interweaving of birdsong and rustling leaves, this touch of breeze, this flutter of moth's wings, this patter of falling spruce needles . . . and always, the possibility of a soft, brown shape moving at the margin of sight.

Halfway through a stretch of woods, something twitches on the mossy groundscape ahead—a marten, loping our way, slinking under huckleberry bushes, flashing through patches of light and dwindling in the shadows. I purse my lips and squeak like a vole or nestling bird, and the marten's head pops up behind a log 30 feet away. After a few more squeaks, he hops onto a fallen tree trunk that angles toward us, and he's perched on the log's slender tip about five feet away.

The marten stares intently, moving his head from side to side like an Egyptian dancer, as if he's searching for a clear view even though we're almost within touching distance. Then he scampers back down the log without making the faintest sound, slips through the undergrowth to see us from another angle, and vanishes again. Enticed by more squeaks, he emerges wraithlike from the thicket and makes a long, effortless, magically suspended leap back up onto the log.

Again he pads out to the windfall's tip, rests on his haunches, and examines us at close range. His body is cat length but lean and cylindrical, with a limber, craning neck and a long, bristly tail; his feet are oversized, with sharp, whitish claws for scrambling through the branches in pursuit of red squirrels; his fur is dense, soft, and needled, hoary tan darkening to mahogany on the legs and feet, every hair shining like a spiderweb in the sunlight; his face is narrower than a mink's, more pointed and foxy, with big round ears extending far down each side; and his bright, black eyes gleam like ebony beads.

The marten leans back and scratches himself while continuing his study. He's probably never seen a human or dog before and considers us a prodigiously mismatched couple. Very slowly, I tilt my head to check on Keta, worrying that she'll make an impulsive grab, like a frog snapping a fly off its twig. She's totally spellbound, her eyes blazing and fervid, her ears tilted forward and shivering, but she makes not the slightest move. I feel proud of her: a young working dog, still learning but already well disciplined and attentive, seemingly motivated by the pleasure she takes in our partnership.

Finally the marten tires of investigating us, jumps down off his log, and disappears in the underbrush.

By late afternoon the air has become vibrant and crystalline, high boughs weave delicate lacework against the sky, and dissipating clouds are fringed in marigold. Figuring to set up camp as evening comes on, I turn back toward the boat with Keta tracking close alongside. The dun-colored muskeg looks arid and brittle, but in fact the vegetation is moist and limber from heavy rains—ideal for the necessary quiet of hunting. Still, I'm careful to not brush my knee-high rubber boots against twiggy plants like Labrador tea and bog laurel and to avoid the crisp deer cabbage leaves.

As we approach a cluster of pines, Keta lifts her nose and reaches into the breeze, her body tensing as if she's found a trickle of scent but hasn't yet seen anything. We slant up into the wind, working very discreetly toward the trees, Keta peering and sniffing as the enticement grows stronger. I try to imagine the lavish bloom of smells in Keta's world: distinctive odors that emanate from every kind of animal, every plant and flower, every patch of earth and water. She moves through a constant intermingling of sweet vapors, glandular musks, balmy aromas, and festering stinks; in heavy banks, sinuous ribbons, or delicate, hazy wisps; wafting and drifting, dense and faint, sharp and hazy; all apparently alluring. By comparison, my pathetic little snout registers virtually nothing, so I must rely on the dog as my only access to this rich, hidden realm.

When it comes to sight, however, I occasionally get an edge on her—and now is one of those times. Forty yards away I catch the fragmentary shape of a large deer, standing behind a tree so that only its bulging flanks and projecting ears are visible, as if it were staring at the trunk. But in fact, by keeping itself screened this way a deer minimizes the chance of being seen while it tracks every sound an interloper makes.

Eventually the deer turns aside and I see its entire head—a doe. It comes as no surprise, because a buck this large would almost certainly have dashed for cover long before we came so close. I watch until my arms shake from holding the binoculars; then at last she moves into plain view, staring at us. Except for remnants of reddish summer fur on her haunches, she's in her smoky-tan winter coat. If this were a younger blacktail, the two white patches on the front of her neck would look dull and indistinct, but hers are strikingly bright, one above the other with a sharp brown band between. I can even see the two whorls between her forelegs where the hair of her neck meets hair laid in the opposite direction on her chest and spins into paired vortices.

A woodpecker's shardlike call splinters from the nearby woods as the doe breaks her rigid pose, strides across open ground less than 100 feet away, and pauses amid a frazzle of grass. All this sets off a jangle inside Keta, but she holds tight and makes not a whimper. Realizing that we've come across a very large doe, and induced by the way she seems to give herself, I ease down onto the moss, slowly lift the rifle, and prop my forearms against my knees.

Just then the deer glides off behind a clump of brush, moving toward our right, lifting and lowering her muzzle the way someone might reach out a hand in darkness. Now I realize what's going on: uncertain about these strange creatures and unable to quell her curiosity, the deer is making her way toward our scent. Before she gets downwind, she pauses in full view, except for a sapling pine directly between us. Leveling the sights, I find a tiny space through its branches, opening a clear and easy shot. If she had a fawn nearby I probably would have seen it by now, so I take a deep breath and steady my aim.

But during the long moments that follow, I'm unable to find the necessary resolve. At last, I raise my head and watch the motionless deer. I cannot exactly account for this decision. Perhaps, after just one day out, it seems too early to end the hunt. Perhaps, after a summer of tracking and following and observing deer at close range, the hunter inside me has not fully emerged. Eventually I will do what I've come for . . . but this isn't the right time.

A raven flaps aimlessly above the distant ridge, gurgling and clunking. He might have been watching from a treetop, waiting for a chance to scavenge, and now he may be scolding, laughing, or commenting on fools.

Finally, the deer becomes impatient with our standoff and circles determinedly until she comes straight downwind, where she collides with the bitter cloud of our scent. A hard spasm runs through her and she springs away, flagging her tail, snorting explosively. Keta watches until she's gone, then licks my face as I pull her against my side, and in the running deer's wake we share a storm of exhilaration.

An hour later, after setting up the tent, I skewer chunks of last year's venison on an alder stick to roast over the campfire. The skiff rides at anchor, secure on slick water inside our cove, while lazy swells roll against offshore rocks. I've kept an eye out for seals or sea otters that often haunt these waters, but the place seems abandoned except for the occasional flight of cormorants and circling gulls. At last, I slice pieces of venison from the stick—browned on the outside, scarlet inside, sizzling, tender, and delicious.

While relaxing against a driftwood log afterward, I hear a faint rushing sound from high overhead, and purely by luck I pick out a dark projectile hurling under the torn remnants of cloud. It must be a peregrine falcon diving after some hapless seabird, I think, grabbing the binoculars. But within seconds I realize it's a bald eagle, much higher than I'd thought, descending at a sheer angle, wings half folded, feathers shuddering in the gale of its own descent. The bird dilates like the pupil of a cat's eye, and in the final moments unfurls its wings to break the fall, dangles its legs, flexes its golden feet, turns its eyes and beak downward, and shapes an inverted arc that intersects the water 100 yards offshore.

At the precise moment of impact, it reaches out and down, and jerks through the shattered surface a fish the length of my forearm, then labors upward, water trailing from its pinions while the gasping fish strokes its tail against the air. The eagle finally regains altitude and flies back toward the forest, where it lands atop a huge spruce. Swaying from side to side, still folding its wings, the bird bends down to fill its beak with living flesh.

How many meetings between predator and prey take place along this shore during the passage of a single day? How many along the thousand-mile reach of the North Pacific coast? How many over the entire North American continent, with its sprawls of forest and desert, farm field and marsh, seacoast and river valley, scrubland and prairie—all aswarm with hunters and prey: owl snatching mouse, snake seizing frog, spider snaring fly, fox grabbing chipmunk, trout striking minnow, shrew nipping beetle, toad snagging cricket, raccoon digging clam, dragonfly capturing moth, bear biting marmot, swallow taking mosquito, weasel clutching vole, mountain lion ambushing deer.

During every moment of every day on earth, there are billions of predatory encounters: life changing hands, creatures of every description devouring and digesting, shaping themselves through the deaths that sustain their existence. I can best comprehend my own place in this living family here on the island where I hunt and fish and gather. Like the eagle, my blood is made from fish. Like the bear, my flesh is made from deer.

On the far side of Haida Strait, amber light bathes the high peaks, then softens to tangerine and fuchsia, to purple, and to gray dusk. I imagine, with a subtle and binding awe, the black immensity of ocean that stares into the heavens like earth's great, unblinking eye.

Morning. Blue patches between drifting puffs of cloud, chickadees and juncos twittering in the woods behind camp, gulls drifting and wheeling above the shore, a river otter's birdlike chirps out beyond the surge, varied thrushes wheezing their pallid autumn song, and the soothing, ceaseless, sensuous rhythm of the waves.

Keta brims with energy, wagging and snuffing, restraining an urge to dash ahead as we slip back through the forest. Every low spot in the muskeg is brightly pooled with fog, and Kluksa Mountain towers beyond the lowlands like a thunderhead over the plains. Patches of frosted vegetation sound like crumpling cellophane under every step, so we keep to the muskeg's fringe, where overhanging boughs have held the temperature above freezing and the soft ground is fairly quiet. We sit for a long time under a big cedar, watching for deer and waiting for the sun to melt the frost. Keta stares at a red squirrel twitching on a low branch, then at a brilliant blue Steller's jay that flashes back and forth in the thicket, apparently inspecting us. Aside from these little events, it's as if our wild surroundings were vacant and inert, at least when compared to the frenetic hive back in town.

Of course, the island is a richly inhabited community where thousands of creatures go about their daily business; it's just that the pace here is extremely slow by modern human standards, more cautious and measured and quiet, in a way that resonates—to my mind, at least—as an abiding sanity. How I envy the creatures who spend their entire lives embedded in this place. What could possibly have impelled our ancestors, who lived in the midst of nature for thousands of millennia, to turn away from it? Should anyone ask for incontrovertible evidence that humankind has gone seriously awry, it's only necessary to enter wild country and pay attention.

A while later, Keta and I find a game trail cutting through a narrow stretch of woods between two muskegs. I've been here many times and couldn't possibly have missed this trail, yet I have never seen it. Not an ordinary path, it's made up of individual footprints—broad hollows in the moss, each a few inches deep and appropriately sized for a brown bear. It takes uncomfortably long strides to walk in these prints, with my legs spread wider than my shoulders. Above timberline I've seen trails like this extending for hundreds of yards, apparently worn by generations of brown bears stepping precisely in each other's tracks until the prints became holes 6 to 10 inches deep.

But this trail has just appeared within the past couple weeks, and a close look reveals a little pile of moss and twigs at the heel of each footprint, showing that the bear intentionally raked it out. My friend Steve Reifenstuhl, a fisheries biologist, once told me he'd come across a trail like this, and he speculated it was a male bear's territorial signpost, much like the trees they scratch and rub to advertise their presence. Possibly that's true, especially in early summer when mating dominates bruin society, but these tracks were made in the fall, shortly before hibernation. In any case, I'm reminded that a single lifetime is only enough to acquire a beginner's understanding of the natural world.

An hour dissipates practically unnoticed, and then another: clouds drift at intervals across the elevating sun, ravens fly above the fringing trees, eagles soar in the blue heights beyond Kluksa Mountain's shoulder. From time to time, Keta picks up a strong scent, but we glimpse only one deer, bounding into a thicket so far off I can't tell if the animal is large or small, doe or buck.

Around midday we squat on a gentle rise amid parklike muskeg with evenly scattered pines. Although it's ideal habitat where I've often seen deer, the place now seems deserted. I've never figured out just why, but on some days our island blacktails turn up almost everywhere and on others—even when conditions are ideal—they keep totally out of sight. Along this coast, you're most likely to see deer around dawn and dusk, but they can turn up anytime, especially when it's cool and cloudy. In rainy weather they prefer sheltering woods, and if it's windy they retire to thickets or ravines, apparently because the commotion makes them vulnerable to an undetected approach. During winter these northern blacktails shift their active time to the warmest, brightest part of the day, particularly when there's snow on the ground. And in rutting season, when madness infests every cranny of their brains, you're likely to encounter deer anywhere, at any time.

At lunchtime, feasting on leftovers from last night's campfire venison, I think of Nita back in town, wishing she were here and reflecting on the ways that harvesting wild food tightens the bonds between us. Whenever we bring home a deer, we hang it from a beam in our cool basement for easy skinning and butchering. For me, this work is another way to experience the elegance of a deer's design and the wonder of transforming its life into my own, as I sever joint from joint, laying aside each part. Next, we spend many hours bent over cutting boards in our kitchen, paring meat from bone. We use virtually everything, from heavy quarters to sinewy leg muscles, even the smallest bits meticulously sliced from ribs, brisket, and backbones. Then we wrap and freeze the venison for our year's supply of roasts, stews, and ground burger. We save all scraps and edible viscera that we don't use ourselves for Keta. The hides and hooves we give to Native American friends who use them for traditional arts.

Nita and I try to follow the example of Koyukon tradition, showing respect toward every part of an animal and remembering our gratitude for the food that gives us life. Also, anything we can't use—mainly bones and fat—we return to a clean, quiet place in the woods. Koyukon elders say this provides food for ravens and other creatures, and it allows the bones to molder back into the soil, ultimately to become plants and food for the animals again. These simple gestures, taught by people whose roots penetrate so deeply into the North American landscape, remind us to nurture in return the world that nurtures us.

On a mild afternoon like this, deer are likely to feed and bed in shady forest, so I follow the rim of a steep, wooded ravine with a narrow stream at the bottom. Except for occasional murmurs of water on rock we're immersed in stillness, a hush perfectly matched to the nature of deer themselves and ideally suited to their keen protective senses. Blacktails (especially does and adolescents) sometimes allow a hurried, noisy hunter to come within close range, apparently tricked by their own curiosity. But in my own hunting I prefer to move slowly and carefully, pausing often to watch and listen, always striving toward silence.

With Keta at my side, I weave through the pillared mazework of trees, working my legs and body around branches to avoid the slightest scuff, easing my feet down between stems and twigs, making every step as gently, as deliberately, as possible. Pausing at intervals, I lean from side to side, sometimes bend down and straighten again, to peer at every angle through shrubs and boughs. In this I'm reminded of the way a horned owl stares, moving its head back and forth, up and down, watching for the flicker of prey. Wherever possible, I follow narrow deer trails like the one skirting this ravine. These are often the easiest and quietest routes, because the animals know enough to avoid dense underbrush and circuit around helter-skelter windfalls.

On a breezy day, I move when gusts in the high branches help to cover any sounds, then pause when it's calm. But now, in the absence of wind, my only recourse is patience and caution. It's always best to presume a deer is bedded somewhere nearby or browsing through the understory, halting every few steps to look around and listen. Should a blacktail hear a twig snap under your boot or glimpse your moving shape, it might dash away, or it might stand watching for five to ten minutes, then settle down again—if you keep very still and make no noise.

Our ravine leads through dense patches of deer cabbage, low-growing plants with stiff, tympanic leaves that rattle beneath every step. The unavoidable noise gets frustrating after a while, but I remind myself that deer cabbage is a staple in the blacktail diet and that I regularly come across swaths of empty stems with their leaves nipped cleanly off. So despite the fact that deer cabbage sometimes warns of my approach, it's also an important part of my personal ecology, helping to sustain the animals who sustain me.

Glancing at my watch, I realize it's been eight hours since we started hunting, much of that time given to hard-muscled exercise and unbroken alertness, yet I haven't felt physically or mentally tired. I suppose it's the concentration, the adrenaline of desire, and the simple fact that I love using my body and mind as tools to nurture my own existence—in a world entirely removed from the supermarket.

I work here to the accompaniment of birdsongs and tumbling water rather than piped-in music; I move among congregations of trees and animals rather than crowds of people; I search for delicately hued creatures designed for elusiveness rather than for bright boxes that shriek for attention; I am surrounded by mountains and sky rather than walls and ceilings; I breathe the clear, unfettered wind rather than exhalations of heating systems and air conditioners; I anticipate the unparalleled intensity of encountering prey rather than the anesthetized drudgery of waiting in a checkout line.

If hunting is an ancient, obsolete, and outmoded way to live, then I will lie down on the blessed earth, let the wet moss saturate my body, open my eyes to the heaven beyond these boughs, and shout aloud my gratitude for the gift of birth in a time before hunting vanishes from the realms of human experience.

A few years back, a government agency promoting the American agrarian ideal shipped baby chickens and piglets to Koyukon Indian villagers—people who have been hunters, trappers, and fishers all their lives. Some folks took to the notion, built pens, raised healthy pigs and successful flocks, and eventually found eggs under their hens. That's when things started going awry. After watching the chickens grow, many couldn't bring themselves to eat the eggs, and it was even worse to think of dining on the birds or pigs. "People felt like they'd be eating their own children," a Koyukon woman told me. "A lot of them said, from now on they would only eat wild game they got by hunting. It felt a lot better that way."

In the trail Keta and I are following, bare dirt patches reveal crisp tracks indicating that a deer had come by ahead of us. From Keta's sniffing, I can tell there's scent not only in the prints but also among freshly nibbled greens alongside the trail—a good sign, though it might be several hours old. Then she starts lifting her nose and peering urgently into the breeze, testing a thick airborne scent. From this I know there's a deer close by, as surely as if I'd seen it walk into plain view.

Keta trails the aroma into a long, flat meadow clothed in sedge with scattered tussocks of bog blueberry and Labrador tea. On this bright afternoon it reminds me of a midwestern hay field, and then I realize: this is our equivalent of farmland, source of the animals that provide our household's staple food. I push my fingers down through feathery moss into the damp, black soil that ultimately nourishes my own life. At the same time, I remember squatting in a cornfield with a Wisconsin farmer who sifted handfuls of dirt while we talked. It was a lovely thing to watch this man of the earth caressing the source of his livelihood.

But that image was not without paradox because his fields lay raw and barren for much of the year, practically devoid of life except during the growing season, when they supported a single species of crop plus whatever fugitive weeds survived his herbicides. On the North American continent, agriculture has almost completely annihilated natural communities from thousands of square miles of land. When compared with the diversified crops and patchwork fields of traditional European or Native American farms, this is a massive ecological cataclysm. Yet we all depend on industrial agriculture, and our modern way of life essentially requires that we participate in it.

Here on the island we are privileged to harvest food from an undiminished natural environment supporting a lavish mosaic of plants and animals, all nourished by the soil and contributing to the soil in turn. Someday I, too, will complete my role in the cycle, become a part of it, and feed the plants that feed the deer.

Standing for a while beside the meadow, I notice a breeze lifting from the southeast and a murky brow of clouds above the seaward horizon—storm signs. Tucking the thought away, I move beneath a tree and blow the deer call a few times, then wait quietly. Ten minutes later a raven drifting over the forest makes two aerial rolls, "dropping his packsack," but the bird keeps quiet rather than shouting "Animal!" to fully affirm the good-luck sign I learned from Grandpa William. After landing in a tree, perhaps to watch our hunt unfold, the raven unwinds a litany of indescribable squawks, clucks, and bubbling croaks that echo from the distant ridge—as if he were talking to himself. Or is he teasing the likes of me, a man who listens but understands nothing?

I have taken seriously all that Koyukon elders teach about nature, I've tried to live in accordance with their instructions, and I accept the wisdom in their belief that everything is filled with spirit and awareness. Because I came to these teachings as an adult from another culture, I cannot *feel* these things wholly and intuitively, to the core of my bones, as they do, but anyone can act according to the principles behind listening to ravens, acknowledging power in trees and mountains, and making gestures of respect to game animals—because they are all founded on treating with honor, humility, and restraint the world that shapes our lives. Motioning Keta to my side, I take the direction indicated by the raven's topsy-turvy flight, an act somewhat blinder than faith, as a skeptic might receive Holy Communion.

Before we've gone 20 yards Keta tenses, focuses on the woods ahead, then stops of her own accord, as if she's locked in place. Kneeling down, I look from her same vantage but detect nothing amid the billowing leaves and boughs. Then I hear a faint noise penetrate the surrounding quiet, something altogether strange—a rapid, hollow thumping that fills the air around us, muffled and directionless as the drumming of a ruffed grouse. The cadence quickens and grows louder, as if the earth itself were throbbing. At first I'm only perplexed, and then, I'll admit, a little spooked. But suddenly I realize: this is the sound of Keta's wildly pounding heart.

I'd heard an almost identical sound once before, but that was the heartbeat of a young, terrified deer captured by researchers on Channel Island. The noise had set my own heart racing with empathy and excitement as it's doing again now. A Koyukon elder once told me that hunters who crawl into the entrance of a black bear's den occasionally hear the animal's pulsing heart, which indicates it's a young bear who isn't likely to put up a fight. An older animal, he said, would never be so afraid. From these experiences, I realize that in the moment when predator and prey converge, their two hearts may rise to a single throbbing chorus. This business of life . . . how tightly we are joined.

As I start inching forward again, I catch another sound: the soft, low, sheeplike bleats of a deer coming from behind a curtain of brush 30 yards away. Keta flares with inconsolable desire, her heartbeats jolting and leaping. At last, I see the deer: a dusky haze of flank and neck, half visible through menziesia bushes at the forest's edge; a single eye shining amid the leaves; an ear turning from side to side; and above it a burnished, two-pronged antler.

I take a few soundless steps, squat against the grass, brace the rifle on a sturdy-trunked pine, and peer through the sights. The deer shifts behind a scramble of branches, showing his rounded gray haunch, the broad ridge of his back, the narrowing shanks of his forelegs. But everything else is partially obscured, including the only place where I would ever aim—a small patch of temple—which is visible but crossed by a single twig the diameter of a pencil.

I have a fetish, an absolute and unwavering conviction, that every death I bring in hunting must be as quick as a blink, as instant as blackness when a light clicks off. My first obligation is to cause no preventable suffering, even for a split second. This requires concentration and care; it demands self-control to overcome the flashfire of excitement when an animal appears; and it depends on the resolution to wait until an adult buck or solitary doe stands at close range, unmoving, in clear view, as if to offer itself. On these things I make no compromise.

After I've held a steady aim for several minutes, the buck abruptly fades into the forest, like an owl taken in by the night. My shoulders slacken a bit, and yet I'm pleased that we stalked quietly enough to come within range of a buck's whispered voice without frightening the animal away. I wonder how many times I've passed a deer at equally close range without looking in the right place to see it. Hunting is so often a matter of happenstance, improbability, and moments of unbridled grace. Small wonder that people like the Koyukon approach it with such humility and believe that success depends more on nature's benevolence than on a hunter's prowess and skill. After centuries of intimate contact with wild animals—who have far keener senses than ours, who know the terrain in finer detail, who move silently and with extraordinary speed, and who usually vanish without being detected at all—how could an astute society of hunters entertain delusions of superiority over nature?

Real wisdom, it seems to me, acknowledges that dominion belongs to the world around us, not to ourselves—as we can see in the immense power of storms, the inevitability of sunrise, the temerity of beetles, the elusiveness of deer. When I come into this wild place, it seems right to shun all notions of power and accept thankfully whatever is given.

By late afternoon thickening overcast blankets the sky, the air becomes dense and clammy, and the breeze increases. During this season, when storms charge in like Brahma bulls from the Pacific, anyone with a lick of sense pays close attention to weather signs. Knowing that the waters in our little cove degrade into chaos during heavy weather, I hurry back to camp, load everything into the skiff, and head several miles up the coast to a well-protected anchorage close to muskegs favored by deer. Right now the sandy shore of this anchorage is inundated by a full-moon tide, so it's impossible to tell if bears have passed here recently. There's no time to worry about it, because evening's coming on and deer should be moving into the open.

We make our way through a dim gallery of spruce and hemlock giants, with sapling trees growing atop long-fallen trunks and a plushy cloak of moss laid over the earth. Keta knows the deer trail that takes us into a narrow, boggy muskeg that eventually broadens to a sweep of semiopen terrain with ample cover for deer but also good visibility for hunting.

She follows a river of scent toward a small patch of trees—just the sort of place where you'd expect to find deer. Perusing every nook through binoculars reveals nothing, so I move ahead very cautiously—but not, as it turns out, cautiously enough. While we're still a fair distance off, a doe unwinds in flight from the trees' edge, tail high and ears pinched back, punctuating each suspended leap with a snort. When I snort back she stops, mistaking us for other deer, but the ruse works only for a few seconds.

Meanwhile, Keta begs desperately to chase, fairly crazed with herd-dog impulses. In this we're much alike: I would love to sprint alongside that deer, to savor at close range her dazzling agility, to watch the flex and spring of her sinewy legs, the moss flying from her hooves, the boughs parting against her neck like water cleaved by a dolphin's prow. Perhaps only a person who hunts can penetrate the seeming paradox of loving a creature that you also stalk and kill and eat.

After the doe, we pass through an occasional trace of scent, but nothing to elevate Keta's interest. Thickening clouds bury the heights of Kluksa Mountain, foggy streamers drift along the lower slopes, and dusk broods in every cleft. Because I haven't set up camp, there's no choice but to hurry back, hoping we might happen onto a careless deer along the way. Dark forest impinges on either side of the narrow muskeg where we started hunting an hour ago. I've often attracted deer to a call in this place, but the light is fading quickly now.

From my hurried, noisy strides, Keta knows our hunting is finished, so she grabs a stick, dashes madly through the grass, crouches ahead of me, and gives me that border collie stare, asking to play. Each time I approach she races off in a wide circle, joyous as a kid erupting from a school bus.

Then, unaccountably, she drops the stick, walks up into the wind testing a scent, and makes one . . . two . . . three suspicious whoofs, hesitates, then whoofs again. I've never heard this breathy, huffing sound from Keta, but I know it well. Koyukon people often describe such barks as a bear warning, and once, in a northern Alaska fishing camp, a sled dog tethered outside my tent made exactly this sound as a black bear approached under cover of twilight. Luckily, the bear ran off after we shouted a few times.

There are no black bears on this island, only the weighty, formidable, and cantankerous brown bear. If Keta were an experienced northern husky, I'd know without question what's going on, but she has yet to encounter one of the big animals at close range. And would a border collie raised in suburban Wisconsin react like a wolfish sled dog to fresh bear scent? Maybe she's just caught a peculiar smell or heard something unusual.

Keta stares across the muskeg toward the place where we met the deer earlier. I see nothing in that direction except an oddly shaped stump; perhaps she's mistaken it for a person or animal. After a few minutes' watching I decide to ease over that way—bullet chambered and rifle ready—to make sure we're not being shadowed. Keta balks at my side, tentative and anxious, not at all the way she'd react to a deer, and when we reach the misshapen stump she ignores it, peering farther into the muskeg. It's getting late, I can't distinguish anything except brush and meadow, and it seems best to turn back. Keta hesitates until I whistle for her, then reluctantly tags along.

Fifty yards ahead of us the muskeg narrows to a cul-de-sac where we'll pick up the trail to our anchorage. As an experiment I toss a stick for Keta. Incredibly, she pays no attention to it, but stays out in front glancing nervously from side to side. Even if she's detected an animal, I think it must be long gone after all the disturbance we've caused, so I let myself relax and watch Keta instead of our surroundings.

Then it happens.

PSHEEEEEEAAAAWWWWWWW! An explosive, wheezy snort shatters the silence, unleashing an electrified jolt that shocks every nerve in my body. Stopping short, acting without thought, I jerk the rifle to my shoulder. And at the same instant, a dark, hulking shape rises 30 yards ahead.

Brown bear!

The animal towers up on thick, bent legs, showing the mass and girth of his body, immense forelegs opened at either side, platter-sized paws hanging down. Staring at us through the impending dusk, his head looms like a stony butte, his chest heaves ponderously, his body sways from side to side.

In a single motion, the bear turns and pitches down on all fours, gathers himself like a landslide, and hurtles off, smashing violently through underbrush at the forest's edge.

Stunned beyond movement, I trace the bear's pounding retreat into the woods—just where I'd beg for him to go—until the bedlam abruptly stops. After a tremendous quiet lasting a few seconds, the animal charges off again, either coming toward us or skirting the muskeg just behind the trees. During these moments I remember Koyukon hunters describing the brown bear's preternatural strength, incredible speed, and vehement temper. And I wonder if this beast will turn away in fear or come bursting out in anger.

At this point I have the presence of mind to speak—or perhaps yell—so the animal knows without question that the thing it saw or heard or smelled is in fact a human. The words are something akin to what Koyukon elders taught me to say:

"Bear.

"I am a man. I don't want trouble!

"If you'll go your way, I'll go mine!

"Bear. I am a human! I didn't come here to bother you!"

The words overflow from a part of my brain that leaves no memory afterward, as someone might forget what he thought in the last instant before colliding with a dump truck.

Again and again I call out, trying to be heard over the cacophony of splintering branches and thundering feet. At one point I realize my voice is so loud and low it could be mistaken for a growl, so I force myself to talk more easily, which helps settle the storm inside my brain. It also allows me to hear the bear, who sounds as if he's bowling over everything in his path except full-sized trees.

There's such fury in all this, I can't help imagining the bear has circled back to teach me a lesson for some nameless offense I've committed against his kind. With this thought, I lift my anchoring feet and scuttle backward, gawking around for a climbable tree. There are none, but of course it wouldn't matter, because I'd be lucky to get off the ground at all—much less the required 15 feet—in the time it would take a bear to get here. The rifle seems equally useless. How could I take lethal aim at an animal rumbling toward me at full speed, head bobbing and shoulders rolling, only half visible in the swarthy light?

Meanwhile, Keta's reaction, as far as I can tell, is totally opposite from mine. She's dancing toward the woods, ears up, ready for a chase. "Get back here!" I shout, and she cringes to my side. "You stay now," I order again and again, not just to get my point across but to make sure the bear hears my voice over his own racket.

At the same time, I've angled toward the exit trail, rifle still at ready, looking ahead so I won't stumble but keeping an eye behind for trouble.

Then everything falls silent. I have no idea if the bear has fled, stopped to reconsider, or slowed to a predatory stalk. I also can't tell if Keta, scampering ahead as we enter the forest trail, has picked up my fear or feels playful after so much excitement. As all this unfolded, I now realize, my hands never got shaky and my heart didn't race; there was only that hard twang of fright, followed by a state of intense concentration and an absolute resolve to do whatever became necessary. By some quirk of instinct, the jitters haven't begun until now.

When we're well inside the woods I stop to catch my breath and settle my brain, figuring the bear is gone. And then, looking down at the muddy trail, I discover the impression of a bear's front paw. More prints reveal that the animal had followed our own freshly scented tracks through this forest and into the muskeg.

Keta snuffles every footstep until we reach the shore, where one of us, at least, is incredibly glad to get out of those murky woods. Here— etched on clean, smooth sand exposed by the falling tide—is a record of how our encounter began. The bear came ambling southward along the shore, got within 30 feet of where Keta and I first landed, then turned abruptly into the woods, laying its tracks atop our own.

These, incidentally, are about the largest bear prints I've ever seen on the island. The hind feet, measured from heel to toe and excluding the claw marks, are a bit longer than my size 11 boots and about twice as wide. Almost certainly it's a male, who followed us more out of curiosity than deadly intent. Possibly he's learned, as bears have on Kodiak Island, to track hunters in hopes of finding leftovers from their kills. Whatever the case, I realize there's a fair chance of meeting this bear again, since we both favor the same territory.

Above all, I marvel that I could have been so lucky. Had we started back 15 minutes earlier I would have blown the deer call, possibly bringing the bear at a full charge expecting a helpless fawn. Or we might have startled the bear at close quarters in the woods. Or if I were carrying a fresh-killed deer, the bear might have come to take it away.

As the bear's chuffing and snorting reverberate in my mind, I understand as never before that I am nothing more than an ordinary member of this island community. I cannot know if this animal was hunting us, or if we've been stalked at other times without realizing it—an ignorance I frankly welcome. And I will say this: Without denying the terror those last moments would bring, I'd rather die as a bear's prey than keel over on my desktop or meet my fate in rush-hour traffic. What an afterlife, to march around as part of a bear's muscles, bones, and brain!

Despite these romantic thoughts, I don't feel like sleeping here in a flimsy tent, being startled by every click and shuffle in the nearby woods, so I pull anchor and head farther up the shore toward an old, mossy-roofed shack in Bear Cove. As we idle away, it seems both prudent and appropriate to thank the bear for going easy on us.

Awake in my sleeping bag, I stare into the black fissure of night, listening to raindrops flail against the cabin roof, gusts hiss in the treetops, waves pound on the nearby rocks. I reassure myself that the skiff is securely anchored and tethered by a safety line to a tree on shore. At last, in the dim light before dawn, I can see the boat still nested in our sheltered cove. Haida Strait, on the other hand, is a pandemonium of whitecaps, with thick-bellied swells pouring across submerged reefs and detonating against bare islets.

Half a mile offshore, there's a flock of several hundred gulls, circling and undulating like mist in a cataract. What inspires these birds to seek out the storm instead of heading for a protected bay? Do the frothing waves stir up food? Or do gulls simply love riding the wind, as I would if I had wings? Never mind such questions, I tell myself: the searing, storm-sung enchantment of the sky is reason enough.

Obviously, Keta and I won't be going home this afternoon as planned. Through a spatter of raindrops on the window, I peer into the gloom, watching black water tremble in the cove. I could fire up the woodstove and hunker inside, since most of the deer will bed in thickets until the wind and rain diminish, but I can't resist the temptation to head outside, drawn by an urge to stalk through the woods and muskegs, and to feel the storm's onrushing power. A full suit of rain gear might seem perfect on a day like this, but wearing nylon or some other noisy outfit makes it almost impossible to approach wildlife. Instead, I'll wear my usual out- fit—wool jacket and polypropylene pants—soft, quiet clothes that keep you fairly warm even when they're soaked.

Keta and I trudge up the long, wooded slope behind Bear Cove, and by the time we reach open muskeg there's sweat on my brow. From then on we set a slower pace, staying near the muskeg's fringe, where forest creates a sheltered lee and deer might abandon cover to feed. Although it's quieter here, the wind and rain make enough noise to help mask our sloshy footsteps.

Everything around us is alive with raindrops—dappling tea-colored ponds, shimmering on gray trunks, clinging to needles and boughs, hanging from cottongrass fluff and withered shooting stars, splashing on mushroom crowns and bog cranberries, running down salmonberry leaves and blades of grass, soaking into sedges, saturating the soil, trick- ling down rivulets and streams.

Half a mile into the muskeg, Keta starts lifting her snout and peering ahead. I'm sure she's caught a rich blacktail scent . . . but has the deer al- ready detected our approach? In hunting or watching wild animals, it's crucial to remember we carry around us a shifting halo of scent that drifts on the breeze, stretches into threads and plumes, gathers in pools and ed- dies, and flows off into the distance—totally beyond our own senses but unmistakable to deer. At the same time, we produce a halo of sound in the pattern of our footsteps, breaths, and scrapes against vegetation; and we create a visual halo that betrays us at ranges varying with cover, light, and terrain.

I try to imagine how far and in what direction our halos disperse, while I stay alert for the muted halos of sound and sight also given off by deer; and at the same time I watch Keta to borrow acuteness from her senses. Both the deer and I strive to conceal ourselves, as we also try to break through the other's concealment. For countless millennia, hunters and prey have carried out this complex interweaving of mind and senses; it lies at the core of our existence; it braids our separate lives together.

Keta's eagerness heightens as we track slowly upwind, immersed in a dense streamer of scent. Finally she hesitates, stiffens, and stares intently. Kneeling beside her, following her gaze, I eventually pick out a doe— smaller than I would hunt—almost perfectly camouflaged amid a backdrop of tawny beige grass, dusky tree trunks, and whirling rain. A pro-longed standoff ensues, the deer absolutely motionless while I struggle to keep almost as still. For 15 minutes she never stirs, never unfastens her eyes, never so much as twitches an ear, until I can't help feeling perplexed and wonder if she'll ever turn us loose. It's as if time moves differently in our two minds, as if this extended wait is nothing but a moment—or nothing in the world at all—for the deer.

When I glance away and then look back, the doe seems to have dis-solved; but then, meticulously searching the spot, I discover she's still there, half lost in the mysterious perceptual veil that always seems to sur-round deer, the marvelously perfected cryptogram shaped by a million years of evolution. Deer are not *supposed* to be seen by predators, after all.

At last the doe breaks our impasse, reaches down to nibble a wet petal, flicks the raindrops from her tail, and struts away in an exaggerated gait reminiscent of a prancing show horse, forelegs raised high and bent ele-gantly above her hooves, as if to render me harmless at the sight of her unalloyed beauty. Then she bursts into a four-footed trampoline stott, hesitates once to glance back at us, and flounces off like tumbling water. I watch her vanish into the forest, rain flowing like a river in my eyes.

In the hours that follow, Keta and I drift along the muskeg's border without coming across another blacktail. Keta's soaked, clinging coat makes her look skinny and a bit wretched, although she's as lively and wagtailed as ever. My clothes are totally waterlogged, but I'm still fairly warm, thanks to steady trekking and southerly gales bringing tempera-tures well up into the forties. Despite the pleasure and excitement of ram-bling around in a storm, I also feel a growing urgency about the hunt. We're short of camp food, so we must head back tomorrow if the wind subsides. At home, last year's venison is about gone, and this is the ideal season for replenishing our supply—a time when bucks, especially, have reached maximum size and prime condition just before the rut.

Around midafternoon I abandon the muskeg and work along a nar-row peninsula of forest with a deeply incised creek rushing through the middle. Here, during a long session with the call, a small, spike-antlered buck emerges from the underbrush, eases in our direction, head high and ears wide, but then flashes away—as if the wind has made him frazzled and hypersensitive.

A bit farther on, we come across a thick cedar tree with long pieces of bark peeled off, as you might tear vertical bands of tape from a wall. Some lie coiled like wet pythons beneath the tree, but others are still at-tached 15 feet above the ground, hanging loosely over the smooth, shiny wood. Undamaged bark covers about half the trunk and the tree looks healthy, although it's too soon to know if it will survive. A wildlife biologist told me that brown bears sometimes pull off cedar bark this way in springtime, then lick the heavy-flowing sap either for a tasty treat or a nutritional boost.

Closer inspection of this tree reveals faint tooth marks, some well above my head, and the surrounding earth is worn raw, indicating the bear stayed here for a while, scraping and rolling and scuffling. Although there's nothing subtle or inconspicuous about these workings, and although I must have passed many trees like this over the years, I never noticed them until I'd talked with the biologist. It's often like this, I think: we're blind to much of the world until someone tells us how to see it.

The storm shows no sign of relenting as afternoon gives way to evening. From a ridgetop, I look out over Haida Strait—still a torrent of whitecaps, the offshore islets half lost in rain squalls, thick stratus surging overhead. I turn my face toward the sky, let the raindrops prickle my skin, and feel grateful to be alive in this saturated kingdom of clouds. After months of tranquil weather, the whole world seems caught up in a boisterous celebration, as if the season isn't just turning, it's doing handsprings. I'm exalted by the wildness of it all, ready for the cold and fire and passion of winter.

At times the gale blows so hard that the rhythm of my tired footsteps seems almost inconsequential, but I still try to keep quiet, staying on the highest, least spongy ground as we trek along the muskeg's edge. Little time remains before nightfall, so there's not much chance we'll come across any more deer. And yet, judging by the abundance of tracks, droppings, and clipped vegetation, more than one blacktail would hear the sound if I clapped my hands.

All around us is lovely parklike heath scattered with bonsai-sized pines, veiled in mist and rain. It's as if everything had been set perfectly in place, according to some meticulous yet whimsical design, and even I—a man freshly rooted here—feel myself a part of it, a single voice in a deafeningly beautiful chorus. I am an *animal*, moving among other animals, surrounded by plants, wrapped in a cloak of rain, breathing wind, feet sunken into the moss, the great earth plunging away below.

With the approach of dusk, I have no choice but to head back toward the cove. We haven't come across fresh bear signs today, but I'm still jittery from last evening's experience and don't care to grope through the woods in darkness. Retracing our earlier route, Keta and I approach the spot where we saw the first doe this morning. It's fairly calm and quiet under the leaning brow of trees, so I move along slowly and pause every few steps to look around . . . but just ahead is a broad, open meadow—not the sort of place where I'd expect to see deer, especially during a storm.

Keta grabs a stick and begs me to play, but I motion her to settle down; if nothing else, stepping along carefully and silently will keep my senses alert, heightening my awareness of the wind, the rain, and the softly dwindling light. I pick my way through a patch of deer cabbage, then look up to scan the area ahead.

In that fraction of a second, everything is changed, and I catch myself in midstep as the truth of it bolts through me. At the same instant, Keta sags into a half crouch, her neck leaning forward, her ears honed and eyes riveted, her legs quivering, one forepaw lifted off the ground.

There, standing atop a low rise about 20 yards ahead, silhouetted above the crowns of two stunted pines, hard edged against the faded, hoary overcast, are the chest and neck and head of a deer, faced directly toward us, eyes shining, ears in a wide V, and a beamy crescent of antlers bending above.

Without hesitating and without conscious thought, I sink onto my knees, raise the rifle to my shoulder, and brace it against a slender tree. During these seconds, I'm taken by a powerful sense of déjà vu. At this same season a few years ago, a buck stood against the evening sky less than a hundred yards from this spot, and I did exactly what I'm doing now.

Perhaps this is why the outcome seems just as certain. There is no tingling apprehension, no pounding heart, no shaking hand. The rifle sights come to rest, unwavering. I breathe deeply, and deeply again, eyes opened wide. It's as if everything were preordained and the animal had come—as Koyukon elders teach—to give itself.

I feel absolutely, jarringly predatory, like a cat splayed against the grass, simmering in ambush. And utterly alive, in a way that defies language, that scarcely renders itself in conscious thought. I am a living creature questing for its food. Whatever ambiguity I feel about the hunt, it now lies far beyond reach. And I say this: No tiller of soil, no herder of flocks, no gatherer of plants, no browser of grocery shelves will ever cross this same emotional terrain. As for me, I would rather be a rock on a hillside than exist without knowing in this way the animal who lives inside me and gives me life.

The buck pumps his head up and down, telegraphing his uncertainty.

Then he stands utterly still, his shape incised above the curving cloud of branches, as if the full truth of him had leapt down into the fluid of my eye.

Lightning flashes brightly in the blackness, and thunder pours away over the land's edge, tumbling and tumbling beneath the storm.

There is a burst and a shock and a jarred half vision of the deer's fall, as if he were completely released, like a puppet whose strings have all been snipped at once. I stand, breathing heavily, and rush toward the empty place between the pines with Keta bounding alongside. She reaches the spot before me, circles, and snuffles the soft edges of the buck. He lies on a mat of crowberry and bog laurel, soft and quiet and midnight-still—as if the gale had instantly grown calm.

At first I hear only silence. Then I hear my heart pounding and the ringing in my ears, and finally Keta panting at my side, the swashing of wind in high boughs, the distant drum of surf.

I kneel beside the deer and touch his warm, silky eye to affirm the certainty of death. Then I run my hand along his flank, whispering words of thanks that seem inadequate and frail against what I've been given here—a life that will enter and sustain my own. Beaded raindrops roll down over the dry, brittle fur.

I am not a guiltless hunter, but neither do I hunt without joy. What fills me now is an incongruous mix of grief and satisfaction, excitement and calm, humility and pride. And the recognition that death is the rain that fills the river of life inside us all.

Keta prances back and forth excitedly, looking in all directions for another deer, as if animals fascinate her only when they're running or might do so. I hold her by my side, rub her fur, and nuzzle her wet face. The deer is a prime, heavy, thick-coated buck, bearing modest but lovely antlers, their slender beams stained dark maroon at the base, fading to polished gray on each of the six elegantly tapered points. I will leave them here, although it's not hard to understand why someone might hang them on a living-room wall.

After dragging the buck to a nearby tree, I fasten a rope around both forelegs, loop it over a branch, then hoist the animal off the ground. With a small pocket knife, I sever the neck and spinal cord, then make a shallow incision, slightly longer than my hand, down the middle of the deer's belly, being careful not to puncture its stomach, which would foul the body cavity with spilled contents. Next I reach up into the hot, moist cavity to pull out the stomach, intestines, and fatty mesenteries, leaving the heart, liver, and kidneys in place. Keta nudges close, trying to lick the blood that drips down, but I shoo her away out of respect for the animal. Later on, when we butcher the deer, Keta will have her share of scraps.

I take some fat from inside the body, plus a few slivers of meat, and leave them with the viscera for the other animals. It's important, Koyukon people say, that wild creatures feed on remnants left in the woods by hunters, but other than small tidbits, nothing should be abandoned except parts we can't use ourselves. The eagles and ravens will come at first light tomorrow and within an hour they'll clean up everything but the skull bones and stomach contents.

To make sure no dirt gets inside the carcass, I cut small holes through the skin around the belly and neck openings, then lace them shut with cord. Next, I half sever the forelegs at their "knee" joints and toggle each front leg through a sliced opening in the hock of the corresponding rear leg. This makes it possible to carry a modest-sized deer as if it were a pack, putting your arms through the fastened legs and hoisting it up so the animal's belly lies against your back. With darkness looming above mountains to the east, I start the final trudge. Keta dances alongside, perhaps anticipating tonight's dinner. I'll cut a few pieces of fresh venison to fry in a skillet atop the wood-burning stove—the most delicious and elemental feast I can imagine, making the deer a part of me.

In the last stretch of muskeg, just before we'll enter the woods behind Bear Cove, I angle over to a small, rain-dappled lake, put my load on the ground, and rest beside the water. Keta slumps against me, finally getting tired. But she perks up a few minutes later, when a large doe ghosts out from the trees directly across the lake from us and steps to the water's edge, nervously switching her tail. She reaches down and touches her nose to the water . . . and it's as if I have drifted into a deer's dream.

I slowly bend over, dip my hand beneath the ripples, and fill it with the same chill water. And there, embraced by the island and the sky, we drink each other down.

EPILOGUE

June 12. A chill northwesterly breeze winnows down over the muskeg, shaking through pearly blossomed Labrador tea and purple-berried juniper. Brown, brittle grass and newly sprouted sedges shiver at the margins of rippling ponds. Above the muskeg and beyond a high, wooded ridge stands the brooding, conical wall of Kluksa Mountain, overcast shrouding its rim. Snow-filled ravines cleave upward through the talus like ivory spokes, giving the mountain a cold, forbidding look. I shrug against gusts that seep through my blue jeans and wool jacket. Yet there's a promise of summer in the wheezy, ethereal notes of a varied thrush chiming first on one pitch and then another, like a rainbow spilling from an indigo cloud.

In spite of rough water that made boating a misery, and regardless of the unseasonably cold weather with passing fits of rain, something impelled me to head out across Haida Strait with Keta this morning. It was partly the simple wish to abandon town and spend a quiet day here on the island. And it was partly a notion about deer; not just that I wanted to see them, but a desire of mine whose fulfillment fell somewhere between extreme unlikelihood and rock-solid impossibility. Along the North Pacific coast—as in most northern regions of the continent—the first half of June is fawning time. And despite the tremendous odds against wandering into the right place at precisely the right moment, I have allowed myself to dream of seeing a wild deer give birth.

To measure the improbability of witnessing this event, consider the experience of Leonard Lee Rue III, writer, naturalist, and preeminent wildlife photographer. Rue spent decades working closely with his favorite subject in both wild and confined situations, and by the mid-1980s, he estimated that he'd taken more than 100,000 photographs of deer. And yet, he writes in his 1978 classic, *The Deer of North America*: "I have been most fortunate in being able to witness the birth of fawns on two different occasions. Both does were semi-tame, living on a deer preserve." In other words, although millions of fawns are born each year in every imaginable cranny of our continent, there's very little chance that anyone is going to see it happen except within a fenced enclosure or perhaps a suburban backyard. On this wild, remote island, I could just as well spend my time searching the woods for stray albatrosses or watching the sky for unknown comets.

However, it's vaguely realistic to imagine stumbling across a sequestered fawn, perhaps seeing an infant blacktail with its mother, even watching it nurse—if not this year, then maybe sometime in the future. Over the past few weeks I've visited the island often, motivated by these peculiar and farfetched ambitions. But in fact, I'd be satisfied to encounter any deer at all, especially to stalk near enough for a glimpse into its daily life.

Trekking slowly toward the center of the muskeg, Keta and I follow an elongated rise that overlooks a grassy, undulating terrain with scattered copses of shore pine, scrubby juniper thickets, and twisting streamlets connecting hundreds of tiny ponds. Somewhere inland from us, a greater yellowlegs pours ceaseless, warbling whistles, growing louder as we hike along the ridge. Eventually I spot the mottled, stilt-legged shorebird fluttering from one dead tree to another, still ranting. Many times I've been scolded by a yellowlegs after inadvertently walking too close to its nest, and I've seen these birds get just as agitated over a deer or bear. The first possibility tempts me to head that way for a closer look, but the second encourages me to mind my own business.

While I ponder this dilemma, Keta picks up a hard scent, not on the ground but drifting in the northwest wind, meaning there's almost certainly a deer close by in a direction opposite from that of the yellowlegs. The aroma must be pretty thick, judging by Keta's fidgety behavior; just when I want her to keep still, she's prancing from side to side, raising and lowering her snout, gazing up into the wind. After she settles down we make our way across lower ground and through patches of deer cabbage—small plants with a single leaf like an umbrella perched on a finger-length stalk. Some are freshly clipped, leaving empty stems with no crowning leaf, and hoofprints sunk deep into the moss identify the nibbler. Keta sniffs eagerly, sampling a mix of smells like a kid eating a dozen kinds of candy at once. From her excited behavior I'd guess a deer browsed here within the hour.

Angling west, still on the scent, we trek along another low rise affording good views on either side, so I stop to peruse the terrain. This muskeg is one of my favorites; I've walked every part of it innumerable times while hunting or bird-watching or exploring, often with friends, and I've had many encounters with the wild animals who live here—especially black-tailed deer. These experiences run through my mind whenever I come here, filling the land with memories, strengthening my attachment to it, rooting it more deeply inside me.

Near this spot, I once found the skeletons of two small bucks, a fork-horn and a spike, lying a few yards apart, and both of them had drastically asymmetrical antlers—long on one side, very short on the other. Another time I found several patches of thick, chalky material mixed with beach gravel lying around like cow pies, unlike anything I'd ever seen before. I finally realized they were droppings of a bear who had eaten blubber from a dead whale on the nearby shore.

From Keta's excitement I know we're still immersed in thick scent, so I stalk meticulously ahead—lifting each foot clear of the crunchy grass, worming through snarled juniper branches, bending and bracing and standing off balance and peering all around—on the assumption that we could come across something at any moment. Again and again Keta reaches for the breeze, delving farther into the trail of scent and urging me closer to whatever made it. I know she wants to turn directly upwind, but that would take us down off the ridge, into a broad meadow that seems too open for deer at midday, especially given my preoccupation with does and fawns. So I keep on as before, figuring our best chance is the ridge with its intermingled grassy swatches, thickets, and pines.

But while I focus on what I presume and infer, Keta focuses on what she *knows*, on the truth of this moment as revealed by her impeccable senses. She probes the air more intently as the scent grows richer and thicker. She swings up into the wind as if she has no choice, as if the pleasure or promise of the smell is more than she can resist. She comes back when I point insistently at the ground beside me but soon veers off again, balancing her own determination against mine.

Eventually I yield, figuring there's no harm in taking a look that way before we get back on course. Respecting the strength of Keta's interest, I give her the lead and pick every step deliberately, trying to make no sound at all, waiting for each little gust and then moving while the wind's bluster conceals the noise of my clumsy feet. I hesitate, study the terrain ahead, and move again. The muskeg looks abandoned and austere in the jostling wind and gray light, beneath the pallid, scudding clouds. In the distance I hear a robin's song, lilting and fading on the breeze. I stop to listen, but keep scanning up into the wind that Keta finds so promising and fertile.

When I'm about to take a step, I notice almost by chance a small tan-colored blotch, bright and sharp edged, incongruous amid the sere grass and ashy trunks and deep-green boughs. I catch myself and ease my foot back to the ground, Keta halting close at my side. Is it a deer, I wonder, as I lift the binoculars, or a patch of dry, faded moss?

Blacktail . . . doe . . . lying in a small oval of bare ground, legs folded tight against her flanks, head raised to keep watch. Because she's curled like a dog, I can see both her front and hind quarters, showing the breadth of her chest, the muscular bulge of her thighs, the broad ridge of her back, the shaggy fur of her tail. She seems very round, partly because she's resting on her side, partly because her belly seems unusually full.

Perhaps it's that look of fullness. Perhaps it's the way this deer has chosen to rest, lying on one side rather than belly down with forelegs tucked under her chest. Perhaps it's just because the season is right and because for so long I've carried this fervent wish. Whatever the reason, a thought flutters through my mind: she's going to have a fawn. Then it vanishes in the flood of reason and sensibility: never in such an open place as this, never just as Keta and I happen along, never would I have such blind, blundering luck.

I lower the binoculars, pleased that we've come across a bedded deer in plain sight and seemingly unaware of us. Instead of trying to stalk closer I sink down onto a dry tussock covered with reindeer lichen and crowberry—an ideal perch. Beside it, within easy reach, is a small muskeg pond a few inches deep, dimpled with water striders. I slip off my little backpack and glance at my watch—2:20 p.m.

Keta sits beside me, pressing heavily against my leg, raising her muzzle urgently to the wind, quivering with excitement. She knows as well as I do there's a deer close by, but luckily she can't see it from her low vantage. I rub her silky black fur, hoping she'll calm down, fearing she might whine or jitter noisily in the dry grass. She resists when I gently force her to lie down, then stands immediately, nose high, leaning toward the deer.

This is a fair-sized doe, as indicated by the brightness of the white patches on her neck and the long, narrow shape of her head. Her luster-less winter coat has just begun to shed, revealing patches of sleek, rust-colored summer fur. She's looking directly toward us, ears in a wide V and funneled to pick up the slightest sound, as if she might have glimpsed us or heard our rustlings. As fate would have it, Keta and I are surrounded by grass and tussocks with no shrubs to screen us from the deer's view or protect us from the wind. If she stays bedded for long, this is going to be an extremely cold watch. The deer's place is better than ours, in the lee of a small mound with a windscreen of waist-high ju-nipers and sapling pines. Between us is a gentle swale fretted with bushes, sapling trees, and mossy patches. Luckily we're straight downwind and the northwester flows unwaveringly—so there's no chance the deer could catch our scent.

After 10 uneventful minutes the doe abruptly stands. Good news, I think, hoping she'll start to browse so we can sneak closer while she's dis-tracted. On the other hand, she may slip off into the concealment of brushier terrain or she might see us from her higher vantage. But the deer just stands there, facing away from us with her back arched and her body strangely hunched. Then she flips up her tail and holds it for a moment curved stiffly over her back, the muscles unnaturally tensed, hairs stand-ing on end as if they'd been stimulated by an electric shock—something altogether different from the waving vertical flag of an alarmed deer. Af-terward she relaxes, walks a few steps, and to my great surprise lies down again, facing us with her head high.

This seems unusual—a bedded deer standing up and then lying back down in the same place. For a while she gazes our way, the great orbs of her eyes opened wide and black as midnight sky. Then she shifts her ears back and forth, visibly slackens, and looks off toward the runneled face of Kluksa Mountain, as if she were wholly at peace.

A bunch of chickadees flits in among the nearby pines, clinging to the boughs, probing their beaks under the loose bark and into the cleavages between needles, hunting for insects. Then, darting from tree to tree, they work their way toward the doe, who twitches her ears but otherwise ignores them. How I envy those little birds, perched within a few feet of her, their chittery notes falling around her like a shower of sequins.

Ten minutes later the doe stands, hunches her body again, turns around a few times with her tail rigidly erect, and then lies back down. Suddenly, my earlier fancy becomes a clear and plausible thought: she must be coming into labor! And yet I'm still convinced fawning is one event in a wild deer's life that I'll never see. Squinting through the binoc-ulars until my arms throb, I now realize there's a conspicuous bulge in her belly, shaped like a basketball and far back near the hips. Is it the cold wind or the hard surge of excitement that sets me shivering?

The deer stands, immediately lies down, then rests for another 10 min-utes before getting up and turning aimlessly, still oddly hunched, tail arched over her back like a drawn bow. And what I see now takes away all remaining doubt: beneath her erect tail is a conspicuous, dark, dilated opening.

Whenever the doe stands Keta picks up a flush of scent, so I press her to the ground and scratch her belly to keep her soothed and distracted. Deer can interrupt labor if they sense danger, so our doe might startle away, and even if she moved a few steps I'd no longer see her. After being totally immobile for almost an hour, lightly dressed and exposed to the wind, I've started shaking uncontrollably, and I'm afflicted with a nearly overpowering urge to move, warm up, sneak closer to her. She's only a few street-widths away, but the scrabble of brush, dry grass, and saturated, squishy moss would be impossible to traverse quietly. Above all, I'd be crazy to risk losing what is being given here.

For a while the doe lies quite still, intermittently flipping her tail; then every few minutes she rolls sharply on her side, straightens and stiffens her neck, and reaches out with her chin, ears laid back, eyes half closed. Although I hear no sound, her movements and expressions telegraph pain. Then she stands and turns several times, once again showing the dilated place beneath her tail.

Slowly, carefully, I pull a short rope from my pack and fasten one end to a shrub, the other to Keta's collar, with very little slack so she can't move around. I'm quaking so hard I can barely tie the knots, and when I tense my muscles to stir up a little warmth, my back and arms threaten to cramp. I've never realized how much a person's nose drips on a cold day until now, when I can't make the tiniest sniffle and don't dare raise a sleeve for the traditional swipe.

The doe paces awkwardly back and forth on her patch of bare ground, then lies down again, keeping very still. Head raised, she glances around constantly as if she's tense and disquieted. From a human standpoint she seems profoundly alone, terribly vulnerable—which of course she is— and this fills me with compassion. A woman in her situation would be surrounded by midwives and companions, or nurses and doctors; she'd be supported, encouraged, touched, consoled, attended, assisted. I would sit with the deer and protect her from harm, if only I could displace her fear. But she can know only the predator inside me, not the watcher.

A light drizzle falls, just enough to set the grass and leaves glistening. In the quiet moments that follow, the deer rolls on her side and sprawls to her fullest length with her neck stretched out, head wavering up and down, tail flashing and tensing. What happens next is so sudden and so unexpected—despite all that's come before—that I am wholly unprepared to see it.

Still lying on one side, she raises her uppermost hind leg off the ground, arches her neck, and reaches her head back. Then, out from beneath the flared white tail slips something long and wet and shining and very dark.

I want to jump and shout aloud for the joy of it, but instead I hold the binoculars to my eyes, arms aching and muscles shivering.

Half visible beside the mother's loins, a dusky-brown mass gathers itself together, moves in confused, spasmodic jerks, and becomes a fawn—a tiny, throbbing, trembling, living fleck of earth.

Reaching back along her flank, the doe begins vigorously licking her child, and as she pulls away the clinging membranes, the fawn thrusts her muzzle into the cold breeze, opens her mouth, and draws her first breath—taking in the same air that sustains every creature on earth, the air that surrounds this unlikely congeries of doe, fawn, dog, and human.

Through newly opened eyes, this tiny deer sees the island where she will live through her seasons of sunshine and rain, blizzard and frost, abundance and hardship; where she will learn the mosaic of landscape and trail, find membership in a society of deer, grow sleek and graceful and quick, present herself to courting bucks, and bring on fawns of her own. During these beginning moments of her life, she sees the prodigious wall of Kluksa Mountain that will loom above her from now until the moment of her death. The deer is born into a home more purely and absolutely than I could ever imagine.

I hear a series of short, high-pitched bleats drifting on the wind, almost surely from the fawn. The doe stands and licks her offspring, then raises her head, flicking her tongue in and out. Her lifted tail reveals the distended pinkish opening from which the fawn was born. A few minutes later she moves back to her original bed and lies down facing our way. The tiny deer—still very dark, wet, and slick—crawls over against her mother's belly and nuzzles up between her legs, as if to begin nursing.

Over the next 15 minutes the doe alternates between licking her child and licking herself, while the little one keeps trying to stand: front end up and back end down, back end up and front end down, wobbling precariously the whole time. At last, she turns so I can see her tiny face and her enormous, blinking eyes. Then she braces up onto her hind legs, straightens her spindly forelegs . . . and stands. But she flops down almost immediately and crawls close to her mother, who licks her once again.

The doe seems almost completely focused on her fawn, and I can't endure the cold any longer, so after whispering stern orders in Keta's ear I begin an excruciatingly careful stalk, keeping myself screened behind bushy pines, holding for long intervals between each step, moving stiffly and awkwardly after the protracted wait, still shaking like grass in the wind.

The fawn's coat is much darker than the doe's and it's aswarm with miniature white spots. She moves around constantly on quaking, rubbery legs, often arching her tail toward her back—much as her mother did in labor—showing a miniature white flash.

I have never approached a deer so fastidiously, twisting between close-grown shrubs, worming under low boughs, parting grass with my hands before bringing down each foot, struggling across murky seeps, creeping in slow motion like a slug on a cold morning. It's taken half an hour to cover 25 yards, but at least the shivering has stopped and I feel gloriously warm inside.

An hour after giving birth the doe still licks her fawn's shoulders, neck, face, and flanks—her raspy tongue tugging at the fur. When the fawn half squats, apparently to urinate or defecate, the mother licks beneath her infant's tail. Again and again the tiny deer stands and flops down . . . this animal destined someday to unleash herself in tremendous, vaulting leaps.

I somehow avoid any serious missteps until I've come within 10 yards of the deer and then a tuft of grass crackles under my boot. The doe stands abruptly and stares, but I'm hidden behind a patch of junipers, bending out just enough to see her. Her eyes blink slowly, her nostrils pinch and flare, her pinkish tongue swipes across her nose. I stay absolutely motionless for 20 minutes, letting her settle down while I figure out a way around the snarled junipers. For much of this time the doe licks her fawn while the little one bumps against her udder, searching for the tiny nipples.

When the deer child is an hour and a half old she clambers atop a small mound beside her mother's head, up into the full clear light and the wind, and there she stands, her forelegs braced like tripod stilts, hind legs bent so her hocks nearly touch the ground, her fur now dry and frizzy and light tawny brown.

I've started to cross a narrow stream—two inches of water flowing over a bed of organic ooze that bubbles noisily as my boots sink into it. This isn't lost on the doe, who watches and listens, trapping me in the little swamp. Future paleontologists might find my bones here, but despite their limber imaginations I doubt they'll ever surmise how it happened.

After browsing halfheartedly the doe reclines beside her fawn, staring at me but showing no trace of fear, while the wobbly infant sniffs her mother's huge gray ear. A burnished-brown streak runs between the fawn's eyes, and another from its forehead to the shiny black of its muzzle, making a distinct cross on its face. Nearby, juncos flit from pine to pine, tittering softly.

I keep looking back, trying to see Keta, hoping she's curled up on the grass, not chewing the rope to free herself and bring all this to an end. But she's completely hidden from view. Of course, I owe this experience to Keta, whose persistence brought me here, so when it's over she'll have the cookie in my pack.

Two hours after the fawn's birth and three hours since we first arrived, I'm still trying to close the distance between myself and the doe. The doe stares and listens intently to the rustling of my jacket sleeves, the grumbling of my empty stomach, the sponging of moss beneath my feet. Under ordinary circumstances she'd have fled long ago. Although I'm mostly hidden, and she probably doesn't know what I am, she knows an intruder is precisely here. Perhaps because of this she walks over to the resting fawn, who stretches up to nurse.

Squirming through the juniper thicket, I can't help making noises that must sound to the doe like crumpling paper. Suddenly, as if I had leapt out in front of her, she jars to full alarm, flags her tail, and struts a short distance, which puts me in plain sight with nothing taller than a blade of grass between us. She gazes first at me, then at her child, who makes a faint sound more like a high-pitched bird's whistle than a deer's bleat. The doe funnels her ears, raises and lowers her head, then returns to gently nuzzle her fawn as if its voice made everything else irrelevant. Now I believe I can come as close as common sense and etiquette allow.

She moves about 20 feet from the fawn and 20 feet from me, then starts nibbling the grass, displacing her nervous energy the way an anxious cat licks herself. Meanwhile, the tiny deer weaves around unsteadily, poking her nose into the scrubby pines, the grass tussocks, the crowberries, the Labrador tea, the sphagnum moss, the marsh marigolds, the arctic starflowers, the pink-blossomed laurel, and crispy-leaved deer cabbage—plants that will soon feed and fatten her, transforming the island's soil and waters into a lovely, bounding creature.

While the fawn keeps busy exploring, the doe's phantom grazing leads to something remarkable. She pulls from the grass a long, flaccid, shiny, crimson ribbon of afterbirth and in less than a minute she's eaten it. Then she moves around the place licking the earth and eating plants soiled with birth fluids, eliminating all signs and odors that could lead a predator to her fawn. For a while, the little deer will have no scent, so even a bear, despite its incomparable sense of smell, might pass within a few yards, yet never realize there's an easy kill nearby.

Finally, I step into the opening where the birth took place and we stand 10 feet apart. The doe walks off, stares for a long minute, then comes determinedly back, her head lowered and ears up, muscles tense and enervated as if she might charge straight into me. For the first time, the fawn turns away from her mother and sees me. Perhaps it's emblematic of the latter twentieth century that a deer born at the wild edge looks into the eyes of a man within two hours of her birth. Showing no trace of fear, she wobbles in my direction, making high-pitched bleats.

The doe comes to intervene, but the fawn keeps on moving toward me, her legs straddled, body wavering awkwardly from side to side, until I have to ease away. The doe watches for a moment, wags her ears, and then steps directly between us to prevent the fawn from advancing closer. I could easily have touched the little deer, but didn't want to afflict her with my scent, and now I could easily touch the mother deer, but it seems inconsiderate and excessive.

The fawn, who surely regards me as an ordinary fixture of the landscape, pushes eagerly for her mother's milk and I hear the soft rhythms of her suckling. Afterward she stands under the doe's belly, peering up at me with great, glinting eyes. I can scarcely believe how endearingly and impossibly tiny she is. The fawn's body is smaller than a cat's, probably weighing around five pounds, perched atop long, gangly legs about the diameter of my thumb. I suppose her back isn't more than 12 inches above the moss. She has a short, snubby face, shining black nose, and great, floppy rabbit ears. Along her backbone is a two-inch-wide strip of plain mahogany brown, with a row of about 20 white spots on either side, and her flanks are densely, randomly speckled. She pokes her snout into a juniper bush, touches brittle twigs and boughs, pulls back and vigorously shakes her head. Then she pinches her ears and slips in among the bushes.

Putting some distance between us, the doe walks easily away, but she pauses to nibble at the grass so her little one stays close. Because the wind holds perfectly, without ebbing or eddying, she's had no chance to catch my scent; otherwise she'd be gone by now. When I try to follow, she faces me and stamps all four feet as if she's running in place, as if she's trying to bluff me away, as if she'd like to drive me off but can't bring herself to do it. Embarrassed by her uneasiness and by the directness of my own intrusion, I slowly back away.

At this point the doe makes a decisive move. Turning abruptly, she circles downwind from me, and there—four hours after I first saw her—she blunders into my dense, flooding scent. She lifts her snout in little twitches, eyes wide and muscles hard, taking in a rank human pungence that tears every trace of ambivalence out of her. She stamps her front hooves, takes a few powerful bounds, stops to look back, then springs away, all four feet aloft, snorting and zigzagging, drumming the earth like a heartbeat. She halts behind a thicket and snorts repeatedly, as if she hopes to lure me away like a bird feigning a broken wing.

I have no choice but to leave quickly, after pausing for one last look at the fawn. Apparently her mother's snorts triggered an instinct to hide and freeze, because the little one is curled up beneath a juniper bush, perfectly still for the first time since she was born. Her tiny brown sides rise and fall, her great eyes stare unblinking, and she waits.

I turn away, look back once more, and hurry off so the mother can return.

The doe is still snorting when I reach the place where I left Keta, still snorting when I untie the dog and give her a grateful hug, still snorting as we hurry off down the muskeg, making plenty of noise so the mother will know we've gone.

My legs seem to fly over the moss as if I've become weightless, and my body is filled with the energy of euphoria. Keta revels back and forth in front of me, happy to be together again and jubilant in her freedom.

How to explain that the impossible has happened? This is what I've most desired for years, although I felt sure it was utterly beyond reach. Even if I'd gone to an enclosure or a zoo the timing was just too implausible. And yet I've now seen a wild deer born, and on this wild island where my love for deer was born. I remember what the Koyukon elders teach: that everything we receive from nature comes to us as a gift.

The fawn and I live from these same earthly gifts—the air we breathe, the water we drink, the food we eat. Looking at the fawn, I see myself, being born and flinging out into the world, to live and grow and die, and someday to feed other life, nurturing further generations in turn. Because I hunt in these muskegs every fall, our fates might someday conjoin. For this I feel neither guilt nor sadness, only gratitude and joyful affinity.

Lovely deer, you are always in my heart, dancing down the dawn into the light. Lovely deer, you are always in my blood, dancing down the dusk into the night.

At the outset I want to express my profound indebtedness to the researchers and writers whose published work I have used for this book. Complete citations for all references can be found in the "Literature Cited" section following these pages.

The opening epigraph is from Nanao Sakaki's poem "Fifth Deer," in *Break the Mirror* (1996). The Yup'ik Eskimo saying quoted in "Beginnings" is from Himmelheber (1993).

Chapter 1: Tracking the Deer

Because I am not a biologist, I've drawn material for this chapter mainly from books and articles by professionals in that field. The opening quote by Archibald Rutledge is from Wegner (1990). I've used Putman (1988) especially for information on evolution, taxonomy, and digestive processes. Putman's book is a readable but authoritative synopsis of the biology of deer worldwide, with emphasis on European species.

Halls's comprehensive volume on white-tailed deer (1984) provided material about evolution, species characteristics and distribution, historical and introduced populations, predation, ecological adaptation, antler development, physiology, nutrition, behavior, and the seasonal cycle. Most biologists consider Halls *the* essential reference on whitetails; I've consulted it during every aspect of my research and writing, and I highly recommend it to anyone seriously interested in these animals. A more technical but equally valuable reference on mule and black-tailed deer is Wallmo (1981), from which I've taken material on species characteristics, the seasonal cycle, and other aspects of deer biology. I've also consulted Taylor (1956), an earlier basic textbook on North American deer that is loaded with fascinating information and written in a less technical style than the Halls or Wallmo volumes.

For general readers who want to know more about the natural history of North American deer I recommend the following books. Cox and Ozoga (1988) offer a combination of exquisite, intimate photographs and a highly readable, authoritative text by an eminent expert on white-tailed deer. I have drawn extensively from Ozoga's text, especially for material on seasonal activities. I used the excellent companion volume by Geist and Francis (1990) for information about the evolution and natural history of mule deer. I've also consulted Rue (1978) for a wide range of material on deer natural history. This is a readable and beautifully photographed work on all North American deer, with some emphasis on material of interest to hunters.

I also recommend the superb volume on North America's deer edited by Gerlach,

Atwater, and Schnell (1994). This book includes essays by leading authorities on every aspect of deer biology, covering a tremendous range of information in a way that any interested person can understand.

This chapter also contains information from Seton (1929) on pre-Columbian deer populations; Klein (1981) on Coronation Island deer and wolves; Mech and Karns (1977) on relationships between wolves and whitetails; Nixon and Hansen (1992) on Illinois farmland deer; Telfer (1988) on the introduced blacktails of Kaua'i; and Hahn (1945) on the homing ability of a relocated Texas deer. Information on deer eating fish and insects is from Case and McCullough (1987), Rue (1978), and Taylor (1956). And I found Claus Chee Sonny's statement that deer "travel on lightning" in Luckert (1981).

I've drawn material on antlers from Petersen's (1991) excellent book on the subject, from Harmel, Williams, and Armstrong (1989) on antler genetics, and from Robinette, Hancock, and Jones (1977) as well as Wallmo (1981) on the relationship between leg injuries and deformed antlers. The discussion of New York coyote predation is mainly from Porter's (1992) article and the Ad Hoc Coyote Committee's report (1991).

For the material about starving deer in Oregon, I am indebted to Barry and Sandra Lopez, and to the following Oregon Department of Fish and Game biologists who generously provided information: James Lemos, Chris Wheaton, Richard Humphreys, and William Olson.

A very special note of thanks to Isabel Stirling, University of Oregon Library, who searched out countless journal and magazine articles that I've used in this and other chapters.

Chapter 2: Crossing the Wild Edge

I am grateful to Thomas Hanley (of the U.S. Forest Service's Pacific Northwest Research Station, in Juneau, Alaska) and to Katherine Parker and Michael Gillingham (both faculty members at the University of Northern British Columbia), for inviting me to visit their study site on Channel Island. I have also used material from discussions with David Klein, Terry Bowyer, and Stephen Lewis (all affiliated with the University of Alaska, Fairbanks), John Schoen (Alaska Department of Fish and Game, Anchorage), and Norman Barichello (guide-naturalist with the Oldsquaw Lodge, Whitehorse, Yukon Territory).

The chapter also contains material from many published sources. I've used Hanley's excellent technical overview (1984) for information on black-tailed deer ecology in southeastern Alaska. For project background, research methods, and goals of the Channel Island study, I have drawn from Hanley (1987), an internal document of the U.S. Forest Service in Juneau, Alaska. Results of the Channel Island study are reported in Parker, DelGiudice, and Gillingham; Parker, Gillingham, and Hanley; and Parker, Gillingham, Hanley, and Robbins (all 1993).

Other reports on deer research by Thomas Hanley include Robbins, Mole, Hagerman, and Hanley (1987); Spalinger, Hanley, and Robbins (1988); and Hanley and McKendrick (1985). Publications specifically related to deer and timber harvesting in southeast Alaska include Hanley, Robbins, and Spalinger (1989); Hanley (1993); and an edited volume by Wallmo and Schoen (1979). Related articles by Katherine Parker and Michael Gillingham include Parker, Robbins, and Hanley (1984); Bunnell, Hovey, McNay, and Parker (1990); Parker and Gillingham (1990); Gillingham (1985); Gillingham and Bunnell (1985); Gillingham and Bunnell (1989).

Material on the longevity of deer trails, as reported by Severinghaus and Rutledge, is contained in two books by Wegner (1987, 1990). Readers interested in further information about deer physiology, nutrition, and winter survival and about methods of research should see the general references listed for chapter 1.

I have not cited articles or named researchers involved with studies in which deer were subjected to cruel or highly intrusive procedures, because it would be unfair to single out a few individuals or institutions among the many who could be criticized for similar practices. It's important to note that standards for ethical treatment of study animals have become stricter, and more biologists have grown concerned about this problem. In professional wildlife journals, articles reporting on studies nearly always include a discussion of the methods used, so interested persons can explore and judge for themselves.

Chapter 3: Excess and Restraint

For almost every section of this chapter, I have drawn material from Halls's (1984) comprehensive sourcebook on white-tailed deer, especially from the fascinating, detailed, and intricately researched historical overview in that volume by Richard McCabe and Thomas McCabe. This is the best source I have found on historical relationships between deer and people in North America. I also consulted Taylor's earlier (1956) volume on North American deer for information on this subject.

The narratives by Claus Chee Sonny are from Luckert's (1981) elegant account of Navajo deer hunting traditions; this material was lightly edited and abridged for use here. Additional sources I've consulted for Native American hunting methods, uses of deer, associated rituals, conservation ethics, and the economic importance of deer include the following: Hill (1938) and Toelken (1976)—Navajo; Beaglehole (1936)—Hopi; McLoughlin (1966)—Cherokee; Turner and Santley (1979)—Huron; Webster (1979)—Huron; Nelson (1983)—Koyukon; Elder (1965)—prehistoric Missouri; Vecsey and Venables (1980)—Native American conservation; McLuhan (1971)—first-person quotes on culture change and dispossession.

Information about Native Americans' use of controlled burning to manipulate plant and animal environments is from Blackburn and Anderson (1993), Lewis (1993, 1982), Stewart (1954), and Day (1953); and material on controlled burning and deer habitat in modern wildlife management is from Dasmann (1971), Halls (1984), and Wallmo (1981).

My principal sources of information about hunting and the development of Euro-American conservation ethics include the detailed history by Reiger (1975), as well as material from Brooks (1980), Norwood (1993), and Fox (1981). The quote from early Plymouth is taken from James (1963).

The regional deer population histories are based on Severinghaus and Brown (1956)—New York; Burke (1973), Caughley (1970), Rue (1978), and Wegner (1990)—Kaibab Plateau; and Halls (1984)—New York and Kaibab.

Material on relationships between deer and logging in the continental United

States and Canada is from Halls (1984); Wallmo (1981); Schoen, Wallmo, and Kirchoff (1981); Kuhlman (1990); Alverson, Waller, and Solheim (1988); and an anonymous historical article in *Forest Watch* magazine (1991). For persons interested in forests and clear-cutting in the American West, I recommend *Last Stand* (1991), by Richard Manning.

For information on clear-cutting in the Tongass National Forest my principal sources were Schoen and Kirchoff (1988, 1990); Schoen, Kirchoff, and Hughes (1988); Kirchoff, Schoen, and Wallmo (1983); Wallmo and Schoen (1979, 1980); Hanley (1984, 1993); Klein (1992); O'Toole (1993), and Finch and Phipps (1993). The scientific and political context for understanding these articles was provided through conversations and interviews with Matthew Kirchoff and John Schoen (both employed by the Alaska Department of Fish and Game); with Thomas Hanley (U.S. Forest Service in Juneau, Alaska); and with Paul Alaback (formerly with the U.S. Forest Service in Juneau, and now with the University of Montana). Matthew Kirchoff also reviewed and edited this chapter section for accuracy and provided additional material.

Chapter 4: Embattled Sanctuaries

I am indebted to Huey Johnson (Aldo Leopold Society, Mill Valley, California), who first brought the history of Angel Island's deer to my attention; and to my friends Lee Swenson and Vijaya Nagarajan (Institute for the Study of Natural and Cultural Resources, Berkeley, California) for helping to make the Angel Island work possible.

This chapter's epigraph is from Leopold (1949). The introductory section contains information from Taylor (1956)—Aransas National Wildlife Refuge; Stokes (1989)—northern Illinois and Wisconsin; Diamond (1992)—Fontenelle Forest in Nebraska; Ad Hoc Committee (n.d.)—Yale-Myers Forest in Connecticut; Connecticut Wildlife Division (1991a, 1991b)—Bluff Point Reserve in Connecticut; and Cobb (1992)—Harriman State Park in New York.

For material on the biology and management of Angel Island's deer, I've drawn from interviews with the following people: Dale R. McCullough (Department of Forestry and Resource Management, University of California–Berkeley), Gene S. Fowler (Department of Zoology, University of Washington), Tom Lindberg and Floyd Lemley (both with the California Department of Parks and Recreation).

I consulted the following reports and articles for published material about Angel Island's deer and their management history: McCullough (1987), O'Bryan and McCullough (1985), Fowler and McCullough (1985), Botti (1985), Smith (1986), Goldsmith (1982), White (1981), and Azevedo (1985). For persons interested in a brief overview of the Angel Island deer management controversy, I especially recommend McCullough's 1987 article, which also includes a summary of conclusions from his George Reserve studies. A more detailed and technical—but quite readable—overview of research on the George Reserve deer is found in the chapter by McCullough in Halls's white-tailed deer compendium (1984).

For the section on Fire Island, I'm grateful to Susan Bergholz, my literary agent, and her husband, Bert Snyder, who made my visit to Fire Island possible and supplied information about issues surrounding deer management in Fire Island National Seashore. The accounts of Fire Island also rely on conversations with Garrett Anger, Pat Sacco, Jim and Marie Pianta, the family of Tom and Terri Carroll, Bob Spencer, and many other people who spoke with me in Davis Park and Ocean Ridge.

In the discussions of ecology, population dynamics, and management history of Fire Island deer, I've drawn extensively from an interview with Mark Lowery (senior wildlife biologist, New York Department of Environmental Conservation), as well as a discussion with Jim Eberts, chief naturalist for the National Park Service, Fire Island National Seashore.

Besides information from his own research, Mark Lowery provided several technical reports that I've used throughout this section—including O'Connell and Sayre (1989), Knoch and Lowery (1989), and two anonymously authored government documents on Fire Island deer management (1990 and n.d.). I've also taken material from National Park Service informational pamphlets about Fire Island National Seashore; from a survey of Fire Island residents' attitudes toward deer, conducted by Bob Spencer of Davis Park; and from two newspaper articles, one summarizing Fire Island's history (Anonymous, 1985) and another detailing a recent sterilization project (Tuma, 1993). The quote about ethics of capture-and-euthanasia versus shooting is from McCullough, n.d. Information about effects of deer on small mammals and songbirds is from Budiansky (1994) and DeCalesta (1994).

Information on the Mary Flagler Cary Arboretum and Center for Ecosystems Studies in Millbrook, New York, is primarily from an interview with Raymond J. Winchcombe, manager of field research facilities. Several articles by Winchcombe (1991, 1992a, 1992b, 1992c) provided further details about the Cary Arboretum's deer management program. For a broader perspective on issues related to deer and habitat in nature preserves, I have drawn from an interview with Mark Ellingwood (wildlife biologist with the New Hampshire Fish and Game Department) and from a pamphlet coauthored by Ellingwood and Caturano (1989), which evaluates different methods for controlling deer populations. This pamphlet, published by the Connecticut Department of Environmental Protection, is useful to anyone interested in management of urban and parkland deer.

My files bulge with newspaper articles about Lyme disease. Two of the most useful are from *The New York Times* (June 15, 1993, and September 21, 1993), by Elizabeth Rosenthal. I also drew material from Daniels and Falco (1989), as well as from two informational pamphlets: *Lyme Disease on Fire Island and Long Island,* prepared by the Fire Island Association, and *The Deer Tick,* published by the Cornell Cooperative Extension. In addition I've drawn facts and perspectives from a discussion with James Kazmierczak, an epidemiologist with the Wisconsin Division of Health.

Persons interested in Lyme disease may wish to contact the Lyme Disease Association of the United States, 268 North Diamond Mill Road, Clayton, Ohio 45315—a union of Lyme disease support groups, associations, networks, and educational organizations, formed in 1993. The association's quarterly newsletter is *Lyme Disease National Clarion.* For a wide-ranging collection of medical updates and patient perspectives on Lyme disease, I recommend Mermin (1991).

Chapter 5: The Backyard Wilderness

Source of the chapter epigraph is an essay titled "North of the C.P. Line," by John McPhee, in his book *Table of Contents* (1985).

In the chapter's introductory section material on establishment of urban deer herds is from an interview with William Ishmael (wildlife biologist with the Wisconsin Department of Natural Resources) and from his article on urban deer (1989). George Washington's letter, in a collection at the official residence of New Jersey's governor, was quoted in a May 1991 issue of *The New York Times Magazine.* I found stories and information about urban deer in the following newspapers: the *Capital Times* and *Wisconsin State Journal,* published in Madison, Wisconsin; the *Times Union* of Albany, New York, and the *Maine Times* of Topsham, Maine. I've drawn material from Tom Horton's excellent article about urban deer in the Northeast, titled "Deer on the Doorstep," published in *The New York Times Magazine,* April 28, 1991. Information about deer at O'Hare Airport in Chicago is from Witham and Jones (1986).

Material on relocation of Los Angeles deer is from Longhurst, Leopold, and Dasmann (1952). James Swanson, a biologist with the California Department of Fish and Game, provided information about the Ardenwood Relocation effort.

For material on Westchester County and New York State, I am indebted to Robert and Chris Reifenstuhl, and to many other Westchester County residents who spoke with me. Information about the biology and ecology of Westchester County deer was provided by Glen Cole, Steven Cook, and David Reihlman, all wildlife biologists with the New York Department of Environmental Conservation. Other information was provided by Vinnie Pascual of the Westchester County Planning Department, as well as Cirincion and Mulligan (1990).

Additional perspectives on urban deer in New York and the northeastern states came from Raymond Winchcombe (Center for Ecosystems Studies, Mary Flagler Cary Arboretum, Millbrook, New York) and from Mark Ellingwood (New Hampshire Fish and Game Department), as well as the informational booklet on urban deer management authored by Ellingwood and Caturano (1989). I also consulted the following sources for information about Westchester County deer: Connelly, Decker, and Wear (1987); Eschweiler et al. (1991); Wear and Schreiner (1987); and Reihlman (1988).

The work in River Hills was made possible by my longtime friends Donald, Elaine, Shana, and Samantha Harvey. I am also indebted to Beverly Bryant (Weir Nature Center, Milwaukee), who generously shared results of her work in River Hills as we toured the area together; and to Tom Isaacs (Wisconsin Department of Natural Resources) for updated information on River Hills deer. Beverly Bryant gave me a thick bundle of her own research materials, which I've used extensively here, including dozens of clippings from the *Milwaukee Journal, Milwaukee Sentinel, North Shore Herald* and other newspapers; reports on the 1990 deer policy survey by Friends of River Hills; her article on River Hills deer relocation (Bryant and Ishmael, 1990); and Ishmael and Rongstad's (1984) article on costs of urban deer relocation.

I've also drawn information from a series of newspaper articles by Andy Hall and Susan Lampert Smith (1991) about problems caused by high whitetail populations in

Wisconsin. For this and other chapters dealing with Wisconsin deer, I have used material generously passed along by Mark Weller of Wisconsin Public Television in Madison. Outcomes of metropolitan deer relocation projects are summarized in Jones and Witham (1990). I've consulted Ishmael and Rongstad (1984) for a cost comparison of various deer control methods.

My visit to Boulder was possible through the kindness of Dewitt Daggett and Julia Brown. Brian Peck, park ranger with the City of Boulder's Mountain Parks, provided much of the material I've used in writing this section. I also received information from Jeannie Scholl and Steve Armstead (Boulder Mountain Parks), Kathy Green and Allen Anderson (biologists with the Colorado Division of Wildlife), and Claire Martin (staff writer for the *Denver Post*), who first told me about the deer and mountain lions inhabiting suburban Boulder.

For specific information on the ecology, population, and management strategies for Boulder's deer, I've consulted two commissioned studies published by the city (City of Boulder, 1987; Western Resource Development Corporation, 1984) and a brochure titled *Boulder's Deer*, published by the city (1987). I've also drawn material from articles and letters to the editor published in the *Denver Post* and *Boulder Daily Camera*.

Information about mountain lions came primarily from the interviews, studies, and articles mentioned above, from a brochure on the subject published by the Colorado Division of Wildlife (n.d.), and from Harley G. Shaw's excellent book on cougars (1989).

Chapter 6: The Deer Capital of Texas

Information, experiences, and perspectives underlying this chapter came through the extraordinary kindness of Bart and Debbie Gillan, who hosted me on the Slator Ranch. I consulted a magazine article by Cox (1991) for additional material about Slator Ranch's deer program. Throughout this chapter, I have drawn from discussions with many hunters—named and unnamed—whose teachings greatly enriched my visit to the Slator Ranch.

Dewitt Daggett, sound recordist and founder of Audio Press, first led me to the subject of deer and hunting in the Texas ranch country. Besides helping with initial contacts, Dewitt joined me for several days in Texas and asked penetrating questions that helped to shape my inquiries.

Much information found in this chapter is based on discussions with a contingent of widely experienced field biologists: Fielding Harwell (Texas Parks and Wildlife Department); William Armstrong, Donnie Harmel, and Joe Johnson (Kerr Wildlife Management Area); and Rodney Marburger (private consultant with Wildlife, Incorporated). All are stationed in or near Kerrville, Texas. Like the Gillans, these practical-minded researchers helped me to gain an entirely new comprehension of wildlife, livestock, and habitat management in ranch country.

For material about deer in the Hill Country economy, business, and lifeway I've drawn from conversations with Bryan Miiller and Chad Parker of Miiller's Meats in Llano, Jackie Hatfield of the Llano Chamber of Commerce, David Willman of the Llano National Bank, owners and operators of the Llano Feed and Supply, and the folks at Heart O' the Hills Taxidermy Shop in Kerrville. Information about the economic importance of deer hunting in Texas is based on a 1994 survey by South-wick Associates, quoted in Merwin (1994), and from Gough (1991). Statistics on Texas statewide and regional deer harvests are from Boydston (1990) and the Texas Parks and Wildlife Department (1991).

I consulted a vintage account by Hahn (1945) and a modern synopsis by Teer (1984) for detailed accounts of whitetail history, ecology, and management in the Ed-wards Plateau region. For the discussion of quality deer management programs, I've drawn from Marburger (1983), Armstrong (1991), Thomas and Marburger (1965), Harwell, Harmel, and Perkins (1986), and Harmel and Litton (1981). An article by Wuerthner (1989) provided useful information about grazing on private and public lands in the United States. I recommend these sources to anyone interested in Hill Country deer or the ways hunting and grazing can be managed to affect the health of deer populations.

Most of my information about Holistic Resource Management came from discus-sions with Bart Gillan. Readers interested in the subject may wish to read Allan Sa-vory's text (1988). An article by Brown (1994) provides a brief overview and critique of Savory's concepts, emphasizing biodiversity concerns in arid environments.

For the discussion of exotic wildlife species I've drawn information from inter-views with William Armstrong and Donnie Harmel of the Kerr Wildlife Manage-ment Area, and from Mike and David Hughes of Exotic Game Ranching in Ingram, Texas. I also consulted the following published sources: Roybal (1987), Armstrong and Harmel (1981), Butts et al. (1982), and Ervin, Demarais, and Osborn (1992). Any-one interested in the breeding, sale, and raising of deer or exotic wildlife from an in-dustry perspective may wish to consult the Exotic Wildlife Association in Ingram, Texas, or the North American Deer Association in Reston, Virginia.

I found information about hunting lease prices in a listing by the Texas Wildlife Association (1991). This organization, located in San Antonio, represents private wildlife management and property rights interests in the state. Published materials I've used to summarize the debate over deer ranching, fee hunting, and "Texas-style game management" include Geist (1987, 1992), Benson (1992), Heberlein (1987a), and Kellert (1984).

For persons interested in any aspect of deer hunting, I strongly recommend the three-volume series by Robert Wegner (1984, 1987, 1990), which I have consulted for material about quality deer management, characteristics of wild venison, and history and sociology of trophy hunting. I also recommend Wegner's immensely useful bib-liography of deer and deer hunting (1994), which contains more than 1,000 annotated entries.

The statistics on American women hunters are from the U.S. Department of the Interior (1988), an exhaustive and detailed compilation of data on hunting, fishing, and other wildlife-related activities in the United States.

For anyone wishing to understand more about personal involvement with hunt-ing and its associated subculture, I recommend the following works by hunters who also happen to be eloquent writers. Bass (1985), Kilgo (1988), and Gish (1992) are sen-sitive and evocative first-person accounts of deer hunting, set respectively in Texas,

South Carolina, and Oklahoma. Kerasote (1993) is a penetrating analysis of hunting in all its modern varieties. Other recent books on North American hunting traditions include Swan (1995), Miller (1992), Marks (1991), and the superb anthology by Petersen (1996).

Chapter 7: Opening Weekend

This chapter's epigraph is from the foreword to Leopold (1949). In tangible and intangible ways far beyond recounting, my late parents, Robert and Florence Nelson, made possible the work underlying this chapter and all others containing material about Wisconsin deer.

For providing the foundation for this chapter, I am deeply grateful to Jim Mlsna and his brother Mark Mlsna; to Janet Mlsna; and to Dan, John, Mike, Ken, Stanley, Pete, Tom, Mike Jr., Matthew, Mark, Ben, and all the others in their hunting group; as well as Donald Harvcy, who came up with the idea.

I have also relied on the knowledge and generosity of many people affiliated with the Wisconsin Department of Natural Resources, especially William Ishmael, John Olson, Harry Libby, Jordan Petchenik, Kevin Wallenfang, Steve Miller, Ralph Christianson, Steve Crary, and Doris Rusch. A large body of information was also kindly provided by Thomas Heberlein, rural sociologist with the University of Wisconsin in Madison.

Published sources I've consulted include the following. On the history and management of Wisconsin deer: Ishmael (1990), McCaffery (1990), Swift (1946), Hofacker (1992), Creed et al. (1984), Creed and Haberland (1980), Isaac (1990), Hall and Smith (1991), and Wegner (1987). On state hunting regulations and hunters' attitudes toward these regulations: Heberlein (1989) and Petchenik (1992). On the economics of Wisconsin deer hunting: Libby (1991) and Heberlein (1991). On poaching: Wegner (1987), Daniel (n.d.), and Jameson (1988). And on hunter safety: Castaneda (1992) and Famighetti (1995). On hunter ethics and stages: Jackson and Norton (1980), Wegner (1984), and Posewitz (1994). Note also that some of these sources cover more than one of the topics listed.

I've drawn material on the sociology, attitudes, and motivations of hunters from Heberlein and Laybourne (1978), Heberlein (1987b), Heberlein and Keplinger (n.d.), Petchenik (1988), Enck and Decker (1991), Decker and Mattfield (1988), Hautaluoma and Brown (1979), More (1973), Jackson and Norton (1980), Wegner (1984), and Potter, Hendee, and Clark (1973). These are only a few references from the voluminous literature on hunter sociology. Persons interested in these subjects might begin with materials published by the Human Dimensions Research Unit, affiliated with Cornell University in Ithaca, New York.

For information related to each of the topics above and for news accounts of Wisconsin's recent deer hunting seasons I have relied on dozens of articles from the *Wisconsin State Journal* and *Capital Times,* both newspapers published in Madison. Other material in this chapter came from the proceedings of a conference on North America's hunting heritage (State of Montana, 1992), especially from articles by Ann S. Causey, Robert T. Delfay, Dennis S. Elliot, Mike Hayden, William P. Horn, John G. Mitchell, and Jim Peterson.

Persons interested in ethical and responsible hunting may wish to contact Orion— The Hunters Institute, P.O. Box 5099, Helena, Montana 59604.

Chapter 8: In Search of Eden

For the information and experiences on which this chapter is based, I am grateful to Buzz Kemper and Jodi Kemper, and to John Barnes, as well as Lu, Penny, Mary, Darcy, and the other members of Alliance for Animals and Voice for Animals who shared their philosophy and beliefs with me and had the generosity of spirit to allow a hunter into their midst.

I have also drawn extensively, here and in other chapters, from the teachings of elders and hunters in Alaskan Native villages where I've spent time over the past 30 years. My profound thanks especially to the people of Wainwright, Chalkyitsik, Huslia, and Hughes, Alaska.

Important and clearly written books setting forth the animal rights viewpoint include Singer (1975) and Regan (1982). For material on the history and philosophy of animal rights and antihunting proponents, and for critiques of these viewpoints, I have drawn from Amory (1992), Conniff (1990), Knox (1991), and Satchell and Schrof (1990). Baker (1985) is the most important sourcebook I have found on antihunting philosophy, presenting both ecological and moral arguments, although this reference is flawed by inaccurate and misleading use of scientific information. Shedd (1991) presents a survey of hunter harassment laws in the United States. The article by Shedd and another by Atwill (1991) offer sympathetic discussions of hunting groups formed in response to antihunt activism.

I have also used, and strongly recommend, an insightful, balanced examination of hunting morality by Causey (1989). A perceptive essay by Dean (1992) explores the moral dimensions of taking plant life, from the perspective of a nonhunter and vegetarian. To understand more about how worldview affects people's attitudes about hunting, I recommend Dizard's book (1994) examining conflicts over managing deer in the Quabbin Reservation.

For sociological material on hunters and antihunters, I consulted Applegate (1975) and Kellert (1978). My principal sources on public attitudes about hunting included Mealey (1994), Satchell and Schrof (1990), and Applegate (1975). The discussion of Walt Disney's film *Bambi* derives from critical retrospectives by Lutts (1992) and Cartmill (1993), and from a beautifully illustrated account of the film's creation, by Johnston and Thomas (1990), who were among its original animators.

Information about feral goats on San Clemente Island is from Knox (1991); and the account of Everglades deer reduction is based on a report by the Florida Game and Fresh Water Fish Commission (1983).

The discussion of Euro-American views of nature and human animality derives from the fascinating historical study by Thomas (1983). Readers interested in traditional hunting and relationships to the natural world among Iñupiaq Eskimos, Gwich'in Indians, and Koyukon Indians may wish to look at Nelson (1969, 1973, 1980, 1983). There are many other books containing excellent descriptions of Eskimo hunting, and a long list of books that eloquently evoke the spirituality of nature in Native American communities.

Chapter 9: The Hidden Harvest

The chapter's introductory section includes material on the whitetail diet from Wegner (1984, 1987), on agricultural lands and deer from Halls (1984), and on the history of California agricultural damage from Longhurst, Leopold, and Dasmann (1952). The quotation about deer damage in early England is from Thomas (1983).

My work in New York was made possible by the kindness and hospitality of Robert and Chris Reifenstuhl in Westchester County, as well as that of my longtime friends George and Sharon Gmelch, of the Anthropology Department at Union College in Schenectady.

To assure their privacy and to protect their livelihoods, I have changed the names of farmers in Wisconsin, New York, and California who contributed information used in this chapter. None of the farmers requested anonymity, so this decision—which I hope they will understand and support—was mine alone.

Material about Westchester County deer and agriculture is mostly from area farmers who were kind enough to discuss their situations with me—especially "Tom Sampson," "Bob Stroud," "Jane Willman," and "John Gellerman." I have also used information provided by New York Department of Environmental Conservation biologists Steven Cook, Glen Cole, and Karl Parker. And I consulted the report by Sayre and Decker (1990) on whitetail damage to commercial nurseries in New York State.

In the section on California, I am grateful for the help and information provided by "Kim Foster"; for kind assistance given by Lee Swenson and Vijaya Nagarajan; and for the broader view of California deer and agriculture offered by Sonke Mastrup of the California Department of Fish and Game. Again in this discussion, I drew historical material from Longhurst, Leopold, and Dasmann (1952).

In the sections on Wisconsin deer and agriculture, I am greatly indebted to Dan Hirchert and Wade Owens, of the U.S. Department of Agriculture's Animal Damage Control agency in Waupun, Wisconsin.

I am also grateful to Jim Heinrich, supervisor of the Waupun office, for his willingness to help in this project and for making the trips with Dan and Wade possible; to Laine Stowell, head of the Wisconsin Department of Natural Resources' deer damage program, for the information he passed along; to William Ishmael, deer biologist with the Wisconsin Department of Natural Resources, for his abundant knowledge and insights; and to John Olson and Steve Miller, also of the Wisconsin DNR, for the information they provided. My thanks to "Carl Burton," "Bill Mackinnon," and the other farmers who kindly took the time to explain their perspectives on balancing agriculture with deer in Wisconsin today.

I have also consulted the following references and documents in compiling the Wisconsin material: Swift (1946)—historical perspectives; Petersen (1994)—history and overview of the U.S. Department of Agriculture's Animal Damage Control program; Wegner (1984, 1987)—information on corn and alfalfa; Hall and Smith (1991)—general information on agricultural damage in the state.

For specific information about Wisconsin's deer damage program, I've drawn from Craven and Hygnstrom (1986), the Wisconsin Agricultural Reporting Service (1984), the Joint Legislative Audit Committee (1988), as well as documents, forms, and newsletters provided by the Wisconsin Department of Natural Resources and the USDA Animal Damage Control program.

Information about crops eaten by deer is from the growers themselves, from wildlife managers in affected regions, and from the following published sources: Halls (1984), Taylor (1956), Wegner (1984), Cox and Ozoga (1988), and Gerlach, Atwater, and Schnell (1994). The brief comments and quotations about soybeans are from Kennedy (1992); the quotation about eating as an agricultural act is from Berry (1990).

Chapter 10: Heart of the Hunter

Source of the epigraph is Gary Snyder's poem "One Should Not Talk to a Skilled Hunter About What Is Forbidden by the Buddha," published in *Turtle Island* (1974).

This chapter happens to recount a time on the island spent only with Keta, but it rests on a foundation of many years afoot in these same places with my partner, Nita Couchman, and with our son, Ethan Esterline. Our dogs, Shungnak and Keta, have added richness to these island experiences, especially by giving us clues about a world of the mind and senses that would otherwise completely elude us.

Many of the pleasures I've found in the island and its deer, and much that I've learned about them, I owe to friends and teachers who have shared in it. I can only mention a few (in no particular order): Mark Gorman and Nancy Knapp, Robert Rose and Barbara Teepe, John and Jan Straley, Steve Reifenstuhl and Andrea Thomas, Jay Zischke and Karen LeGrand, Dave and Paulla Hardy, James Mahan, and Ronald Kreher.

My entire sense for the natural world, and what little I know of the hunter's way, I owe to my Native American teachers in the villages of Wainwright, Point Hope, Huslia, Hughes, Chalkyitsik, Ambler, and Shungnak, Alaska. Among those who have been most important to me are Steven and Catherine Attla, Edwin and Lydia Simon, Chief Henry, Eliza Jones, Fred Bifelt, Lavine Williams, Joe Beetus, and Tony Sam; Waldo Bodfish and his sons, Wesley Ekak and Weir Negovanna; Sam Herbert Jr., Harry Carroll, and Moses Peter. In this chapter, I have specifically paraphrased or quoted teachings from Catherine Attla (Koyukon), Eliza Jones (Koyukon), Lavine Williams (Koyukon), and Mo Johnson (Tlingit).

Whatever I have seen and written about deer, bears, and other wildlife in this part of the world is much influenced by the insights of biologists who have studied these animals, written about them, and passed some of their knowledge along to me. These people include Matthew Kirchoff, John Schoen, Thomas Hanley, Katherine Parker, Michael Gillingham, Steven Reifenstuhl, David Hardy, Loyal Johnson, David Klein, and Olof Wallmo.

Ad Hoc Committee. "Ad Hoc Committee on the Management of the Yale-Myers Forest." New Haven: Yale University, n.d. Mimeographed.

Ad Hoc Coyote Committee. *The Status and Impact of Eastern Coyotes in Northern New York.* Albany and Ithaca: New York State Department of Environmental Conservation and Cornell Cooperative Extension, 1991.

Alaback, Paul B. "Forest Community Structural Changes During Secondary Succession in Southeast Alaska." In *Forest Succession and Stand Development Research in the Northwest: Proceedings of the Symposium.* Corvallis, Ore.: Forest Research Laboratory, 1982.

Alverson, William S., Donald M. Waller, and Stephen L. Solheim. "Forests Too Deer: Edge Effects in Northern Wisconsin." *Conservation Biology* 2:4, 1988.

Amory, Cleveland. Response to a question: "If you had absolute power . . . ?" *Sierra,* May–June 1992.

Anonymous. "Fire Island: The Lonely History of a Barrier Beach." *Fire Island Tide,* July 12, 1985.

———. *Statement of Deer and Vegetation Management Options.* Patchogue, N.Y.: Fire Island National Seashore, n.d.

———. *Comments on the Deer and Vegetation Management Plan Proposed for Fire Island National Seashore.* Stony Brook: New York State Department of Environmental Conservation, 1990.

———. "The Citizen's Guide to the Timber Industry." *Forest Watch* 12:1, 1991.

Applegate, James E. "Attitudes Toward Deer Hunting in New Jersey: A Second Look." *Wildlife Society Bulletin* 3:1, 1975.

Armstrong, William E. *Managing Habitat for White-Tailed Deer in the Hill Country Area of Texas.* Austin: Texas Parks and Wildlife Division, 1991.

Armstrong, William E., and Donnie Harmel. "Exotic Mammals Competing with the Natives." *Texas Parks and Wildlife Magazine,* February 1981.

Atwill, Lionel. "What Is the UBNJ? And How Is It Converting Anti-Hunters?" *Field and Stream,* November 1991.

Azevedo, Margaret. "Thinning the Herds of Deer on Angel Island." *Mill Valley Record/Marin Messenger,* October 2, 1985.

Baker, Ron. *The American Hunting Myth.* New York: Vantage Press, 1985.

Bass, Rick. *The Deer Pasture.* New York: W. W. Norton, 1985.

Beaglehole, Ernest. *Hopi Hunting and Hunting Ritual.* Yale University Publications in Anthropology, No. 4. New Haven: Yale University Press, 1936.

Beals, Ralph L. "Aboriginal Culture of the Cahita Indians." *Ibero-America* 19. Berkeley: University of California Press, 1943.

Benson, Delwin E. "Commercialization of Wildlife: A Value-Added Incentive for Conservation." In Robert D. Brown, ed., *The Biology of Deer.* New York: Springer-Verlag, 1992.

Berry, Wendell. "The Pleasures of Eating." In Robert Clark, ed., *Our Sustainable Table.* San Francisco: North Point Press, 1990.

Blackburn, Thomas C., and Kat Anderson. *Before the Wilderness: Environmental Management by Native Californians.* Menlo Park, Calif.: Ballena Press, 1993.

Botti, Fred L. "Chemosterilants as a Management Option for Deer on Angel Island: Lessons Learned." *Cal-Neva Wildlife Transactions,* 1985.

Boydston, Glenn. *White-tailed Deer Harvest Surveys: Federal Aid Project No. W-125-R-1.* Austin: Texas Parks and Wildlife Department, October 20, 1990.

Brooks, Paul. *Speaking for Nature.* San Francisco: Sierra Club Books, 1980.

Brown, David E. "Out of Africa." *Wilderness,* Winter 1994.

Brown, Lester R., Hal Kane, and Ed Ayers. *Vital Signs 1993.* Washington, D.C.: Worldwatch Institute, 1993.

Bryant, Beverly K., and William Ishmael. "Movement and Mortality Patterns of Resident and Translocated Suburban White-Tailed Deer." *Proceedings of the National Urban Wildlife Conference,* Columbia, Md., 1990.

Budiansky, Stephen. "Deer, Deer Everywhere." *U.S. News & World Report,* November 21, 1994.

Bunnell, F. L., F. W. Hovey, R. S. McNay, and K. L. Parker. "Forest Cover, Snow Conditions, and Deer." *Canadian Journal of Zoology* 68, 1990.

Burke, C. John. "The Kaibab Deer Incident: A Long-Persisting Myth." *BioScience* 23:2, 1973.

Butts, Gregory L., Melvin J. Anderegg, William C. Armstrong, Donnie E. Harmel, Charles W. Ramsey, and Silvestre H. Sorola. *Food Habits of Five Exotic Ungulates on Kerr Wildlife Management Area, Texas.* Austin: Texas Parks and Wildlife Department, Technical Series No. 30, 1982.

Cartmill, Matt. "The Bambi Syndrome." *Natural History,* June 1993.

Case, David J., and Dale R. McCullough. "The White-Tailed Deer of North Manitou Island." *Hilgardia* 55:9, 1987.

Castaneda, Carol J. "Carelessness, Hunters, Equal a Deadly Season." *USA Today,* December 2, 1992.

Caton, John D. *The Antelope and Deer of North America.* New York: Hurd and Houghton, 1877.

Caughley, Graeme. "Eruption of Ungulate Populations, with Emphasis on the Himalayan Thar in New Zealand." *Ecology* 51:1, 1970.

Causey, Ann S. "On the Morality of Hunting." *Environmental Ethics* 11:4, 1989.

Cirincion, William G., and Jerry Mulligan. *Land Use Trends in Westchester County: 1978–1988.* White Plains, N.Y.: Westchester County Department of Planning, 1990.

City of Boulder. *Mule Deer Study: Update.* Boulder, Colo.: City of Boulder, Parks and Recreation Department, 1987.

Cobb, Thomas L. "Deer Management Unit-53: A Chronicle of an Interagency Cooperative Effort to Protect Harriman State Park from the Ravages of Deer Overpopulation and Habitat Degradation." *The Conservationist,* September–October, 1982.

Colorado Division of Wildlife. *Living with Wildlife in Lion Country.* Denver, Colo.: Colorado Division of Wildlife, n.d.

Connecticut Wildlife Division. "Bluff Point Controlled Deer Reduction." *Scope: Connecticut's Wildlife Publication* 11:1, 1991a.

———. "A Response to the Bluff Point Deer Hunt." *Scope: Connecticut's Wildlife Publication* 11:4, 1991b.

Connelly, Nancy A., Daniel J. Decker, and Sam Wear. *White-tailed Deer in Westchester County, New York: Public Perceptions and Preferences.* Ithaca, N.Y.: Human Dimensions Research Unit, Cornell University, 1987.

Conniff, Richard. "Fuzzy-Wuzzy Thinking About Animal Rights." *Audubon,* November 1990.

Cox, Daniel J., and John J. Ozoga. *Whitetail Country.* Minoqua, Wis.: NorthWord Press, 1988.

Cox, Jim. "Bucking Tradition: Llano County Ranch Finds the Formula for Growing Bigger Whitetail." *Texas Parks and Wildlife Magazine,* June 1991.

Craven, Scott, and Scott Hygnstrom. *Controlling Deer Damage in Wisconsin.* Madison: University of Wisconsin, Cooperative Extension Service, 1986.

Creed, William A., and Frank Haberland. "Deer Herd Management: Putting It All Together. In Ruth L. Hine and Susan Hchls, eds., *White-Tailed Deer Population and Management in the North Central States: Proceedings of a Symposium.* The Wildlife Society, 1980.

Creed, William A., Frank Haberland, Bruce E. Kohn, and Keith R. McCaffery. "Harvest Management: The Wisconsin Experience." In Lowell K. Halls, ed., *White-tailed Deer: Ecology and Management.* Harrisburg, Pa.: Stackpole Books, 1984.

Daniel, John. "Impacts of Wisconsin's High Fines on Deer Poaching." Madison: Wisconsin Bureau of Law Enforcement, n.d. Mimeographed.

Daniels, Thomas J., and Richard C. Falco. "The Lyme Disease Invasion." *Natural History,* July 1989.

Dasmann, William. *If Deer Are to Survive.* Harrisburg, Pa.: Stackpole Books, 1971.

Day, Gordon M. "The Indian as an Ecological Factor in the Northeastern Forest." *Ecology* 34:2, 1953.

Dean, Barbara. "Hunting a Christmas Tree." *Orion,* Winter 1992.

DeCalesta, David. "Impact of Deer on Interior Forest Songbirds in Northwestern Pennsylvania." *Journal of Wildlife Management* 58, 1994.

Decker, Daniel J., and George F. Mattfeld. *Hunters and Hunting in New York.* Ithaca, N.Y.: Human Dimensions Research Unit, Cornell University, 1988.

Diamond, Jared. "Must We Shoot Deer to Save Nature?" *Natural History,* August 1992.

Dizard, Jan E. *Going Wild: Hunting, Animal Rights, and the Contested Meaning of Nature*. Amherst: University of Massachusetts Press, 1994.

Elder, William H. "Primeval Deer Hunting Pressures Revealed by Remains from American Indian Middens." *Journal of Wildlife Management* 29:2, 1965.

Ellingwood, Mark R., and Suzanne L. Caturano. *An Evaluation of Deer Management Options*. Connecticut Department of Environmental Conservation, Wildlife Bureau, 1989.

Enck, Jody W., and Daniel J. Decker. *Hunters' Perspectives on Satisfying and Dissatisfying Aspects of the Deer-Hunting Experience*. Ithaca, N.Y.: Human Dimensions Research Unit, Cornell University, 1991.

Ervin, R. Terry, Stephen Demarais, and David A. Osborn. "Legal Status of Exotic Deer Throughout the United States." In Robert D. Brown, ed., *The Biology of Deer*. New York: Springer-Verlag, 1992.

Eschweiler, Peter Q., et al. *White-Tailed Deer Report*. White Plains, N.Y.: Westchester County Department of Planning, 1991.

Evers, Larry, and Felipe S. Molina. *Yaqui Deer Songs: Maso Bwikam*. Tucson: University of Arizona Press, 1987.

Famighetti, Robert, ed. *World Almanac and Book of Facts*. Mahwah, N.J.: Funk and Wagnalls, 1995.

Finch, Chris, and Allan Phipps. *Alaska Rainforest Atlas: The Ecosystem, the People, the Challenge*. Juneau, Alaska: Southeast Alaska Conservation Council and Alaska Center for the Environment, 1993.

Florida Game and Fresh Water Fish Commission. *Everglades Emergency Deer Hunt Controversy*. Tallahassee: Florida Game and Fresh Water Fish Commission, 1983.

Fowler, Gene S., and Dale R. McCullough. Angel Island Deer Sterilization Follow-up Study. Berkeley: University of California, Department of Forestry and Research Management, unpublished research proposal, 1985.

Fox, Stephen. *The American Conservation Movement*. Madison: University of Wisconsin Press, 1981.

Geist, Valerius. "Three Threats to Wildlife Conservation." *Deer and Deer Hunting*, February 1987.

———. "Deer Ranching for Products and Paid Hunting: Threat to Conservation and Biodiversity by Luxury Markets." In Robert D. Brown, ed., *The Biology of Deer*. New York: Springer-Verlag, 1992.

Geist, Valerius, and Michael H. Francis. *Mule Deer Country*. Minoqua, Wis.: NorthWord Press, 1990.

Gerlach, Duane, Sally Atwater, and Judith Schnell, eds. *Deer*. Mechanicsburg, Pa.: Stackpole Books, 1994.

Gillingham, Michael P. *Foraging Behaviour of Captive Black-Tailed Deer*. Vancouver, B.C.: University of British Columbia, Ph.D. thesis, 1985.

Gillingham, Michael P., and F. L. Bunnell. "Reliability of Motion-Sensitive Radio-Collars for Estimating Activity of Black-Tailed Deer." *Journal of Wildlife Management* 49, 1985.

———. "Black-Tailed Deer Foraging Bouts: Dynamic Events." *Canadian Journal of Zoology* 67, 1989.

Gish, Robert F. *Songs of My Hunter Heart: A Western Kinship.* Ames, Iowa: Iowa State University Press, 1992.

Goldsmith, Audrey E. "The Angel Island Deer Herd: A Case History of Wildlife Management Controversy." *Cal-Neva Wildlife Transactions,* 1982.

Gough, Buddy. "Deer Season Means Big Bucks for Area." *San Antonio Light,* November 10, 1991.

Hahn, Henry C., Jr. *The White-Tailed Deer in the Edwards Plateau Region of Texas.* Austin: Texas Game, Fish, and Oyster Commission, 1945.

Hall, Andy, and Susan Lampert Smith. "The Deermakers: Wisconsin's Runaway Herd." *Wisconsin State Journal,* November 17–20, 1991.

Halls, Lowell K., ed. *White-Tailed Deer: Ecology and Management.* Harrisburg, Pa.: Stackpole Books, 1984.

Hanley, Thomas A. *Relationships between Sitka Black-Tailed Deer and their Habitat.* Portland, Ore.: U.S. Forest Service, Pacific Northwest Forest and Range Experiment Station, General Technical Report PNW-168, 1984.

———. "Study Plan: The Nutritional Basis for Habitat Selection by Black-Tailed Deer." Juneau, Alaska: U.S. Forest Service, 1987.

———. "Balancing Economic Development, Biological Conservation, and Human Culture: The Sitka Black-Tailed Deer as an Ecological Indicator." *Biological Conservation* 66, 1993.

Hanley, Thomas A., and J. D. McKendrick. "Potential Nutritional Limitations for Black-Tailed Deer in a Spruce-Hemlock Forest, Southeastern Alaska." *Journal of Wildlife Management* 49:1, 1985.

Hanley, Thomas A., Charles T. Robbins, and Donald E. Spalinger. *Forest Habitats and the Nutritional Ecology of Black-Tailed Deer: A Research Synthesis with Implications for Forest Management.* Portland, Ore.: U.S. Department of Agriculture, Forest Service, Pacific Northwest Research Station, 1989.

Harmel, Donnie E., and George W. Litton. *Deer Management in the Edwards Plateau of Texas.* Austin: Texas Parks and Wildlife Department, 1981.

Harmel, Donnie E., John D. Williams, and William E. Armstrong. *On Antler Development and Body Size of White-Tailed Deer.* Texas Parks and Wildlife Department, FA Report Series, No. 26, 1989.

Harwell, Fielding, Donnie Harmel, and Jim Perkins. *A Tale of Two Deer Herds.* Texas Parks and Wildlife Department, 1986.

Hasselton, William T., C. W. Severinghaus, and John E. Tanck. "Deer Facts from Seneca Depot." *The New York State Conservationist,* October–November 1965.

Hautaluoma, Jacob, and Perry J. Brown. "Attributes of the Deer Hunting Experience: A Cluster-Analytic Study." *Journal of Leisure Research,* 4th Quarter, 1979.

Heberlein, Thomas A. "Leasing and Fee Hunting in the United States." Paper Presented at the 18th Congress of the International Union of Game Biologists, Krakow, Poland, 1987a.

———. "Stalking the Predator: A Profile of the American Hunter." *Environment* 29:7, 1987b.

———. "Attitudes and Environmental Management." *Journal of Social Issues* 45:1, 1989.

————. "Changing Attitudes and Funding for Wildlife: Preserving the Sport Hunter." *Wildlife Society Bulletin* 19:4, 1991.

Heberlein, Thomas A., and Bruce Laybourne. "The Wisconsin Deer Hunter: Social Characteristics, Attitudes, and Preferences for Proposed Hunting Season Changes." Madison: University of Wisconsin, School of Natural Resources, working paper No. 10, 1978.

Heberlein, Thomas A., and Kent E. Keplinger. "Hunter Surveys and Wildlife Management: Wisconsin's Experience." *Transactions of the Forty-ninth North American Wildlife and Natural Resources Conference,* n.d.

Hill, W. W. *The Agricultural and Hunting Methods of the Navajo Indians.* New Haven: Yale University Publications in Anthropology, No. 18, 1938.

Himmelheber, Hans. *Eskimo Artists.* Fairbanks: University of Alaska Press, 1993.

Hofacker, Al. "Where Were Those 1.35 Million Deer?" *Wisconsin Deer Report.* Appleton, Wis.: Stump Sitters, 1992.

Horton, Tom. "Deer on the Doorstep." *New York Times Magazine,* April 28, 1991.

Isaac, Tom. "Whitetail Forecast: 1990." *Wisconsin Natural Resources,* August 1990.

Ishmael, William E. "In a Rut." *Wisconsin Natural Resources,* October 1989.

————. "Counting Heads in the Herd." *Wisconsin Natural Resources,* October 1990.

Ishmael, William E., and Orrin J. Rongstad, "Economics of an Urban Deer-Removal Program." *Wildlife Society Bulletin* 12:4, 1984.

Jackson, Robert M., and Robert Norton. "Phases: The Personal Evolution of the Sport Hunter." *Wisconsin Sportsman* 9:6, 1980.

James, Sydney V., Jr., ed. *Three Visitors to Early Plymouth.* Plymouth, Mass.: Plimouth Plantation, 1963.

Jameson, Dennis. "Deer Diary: Travel with a Warden." *Wisconsin Natural Resources,* 1988.

Johnston, Ollie, and Frank Thomas. *Walt Disney's Bambi: The Story and the Film.* New York: Stewart, Tabori, and Chang, 1990.

Joint Legislative Audit Committee. *An Evaluation of Wildlife Damage Abatement and Claims Program.* Madison: Wisconsin State Legislature, 1988.

Jones, Jon M., and James H. Witham. "Post-Translocation Survival and Movements of Metropolitan White-Tailed Deer." *Wildlife Society Bulletin* 18:4, 1990.

Kellert, Stephen R. "Attitudes and Characteristics of Hunters and Anti-Hunters." *Transactions of the North American Wildlife and Natural Resources Conference* 43, 1978.

————. "Wildlife Values and the Private Landowner." *American Forests,* November 1984.

Kennedy, Pagan. "Soy Anything." *Voice,* May 5, 1992.

Kerasote, Ted. *Blood Ties: Nature, Culture, and the Hunt.* New York: Random House, 1993.

————. "The Overpopulating of America." *Sports Afield,* January 1993.

Kilgo, James. *Deep Enough for Ivorybills.* New York: Doubleday, 1988.

Kirchoff, Matthew, and John W. Schoen. "Forest Cover and Snow: Implications for Deer Habitat in Southeast Alaska." *Journal of Wildlife Management* 51:1, 1987.

Kirchoff, Matthew, John W. Schoen, and Olof C. Wallmo. "Black-tailed Deer Use in Relation to Forest Clear-Cut Edges in Southeastern Alaska." *Journal of Wildlife Management*: 47:2, 1983.

Klein, David R. "The Problems of Overpopulation of Deer in North America." In Robert D. Brown, ed., *Problems in Management of Locally Abundant Wild Mammals*. San Diego: Academic Press, 1981.

———. "The Status of Deer in a Changing World Environment." In Robert D. Brown, ed., *The Biology of Deer*. New York: Springer-Verlag, 1992.

Knoch, Harold W., and Mark D. Lowery. *The 1988/89 Deer Hunt on Fire Island National Seashore*. Stony Brook: New York Department of Environmental Conservation, 1989.

Knox, Margaret L. "The Rights Stuff." *Buzzworm*, May–June 1991.

Kuhlman, Walter. "A Biological Attack on Timber Primacy." *Forest Watch* 11:1, 1990.

Leopold, Aldo. *A Sand County Almanac*. New York: Oxford University Press, 1949.

Lewis, Henry T. "Fire Technology and Resource Management in Aboriginal North America and Australia." In Nancy M. Williams and Eugene S. Hunn, eds., *Resource Managers: North American and Australian Hunter-Gatherers*. Washington, D.C.: American Association for the Advancement of Science, 1982.

———. "Patterns of Indian Burning in California." In Thomas C. Blackburn and Kat Anderson, eds., *Before the Wilderness*. Menlo Park, Calif.: Ballena Press, 1993.

Libby, Harry. "1991 Deer Hunting Forecast: Lots of Deer and a Boost to Local Economies." Madison: Wisconsin Department of Natural Resources, 1991. Mimeographed.

Longhurst, William M., A. Starker Leopold, and Raymond F. Dasmann. *A Survey of California Deer Herds*. Sacramento: California Department of Fish and Game, Game Bulletin No. 6, 1952.

Luckert, Karl W. *The Navajo Hunter Tradition*. Tucson: University of Arizona Press, 1981.

Lutts, Ralph H. "The Trouble with Bambi: Walt Disney's Bambi and the American Vision of Nature." *Forest and Conservation History* 36, October 1992.

Manning, Richard. *Last Stand: Logging, Journalism, and the Case for Humility*. Salt Lake City: Peregrine Smith, 1991.

Marburger, Rodney G. *The King of Deer*. Kerrville, Texas: Wildlife Publications, 1983.

Marks, Stuart A. *Southern Hunting in Black and White: Nature, History, and Ritual in a Carolina Community*. Lawrenceville, N.J.: Princeton University Press, 1991.

Martin, Claire. "Deer Chomp Boulder Roses as Buck Passes to Council." *Denver Post*, July 22, 1988.

McCabe, Richard E., and Thomas R. McCabe. "Of Slings and Arrows: An Historical Retrospective." In Lowell K. Halls, ed., *White-Tailed Deer: Ecology and Management*. Harrisburg, Pa.: Stackpole Books, 1984.

McCaffery, Keith R. "Wisconsin Deer Status Report—1989." *Proceedings of the Midwest Deer and Turkey Study Group*, 1990. Mimeographed.

McCullough, Dale R. "Lessons from the George Reserve, Michigan." In Lowell K. Halls, ed., *White-Tailed Deer: Ecology and Management*. Harrisburg, Pa.: Stackpole Books, 1984.

————. "North American Deer Ecology: Fifty Years Later." In Thomas Tanner, ed., *Aldo Leopold: The Man and His Legacy.* Ankeny, Ohio: Soil Conservation Society of America, 1987.

————. "Demography and Management of Wild Populations by Reproductive Intervention," n.d.

McLeod, Ramon G. "Polluting the Globe with People." *San Francisco Chronicle,* March 20, 1992.

McLoughlin, William G. *Cherokee Renascence in the New Republic.* Lawrenceville, N.J.: Princeton University Press, 1966.

McLuhan, T. C. *Touch the Earth: A Self-Portrait of Indian Existence.* New York: Simon and Schuster, 1971.

McPhee, John. *Table of Contents.* New York: Farrar, Straus and Giroux, 1985.

Mealey, Stephen P. "Ethical Hunting: Updating an Old Heritage for America's Hunting and Wildlife Conservation Future." Address to the Foundation for North American Wild Sheep Conference, San Antonio, Texas, 1994.

Mech, L. D., and P. D. Karns. *Role of the Wolf in a Deer Decline in the Superior National Forest.* St. Paul, Minn.: U.S. Forest Service, North Central Forest Experiment Station, Research Paper NC-148, 1977.

Mermin, Lora, ed. *Lyme Disease 1991: Patient/Physician Perspectives from the U.S. and Canada.* Madison, Wis.: Lyme Disease Information Project, Inc.

Merwin, John. "The Sportsman's Dollar." *Field and Stream,* May 1994.

Miller, John M. *Deer Camp: Last Light in the Northeast Kingdom.* Cambridge: MIT Press, 1992.

More, Thomas A. "Attitudes of Massachusetts Hunters." *Human Dimensions in Wildlife Programs,* Thirty-eighth North American Wildlife Conference, 1973.

Nelson, Richard K. *Hunters of the Northern Ice.* Chicago: University of Chicago Press, 1969.

————. *Hunters of the Northern Forest.* Chicago: University of Chicago Press, 1973.

————. *Shadow of the Hunter.* Chicago: University of Chicago Press, 1980.

————. *Make Prayers to the Raven.* Chicago: University of Chicago Press, 1983.

————. *The Island Within.* New York: Vintage Books, 1990.

New York Department of Environmental Conservation. *The Status and Impact of Eastern Coyotes in Northern New York.* Albany: Division of Fish and Wildlife, New York Department of Environmental Conservation, 1991.

Nixon, Charles M., and Lonnie P. Hansen. "Habitat Relationships and Population Dynamics of Deer in the Intensively Farmed Midwestern United States." In Robert D. Brown, ed., *The Biology of Deer.* New York: Springer-Verlag, 1992.

Norwood, Vera. *Made from This Earth: American Women and Nature.* Chapel Hill: University of North Carolina Press, 1993.

O'Bryan, Mary K., and Dale R. McCullough. "Survival of Black-Tailed Deer Following Relocation in California." *Journal of Wildlife Management* 49:1, 1985.

O'Connell, Allan F., and Mark W. Sayre. *White-Tailed Deer Management Study: Fire Island National Seashore.* National Park Service, Office of Scientific Studies, North Atlantic Region, Report OSS 89-1, 1989.

O'Toole, Randal. "The $64 Million Question: How Taxpayers Pay Pulpmills to Clearcut the Tongass National Forest." Portland, Ore.: Cascade Holistic Economic Consultants, 1993.

Parker, Katherine L., G. D. DelGuidice, and Michael P. Gillingham. "Do Urinary Urea Nitrogen and Cortisol Ratios of Creatinine Reflect Body Fat Reserves in Black-Tailed Deer?" *Canadian Journal of Zoology,* 1993.

Parker, Katherine L., and Michael P. Gillingham. "Estimates of Critical Thermal Environments for Mule Deer." *Journal of Wildlife Management* 43, 1990.

Parker, Katherine L., Michael P. Gillingham, and Thomas A. Hanley. "An Accurate Technique for Estimating Forage Intake of Tractable Animals." *Canadian Journal of Zoology,* 1993.

Parker, Katherine L., Michael P. Gillingham, Thomas A. Hanley, and Charles T. Robbins. "Seasonal Patterns in Body Weight, Body Condition, and Water Transfer Rates of Free-Ranging and Captive Black-Tailed Deer in Alaska." *Canadian Journal of Zoology,* 1993.

———. "Foraging Efficiency: Energy Expenditure Versus Energy Gain in Free-Ranging Black-Tailed Deer." *Canadian Journal of Zoology,* 1996.

Parker, Katherine L., Charles T. Robbins, and Thomas A. Hanley. "Energy Expenditures for Locomotion by Mule Deer and Elk." *Journal of Wildlife Management* 48, 1984.

Petchenik, Jordan B. *Wisconsin's Wildlife Constituency Study.* Madison: University of Wisconsin, Cooperative Extension Service, 1988.

———. *Public Opinion of Proposed 16-Day Deer Seasons.* Madison: Wisconsin Department of Natural Resources, 1992.

Petersen, David. *Racks: The Natural History of Antlers and the Animals That Wear Them.* Santa Barbara: Capra Press, 1991.

———. "The Killing Fields." *Wilderness,* Summer 1994.

David Petersen, ed. *A Hunter's Heart: Honest Essays on Blood Sport.* New York: Henry Holt, 1996.

Potter, Dale R., John Hendee, and Roger Clark. "Hunting Satisfaction: Game, Guns, or Nature?" *Human Dimensions in Wildlife Programs,* proceedings of the Thirty-eighth North American Wildlife Conference, 1973.

Porter, William F. "High-Fidelity Deer." *Natural History,* May 1992.

Posewitz, Jim. *Beyond Fair Chase: The Ethic and Tradition of Hunting.* Helena, Mont.: Falcon Press, 1994.

Putman, Rory. *The Natural History of Deer.* Ithaca, N.Y.: Comstock Publishing Associates, 1988.

Regan, Tom. *All That Dwell Therein: Essays on Animal Rights and Environmental Ethics.* Berkeley: University of California Press, 1982.

Reiger, John F. *American Sportsmen and the Origins of Conservation.* Norman: University of Oklahoma Press, 1985.

Reihlman, David. "Westchester County Deer: Status and Management Needs." White Plains: New York Department of Environmental Conservation, 1988. Mimeographed.

Robbins, C. T., S. Mole, A. E. Hagerman, and T. A. Hanley. "Role of Tannins in De-

fending Plants Against Ruminants: Reduction in Dry Matter Digestion?"
   Ecology 68:6, 1987.

Robinette, Leslie, Norman V. Hancock, and Dale A. Jones. *The Oak Creek Mule Deer
   Herd in Utah.* Salt Lake City: Utah State Division of Wildlife Resources,
   Publication No. 77-15, 1977.

Roybal, Joe. "Have Game? We'll Travel." *Beef,* July 1987.

Rue, Leonard Lee III. *The Deer of North America.* New York: Crown Publishers, 1978.

Satchell, Michael, and Joannie Schrof. "The American Hunter Under Fire." *U.S.
   News & World Report,* February 5, 1990.

Savory, Allan. *Holistic Resource Management.* Washington, D.C.: Island Press, 1988.

Sayre, Roger W., and Daniel J. Decker. *Deer Damage to the Ornamental Horticulture
   Industry in Suburban New York: Extent, Nature and Economic Impact.* Ithaca,
   N.Y.: Human Dimensions Unit, Cornell University, 1990.

Schoen, John W., and Matthew D. Kirchoff. "Little Deer in the Big Woods." *Natural
   History,* August 1988.

———. "Seasonal Habitat Use by Sitka Black-Tailed Deer on Admiralty Island,
   Alaska." *Journal of Wildlife Management* 54:3, 1990.

Schoen, John W., Matthew D. Kirchoff, and Jeffrey H. Hughes. "Wildlife and Old-
   Growth Forests in Southeastern Alaska." *Natural Areas Journal* 8:3, 1988.

Schoen, John W., Olof C. Wallmo, and Matthew D. Kirchoff. "Wildlife-Forest
   Relationships: Is a Reevaluation of Old Growth Necessary?" *Transactions
   of the 46th North American Wildlife and Natural Resource Conference,* 1981.

Seton, Ernest Thompson. *Lives of Game Animals.* Garden City, N.Y.: Doubleday,
   Doran, and Company, 1929.

Severinghaus, C. W., and C. P. Brown. "History of the White-Tailed Deer in New
   York." *New York Fish and Game Journal* 3:2, 1956.

Shaw, Harley G. *Soul Among Lions: The Cougar as Peaceful Adversary.* Boulder, Colo.:
   Johnson Books, 1989.

Shedd, Warner. "The Giant Stirs." *Outdoor Life,* October 1991.

Singer, Peter. *Animal Liberation: A New Ethics for Our Treatment of Animals.* New
   York: Avon Books, 1975.

Smith, Dabney Jane. "Deer Management on Angel Island." Berkeley: University of
   California, 1986.

Snyder, Gary. *Turtle Island.* New York: New Directions Books, 1974.

Snyder, Phillip V. *The Christmas Tree Book.* New York: Viking Press, 1976.

Spalinger, D. E., T. A. Hanley, and C. T. Robbins. "Analysis of the Functional Response in Foraging in the Sitka Black-tailed Deer." *Ecology* 69:4, 1988.

State of Montana. *The Governor's Symposium on North America's Hunting Heritage:
   Proceedings.* Wildlife Forever and North American Hunting Club, Min-
   netonka, Minn: 1992.

Stewart, Omar C. "The Forgotten Side of Ethnography." In R. F. Spencer, ed.,
   Method and Perspective in Anthropology. Minneapolis: University of Minnesota Press, 1954.

Stokes, Bill. "The Dark Side of Bambi." *The Chicago Tribune Magazine,* August 6,
   1989.

Swan, James A. *In Defense of Hunting.* San Francisco: HarperCollins San Francisco, 1995.

Swift, Ernest. *A History of Wisconsin Deer.* Madison: Wisconsin Conservation Department, 1946.

Taylor, Walter W., ed. *The Deer of North America: Their History and Management.* Harrisburg, Pa.: Stackpole Company, 1956.

Teer, James G. "Lessons from the Llano Basin, Texas." In Lowell K. Halls, ed., *White-Tailed Deer: Ecology and Management.* Harrisburg, Pa.: Stackpole Books, 1984.

Telfer, Thomas C. "Status of Black-Tailed Deer on Kauai." *Transactions of the Western Section of the Wildlife Society* 24, 1988.

Texas Parks and Wildlife Department. *Big Game Harvest Survey Results.* Austin, March 25, 1991.

Texas Wildlife Association. *Hunting Lease Registry: A Listing of Managed Leases.* San Antonio: Texas Wildlife Association, 1991.

Toelken, Barre. "Seeing with a Native Eye: How Many Sheep Will It Hold?" In Walter Holden Capps, ed., *Seeing with a Native Eye: Essays on Native American Religion.* New York: Harper and Row, 1976.

Thomas, Jack Ward, and R. G. Marburger. "Quantity vs Quality." *Texas Parks and Wildlife Magazine,* October 1965.

Thomas, Keith. *Man and the Natural World: A History of the Modern Sensibility.* New York: Pantheon, 1983.

Tuma, Debbie. "Birth Control for Mama Deer." *Long Island Daily News,* November 14, 1993.

Turner, E. Randolph, and Robert S. Santley. "Deer Skins and Hunting Territories Reconsidered." *American Antiquity* 44:4, 1979.

United States Department of the Interior. *1985 National Survey of Fishing, Hunting, and Wildlife Associated Recreation.* Washington, D.C.: U.S. Fish and Wildlife Service, 1988.

Vecsey, Christopher, and Robert W. Venables. *American Indian Environments: Ecological Issues in Native American History.* Syracuse, N.Y.: Syracuse University Press, 1980.

Wallmo, Olof C., ed. *Mule and Black-Tailed Deer of North America.* Lincoln: University of Nebraska Press, 1981.

Wallmo, Olof C., and John W. Schoen, eds. *Sitka Black-Tailed Deer: Proceedings of a Conference.* Juneau, Alaska: U.S. Department of Agriculture, Forest Service, 1979.

Wallmo, Olof C., and John W. Schoen. "Response of Deer to Secondary Forest Succession in Southeast Alaska." *Forest Science* 26:3, 1980.

Wear, Sam, and Richard A. Schreiner. *The Wildlife Resources of Westchester County.* White Plains, N.Y.: Westchester County Department of Planning, 1987.

Webster, Gary S. "Deer Hides and Tribal Confederacies: An Appraisal of Gramly's Hypothesis." *American Antiquity* 44:4, 1979.

Wegner, Robert. *Deer and Deer Hunting.* Harrisburg, Pa.: Stackpole Books, 1984.

———. *Deer and Deer Hunting: Book 2.* Harrisburg, Pa.: Stackpole Books, 1987.

————. *Deer and Deer Hunting: Book 3.* Harrisburg, Pa.: Stackpole Books, 1990.

————. *Wegner's Bibliography on Deer and Deer Hunting.* DeForest, Wis.: St. Hubert's Press, 1994.

Western Resource Development Corporation. *Mule Deer Study: Current Conditions and Management Options.* Boulder, Colo.: City of Boulder, 1984.

White, Jack. "Trouble on Angel Island." *Outdoor California* 42:5, 1981.

Winchcombe, Raymond J. "Deer Management at the Institute of Ecosystem Studies, Mary Flagler Cary Arboretum." *New York Wildlife Damage News* 2, 1991.

————. "Minimizing Deer Damage to Forest Vegetation Through Aggressive Deer Population Management." *Proceedings of the Eastern Wildlife Damage Control Conference,* vol. 5, 1992a.

————. "Report on the 1992 Deer Hunt." Millbrook, N.Y.: Mary Flagler Cary Arboretum, 1992b.

————. "Participation in a Controlled Deer Management Program: How the Hunters Responded," 1992c.

Wisconsin Agricultural Reporting Service. *Wisconsin Deer Population and Damage Survey.* Madison: Wisconsin Department of Agriculture, Trade and Consumer Protection, 1984.

Witham, James H., and Jon M. Jones. "Deer-Human Interactions and Research in the Chicago Metropolitan Area." In L. W. Adams and D. L. Leedy, eds., *Integrating Man and Nature in the Metropolitan Environment.* Columbia, Md.: National Institute for Urban Wildlife, 1986.

Wuerthner, George. "Public Lands Grazing: What Benefits at What Cost?" *Western Wildlands,* Fall 1989.

accidents, hunting: and orange clothing, 219, 237, 238; frequency of, 144,
237–8; preventing, 160, 219, 223, 229;
versus other activities, 238; *see also*
collisions, hunter education, hunting
adaptability, of deer, 19–24
Adirondacks, 104, 108
age, of deer: and hunting, 226, 230,
234; and reproduction, 33; average
and maximum, 37, 208, 212, 226;
determining, 37–8, 208, 232
aggression: and food competition,
44–5; during rut, 39–41 passim, 82–3;
submission and dominance, 38, 42,
69 70, 77; toward humans, 77, 128,
155; toward predators, 34, 173; *see also*
communication, rutting
agricultural damage, by deer: and agricultural economy, 309–11; and deer
abundance, 294, 299, 308; and deer
density, 309–10; and deer diet, 290;
and hunting attitudes, 294, 304, 309;
and organic farming, 295–8; and
perceptions of deer, 291, 294, 298,
302, 304 5; assessing, 298–301,
306–7; compensation for, 291, 301–2,
303; control by hunting, 291, 292,
294–5, 297, 298, 301, 302, 303, 304,
306, 309–11; cost of, 290–1, 293, 294,
299, 301–2, 307, 308; crop types
affected, 290, 292–3, 295, 296, 297,
301–2, 307, 309; history of, 108, 291,
301; nonlethal control of, 291, 294;
references on, 363–4; *see also* agriculture, fencing, repellents

Agricultural Damage Control (agency),
299, 301, 363
agriculture: and deer populations,
22–3, 291–2, 308; and forests, 110–1,
112, 158; and importance of hunting,
309–11; and natural habitat, 291–2,
295, 296, 299, 328; compared to
hunting, 327–8; *see also* agricultural
damage, livestock, ranching, Slator
Ranch
Alaback, Paul, 118
Alabama, 25, 102
Alaska. *See* Channel Island, hunting,
Iñupiaq Eskimos, Koyukon Indians,
Tongass National Forest
alfalfa: deer damage to, 296, 303,
306–7; in deer diet, 306–7
Amory, Cleveland, 133–4, 275
Angel Island, California: culling deer
on, 133–6; deer population on, 127,
130–1, 133, 135; deer starvation on, 125;
described, 124–5, 126–7; habitat condition on, 127, 128, 132, 134; history
of, 126; references on, 356; relocating
deer from, 129–31, sterilizing deer on,
131–3; *see also* Fire Island, preserves
animal rights: and environmentalism,
276; and religion, 265; in Native
American tradition, 284–6; philosophy of, 252–3, 265, 274–6; references
on, 362; *see also* antihunting, Bambi,
humane organizations, hunters,
hunting
antihunting: and deer management, 254, 259–60, 264–5; and

antihunting (*continued*): environmentalism, 276; and hunter harassment laws, 251, 256, 269; and
hunters' motivations, 278–81; and
urban-rural background, 177,
249–50, 277; and vegetarianism, 254,
260, 261, 280, 288; and view of
nature, 271–81 passim; attitudes
regarding, 144, 250; description of
protest for, 251–71 passim, 286–8;
hunter reactions to, 255–6, 262–4,
265–9, 270; media coverage of, 252,
257, 262, 269–70; philosophy of,
252–3, 258–61 passim, 265, 266–7,
271–80 passim, 277–8, 287–8; sociological information on, 277–8; *see
also* animal rights, Bambi, humane
organizations, hunters, hunting
antlers: and age, 37, 193–4, 212; and
nutrition, 37; and testosterone, 37,
193; deformations of, 32, 197; effects
of removing, 86; evolution of, 12–13;
function of, 13; genetic influence on,
31–2, 37; growth of, 13, 31–2, 37, 39,
43; hunter valuation of, 192–3,
206–7, 208; identifying species by,
16–17; individuality of, 17, 37, 193,
208; loss of, 43; of Irish elk, 12–13; on
does, 32; structure of, 12–13, 32, 37;
typical vs. nontypical, 208; uses of,
93, 97, 101; *see also* Boone and
Crockett Club, bucks, rubs, rutting,
trophy hunting
apples, deer damage to, 292, 301
Aransas National Wildlife Refuge, 36,
123
arboretum: Mary Flagler Cary, 151–2;
University of Wisconsin, 151; *see also*
preserves
Arizona, 22, 99, 108–11
Arkansas, 99
Armstrong, William, 202–3, 360
Assateague Island National Seashore,
153, 154, 204

attitudes. *See* animal rights, antihunting, hunters, hunting, motivations,
nature, suburban deer, values
Audubon Society, 106
axis deer, 203

Bambi: history of, 271–2; influence of,
271–3; *see also* animal rights, antihunting
Barnes, John, 259, 265
bear: danger of, 180, 314–15, 318, 320,
331–5; encounter with, 312–15, 331–5;
logging effects on, 116; mentioned,
5, 103, 114, 301; predation on deer, 29,
34, 87, 313–14; signs of, 312, 313, 317,
324–5, 334, 337–8; spirituality of, 285,
315; *see also* predators
bed, deer, 35, 44, 63, 67, 72, 84
birds, grooming deer, 176
birth: description of, 32, 345–52; mentioned, 176; season of, 32, 42, 342;
seclusion for, 32, 342–3; *see also*
fawns, gestation
black-tailed deer: distribution, 15–16,
20–1; identifying, 16–19 passim, 21; in
Hawaii, 23; scientific name of, 13; size
of, 17; *see also* logging, mule deer,
research, Tongass National Forest
Blooming Grove Park, 104
bobcat, 29, 109
Boone and Crockett Club: and conservation movement, 106; and trophy
deer, 164, 191, 192, 198–9, 208;
founding of, 106; *see also* Pope and
Young, trophy hunting
Boulder, Colorado: car-deer collisions
in, 174–5; control of deer numbers
in, 174, 175, 177; deer population in,
172, 174, 178; described, 171; history
of deer in, 173–4; mountain lions in,
178–80; public attitudes in, 172–3,
175–8; references on, 359; *see also*

collisions, damage, River Hills, suburban deer
bow and arrow: hunting effectiveness
of, 160, 294; mentioned, 188; use by
Native Americans, 94, 95, 96
British Columbia, 22, 37, 118
browse line, 45, 127; *see also* overpopulation, starvation
Bryant, Beverly, 162–9 passim, 358
bucks: and American slang, 101; danger
of, 128, 155; hunter attitudes toward,
187–8, 192–3, 198–9, 223, 230; hunting management for, 186–7, 190,
207, 208, 213, 223; nutritional cycle
of, 31, 42–3, 76; size of, 17, 36; social
behavior of, 32, 35, 38, 39, 44–5, 83;
see also antlers, does, rutting, trophy
hunting
buffalo, 98, 103, 106, 184, 200–1, 203

California: agricultural damage in, 291,
295–8, 306; deer population in, 296;
deer species in, 15, 17; habitat characteristics of, 49, 99, 125–6, 296; mentioned, 22, 26, 43, 179, 180, 275;
references on, 356, 363; suburban deer
in, 157, 161–2; *see also* Angel Island
calling deer, methods of, 38–9, 49, 94–5,
318, 331; *see also* communication,
voice
caribou, 13, 283, 284
carrying capacity, biological vs. social,
24, 241, 309–10; *see also* overpopulation, population, starvation
cattle. *See* livestock, ranching
census, deer, 141
Channel Island, Alaska: deer research
on, 53–90 passim; described, 56;
publications on, 354–5; *see also* diet,
nutrition, research, Tongass National
Forest
Chee Sonny, Claus, 27, 91, 354

Christmas trees, deer damage to, 293,
301–2, 304, 310
coat: cleanliness of, 84; of fawn, 32;
seasonal changes of, 35, 39; *see also*
hide, tail
collisions, car-deer: cost of, 167, 175;
danger of, 159; frequency of, 166–7,
175; human injuries from, 164, 165;
of relocated deer, 130, 165, 168; preventing, 160, 166, 174–5; seasonality
of, 175; use of deer, 224
Colorado, mentioned, 15, 18, 205; *see
also* Boulder
communication: by fawns, 34, 78; by
postures, 38, 40, 87; by rubs and
scrapes, 40; by scent, 40–2 passim;
by voice, 38
Connecticut, 102, 158
conservation: among Native Americans, 98–100; and deer habitat, 43–4,
107; modern history of, 101–7, 355;
see also habitat, management
corn: deer damage to, 289–90, 298–300
passim, 303, 307; in deer diet, 189, 290
Coronation Island, Alaska, 27–8
cougar. *See* mountain lion
coyote: control of, 103, 109, 301; mentioned, 129; predation on deer, 28–9,
48, 129; *see also* predators
Crane Wildlife Refuge, 150
crops. *See* agricultural damage, agriculture, alfalfa, apples, corn, soybeans
culling, of deer: by euthanasia, 150–1,
165–6; cost of, 134; feasibility of,
133–6, 150–1, 165; in natural preserves, 123–4, 127, 132–6, 143, 151–2;
methods of, 133–4, 164; *see also* hunting, predators, relocation, sterilization, suburban deer

dairy products, and deer damage,
307

damage, by deer. *See* agricultural damage, collisions, garden and yard damage, habitat, preserves, suburban deer
danger, of deer. *See* aggression, collisions
deer: adaptability and distribution,
19–24 passim; annual U.S. harvest of,
210; attitudes toward, 19, 145, 250–1,
294, 298, 302; distinguishing species
of, 15–19; economic value of, 185;
encounters described, xi-xii, 5–9,
15–19, 49–52, 65–8, 82–5, 138–9, 140,
155–6, 170–1, 172–3, 181–2, 192,
199–200, 216–17, 230–1, 289–90,
317–19, 321–3, 329–30, 336–7; grooming by birds, 176; Native American
knowledge of, 93, 94; North American species, 13–14; physical characteristics of, 12, 15–19 passim; quietness
of, 67; reference books on, 353–4,
355, 356; total population of, 24;
worldwide species, 12, 13; *see also*
black-tailed deer, evolution, mule
deer, white-tailed deer
deer yards. *See* yarding
diet, deer: and evolution, 12; and farm
crops, 290, 296, 306; and foraging
efficiency, 55–6, 89; and garden
plantings, 173–4; and nutrition, 35,
39, 69, 173–4; diversity and selectiv-
ity of, 22, 35, 66, 144; meat and fish
in, 22; of fawns, 34; seasonality of, 31,
39, 44–5, 63, 68; studies of, 55, 60; *see
also* digestion, feeding, metabolism,
nutrition, starvation
digestion, process of, 12, 34, 67–8, 78,
118; *see also* diet, feeding
diseases, 26, 204
distribution, of deer species. *See* range
District of Columbia, 158, 159
does: antlers on, 32; hunting of, 230;
maternal behavior of, 32–4, 39–40,
78, 90, 348–52; nutritional cycle of,
31, 77; reproductive age of, 33; size of,

17; social behavior of, 32, 35, 38,
69–70; *see also* bucks, fawns, social
groups
dog: as predator protection, 5, 179,
332–5; finding or hunting deer with,
3–9 passim, 49–52 passim, 317–20,
321–3, 328, 329–30, 343–5; killed by
deer, 173; predation on deer, 29;
preventing deer damage, 297, 303–4
drives, deer: by Native Americans,
95–6; described, 108–11, 237–44
passim; in modern hunting, 227,
228; mentioned, 109, 245; *see also*
stands
droppings: judging age of, 68; of bear,
313; seasonal changes in, 44, 77–8

eagle, 29, 114, 116, 323, 341
ecology. *See* personal ecology
elk, 13, 103
Ellingwood, Mark, 357
estrus. *See* mating
ethics. *See* animal rights, hunting,
research
Everglades, deer conflicts in, 275–6
evolution: and predators, 15, 26–7; and
silence, 27; of deer, 11–15 passim; of
North American deer species, 14, 18
exotic wildlife: biologists' view of, 204;
commercial uses of, 204; competition with deer, 203–4; hunting of,
203, 204; references on, 360; species
in North America, 13, 203

fallow deer, 203
farm, deer, 162, 170, 204; *see also* agricultural damage, agriculture
fat. *See* nutrition
fawns: behavior of, 33–4, 36, 43, 50,
348–52; coat and color, 32, 36, 349,

351; feeding and diet, 33–4, 348; number per doe, 33; predation on, 28, 29; scent of, 33, 350–1; size and growth, 32, 34, 36, 351; survival of, 33, 187; voice of, 350; weaning, 78; *see also* birth, does, gestation

fee hunting: and deer management, 187–8, 191; and habitat protection, 205; attitudes toward, 205; debate over, 191, 204–5; economics of, 187–8; history of, 185; references on, 360

feeding, artificial: effects on behavior, 137, 138–9, 148–9, 164; mentioned, 168; problems with, 48, 68, 128, 139, 142, 149; prohibitions against, 164, 178; *see also* stands, starvation

feeding activity, patterns of, 63, 67, 72, 77; *see also* diet, digestion, metabolism

fence, deer: cost of, 296–7, 303; effectiveness of, 203, 293, 294, 298, 302–3; for crop protection, 293, 296, 297–8, 302; for yard protection, 160, 178; types of, 160, 178, 213, 293, 297–8, 302–3; *see also* repellents

fighting. *See* aggression, rutting

finding and approaching deer, 3–9 passim, 50, 93–4, 317–20, 321–3, 325, 326–7, 328–30, 335–7, 338–40, 342–52; *see also* dog

fire: habitat manipulation by, 99, 107, 110, 184, 202–3, 355; use in hunting, 96; *see also* conservation, habitat

Fire Island, New York: culling deer on, 141, 143–4, 151; deer behavior on, 138–40, 148–9, 155; deer condition on, 143, 144–5, 149; deer population on, 141–2; described, 124, 137–8, 140; feeding deer on, 139, 142, 148–9; habitat condition on, 140–1, 142–3, 145–6, 152–3; public attitudes on, 145, 146, 148, 149, 152, 155; publications on, 357; settlements on, 138, 140;

sterilizing deer on, 153–4; *see also* Angel Island, preserves

Fire Island National Seashore. *See* Fire Island

firearms, and early trade, 98, 101

fishing, 104

Florida, 17, 93–4, 168

food: and connection to nature, 71, 215, 246, 278–81, 283–4, 327; and significance of hunting, 309–11; as hunting motivation, 210–11, 228, 236, 246–7, 278–81; *see also* diet, feeding, nutrition, personal ecology, venison

forest: deer damage to, 310; importance to deer, 110, 111–13; loss of, 100, 104, 105, 107–8, 110, 112–13; old growth vs. second growth, 112, 113, 117–18, 120–1; regrowth of, 108, 110, 118; *see also* fire, habitat, logging, Tongass National Forest

Fowler, Gene, 131–2

game wardens, history of, 103, 108; *see also* poaching, regulations

garden and yard damage, by deer: examples of, 108, 146, 159–60, 167, 174, 175, 293; nonlethal control of, 160, 169, 175, 178; *see also* hunting, relocation, sterilization, suburban deer

Geist, Valerius, 14, 204–5, 279, 353, 360

George Reserve: deer studies in, 25, 356; *see also* research

Georgia, 25, 158

gestation, length of, 31; *see also* birth, fawns

Gillan, Bart and Debbie, 185–217 passim

Gillingham, Michael, 31, 57–89 passim, 354–5

goose, Canada, 301

Grinnell, George Bird, 104–5

Gwich'in Indians, 279

habitat: damage by deer, 48, 123–4, 127, 128, 142–3, 146, 187, 275–6; effects of change in, 16, 22–3, 25, 110–21, 158, 168–9, 205, 214, 296, 328; historic changes of, 100, 107–8, 110–11, 184; manipulation of, 99, 107, 185, 200–3; protection of, 44, 48, 205, 276; regional differences in, 22, 49; selection by bucks vs. does, 35; species preferences for, 16, 35; *see also* agriculture, fire, forest, logging, management, overpopulation, population, ranching, range

Halls, Lowell K., 353

Hanley, Thomas, 54–60 passim, 88–9, 118, 354–5, 356

harems, of deer, 42; *see also* rutting

Harwell, Fielding, 186–7, 191

Hawaii, 23

hearing, of deer, 27, 197, 327, 336

Heberlein, Thomas, 225, 361

hide, deer: and frontier trade, 98, 100–1; as hunting disguise, 93–4; economic value of, 223; skinning of, 210; uses of, 95, 97, 210; *see also* coat

Hill Country, Texas: deer harvest in, 184–5; deer population in, 184–5; described, 183–4; *see also* Llano, Slator Ranch, Texas

Hirchert, Dan, 298–305 passim

home range: and social groups, 32; fidelity to, 36, 39–40, 79, 130, 163–4; rural and urban deer, 174; size of, 35, 36, 163–4; *see also* range, relocation

hooves, 11, 12

horses, and deer population, 110

humane organizations, 128–33 passim, 144, 154, 274, 276; *see also* animal rights, antihunting

hunter education, 238, 244, 362

hunters: and alcohol, 188, 246–7; and deer management, 223, 241; attitudes toward, 144, 228, 246, 249–50, 260–1, 277–81 passim; density of, 225, 226, 234; learning skills, 218–19, 220–1, 227–8, 229, 243–4, 246; number of, 205, 212, 218, 219, 227; rural vs. urban perspectives, 228, 243, 246, 276–7, 278, 284, 294; sociological information on, 219, 226, 227, 228, 243, 276–9 passim; *see also* hunter education, hunting, motivations, values, Wisconsin

Hunters for the Hungry, 211

hunting: and attentiveness, 320, 336; and deer evolution, 15, 172, 336, 337; and deer population, 23, 25–6, 29, 37, 164, 225, 228, 232–3, 234, 235, 259, 275–6; and origin of conservation, 100–7; and uses of deer, 199, 210; and valuation of deer, 71; and viability of agriculture, 309–11; and wildness, 180–1, 189, 190; as biological process, 279–81, 314, 323–4, 327; as deer population control, 132–6, 151–2, 186–8, 202, 220, 241, 254–5, 291, 292, 294, 303; attitudes toward, 144–5, 150, 177, 180–1, 219, 249–50, 259–61, 277–81 passim, 294, 304, 309, 327; author's background in, 220, 250, 281–6 passim; by Native Americans, 93–8; conflicts over, 123–4, 127–8, 141, 143–4, 160, 164–5, 169, 275–6; economic significance of, 185, 195–6, 223–4, 309; ethics of, 104, 189–90, 194, 206–7, 231, 243–4, 284–6, 318, 326, 327–8, 330, 361, 362; future of, 228, 244; methods of, 93–7, 189, 194–5, 196, 222–3, 227, 228, 317–20, 321–3, 325, 326–7, 328–30, 335–7, 338–40; references on, 360–2; religious dimensions of, 224, 244, 284–6; safety of, 144, 160, 223, 231; use of fees from, 223–4, 301; *see also* bow and arrow, calling deer, culling, drives, fee hunting, finding deer, food, hunters, market hunting, moti-

vations, regulations, Slator Ranch, values, Wisconsin
hybridization: and species origins, 14; between deer species, 14, 16, 17

Idaho, 22, 99
Illinois, 22, 101, 157, 159, 168
Indians. *See* Iñupiaq Eskimos, Koyukon Indians, Native Americans, Navajo Indians, Tlingit Indians
individuality: of deer personality, 57, 61, 65, 69–70, 81–2, 163; of deer physiology, 55
Iñupiaq Eskimos: and animal research, 66; environmental knowledge of, 283; hunting motivations of, 279; learning from, 282–4
Iowa, 290, 307
irrigation, and deer, 173, 292; *see also* agriculture, habitat
Ishmael, William, 158, 165, 241, 358, 361, 363

jumping ability, 27; *see also* speed

Kaibab Plateau, deer history of, 108–11
Kansas, 26, 103, 112, 290
Kellert, Stephen, 276–7, 362
Kemper, Bernard, 252–61 passim, 265, 287–8
Kemper, Jodi, 252–61 passim
Kentucky, 24, 102, 108, 168
Kerr Wildlife Management Area, Texas, 202–3, 360
Keta. *See* dog
Key deer, size of, 17
Kirchoff, Matthew, 113, 116–18, 356
Klein, David, 27–8, 81, 120

Koyukon Indians: and animal research, 66; conservation practices of, 98–9, 286; hunting motivations of, 279, 327–8; references on, 362; relationship to nature, 284–6, 318–19, 326, 329, 330, 333, 352

Lacy Act, 103, 106
livestock: and deer damage, 296, 306, 307; and deer populations, 25, 26, 28, 202, 296; compared to buffalo, 200–1; ecological effects of, 184, 200–1; managed grazing of, 200–3; *see also* ranching
Llano, Texas: described, 186; hunting in economy of, 195–6, 211
logging: alternative methods of, 112, 119; described, 75, 84, 114; effects on deer, 54, 110–21 passim; effects on other wildlife, 111, 116, 355–6; government subsidies for, 119; history of, 99, 104, 110; *see also* forest
Long Island, New York, 108, 137, 140, 141
Louisiana, 15, 102, 111
Lowery, Mark, 140–5 passim, 154, 357
Lyme disease: and deer, 146–7, 154; and relocation of deer, 150; distribution of, 167, 176; mentioned, 292; prevention of, 136, 148, 154, 169; symptoms and effects of, 146, 147–8; transmission of, 26; treatment of, 147–8
Lyme Disease Association of the United States, 357

magazines, outdoor, 104, 105
Maine, 102, 108, 158
management of deer: and hunting fees, 223–4, 255; and regulation of hunting, 186–7, 190, 207, 208, 213, 223,

management of deer (*continued*):
232–5 passim; and viability of agriculture, 309–11; antihunting view of,
254–5, 259–60, 267; references on,
360, 361, 363; use of hunting data
for, 38, 134, 143, 232–3; *see also*
habitat, overpopulation, population,
research, starvation
Manitoba, 15
market hunting, history of, 100–3, 104,
108, 355
marten, 320–1
Maryland, 153
Massachusetts, 102, 103, 150
mating, 41–2
McCullough, Dale, 25, 128–36 passim,
151, 356
meat. *See* venison
Mech, David, 28
metabolism: and energy balance, 55–6,
62, 63, 72, 89; seasonal changes in,
30, 31, 45, 48, 63; *see also* diet, digestion, nutrition, weight
Michigan, 22, 25, 32, 33, 101, 108
migration, seasonal, 30, 35, 43, 174
milk, deer, 34
Minnesota, 15, 17, 28, 44, 101, 111, 157,
306–7
Missouri, 99, 101, 290
Mlsna, Jim, 218–48 passim
Montana, 15, 112, 113, 158
moose, 13, 285
motivations, of hunters: and attitudes
toward hunting, 278–81; closeness to
nature, 185, 219, 234, 245, 269, 277–8,
279–81 passim; escape, 185; food, 185,
188, 199, 210–11, 212–19, 224, 245–6,
268, 276–7, 278–81 passim; recreation, 104, 277–9; references on, 361;
skill and knowledge, 199, 219, 230,
236; social and cultural, 185, 195, 216,
219, 222, 224, 229, 235–6, 279; trophy, 185, 187, 192–3, 199, 206–7, 212,
277; *see also* hunters, hunting, trophy
hunting, values

mountain lion: control of, 103, 109;
danger of, 149–50, 179–80; in suburbs, 178–80; mentioned, 123; predation on deer, 29, 161–2, 180;
protection from, 179; size of, 178; *see
also* predators
Muir, John, 94, 104–5, 106
mule deer: described, 181–2; distribution, 15–6, 19–22; identifying, 16–19
passim, 20; personality of, 18; scientific name of, 13; size of, 17; subspecies of, 17; *see also* black-tailed
deer

national forests: and deer habitat,
111–12; origin of, 106; *see also* forest,
preserves, Tongass National Forest
National Park Service, deer control
policies of, 141, 152; *see also* Fire Island, preserves
Native Americans: and anthropology,
282; deer in economy of, 95, 97–8;
deer in religious traditions of, 91–3,
94, 96–7, 98; hunting methods of,
93–7; traditional conservation
among, 98–100, 107, 119, 286; uses of
deer by, 97–8; *see also* Gwich'in Indians, Iñupiaq Eskimos, Koyukon
Indians, Navajo Indians, Tlingit
Indians
natural history, 281–2
nature: and hunter motivations, 219,
277, 279; attitudes toward, 170, 177,
250–1, 310; humans' place in, 150;
quietness of, 67, 324; spirituality of,
284–6, 315, 319; *see also* animal rights,
Bambi
Navajo Indians: deer traditions of, 91–3,
94, 96; mentioned, 109
Nebraska, 26, 112, 290, 307
New Hampshire, 17
New Jersey, 26, 108, 158
New Mexico, 168

New York: agricultural damage in,
292–5, 303; deer populations in, 25;
history of deer in, 95, 96, 98, 107–8,
110; mentioned, 27, 29, 101, 105,
151–2, 158, 159, 160–1, 162, 205; references on, 355, 356–7, 358, 363; size of
deer in, 17, 31; *see also* Fire Island,
Westchester County
New Zealand, deer in, 23, 204
North Carolina, 102, 103
nurseries, deer damage to, 293
nursing, deer, 33–4; *see also* does, fawns
nutrition: and fat cycle, 31, 39, 55, 89;
and fawn survival, 33; and garden
plants, 173–4; and mating, 42–3; and
nursing, 33; effect on antlers, 37;
effect on size, 18; seasonal changes in,
45; *see also* diet, feeding, metabolism,
starvation

O'Bryan, Mary, 129–30
Ohio, 99
Ontario, 95
orchards, deer damage to, 294, 296
Oregon, 15, 23, 46–8, 102, 114, 157
Orion—The Hunters Institute, 362
overpopulation, deer: and artificial feeding, 48, 128; and deer size, 187, 191;
causes of, 107; ecological effects of, 48,
123–4, 127, 128, 142–3, 146, 187, 275–6;
history of, 123; impact on other animals, 111, 143; in natural preserves,
123–4, 254; mentioned, 191; *see also*
agricultural damage, carrying capacity,
hunting, Kaibab Plateau, population,
relocation, starvation, sterilization
Owens, Wade, 305–9 passim
Ozoga, John, 29, 40, 43, 353

parasites, 26, 176; *see also* diseases
Parker, Katherine, 31, 57–89 passim, 354–5

Peck, Brian, 173–9 passim
Pennsylvania: deer populations in, 25,
108, 159; mentioned, 102, 104, 143,
158, 206, 307
personal ecology: and food, 280–1,
283–4, 327–8; and hunting, 309–11,
323–4, 338–41 passim; *see also* food
poaching: and deer population, 242; for
trophy deer, 206; laws regarding,
241–2; mentioned, 104, 130; sociological data on, 242; *see also* game wardens
Pope and Young, 206; *see also* Boone
and Crockett Club, trophy hunting
population, deer: and agricultural
economy, 309; effect of predators on,
26, 27–9 passim, 108–9, 129, 175;
growth potential of, 25–6, 130–1, 152,
302; influences on, 26, 27–30 passim,
108–9; lethal control of, 123–4, 127,
132–6, 143, 151–2, 186–8, 202, 220,
241, 254–5, 291, 292, 294, 303; modern total, 24; "natural" control of,
149–50, 225, 259; near-extinction of,
107–8, 234; North American history
of, 24, 100–10, 123, 158, 184, 230,
234–5, 355; short-term fluctuations
of, 25, 28, 29; studies of, 25, 38,
232–3; *see also* agricultural damage,
carrying capacity, habitat, hunting,
Kaibab Plateau, management, overpopulation, population density,
relocation, starvation, sterilization
population density, of deer, in specific
habitats, 24–5, 127, 142, 164, 174, 184,
191, 225, 235, 309–10; *see also* overpopulation, population
population, human, 100, 111, 228
predators: and deer populations, 26,
27–9 passim, 108–9, 163; and deer
yards, 44; and fawns, 28, 33; and
livestock, 180, 214; and natural
process, 323–4; as deer population
control, 180, 259; attitudes toward,
129, 149–50, 180; control of, 109, 301;

predators (*continued*): hunting of, 180–1, 184; in natural preserves, 123, 129; types of, 27–30 passim; *see also* coyote, dog, mountain lion, wolf

preserves, natural: and deer history, 123; deer population control in, 129–36 passim, 150–5, 275–6, 295–6; hunting in, 254, 269; optimal deer numbers in, 133; origins of, 104–5, 106; significance of, 123; wildness of, 124, 139–40; *see also* Angel Island, arboretum, conservation, Fire Island, Tongass National Forest

private land: access to, 205; amount of, 205; fragmentation of, 213–15; posting of, 205; *see also* public land

public land: access to, 205; amount in U.S., 205; grazing on, 215; *see also* preserves, private land

radio collar: description of, 59; ethics of, 66; mentioned, 129; use of, 59, 61, 64–5, 81, 130, 161, 163, 165; *see also* research

ranching: and deer management, 186, 190, 191, 202–4; and fee hunting, 185, 187–8, 199; and habitat fragmentation, 214; and overgrazing, 214–15; and public land, 215; and wildland protection, 200–3, 213–15; *see also* agriculture, exotic wildlife, livestock, Slator Ranch

range, of deer species, 19–22; *see also* habitat

raven, 285, 318–9, 329, 341

refuge. *See* preserve, wildlife refuge

regulations, hunting: and private land, 187, 223; and safety, 160, 219, 237–8, 243–4; enforcement of, 103; examples of, 191, 204, 222–3, 227, 232–5 passim, 241; history of, 102–3, 104, 184,

230; *see also* game wardens, hunter education, poaching

Reiger, John, 104, 355

relocation, deer: cost of, 130, 161, 168; examples of, 108, 123, 126, 165, 169–70; feasibility of, 36, 124, 129–31, 150, 159, 161–2, 165, 168, 169–70, 275–6; methods of, 79–82, 85–8, 130, 168; studies of, 163, 165; *see also* culling, hunting, overpopulation, preserves, sterilization

repellent, deer: dogs as, 297, 303–4; types of, 160, 293, 294, 297, 301; uses of, 291, 293; *see also* agricultural damage, fence, garden and yard damage

reproduction. *See* birth, gestation, mating, population, rutting

research, on deer: abundance of, 11, 25; and hunting, 186–7, 232–3; ethics of, 60–1, 63–4, 66, 72–4, 79–82 passim, 85–8, 120, 354; examples of, 161–2, 203; in suburban areas, 167–8, 174; methods of, 38, 60, 62–3, 69–70, 78–9, 80–1, 88–9, 129–36 passim, 141, 143

Rhode Island, 102

River Hills, Wisconsin: car-deer collisions in, 166; culling deer in, 164–5, 169; deer damage in, 167; deer population in, 164; described, 162–3; feeding deer in, 164, 168–9; public attitudes in, 164–5, 167–8, 169; publications on, 358; relocating deer from, 165, 169–70; *see also* Boulder, collisions, damage, suburban deer

Roosevelt, Theodore, 106, 109

rubs, 40, 83; *see also* rutting, scrapes

Rue, Leonard Lee, 342, 353

rumination. *See* digestion

rutting: and agricultural damage, 296; and hunting, 95; and social behavior, 32; described, 38, 39–43, 82–3; seasonality of, 23, 38, 39, 41, 42, 43; *see also* aggression, antlers, bucks, mating

safety, hunting. *See* accidents, hunter education

salmon, 114, 116, 121

scent: and fear of humans, 8, 352; and finding deer, 5, 321, 328, 331, 336, 343–5; communication by, 40–2 passim, 83; glands producing, 40, 83; importance to deer, 41; of fawns, 33, 350–1

Schoen, John, 113, 116, 120–1, 356

scrapes, 40; *see also* rubs, rutting

senses, acuity of, 26–7, 197, 336; *see also* hearing, scent

Severinghaus, C. W., 84

sex ratios, of deer, 186–7, 233; *see also* management, population

sika deer, 203

size: and age, 37, 233; and climate, 18; and diet, 18, 27–8, 233; of North American deer, 17–18; *see also* weight

Slator Ranch, Texas: deer management on, 186–7, 190, 207, 208, 213; deer population on, 187, 191; described, 185–6; fee access to, 188; hunting program of, 186–8, 193–4, 198–9, 204; livestock management on, 200–2; *see also* Hill Country, livestock, private land, ranching

smell. *See* scent

snaring deer, 95; *see also* trapping deer

snow: and clear-cut logging, 112, 116, 117–18; effects on deer, 28, 43–5 passim, 48, 55–6, 62, 72, 76–7, 89, 94, 112, 116, 117, 172, 176; *see also* diet, habitat, starvation

social behavior: and fawning, 32; general patterns, 38, 39–43 passim, 44–5, 69–70; of does vs. bucks, 32, 35, 38; *see also* aggression, bucks, communication, does, individuality, rutting

South Carolina, 98, 99

soybeans: and hunting, 310; and land clearing, 111; deer damage to, 302, 310

SPCA (Society for the Prevention of Cruelty to Animals). *See* humane organizations

speed, of deer, 27, 34; *see also* jumping ability

spirituality, and hunting, 224, 244, 284–6; *see also* Koyukon Indians, Navajo Indians, values

sport hunting: and conservation, 106; and hunter motivations, 277–9; attitudes toward, 277–9; origins of, 104; *see also* motivations, trophy hunting, values

stands, hunting: and bait stations, 189; described, 189, 196, 206, 229–31; ethics of, 189–90; use of, 151, 161, 227, 228; *see also* drives

starvation, deer: and artificial feeding, 48, 68, 149; and fawn survival, 33, 45, 72–3; and winter stress, 45, 60–1, 89, 235; as population control, 259, 264; attitudes toward, 149; described, 46–8; effect on marrow, 46; in natural preserves, 123, 125, 127, 128, 144–5, 149, 152, 275–6; mentioned, 191; numbers killed by, 45, 109, 144–5; recovery from, 76; studies of, 72–4; *see also* diet, metabolism, nutrition

sterilization, of deer: cost of, 132; feasibility of, 131–3, 153, 154, 161, 178; methods of, 131–2, 153; *see also* culling, hunting, predators, relocation, starvation

stotting, 18

suburban deer: and hunting, 160–1; and relocation, 161–2; attitudes toward, 162, 164–5, 167–8, 169, 172–3, 175–8; habitat of, 158, 161, 163, 173–4; history and origins of, 158–62 passim, 164, 173; *see also* Boulder, collisions, garden and yard damage, River Hills

swimming, by deer, 27

tail: as alarm indicator, 16; identifying
    species by, 16, 18
tameness: and artificial feeding, 138–9;
    and danger to humans, 77, 128; and
    fear of strangers, 65, 68–71 passim; of
    deer in preserves, 127, 128, 137, 145,
    148, 155–6; of farmland deer, 293,
    304–5; of hand-raised deer, 60, 62; of
    suburban deer, 158, 166, 172, 181–2;
    see also wariness, wildness
Taylor, Walter W., 353
teeth: and deer survival, 37; and feed-
    ing, 62; use for aging, 37–8, 208, 232
telemetry. *See* radio collar
temperature, effects on deer, 72, 89; *see
    also* snow
Tennessee, 100, 102, 103
Texas: deer harvests in, 184–5; deer
    populations in, 25, 184–5, 191; deer
    studies in, 31; exotic wildlife in,
    203–4; history of deer in, 123, 184;
    hunting in economy of, 196; hunting
    regulations in, 102, 191; mentioned,
    15, 36, 37, 99, 157, 168; number of
    hunters in, 205; private land in,
    205; references on, 359–60; *see also*
    Hill Country, ranching, Slator
    Ranch
Thomas, Keith, 279, 362
tick, deer. *See* Lyme disease
Tlingit Indians, 95, 119, 315
Toelken, Barre, 94
Tongass National Forest: and Native
    corporations, 115, 119; biological
    research in, 54–5, 120–1, 356; clear-
    cutting in, 55, 75, 84, 114–21; de-
    scribed, 114, 115–16; local economies
    in, 118–19, 121; loss of wildlife habitat
    in, 114, 115, 116, 118–21; rate of re-
    growth in, 118; subsidized logging in,
    119; *see also* forest, logging, preserves
tracks, aging, 66; *see also* trail
trail: bear, 324–5; deer, 84–5, 326; *see
    also* tracks

trapping deer, 131, 132, 168; *see also* snar-
    ing deer
trophy hunting: and deer farms, 170;
    and hunter values, 187–8, 192, 198–9,
    206, 207–8; and use of meat, 199,
    213; attitudes toward, 278; deer man-
    agement for, 187–8, 191, 193–4; ethics
    of, 206–7; frequency of, 206; history
    of, 206; methods of, 190; *see also*
    Boone and Crockett Club, motiva-
    tions, Pope and Young, values
turkey, 98, 103, 240

ungulates: characteristics of, 11; types
    and distribution, 11–12
urine, communication by, 40–2 passim

values, of hunters: and bucks, 187–8,
    192–3, 223, 230; and crowding, 225,
    226, 234; and responsibility, 188,
    243–4, 246–7; and success, 226,
    234–6 passim, 241; references on, 361;
    toward deer, 71, 241; toward hunting,
    224, 229, 235–6, 268–9, 276–81 pas-
    sim; *see also* food, hunter education,
    hunters, hunting, motivations, per-
    sonal ecology, trophy hunting, veni-
    son
venison: and frontier trade, 100–3;
    annual amount taken, 210, 223;
    commercial use of, 162, 170, 204;
    donations to homeless, 134, 211, 292;
    economic value of, 223; Native
    American use of, 97–8; processing of,
    209–11, 215–16, 231–2, 325–6; quali-
    ties of, 210–11, 212; sharing, 229, 244;
    see also food, motivations, values
Vermont, 108
vineyards, deer damage to, 296; *see also*
    orchards

Virginia, 14, 24, 103, 108, 153

voice, of deer, 38, 49, 350, 352; *see also* communication

Wallmo, Olof, 113, 120, 353, 356

wariness: of bucks vs. does, 317; of hunted deer, 189, 197–8, 216–17, 231; seasonal changes in, 63; species differences in, 18, 19; *see also* tameness, wildness

Washington, 15, 114, 158, 242

Wegner, Robert, 206, 244, 360

weight: seasonal changes in, 45, 76–7; *see also* size

West Virginia, 98

Westchester County, New York, 167–8, 292–5, 358

white-tailed deer: adaptability of, 16, 20–4 passim, 25; and exotic deer, 203–4; distribution, 15–16, 19–22; identifying, 16–19 passim, 21; in Europe and New Zealand, 23; personality of, 18–19; scientific name of, 13; seasonal cycle of, 30–52 passim; size of, 17; subspecies of, 17

wildlife refuges, origin of, 106; *see also* conservation, preserves

wildness: and hunting, 180–1, 189, 190; as quality of deer, 138–9, 155–6, 172, 291; of natural preserves, 124; thoughts on, 190; *see also* tameness, wariness

Winchcombe, Raymond, 151–2, 357

winter. *See* diet, nutrition, snow, temperature

Wisconsin: car-deer collisions in, 166–7; deer management in, 223, 232–5; deer populations in, 24, 164, 225, 226, 230, 234–5; forests and logging in, 111; history of hunting in, 94, 95, 230; hunter density in, 225, 234; hunter success in, 236, 247, 266; hunting in state parks of, 254; hunting regulations in, 102, 222–3, 230, 235, 241, 266; importance of hunting in, 219, 222–4; Lyme disease in, 167; mentioned, 151, 157, 159; references on, 358–9, 361, 363–4; *see also* agricultural damage, antihunting, hunting, River Hills, suburban deer

wolf: and deer populations, 28, 180; control of, 109, 301; mentioned, 114, 123; predation on deer, 27–8, 44; spirituality of, 285; *see also* predators

women: and bears, 315; and origins of conservation, 105; hunting by, 212–13, 227–8, 360

world view, Western: and biological processes, 279–81; and nature, 319; *see also* Koyukon Indians, nature

wounding deer, 190, 231, 240–1

Wyoming, 15, 26

yarding, deer, 43–4

Yellowstone National Park, 104, 106

A Note About the Author

Richard Nelson, a cultural anthropologist who lived for years in Native American communities, writes about the relationships between people and nature. His previous books include *Shadow of the Hunter, Hunters of the Northern Forest, Hunters of the Northern Ice, The Island Within,* and *Make Prayers to the Raven,* which was developed into an award-winning PBS series narrated by Barry Lopez. His work has appeared in *Life, Harpers, Outside, Audubon, Orion, Wilderness,* the *Los Angeles Times,* and many nature writing anthologies.

A Note on the Type

This book was set in Adobe Garamond. Designed for the Adobe Corporation by Robert Slimbach, the fonts are based on types first cut by Claude Garamond (c. 1480–1561). Garamond was a pupil of Geoffroy Tory and is believed to have followed the Venetian models, although he introduced a number of important differences, and it is to him that we owe the letter we now know as "old style." He gave to his letters a certain elegance and feeling of movement that won their creator an immediate reputation and the patronage of Francis I of France.

Composed by North Market Street Graphics,
Lancaster, Pennsylvania
Printed and bound by The Haddon Craftsmen,
Scranton, Pennsylvania
Drawings by Robert H. Rose
Photographs by the author
Designed by Anthea Lingeman